THE FATHERS
OF THE CHURCH

MEDIAEVAL CONTINUATION

VOLUME 5

THE FATHERS OF THE CHURCH

MEDIAEVAL CONTINUATION

PETER DAMIAN
LETTERS
91–120

Translated by

OWEN J. BLUM, O.F.M.
Quincy University
Quincy, Illinois

THE CATHOLIC UNIVERSITY OF AMERICA PRESS
Washington, D.C.

LIBRARY OF CONGRESS CATALOGING-IN-PUBLICATION DATA
Peter Damian, Saint, 1007–1072.
    [The letters of Peter Damian.
    (The Fathers of the Church, mediaeval continuation ; vv. 1–3, 5)
    Translation of the Latin letters of Peter Damian.
    Includes bibliographical references and indexes.
    Contents: [1] 1–30 — [2] 31–60 — [3] 61–90 — [5] 91–120.
    1. Peter Damian, Saint, 1007–1072—Correspondence.
  2. Christian saints—Italy—Correspondence. I. Blum, Owen J.,
1912– . II. Series: Fathers of the Church, mediaeval continuation ;
v. 1, etc.
BX4700.P77A4 1998   270.3   88-25802
ISBN 0–8132–0702–9 (v. 1)
ISBN 0–8132–0707–X (v. 2)
ISBN 0–8132–0750–9 (v. 3)
ISBN 0–8132–0816–5 (v. 5)

CONTENTS

PREFACE

Letters 91–120 (written during the years 1062–66) comprise the fourth volume in this series. In this section of his correspondence, Peter Damian deals with a wide variety of subjects, some with a limited historical interest, others that approach the size and scope of philosophical or theological treatises. His correspondents range from simple hermits in his community to abbots, bishops, cardinals, and even to Pope Alexander II. Among these letters are to be found one addressed to the patriarch of Constantinople, two to his sisters, one to the empress Agnes, and even a few to such distant personages as the young King Henry IV and his gray eminence, the archbishop Anno of Cologne.

Clearly, the *pièce de résistance* of this collection is *Letter* 119, written in 1063 to Abbot Desiderius of Monte Cassino and his monks, on the omnipotence of God. Like Damian's *Book of Gomorrah*, this text was often separately published in various languages. It is translated here for the first time into English.

As in his earlier works, *On the Catholic Faith* (*Letter* 81), the *Position Paper Against the Jews* (*Letter* 1), the *Book of Gomorrah* (*Letter* 31), and *The Most Free Book* (*Letter* 40), Damian's piece on *Divine Omnipotence* (*Letter* 119) demonstrates his control of both theological and philosophical methodology (see, for example, sect. 80). His opponents are contemporary rhetoricians, whose denial of God's total potency in dealing with his creatures' contingencies in time past, present, and future opens them to the charge of heresy.

Professor Kurt Reindel, editor of the Latin text, remarked that, while the Latin edition will make its mark in the world of scholarship, it is the English translation that will guarantee its transmission to all levels of readers throughout the world. In addition, some scholars have noted that, because of the lexicographical difficulties presented by the *hapax legomena* in Damian's Latin, the English version will assist historical and theological specialists as well. The translator will be the first to admit that Damian's vocabulary frequently challenged the combined dictionary resources of classical, patristic, and mediaeval Latin orientation, but with some imagination and philological acumen the problems proved to be surmountable.

Having now reached *Letter* 120 (of the 180 total), the translator entertains a certain suspicion that Damian's correspondence may well represent a literary device for expressing his views. Perhaps the letters were meant to grow into a *summa theologica* in epistolary form. To what extent they actually left his home monastery at Fonte Avellana in Damian's lifetime is not clear. On occasion, both the editor and the translator refer to certain pieces as "open letters," especially those addressed to Bishop Cadalus of Parma, the antipope Honorius II.

We are still in the dark regarding details of the transmission of Damian's works. They moved out across Europe through the "publishing" work of monastic scriptoria that produced their own copies of a letter or letters originally borrowed from Fonte Avellana; these monasteries in turn loaned out copies to others. In all probability, the work of the highly respected cardinal bishop of Ostia was avidly reproduced. Through this process, copies of the letters may well have reached the original addressees. How Damian's *Letter* 99 to Anno of Cologne (suggesting that he use his good offices to convene a general council for ending the Cadalus schism) reached the attention of Cardinal Hildebrand and Pope Alexander II remains a mystery. This letter was written in June 1063. By the Lent of 1064 (*Letter* 107), Damian was sending a copy of it to the authorities in Rome at their request. Thus the letters are still problematic and will provide future researchers with much grist for their mills.

The translator wishes here again to thank the editor of the Latin text, Professor Kurt Reindel (now in retirement), for his continued interest and the encouragement to complete the translation of the entire collection of letters. The translator's colleagues at Quincy University also provide a constant stimulus for getting on with the work, and are always at hand to answer queries about difficulties encountered along the way. To them too he expresses his deepest appreciation.

Quincy University, November 1997   OWEN J. BLUM, O.F.M.

ABBREVIATIONS

AA SS	*Acta Sanctorum*. 70 vols. Paris, 1863–1940.
Abh B	*Abhandlungen der Preussischen Akademie der Wissenschaften*
AUF	*Archiv für Urkundenforschung*
Beuron	*Vetus Latina. Die Reste der altlateinischen Bibel.* Ed. Archabbey of Beuron, 1949–.
BHL	*Bibliotheca Hagiographica Latina*
Biblia sacra	*Biblia sacra iuxta Latinam vulgatam versionem iussu Pii Papae XI ... edita*, 1926–.
CC	*Corpus Christianorum, Series Latina.* Brepols, 1954–.
CCCM	*Corpus Christianorum, Continuatio Mediaevalis.* Brepols, 1971–.
CSEL	*Corpus Scriptorum Ecclesiasticorum Latinorum.* Vienna.
DA	*Deutsches Archiv für Erforschung des Mittelalters*
DACL	*Dictionnaire d'archéologie chrétienne et de liturgie.* Ed. Fernand Cabrol et Henri Leclerq. 15 vols. Paris, 1907–1953.
DHGE	*Dictionnaire d'histoire et de géographie ecclésiastiques.* Ed. Alfred Card. Baudrillart. Paris. 1912–.
DTC	*Dictionnaire de théologie catholique.* 15 vols. Paris 1903–1950.
DuCange	*Glossarium mediae et infimae Latinitatis.* Ed. Charles de Fresne DuCange. 10 vols. Paris, 1883–1887.
FOTC	The Fathers of the Church. New York and Washington, D.C., 1947–.
Gaetani	*S. Petri Damiani ...Opera omnia.* 4 vols. 1606–1640. Later editions will be cited by year of publication.
HJb	*Historisches Jahrbuch*
HV	*Historische Vierteljahrschrift*
HZ	*Historische Zeitschrift*
Itala	*Itala: Das Neue Testament in altlateinischer Überlieferung.* Ed. A. Jülicher. 4 vols. 1963–1976.
ItPont	*Italia Pontificia.* Ed. P. F. Kehr. Berlin, 1906–1935.
JE	Jaffé-Ewald ⎫
JK	Jaffé-Kaltenbrunner ⎬ Regesta Pontificum Romanorum
JL	Jaffé-Löwenfeld ⎭
LThK	*Lexikon für Theologie und Kirche*
Mansi	*Sacrorum conciliorum nova et amplissima collectio.* Ed. Joannes Dominicus Mansi. 53 vols. Paris, 1900–1927.
MGH	Monumenta Germaniae Historica
Auct.ant.	Auctores antiquissimi

Capit.	Capitularia regum Francorum
Conc.	Concilia
Const.	Constitutiones et acta publica imperatorum
D—DD	Diploma—Diplomata
Epp.	Epistolae (in Quarto)
Ldl	Libelli de lite
LL	Leges (in folio)
Necr.	Necrologia Germaniae
Poetae	Poetae Latini medii aevi
SS	Scriptores (in folio)
Ss rer. Germ.	Scriptores rerum Germanicarum in usum scholarum
Ss rer. Merov.	Scriptores rerum Merovingicarum
MIÖG	Mitteilungen des Instituts für österreichische Geschichtsforschung. 1923–1942.
Muratori	*Rerum Italicarum Scriptores.* Ed. Muratori. 2d ed. 1900ff.
NA	*Neues Archiv der Gesellschaft für ältere deutsche Geschichtskunde*
NCE	*New Catholic Encyclopedia*
PL	*Patrologia Latina.* Ed. J. P. Migne. Paris, 1844–1855.
RE	*Real-Encyclopädie der Classischen Alterumswissenschaft.* Ed. Pauly-Wissowa.
RHE	*Revue d'Histoire Ecclésiastique*
Sabatier	*Bibliorum sacrorum Latinae versiones antiquae.* Ed. P. Sabatier. 3 vols. Paris, 1743.
SBA	*Sitzungsberichte der Bayerischen Akademie der Wissenschaften*
SC	Sources chrétiennes. Paris, 1942–.
StMGBO	*Studien und Mitteilungen zur Geschichte des Benediktiner-Ordens und seiner Zweige*
TU	Texte and Untersuchungen zur Geschichte der Altchristlichen Literatur. Berlin, 1882–.
Vulg	*Biblia sacra iuxta vulgatam versionem.* Ed. Robert Weber. 2 vols. 2d ed., 1975.
ZKG	*Zeitschrift für Kirchengeschichte*
ZRG	*Zeitschrift der Savigny-Stiftung für Rechtsgeschichte, Kanonistische Abteilung*

SELECT BIBLIOGRAPHY

Sources

Amalarius. *Liber officialis.* Ed. J. M. Hanssens, Studi e testi 139 (1948).

Ambrose. *De Spiritu Sancto libri tres.* Ed. O. Faller, CSEL 79 (1964) 1.222.

———. *Exameron.* Ed. C. Schenkl, CSEL 32.1 (1897) 1–261.

———. *Explanatio Psalmorum XII.* Ed. M. Petschenig, CSEL 64 (1919).

Augustine. *De civitate Dei.* Ed. B. Dombart and A. Kalb, CC 47 and 48 (1955).

———. *De Genesi ad litteram libri duodecim.* Ed. J. Zycha, CSEL 28.1 (1894).

———. *De trinitate libri XV.* Ed. W. J. Moutain and F. Glorie, 2 vols., CC 50 and 50A (1968).

———. *Enarrationes in psalmos.* Ed. E. Dekkers and J. Fraipont, 3 vols., CC 38–40 (1956).

Bede. *Retractatio in actus apostolorum.* Ed. M. L. W. Laistner, CC 121 (1983) 100–163.

Benedicti Regula. Ed. R. Hanslik, CSEL 75 (1977).

Boethius. *Philosophiae consolatio.* Ed. L. Bieler, CC 94 (1957).

Burchard of Worms. *Decretorum libri XX.* PL 140.537–1058.

Cassiodorus. *Expositio Psalmorum.* Ed. M. Adriaen, 2 vols., CC 97 and 98 (1958).

Collectio Dionysio-Hadriana. PL 67.39–346.

Concilium Carthaginense. Canones in Causa Apiarii. Ed. C. Munier, CC 149 (1974).

De Gallica Petri Damiani profectione et eius ultramontano itinere. Ed. G. Schwartz and A. Hofmeister, MGH SS 30.2 (1926) 1034–1046 (=Iter Gallicum).

(Pseudo) Dionysios Areopagita. *De divinis nominibus.* PL 122.1111–1172. Ed. Ph. Chevallier, *Dionysiaca* 1 (1936) 5–561.

Eutropius. *Breviarium ab urbe condita.* Ed. H. Droysen, MGH Auct. ant. 2 (1879).

Gelasius. *Tractatus.* Ed. A. Thiel, *Epistolae Romanorum pontificum genuinae* 1 (1867–1868) 510–607.

Gregory I. *Dialogi.* 3 vols. Ed. A de Vogüe, Sources chrétiennes 251, 260 and 265 (1978–1980).

———. *Registrum epistolarum.* 2 vols. Ed. P. Ewald and L. M. Hartmann, MGH Epp. 1 and 2 (1891/1899). Ed. D. Norberg, CC 140 (1892) (cites from MGH).

Gregory VII. *Register.* Ed. E. Caspar, MGH Epp. sel. 2.1 (1920).

Haimo of Auxerre. *Expositio in epistolas ad Thessalonicenses.* PL 117.765–784.

Hrabanus Maurus. *De universo libri viginiti duo.* PL 111.9–614.

Institutio canonicorum Aquisgranensis. Ed. A. Werminghoff, MGH Conc. 2.1.2 (1908) 308–421.

Isidore of Seville. *De natura rerum.* Ed. J. Fontaine, *Isidore de Seville, Traité de la nature.* Bibliothèque de l'école des hautes études Hispaniques 28 (1960).
———. *Etymologiarum sive originum libri XX.* Ed. W. M. Lindsay, Oxford (1911).
Jerome. *Adversus Iovinianum libri duo.* PL 23.221–352.
———. *Commentariorum in Danielem libri III (IV).* Ed. F. Glorie, CC 75A (1964).
———. *Epistulae.* 3 vols. Ed. I. Hilberg, CSEL 54–56 (1910–1918).
———. *Liber interpretationis hebraicorum nominum.* Ed. P. de Lagarde, CC 72 (1959).
John of Lodi. *Vita Petri Damiani.* Text and Kommentar. Ed. S. Freund (Master's Thesis University of Regensburg, 1988).
John the Deacon. *Sancti Gregorii Magni vita.* PL 75.59–242.
Liber pontificalis. 3 vols. Ed. L. Duchesne. Paris, 1886–1957.
Manegold von Lautenbach. *Liber contra Wolfelmum.* Ed. W. Hartmann, MGH Quellen zur Geistesgeschichte des MA 8 (1972).
Orosius. *Historiarum adversus paganos libri VII.* Ed. A. Lippold, *Orosio, Le storie contro i pagani,* 2 vols. Milan, 1976. For an English translation see R. Deferrari, *Paulus Orosius: The Seven Books of History against the Pagans,* FOTC 50 (1964).
Papstwahldekret. Ed. D. Jasper, *Das Papstwahldekret von 1059.* Überlieferung und Textgestalt. Beiträge zur Geschichte und Quellenkunde des MA 12 (1986) 98–119.
Paul the Deacon. *Historia Romana.* In Eutropius, *Breviarium ab urbe condita.* Ed. H. Droysen, MGH Auct. ant. 2 (1879) 183–224; or, ed. A. Crivellucci, *Fonti per la storia d'Italia* 51 (1914).
Petrus Damiani. *Die Briefe des Petrus Damiani,* 4 vols. Ed. K. Reindel. In MGH *Die Briefe der deutschen Kaiserzeit* (1983–1993).
———. *Sermones.* Ed. G. Lucchesi, CC Continuatio Mediaeualis 57 (1983).
———. *Vita Sancti Odilonis.* PL 144.925–944.
———. *Vita Beati Romualdi.* Ed. G. Tabacco, *Fonti per la storia d'Italia* 94 (1957).
Pomerius, Iulianus. *De vita contemplativa libri tres.* PL 59.415–520.
Pseudo-Isidore. Ed. P. Hinschius, *Decretales Pseudo-Isidorianae et capitula Angilramni* (1863). Fuhrmann, *Fälschungen* 153ff. and 168ff. notes that the edition of Hinschius is incomplete.
Pseudo-Jerome. *Epistolae.* PL 30.13–308.
Smaragdus. *Libellus de processione sancti Spiritus.* Ed. A. Werminghoff, MGH Conc. 2.1 (1906).
Vitae patrum sive historiae eremiticae libri decem. I-VIII, PL 73 (=*Vitas patrum*).

Literature

Andreoletti, M. "Liberta e valori nel volontarismo di S. Pier Damiani," *Giornale di metafisica* 15 (1960) 297–320.
Barstow, Anne L. *Married Priests and the Reforming Papacy: The Eleventh-Century Debates.* Texts and Studies in Religion 12 (1982).
Bloch, Herbert. *Monte Cassino in the Middle Ages* 1 (1986).

Blum, Owen J. *The Letters of Peter Damian*. The Fathers of the Church, Mediaeval Continuation, vols. 1–3 (1989–1992).

———. "The Monitor of the Popes: St. Peter Damian," *Studi Gregoriani* 2 (1947) 459–476.

———. *St. Peter Damian: His Teaching on the Spiritual Life*. The Catholic University of America. Studies in Mediaeval history N.S. 10 (1947).

Borino, Giovanni Battista. "Cencio del prefetto Stefano, L'attentatore di Gregorio VII," *Studi Gregoriani* 4 (1952) 373–440.

Brezzi, Paolo and Bruno Nardi (ed.), *S. Pier Damiani. De divina omnipotentia e altri opuscoli* (1943).

Bulst-Thiele, Marie Luise. *Kaiserin Agnes*. Beiträge zur Kulturgeschichte des MA und der Renaissance 52 (1933).

Bultot, Robert. *Pierre Damien*. In *Christianisme et valeurs humaines. A. La doctrine du mépris du monde, en occident, de S. Ambroise à Innocent III*, 4.1. (1963).

Cacciamani, Guiseppe. "La nomina di S. Pier Damiano a Vescovo et a Cardinale di Ostia." In *San Pier Damiano nel IX centenario della morte (1072–1972)* 1 (1972) 181–193.

———. "Le fondazioni eremitiche e cenobitiche di S. Pier Damiano. Inizi della Congregazione di S. Croce di Fonte Avellana," *Ravennatensia* 5 (1976) 5–33.

Calamoneri, Antonio. "San Pier Damiani agiografo." In *San Pier Damiano nel IX centenario della morte (1072–1972)* 4 (1978) 147–210.

Cantin, A. *Pierre Damien. Lettre sur la toute-puissance divine*. Sources chrétiennes 191 (1972).

———. *Les sciences seculieres et la foi. Les deux voies de la science au jugement de S. Pierre Damien (1007–1072)*. Centro Italiano di studi sull'alto medioevo 5 (1975).

Dereine, Charles. "La problème de la vie commune chez les canonistes, d'Anselme du Lucques Gratien," *Studi Gregoriani* 3 (1948) 219–352.

Dobmeier, Heinrich. *Montecassino und die Laien im 11. und 12. Jahrhundert*. Schriften der MGH 27 (1979).

Dressler, Fridolin. *Petrus Damiani. Leben und Werk*. Studia Anselmiana 34 (1954).

Endres, Joseph Anton. *Petrus Damiani und die weltliche Wissenschaft*. Beiträge zur Geschichte der Philosophie des MA VIII 3 (1910).

Fonseca, Cosimo Damiano. "Le canoniche regulari riformate dell'Italia nord-occidentale. Ricerche e problemi." In *Monasteri in alta Italia dopo de invasioni Saracene e Magiare (sec. X–XII.) III Convegno di storia della Chiesa in Italia 1964* (1966) 335–382.

Freund, Stephan. *Studien zur literarischen Wirksamkeit des Petrus Damiani*. Anhang: *Johannes von Lodi, Vita Petri Damiani*. Monumenta Gemaniae historica: Studien und Texte. Hannover, 1995.

Frugoni, Chiara. "Letteratura didattica ed esegesi scritturale nel De bono religiosi status di S. Pier Damiani," *Rivista di Storia della Chiesa in Italia* 34 (1980) 7–59.

Fuhrmann, Horst. *Einfluss und Verbreitung der pseudo-isidorischen Fälschungen. Von ihrem Auftauchen bis in die neuere Zeit*. Schriften der MGH 24 (1972–1974) (=Fuhrmann, Fälschungen).

Gaudenzi, Augusto. "Lo svolgimento parallelo del diritto longobardo e del diritto romano a Ravenna." In *Memorie della regia accademia delle scienze dell'istituto di Bologna, Classe di scienze morali, sezione giuridica* I, 1 (1906–7) 37–164.

Gonsette, Jean Albert Denis. *Pierre Damien et la culture profane.* Essais philosophiques 7 (1956).

Gougaud, Louis. *Dévotions et pratiques ascétiques du moyen âge.* Collection Pax 21 (1925).

Granata, Aldo (ed.), *Pier Damiani. Lettere ai monaci di Montecassino.* Di fronte e attraverso 202 (1987) (=Granata, Montecassino).

Hall, Stuart George and Joseph H. Crehan. "Fasten/Fasttage III. Biblisch und kirchenhistorisch," *Theologische Realenzyklopädie* 11 (1983) 48–59.

Hefele, Carl Joseph and Henri Leclercq. *Histoire des conciles.* 11 vols. Paris, 1907–52.

Heist, Wilhelm W. *The Fifteen Signs before Doomsday* (1952).

Hunt, Noreen. *Cluny under Saint Hugh 1049–1109* (1967).

Jenal, Georg. *Erzbishof Anno II. von Köln (1056–75) und sein politisches Wirken. Ein Beitrag zur Geschichte der Reichs- und Territorialpolitik im 11. Jh.* Monographien zur Geschichte des MA 8 (1974–75).

Jungmann, Josef Andreas. *Missarum sollemnia. Eine genetische Erklärung der römischen Messe.* 2. vols. (1962).

Kötting, Bernhard. "Die Beurteilung der zweiten Ehe in der Spätantike und im frühen MA." In *Tradition als historische Kraft. Interdisziplinäre Forschungen zur Geschichte des frühen MA.* Ed. N. Kamp and J. Wollasch (1982) 43–52.

Laqua, Hans Peter. *Traditionen und Leitbilder bei dem Ravennater Reformer Petrus Damiani (1042–1052).* Münstersche Mittelalter-Schriften 30 (1976).

Laudage, Johannes. *Priesterbild und Reformpapsttum im 11. Jh.* Archiv für Kulturgeschichte, Beiheft 22 (1984).

Lentini, Anselmo. "Il 'cursus' nella prosa di Pier Damiani," *Benedictina* 19 (1972) 239–251.

Lohmer, Christian. "Ausgewählte Aspekte der mittelalterlichen Ernährung für Mönche, untersucht am Beispiel der monastischen Bestimmungen des Petrus Damiani," *Aktuelle Ernährungsmedizin* 13 (1988) 179–182.

———. *Heremi conversatio. Studien zu den monastischen Vorschriften des Petrus Damiani.* Beiträge zur Geschichte des alten Mönchtums und des Benediktinertums 39 (1991).

Lokrantz, Margareta. *L'opera poetica di S. Pier Damiani.* Studia Latina Stockholmiensia 12. Stockholm, 1964.

Lubac, Henri de. *Exégèse médiévale. Les quatre sens de l'écriture.* 3 vols. (Theologie 41, 42, 59, 1959–1964).

Lucchesi, Giovanni. *Clavis S. Petri Damiani.* Faenza, 1970.

———. "Giovanni da Lodi, il discepolo." In *San Pier Damiano nel IX centenario della morte (1072–1972)* 4 (1978) 7–68.

———. "I viaggi di S. Pier Damiani." In *S. Pier Damiani. Atti del Convegno di studi nel IX centenario della morte,* Faenza (1972) 71–91.

———. "Per una vita di San Pier Damiani. Componenti cronologiche e topografiche." In *San Pier Damiano nel IX centenario della morte (1072–1972)* 1

(1972) 13–179 (Nos. 1–153) and 2 (1972) 13–160 (Nos. 154–231) (=Lucchesi, *Vita*).

———. "La 'Vita S. Rodulphi et. S. Dominici Loricati' di S. Pier Damiano," *Rivista di Storia della Chiesa in Italia* 9 (1965) 166–177.

Maccarrone, Michele. "La teologia del primato romano del seculo XI." In *Le istituzioni ecclesiastiche della "societas christiana" dei secoli XI–XII: Papato, cardinalato ed episcopato*. Miscellanea del centro di studi mediaevali 7 (1974) 21–122.

Manacorda, Guiseppe. *Storia della scuola in Italia*. 2 vols. Athenaeum. Biblioteca di storia della scuola e della universita 18 (1913; reprint 1978).

Meyer, Heinz. *Die Zahlenallegorese im MA*. Münstersche Mittelalter-Schriften 25 (1975).

Meyer, Heinz and Rudolf Suntrup. *Lexikon der mittelalterlichen Zahlenbedeutung*. Münstersche Mittelalter-Schriften 56 (1987).

Meyer von Knonau, Gerold. *Jahrbücher des Deutschen Reiches unter Heinrich IV und Heinrich V*. 7 vols. Jahrbücher der Deutschen Geschichte, 1890–1929 (=Meyer von Knonau, Heinrich IV.).

Miccoli, Giovanni. "Ecclesiae primitivae forma," *Studi medievali 3ª serie* 1 (1960) 470–498.

———. "Chiesa Gregoriana. Ricerche sulla riforma del secolo XI," *Storici antichi e moderni*, N.S. 17 (1966) 101–167.

Mittarelli, Johannes-Benedictus and Anselmus Costadoni. *Annales Camaldulenses ordinis sancti Benedicti*, 9 vols. Venice, 1755–1773.

Monasticon Italiae 1. Ed. F. Garaffa, Rome and Latium (1981).

Neukirch, Franz. *Das Leben des Petrus Damiani* (1875).

Reindel, Kurt. "Petrus Damiani und seine Korrespondenten," *Studi Gregoriani* 10 (1975) 203–219.

———. "Studien zur Überlieferung der Werke des Petrus Damiani I–III." DA 15 (1959) 23–102; 16 (1960) 73–154; 18 (1962) 317–417.

Resnick, Irven M. "Peter Damian on the Restoration of Virginity. A Problem for Medieval Theology," *The Journal of Theological Studies* N.S. 9 (1988) 125–134.

Roth, Ferdinand Wilhelm Emil. "Der hl. Petrus Damiani O.S.B. Cardinalbischof von Ostia," StMGBO 7.1 (1886) 110–134, 357–374; 7.2 (1886) 43–66, 321–336; 8 (1887) 56–64, 210–216.

Ryan, J. Joseph. *Saint Peter Damian and His Canonical Sources. A Preliminary Study in the Antecedents of the Gregorian Reform*. Pontifical Institute of Mediaeval Studies. Studies and Texts 2 (1956) (=Ryan, *Sources*).

Schmale, Franz Josef. "Synoden Papst Alexanders II. (1061–1073). Anzahl, Termine, Entscheidungen," *Annuarium historiae conciliorum* 11 (1979) 307–338.

Schmidt, Tilmann. *Alexander II. (1061–1073) und die römische Reformgruppe seiner Zeit*. Päpste und Papsttum 11 (1977).

Schramm, Percy Ernst, "Das Alte und das Neue Testament in der Staatslehre und Staatssymbolik des MA." In P. E. Schramm, *Kaiser, Könige und Päpste. Gesammelte Aufsätze zur Geschichte des MA* 4.1 (1970) 124–140.

———. et. al., *Herrschaftszeichen und Staatssymbolik. Beiträge zu ihrer Geschichte vom 3. zum 16. Jahrhundert* 3 vols. (Schriften der MGH 13.1–3, 1954–1956).

————. *Kaiser, Rom und Renovatio. Studien und Texte zur Geschichte des römischen Erneuerungsgedankens vom Ende des karolingischen Reiches bis zum Investiturstreit.* 2 vols. (1929).

Schubert, Hans von. "Petrus Damiani als Kirchenpolitiker." In *Festgabe für Karl Müller* (1922) 83–102.

Schwartz, Gerhard. *Die Besetzung der Bistümer Reichsitaliens unter den sächsischen und salischen Kaisern mit den Listen der Bischöfe 951–1122* (1913) (=Schwartz, *Bistümer*).

Struve, Tilman. "Die Romreise der Kaiserin Agnes," HJb 105 (1985) 1–29.

Ughelli, Ferdinando. *Italia sacra.* 10 vols. (1717–1722; reprint 1970).

Wemple, Suzanne Fonay. *Atto of Vercelli. Church, State and Christian Society in Tenth Century Italy.* Temi e testi 27 (1979).

Wilmart, André. "Une lettre de S. Pierre Damien à l'impératrice Agnes," *Revue Bénédictine* 44 (1932) 125–146.

Wippel, John F. and Allan B. Wolter. *Medieval Philosophy: From Augustine to Nicholas of Cusa.* New York, c1969.

Zimmermann, Gerd. *Ordensleben und Lebensstandard. Die Cura Corporis in den Ordensvorschriften des abendländischen Hochmittelalters.* Beiträge zur Geschichte des alten Mönchtums und des Benediktinerordens 32 (1973).

CONCORDANCE

Since the new edition of Damian's letters in Kurt Reindel, *Die Briefe der Petrus Damiani*, MGH Die Briefe der deutschen Kaiserzeit (München, 1983) has assigned new numbers in chronological order, the old system of number for *epistolae* and *opuscula* is now outmoded. To correlate the new with the old, the following concordance is herewith provided. There is no longer a distinction between "letters" and "works," and *Letters* 171–180 are placed at the end of the series because they are undatable.

MGH (Chronological) Numeration in Earlier Editions

Reindel	Migne Number	Reindel	Migne Number
1	opsuc. 2 and 3	27	epist. 6, 24 = opusc. 48
2	epist. 7, 15	28	opusc. 11
3	epist. 3, 2	29	epist. 6, 15
4	epist. 3, 3	30	epist. 4, 4
5	epist. 4, 2	31	opusc. 7
6	epist. 6, 6	32	epist. 4, 13
7	epist. 3, 5	33	epist. 1, 4
8	epist. 5, 12	34	epist. 4, 10
9	epist. 6, 28	35	epist. 5, 6
10	epist. 6, 23	36	epist. 5, 17 = opusc. 8/2
11	epist. 2, 19	37	epist. 6, 7
12	epist. 4, 6	38	opusc. 16
13	epist. 1, 1	39	epist. 5, 9 = opusc. 27
14	epist. 4, 7	40	opusc. 6
15	epist. 8, 4	41	Ad Heinricum
16	epist. 1, 2	42	Ad Odalricum
17	opusc. 10	43	epist. 7, 1
18	opusc. 14	44	epist. 6, 30 = opusc. 51
19	opusc. 8/1	45	epist. 5, 8
20	epist. 7, 2	46	epist. 1, 5
21	epist. 8, 8	47	epist. 4, 14 = opusc. 26
22	epist. 4, 5	48	epist. 2, 1
23	epist. 8, 9 = opusc. 58	49	epist. 2, 5
24	epist. 6, 14 = opusc. 29	50	opusc. 15
25	epist. 8, 7 = opusc. 42/2	51	epist. 7, 14
26	epist. 1, 3	52	epist. 2, 4

Reindel	Migne Number	Reindel	Migne Number
53	Ad Iohannem	97	epist. 2, 2 = opusc. 31
54	epist. 6, 18 = opusc. 46	98	epist. 1, 18 = opusc 24
55	epist. 6, 19	99	epist. 3, 6
56	epist. 6, 27	100	epist. 6, 5
57	epist. 1, 10 = opusc. 20	101	epist. 3, 7
58	epist. 3, 4	102	epist. 2, 15 = opusc. 34/1
59	epist. 3, 9 = opusc. 25	103	epist. 6, 2
60	epist. 1, 7	104	epist. 7, 5 = opusc. 56
61	epist. 1, 6 = opusc. 17	105	epist. 6, 8 = opusc. 21
62	epist. 4, 11	106	epist. 2, 14 = opusc. 33
63	epist. 2, 9	107	epist. 1, 16
64	epist. 7, 9	108	epist. 1, 17 = opusc. 23
65	opusc. 5	109	epist. 1, 19 = Vita Rodulphi
66	epist. 7, 19 = opusc. 50		et Dominici
67	epist. 7, 11 = opusc. 57/1	110	opusc. 9
68	epist. 7, 12 = opusc. 57/2	111	epist. 3, 8 = opusc. 39
69	epist. 2, 3 = opusc. 22	112	epist. 4, 3 = opusc. 18/2
70	epist. 5, 16 = opusc. 42/1	113	epist. 6, 4
71	epist. 7, 4	114	epist. 7, 16 = opusc. 18/3
72	epist. 1, 9 = opusc. 19	115	epist. 4, 16
73	epist. 4, 1	116	epist. 6, 10
74	epist. 4, 12	117	epist. 6, 17 = opusc. 45
75	epist. 2, 8	118	epist. 6, 35 = opusc 55
76	epist. 6, 31 = opusc. 53	119	epist. 2, 17 = opusc 36
77	epist. 5, 5	120	epist. 7, 3
78	epist. 6, 11 = opusc. 44	121	epist. 5, 1
79	epist. 1, 8	122	epist. 1, 11
80	epist. 4, 17 = opusc. 40	123	epist. 6, 21 = opusc. 47
81	opusc. 1	124	epist. 7, 6
82	epist. 2, 12	125	epist. 6, 3
83	epist. 8, 5	126	epist. 2, 20 = opusc. 37/1
84	epist. 5, 7	127	epist. 2, 21 = opusc. 37/2
85	epist. 8, 3	128	Ad Ambrosium et
86	epist. 2, 18 = opusc. 52		Liupardum
87	epist. 4, 9	129	epist. 5, 14 and 5, 15
88	epist. 1, 20	130	epist. 7, 7
89	epist. 1, 21 and opusc. 4	131	epist. 6, 13
90	epist. 2, 13	132	epist. 6, 26 = opusc. 49
91	epist. 3, 1 = opusc. 38	133	epist. 6, 34
92	epist. 6, 16 = opusc. 59	134	epist. 6, 36
93	epist. 8, 13	135	Ad Cinthium
94	epist. 8, 14	136	epist. 8, 12
95	epist. 2, 11	137	epist. 6, 33 = opusc. 54
96	epist. 1, 15	138	epist. 5, 2

Numeration of Earlier Editions in MGH

Migne Number	Reindel	Migne Number	Reindel
epist. 2, 13	90	epist. 5, 8	45
epist. 2, 14 = opusc. 33	106	epist. 5, 9 = opusc. 27	39
epist. 2, 15 = opusc. 34/1	102	epist. 5, 10	147
epist. 2, 16 = opusc. 35	159	epist. 5, 11 = opusc. 41	172
epist. 2, 17 = opusc. 36	119	epist. 5, 12	8
epist. 2, 18 = opusc. 52	86	epist. 5, 13	141
epist. 2, 19	11	epist. 5, 14	129
epist. 2, 20 = opusc. 37/1	126	epist. 5, 15	129
epist. 2, 21 = opusc. 37/2	127	epist. 5, 16 = opusc. 42/1	70
epist. 3, 1 = opusc. 38	91	epist. 5, 17 = opusc. 8/2	36
epist. 3, 2	3	epist. 5, 18	177
epist. 3, 3	4	epist. 5, 19 = opusc. 28	spuria
epist. 3, 4	58	epist. 6, 1 = opusc. 43	161
epist. 3, 5	7	epist. 6, 2	103
epist. 3, 6	99	epist. 6, 3	125
epist. 3, 7	101	epist. 6, 4	113
epist. 3, 8 = opusc. 39	111	epist. 6, 5	100
epist. 3, 9 = opusc. 25	59	epist. 6, 6	6
epist. 3, 10 = opusc. 34/2	168	epist. 6, 7	37
epist. 4, 1	73	epist. 6, 8 = opusc. 21	105
epist. 4, 2	5	epist. 6, 9	176
epist. 4, 3 = opusc. 18/2	112	epist. 6, 10	116
epist. 4, 4	30	epist. 6, 11 = opusc. 44	78
epist. 4, 5	22	epist. 6, 12	152
epist. 4, 6	12	epist. 6, 13	131
epist. 4, 7	14	epist. 6, 14 = opusc. 29	24
epist. 4, 8	157	epist. 6, 15	29
epist. 4, 9	87	epist. 6, 16 = opusc. 59	92
epist. 4, 10	34	epist. 6, 17 = opusc. 45	117
epist. 4, 11	62	epist. 6, 18 = opusc. 46	54
epist. 4, 12	74	epist. 6, 19	55
epist. 4, 13	32	epist. 6, 20	150
epist. 4, 14 = opusc. 26	47	epist. 6, 21 = opusc. 47	123
epist. 4, 15	174	epist. 6, 22	158
epist. 4, 16	115	epist. 6, 23	10
epist. 4, 17 = opusc. 40	80	epist. 6, 24 = opusc. 48	27
epist. 5, 1	121	epist. 6, 25	169
epist. 5, 2	138	epist. 6, 26 = opusc. 49	132
epist. 5, 3	163	epist. 6, 27	56
epist. 5, 4 = part of opusc. 18/1	162	epist. 6, 28	9
epist. 5, 5	77	epist. 6, 29	166
epist. 5, 6	35	epist. 6, 30 = opusc. 51	44
epist. 5, 7	84	epist. 6, 31 = opusc. 53	76
		epist. 6, 32	142

Migne Number	Reindel	Migne Number	Reindel
epist. 6, 33 = opusc. 54	137	opusc. 7	31
epist. 6, 34	133	epist. 8/1	19
epist. 6, 35 = opusc. 55	118	opusc. 8/2 = epist. 5, 17	36
epist. 6, 36	134	opusc. 9	110
epist. 7, 1	43	opusc. 10	17
epist. 7, 2	20	opusc. 11	28
epist. 7, 3	120	opusc. 12	165
epist. 7, 4	71	opusc. 13	153
epist. 7, 5 = opusc. 56	104	opusc. 14	18
epist. 7, 6	124	opusc. 15	50
epist. 7, 7	130	opusc. 16	38
epist. 7, 8	144	opusc. 17 = epist. 1, 6	61
epist. 7, 9	64	opusc. 18/1 = epist. 2, 10	162
epist. 7, 10	154	opusc. 18/2 = epist. 4, 3	112
epist. 7, 11 = opusc. 57/1	67	opusc. 18/3 = epist. 7, 16	114
epist. 7, 12 = opusc. 57/2	68	opusc. 19 = epist. 1, 9	72
epist. 7, 13	148	opusc. 20 = epist. 1, 10	57
epist. 7, 14	51	opusc. 21 = epist. 6, 8	105
epist. 7, 15	2	opusc. 22 = epist. 2, 3	69
epist. 7, 16 = opusc. 18/3	114	opusc. 23 = epist. 1, 17	108
epist. 7, 17	151	opusc. 24 = epist. 1, 18	98
epist. 7, 18	143	opusc. 25 = epist. 3, 9	59
epist. 7, 19 = opusc. 50	66	opusc. 26 = epist. 4, 14	47
epist. 8, 1	145	opusc. 27 = epist. 5, 9	39
epist. 8, 2	155	opusc. 28 = epist. 5, 19	spurium
epist. 8, 3	85	opusc. 29 = epist. 6, 14	24
epist. 8, 4	15	opusc. 30 = epist. 8, 11	146
epist. 8, 5	83	opusc. 31 = epist. 2, 2	97
epist. 8, 6	179	opusc. 32 = epist. 2, 7	160
epist. 8, 7 = opusc. 42/2	25	opusc. 33 = epist. 2, 14	106
epist. 8, 8	21	opusc. 34/1 = epist. 2, 15	102
epist. 8, 9 = opusc. 58	23	opusc. 34/2 = epist. 3, 10	168
epist. 8, 10	170	opusc. 35 = epist. 2, 16	159
epist. 8, 11 = opusc. 30	146	opusc. 36 = epist. 2, 17	119
epist. 8, 12	136	opusc. 37/1 = epist. 2, 20	126
epist. 8, 13	93	opusc. 37/2 = epist. 2, 21	127
epist. 8, 14	94	opusc. 38 = epist. 3, 1	91
epist. 8, 15	171	opusc. 39 = epist. 3, 8	111
opusc. 1	81	opusc. 40 = epist. 4, 17	80
opusc. 2	1	opusc. 41 = epist. 5, 1	172
opusc. 3	1	opusc. 42/1 = epist. 5, 16	70
opusc. 4	89	opusc. 42/2 = epist. 8, 7	25
opusc. 5	65	opusc. 43 = epist. 6, 1	161
opusc. 6	40	opusc. 44 = epist. 6, 11	78

Migne Number	Reindel	Migne Number	Reindel
opusc. 45 = epist. 6, 17	117	opusc. 53 = epist. 6, 31	76
opusc. 46 = epist. 6, 18	54	opusc. 54 = epist. 6, 33	137
opusc. 47 = epist. 6, 21	123	opusc. 55 = epist. 6, 35	118
opusc. 48 = epist. 6, 24	27	opusc. 56 = epist. 7, 5	104
opusc. 49 = epist. 6, 26	132	opusc. 57/1 = epist. 7, 11	67
opusc. 50 = epist. 7, 19	66	opusc. 57/2 = epist. 7, 12	68
opusc. 51 = epist. 6, 30	44	opusc. 58 = epist. 8, 9	23
opusc. 52 = epist. 2, 18	86	opusc. 59 = epist. 6, 16	92

Letters That Are Not Found in Migne

To Abbot A.	178	To Honestus	175
To Agnes	149	To John	53
To Ambrose and Liupardus	128	To Odalricus	42
To Bucco	173	To Tebaldus	139
To Cinthius	135	To Bishop W.	180
To Henry	41		

LETTERS
91–120

LETTER 91

Peter Damian to Constantine Lichoudes, the patriarch of Constantinople (1059–1063). This gently worded letter may have been inspired by Desiderius, the abbot of Monte Cassino, who in 1058 was on mission to Constantinople. Its subject was the burning issue of the Filioque. While the Greek Church held that the Holy Spirit proceeds only from the Father, the Roman Church believed in a double procession, from both the Father and the Son. Damian defends the Roman position using both Latin and Greek sources. In the course of his argument, he clearly affirms the magisterial primacy granted by God, universally and for all time, to Peter and his successors.

(1062)[1]

O SIR L<ICHOUDES>, the most blessed patriarch,[2] the monk Peter the sinner offers his servitude.

(2) The devout bishop of the church at Forlimpopoli[3] related to me that he had heard from the lips of the most reverend Dominic, patriarch of Grado,[4] that you had posed a question of great importance for the Catholic faith in your letter to the Apostolic See, and that with vigilance becoming the episcopal office, you had requested of Pope Alexander that it be resolved with unimpeachable evidence from the testimonies of the Scriptures. This question was: Why do the Latins say that the Holy Spirit proceeds from the Father and from the Son, while the Greeks believe that he proceeds only from the Fa-

---

1. The dating follows Lucchesi, *Vita* no. 160.
2. On Constantine Lichoudes, see *Les regestes des actes du patriarchat de Constantinople* nos. 887–892, ed. V. Grumel, *Le patriarcat Byzantin* series 1.1.3 (1947) 17ff.; Joan Mervy Hussey, *The Orthodox Church in the Byzantine Empire* (1986) 138.
3. On the see of Forlimpopoli, see Ughelli, *Italia sacra* 2.589–618, esp. 600, where an Honestus is named as incumbent for 1032, 1059, and 1062. According to Schwartz, *Bistümer* 177, the issue is unclear.
4. Dominicus Marango, patriarch of Grado (see Drehmann, *Leo IX* 35f.) seems to be the most likely occupant of the see in 1062.

ther?[5] I now make bold to demonstrate what I think about this question with the help of the same Holy Spirit here under discussion. It is not that I have been put under obligation by you in this matter, or that it was commanded by the authority of the Roman pontiff. For why would he deign to assign such a weighty subject to an unskilled person, when it cannot be doubted that there are so many holy and very skillful men always at his side? But even though I am a slothful and useless servant in the household of my Lord Jesus, since it was inconvenient for them to accept his request, I am pleased to undertake the task, and no one has seen fit to challenge me.

(3) Your Holiness is to be exalted for his laudable prudence, with deserved acclamation, that in resolving this question about the Holy Spirit you came to not just anyone, but specifically to Peter, whom you undoubtedly recognize as having received the keys of heavenly wisdom and power. Nor was it proper that you, a man of such dignity and wisdom, should seek out from any other the hidden things of heavenly mystery, but from him especially, whom flesh and blood could not instruct, but to whom God himself saw fit to reveal his secrets directly. "Simon, son of Jonah," he said, "blessed are you because flesh and blood did not reveal this to you, but my Father who is in heaven."[6] For the Creator of the world chose him in preference to all other mortals on earth, and granted to him for all time the privilege of magisterial primacy within the Church, so that anyone who wishes to know anything profound about God might have recourse to the divine pronouncements and doctrine of this teacher. One should not be ashamed humbly to present a problem to him for his solution, even though one is not ignorant of what is sought. Was the angel that came from heaven not able to teach Cornelius? Yet he sent him to Peter to learn what he should do. "Send men to Joppa," he said, "to Simon who is called Peter, and ask him to come. He

5. Damian's role in this controversy is discussed by Stefano Belli, "La processione dello Spirito Santo nell' op. 38 [=Letter 91] di S. Pier Damiano primo apostolo dell' unione dei Greci con Roma," *Studi su S. Pier Damiano* 5 (1961) 21–38. The presentation is merely a summary or synopsis, without discussing fully the sources of the two positions. See Hans-Georg Beck, *Kirche und theologische Literatur im byzantinischen Reich* (1959) 306ff.

6. Matt 16.17.

is lodging in the house of Simon the tanner by the sea. He will tell you what you should do."[7] The holy angel could obviously have taught this Gentile what was necessary for his salvation, but he did not wish to usurp the teaching office he knew had been entrusted to Peter.

(4) Why, therefore, should we wonder that a bishop, even though he is outstanding for holiness and thoroughly instructed in the Word of God, should approach the teaching authority of the prince of the apostles, when even an angel sent Cornelius, the first-fruits of the Gentiles, to him for instruction? These are the words that Paul wrote to the Galatians, "Paul, an apostle," he said, "not by men nor through man, but through Jesus Christ and God the Father, who raised him from the dead."[8] And so he, who had been made an apostle, not by men but by Christ himself and God the Father, and who had been adequately instructed by the author of wisdom, still went to the teaching authority of Peter, not for a brief time only, but remaining with him for several days as if he were in a heavenly school. "I went to Jerusalem," he said, "to see Peter, and stayed with him for fifteen days."[9] It was, therefore, by the mystic numbers[10] seven and eight that he learned the hidden mysteries of the Old Testament along with the New.

(5) Hence it was proper that your holy prudence should direct the question for solution to the see of him to whom a man uneducated in the faith was sent by the angel, and by whom also the apostle Paul, who had already been instructed by God, was more thoroughly taught. And besides, it was said through Moses, "You have Aaron and Hur with you; if any dispute should arise, you shall refer it to them."[11]

(6) May Aaron be present, that is, Christ, "the mountain of fortitude"; may Hur also be present, namely, the "fire"[12] which is the Holy Spirit himself of whom I write, that he might use me, the

---

7. Acts 10.32, 9.7. See also Sabatier 3.536, with reference to Bede, *Retractatio* 10.32, 141.

8. Gal 1.1.   9. Gal 1.18.

10. For the meaning of the numbers seven and eight, see Meyer-Suntrup, *Lexicon* 479–580.

11. Exod 24.14.

12. Cf. Jerome, *Nom. hebr.* 12.6 (CC 72.73) and 15.5 (CC 72.77).

least member of the Roman Church, to clarify what is hidden to some, and that Christ, the key of David,[13] might unlock this difficult question as if it were a seal that closes the mystic book.

(7) First of all, therefore, let me explain the source of this ignorance that allows almost all the Greeks and some Latins to maintain that the Holy Spirit does not proceed from the Son, but only from the Father. This they assert from the words of the Lord by which he says, "For it is not you who speak, but it is the Spirit of your Father who speaks in you."[14] And again, "Behold, I send to you the promise of my Father."[15] And this statement, "But when the Advocate has come, whom I will send to you from the Father—the Spirit of truth who proceeds from the Father—he will bear witness about me."[16] Again the Lord says of him, "I will ask the Father, and he will give you another Advocate to be with you forever—the Spirit of truth."[17] And elsewhere he says, "But the Advocate, the Holy Spirit whom the Father will send in my name, will teach you everything."[18] And again, "If you, then, though you are bad, know how to give your children what is good for them, how much more will your heavenly Father give the good Spirit to those who ask him."[19]

(8) Citing these texts, therefore, and the like, not only from the Gospels but from other scriptural evidence as well, they assert that the Holy Spirit in no way proceeds from the Son, but only from the Father. Some such statement which seems to agree with this opinion is often found even in the doctors who use the Latin language. Clearly blessed Jerome, in his explanation of the faith sent to the bishops Alippius and Augustine, says among other things, "We believe also in the Holy Spirit, true God, who proceeds from the Father, equal in all things to the Father and to the Son."[20] Augustine also, inveighing against Maximus the

---

13. Cf. Rev 3.7.   14. Matt 10.20.
15. Luke 24.49.   16. John 15.26.
17. John 14.16–17.   18. John 14.26.

19. Matt 7.11; but cf. Sabatier 3.40, where Ambrose adds: "will give the good Spirit," taken from Luke 11.13.

20. Ryan, *Sources* no. 271, cites Pelagius, *Libellus fidei* 3 (PL 45.1716; PL 48.489B). The *Libellus* was also ascribed to Jerome (=Pseudo-Jerome, *Epist.* 16, PL 30.176B). Where Damian found the addressees as Alippius and Augustine is unknown. See also Damian, *Letter* 81, n. 88.

heretic, says, "The Son is from the Father, the Holy Spirit is from the Father."[21] Even Pope St. Leo, on the silver plaque erected before the most sacred body of St. Paul the Apostle, says among other formulations of his faith, "And [we believe] in the Holy Spirit, the Lord and giver of life, who proceeds from the Father—with the Father and the Son to be jointly adored and glorified."[22] In the creed of the Council of Nicaea, moreover, it says, "We also believe in the Holy Spirit, who proceeds properly from the Father, and who just as the Son is true God"; and a little further on, "And that the Holy Spirit is also true God we find in Scripture, and that he proceeds properly from the Father, and that he always exists with the Father and the Son." And again it says, "The Son is from the Father, and the Holy Spirit proceeds properly and truly from the Father."[23]

(9) Yet these and similar testimonies from the Scriptures or the words of the holy doctors are not prejudicial to the Catholic faith, by which, just as we believe that the Holy Spirit proceeds from the Father, so we maintain nonetheless that he proceeds from the Son as well. For while both the Lord himself and the holy doctors of the Church agree in asserting that the Holy Spirit proceeds from the Father, never do they hold that he does not proceed from the Son. Rather, when the Holy Spirit is said to proceed from the Father, it must be believed that he proceeds also from the Son, because there is no doubt that the Father and the Son are of one and the same substance. For when the Son says, "The Father and I are one,"[24] how can the Holy Spirit both proceed and not proceed from that which is one?

(10) But something ineffable, which cannot be conceived by any natural capacity of human reason and cannot be discerned

---

21. Ryan, *Sources* no. 272, cites Smaragdus, *Libellus de processione sancti Spiritus* (MGH Conc. 2.1.239); Augustine, *Contra Maximinum* 2.14.1 (PL 42.770).

22. Ryan, *Sources* 125f. no. 273, conjectures that Damian cited the Latin text before the image of St. Paul on the authority of the *Liber pontificalis* cap. 98, 2.26. Ryan is not certain that Damian is reporting the inscription based on his own knowledge.

23. Ryan, *Sources* 126 no. 274, refers to Pseudo-Jerome, *Epistola* 17, c. 1 (PL 30.176D) and c. 3 (PL 30.179D), in which, as well as in Damian's citation, the word *filioque* is omitted. Thus, we are dealing with an interpolation.

24. John 10.30.

by any insight or application of the mind, must be gathered only
from statements found in the Word of God. For as the Apostle
says, "The Holy[25] Spirit searches everything, even the depths of
God. Who among men knows the things which pertain to man
except man's own spirit within him? In the same way, no one
knows the things which pertain to God except the Spirit of God.
We, moreover, have not received the spirit of this world, but the
Spirit who is from God, so that we may know all that we have
been given by God; we utter these things not in words taught by
human wisdom but in the teaching of the Spirit."[26] For how can
human insight attain to the knowledge of how the Father ineffably begets the Son, of how the Holy Spirit proceeds from the Father or from both, unless almighty God reveal it to mortal men
through the instrumentality of the prophets or through his in-
carnate Word? "For faith," as the Apostle says, "is the substance of
things hoped for, the evidence of things not seen."[27] Moreover,
we have the solid statement of John that says, "Here and now,
dearest friends, we are God's children; what we shall be has not
yet appeared. We know that when it appears, we shall be like
him, because we shall see him as he is."[28] Therefore, to comprehend this supreme and ineffable mystery of the true faith, let us
not follow the investigation of what men think, but embrace only
the truth of the heavenly message, that above all else we believe
about God what is divinely revealed, and that the constancy of
our faith may not falter in those things which the supreme and
incomprehensible Truth asserts.

(11) Moreover, neither among the Greeks nor among the
Latins is there any question that the Holy Spirit proceeds from
the Father. Nor need one cite evidence for this, since the texts
we quoted above declare this very thing. But that he proceeds
from the Father, and at the same time, from the Son, which is
the question we are addressing, we learn from the authority of
the Gospels, for the Lord says, "But the Advocate, the Holy Spirit
whom the Father will send in my name, will teach you everything."[29] And elsewhere, "When the Advocate has come whom I

---

25. The word "Holy" is an addition of Damian.
26. 1 Cor 2.10–13.   27. Heb 11.1.
28. 1 John 3.2.   29. John 14.26.

will send you from the Father."[30] Since, therefore, the Father sends the Advocate in the name of the Son, and the Son sends him from the Father, it is evident that because he is sent by both who are undoubtedly one, he also surely proceeds from both. And since he is often called the Spirit of Truth, and since Christ is the Truth, he who is the Spirit of Truth is undoubtedly the Spirit of the Son. And so elsewhere the Lord says, "He will glorify me, because he will receive from what is mine."[31] He will indeed receive from what is mine, because he is also in me. Thus also in Isaiah the voice of the Father said to the Son, "My Spirit which is in you and my words which I have put in your mouth shall never depart from your mouth and from the mouth of your descendants forever."[32] This same Spirit is the power that went out from him, as we read in the Gospel,[33] and cured them all.

(12) And again he said of the woman cured of her hemorrhages, "I felt that power had gone out from me."[34] And so the Apostle wrote to the Galatians, "Because you are the sons of God," he said, "God has sent into your hearts the Spirit of his Son, crying 'Abba! Father!' "[35] And elsewhere, "If a man does not possess the Spirit of Christ, he does not belong to him."[36] Note that the Apostle here says, "The Spirit of his Son," or "the Spirit of Christ." Does he even add, "and of the Father," so as to say "the Spirit of Christ and of the Father"? In speaking of the Spirit of the Son without mentioning the Father, does it follow that he is denying that the Spirit belongs to the Father? The same Apostle also says to the Philippians, "I know that this will profit me unto salvation through your prayer and the assistance of the Spirit of Jesus Christ."[37] So it is that the Wisdom of God, which is undoubtedly Christ himself, says, "My spirit is sweeter than honey, and my inheritance sweeter than dripping honey and the honey-comb."[38]

(13) Therefore, just as when we speak of the Spirit of the Son or of Christ, it does not immediately follow that we can disunite him from the Father, so too when we call him the Spirit of the Fa-

---

30. John 15.26.
31. John 16.14.
32. Isa 59.21.
33. Cf. Luke 6.19.
34. Luke 8.46.
35. Gal 4.6. For Damian's variant from the Vulgate, see Sabatier 3.775.
36. Rom 8.9.
37. Phil 1.19.
38. Sir 24.27.

ther, we cannot separate him from the Son. Blessed Peter also says, "This salvation was the theme which the prophets sought out and explored, those who prophesied about the glory[39] which is to come in you. They tried to find out to what time and what circumstances the Spirit of Christ in them was pointing at while foretelling the sufferings in Christ and the glories to follow."[40] But that the Son sent the same Spirit upon the disciples is stated by Peter in the Acts of the Apostles, when he says, "Exalted thus at God's right hand, he received the promise of the Holy Spirit from the Father and then poured out this gift, which you see and hear."[41] And so it was that when he had risen from the dead and had appeared to the disciples, that he might clearly show that the Spirit proceeds from him, he breathed on them and said, "Receive the Holy Spirit."[42]

(14) Nor must we think that this bodily breathing, which then disturbed the air, was the Holy Spirit, but by this apt figure he fitly indicated that the Holy Spirit proceeded from him. In speaking of the Son of God, Isaiah also added, "The rod of his mouth shall strike the earth, and with the Spirit from his lips he shall slay the wicked."[43] Agreeing with this statement, Paul says in the epistle to the Thessalonians, "Then he will be revealed, that wicked one, whom the Lord Jesus will destroy with the Spirit from his mouth and annihilate by the radiance of his coming."[44] This is also mystically described in the book of blessed Job, when it is said, "He will listen to what is heard in the terror of his voice, and to the sound that proceeds from his mouth."[45] In this passage then, the mouth of the Father means the Son, through whom in this case the establishment of God's law is promulgated for us. But the sound that proceeds from his mouth is the Holy Spirit, who resounded in a marvelous fashion as he came forth from the Son, and with a sudden noise, speaking in a variety of tongues, descended upon the apostles. "And suddenly," we read,

---

39. For variants from the Vulgate, see Sabatier 3.946 and *Beuron Vetus Latina* 26.1 (1956–69) 79.

40. 1 Pet 1.10–11.

41. Acts 2.33. For variants, again see Sabatier 3.505.

42. John 20.22.   43. Isa 11.4.

44. 2 Thess 2.8.

45. Job 37.2. For this variant, see *Biblia Sacra* 9.188.

"there came from the sky a sound like that of a wind arriving in great vehemence."[46] Now this sound that came forth from the mouth of Christ is undoubtedly the two-edged sword which in the Apocalypse John saw coming out from his lips.[47] And the psalmist also says of him, "By the Lord's word the heavens were established, and by the Spirit from his mouth all their host was made."[48] Therefore, as I have said, since the mouth of the Father is the Son, we can only interpret the Spirit from the mouth of God to be the Spirit of Christ.

(15) But if one should ask, "Since the Son is of the substance of the Father, and the Holy Spirit is also of the substance of the Father, why is one the Son and the other not also the Son?" it would not be inconsistent to reply as follows. The Son is from the Father, the Holy Spirit is from the Father, but the former is begotten, while the latter proceeds; and therefore the former is the Son of the Father, from whom he is begotten, while the latter is the Spirit of both because he proceeds from both. Nevertheless, this begetting and procession are not only ineffable but also totally incomprehensible. But in those things which we are unable to penetrate with the power of our mind, we apply a sure faith to those through whom the Holy Spirit has spoken, just as if the matter lay clearly before our eyes. And even though these hidden mysteries of profound depth are unknown to us, still we are not in doubt about what the Lord has spoken, we are also not uncertain about what is found in the pronouncements of the prophets.

(16) But perhaps you will object to what I have said [in the following terms]: You do not understand the Gospel and do not know the import of the oracular statements made by the prophets, which on the surface often mean one thing literally while they contain something else in the truth of the spiritual understanding. To this I find no difficulty in replying that before our time there were many apostolic and Catholic men of whose attested devotion and sanctity there remained absolutely no doubt because of the many signs of virtue which they showed. It was these men who explained the orthodox faith in simple

46. Acts 2.2.   47. Cf. Rev 1.16.
48. Ps 32.6.

terms, and left to posterity a record [of their teaching] in written
form. It was clearly their task to derive these matters from the
statements of the apostles and the prophets, and there is nothing else left for us to do but only to obey the definitions [of doc-
trine] which they have determined beforehand. Surely they were
under obligation to investigate these matters carefully and diligently, and to define the rule of faith with certainty; we must
simply follow the path along which our forefathers have preceded us.

(17) That which in their day they avidly drew from the foun-
tainhead of the Gospels, the prophets, and also the apostles they
faithfully passed on that we, coming after them, might drink, as
the psalmist says, "In the assemblies, bless the Lord God from
the fountains of Israel."[49] And now we, secure indeed and totally
without fear, receive with the purity of faith that which came to
us from them as through streams of truth, and we gladly accept
this drink as if it were drawn from the primary source of the divine fountain.

(18) So let us hear what blessed Ambrose says about the procession of the Holy Spirit in the sixth book *On the Faith* that he
sends to the emperor Gratian. "It is not," he says, "as if the Spirit
is sent from some place, or as if he proceeds from some place,
when he proceeds from the Son." And a little further on, "In proceeding from the Father, the Holy Spirit goes out from the
Son."[50] Nor is it improper for him to proceed from both, since he
is equally in both, as Ambrose also states in book eight of the
same work, "Just as the Father is in the Son, and the Son is in the
Father, thus the Spirit of God is both in the Father and in the
Son."[51] Although throughout almost the entire work he composed on the holy Trinity Augustine asserts on countless occa-

---

49. Ps 67.27.
50. Ryan, *Sources* 127 no. 275, cites Ambrose, *De Spiritu Sancto* 1.11 no. 119
(CSEL 79.66) and no. 120 (CSEL 79.67). In the second citation, Ambrose has:
"and the Holy Spirit, when he proceeds from the Father and from the Son." This
citation is found also in Smaragdus, *Libellus* (MGH Concil. 2.1.238.30), likewise
known to Damian, but he fails here to mention "in the sixth book."
51. Ambrose, *De Spiritu Sancto* 3.1 no. 6 (CSEL 79.151), where Ambrose has:
"thus the Spirit of God and the Spirit of Christ is both in the Father and in the
Son." Cf. Ryan, *Sources* 127 no. 276.

sions that the Holy Spirit proceeds from the Father and at the same time from the Son, I will cite at least one of his statements, lest I appear to have neglected him and completely passed him by. "In this holy Trinity," he says, "there is one Father who alone from himself essentially begot one Son, and the one Son who alone is born essentially of the one Father, and one Holy Spirit who alone essentially proceeds from the Father and the Son."[52] Jerome also is said to have written the following, "The Spirit who proceeds from the Father and from the Son is coeternal and in all things coequal to the Father and the Son. This is the holy Trinity, that is, the Father and the Son and the Holy Spirit: it is one deity and power, one essence, that is, the Father who has begotten, the Son who is begotten, and the Holy Spirit who proceeds from the Father and from the Son."[53] This statement, however, cannot be found in his exposition of the faith, at least not in that version which I read. Also blessed Pope Gregory had this to say in the creed of his confession, "I believe in the unbegotten Father, in the begotten Son, and in the Holy Spirit, neither begotten nor unbegotten, but coeternal, proceeding from the Father and from the Son."[54]

(19) But if, on the other hand, those who are acquainted only with Greek and know no Latin should say that doctors in the Roman tongue do not suffice for them unless I also use Greek-speaking Fathers, let them hear what blessed Athanasius states in the book he wrote against Arius. "I believe," he said, "that the Son is in the Father, and the Father in the Son, and also that the Spirit, the Advocate who proceeds from the Father, is of the Son as well as of the Father, because he proceeds from the Son, as it is written in the Gospel that by his breathing upon them he gave the Holy Spirit to the disciples."[55] Also blessed Cyril says of this

---

52. Ryan, *Sources* 127 no. 277. But Damian was citing from Smaragdus, *Libellus* (MGH Concil. 2.1.238.37–40). The text is from Fulgentius of Ruspe, *De fide ad Petrum* c. 6, 139 (CC 91A, 715–716).

53. Smaragdus, *Libellus* (MGH Concil. 2.1.238.32); cf. Ryan, *Sources* no. 278.

54. John the Deacon, *Vita Gregorii* 2.2 (PL 75.87f.) = Gregory I, *Symbolum fidei* (PL 77.1327D); cf. Ryan, *Sources* no. 279.

55. Cf. Ryan, *Sources* 128 no. 280, citing Smaragdus, *Libellus* (MGH Concil. 2.1.238.20) and Pseudo-Athanasius, *Professio Ariana et confessio catholica* in Theodulfus, *De Spiritu Sancto* (PL 105.242A).

same procession of the Spirit in writing against Nestorius, "For even though in his substance he is his Spirit, and is understood to have his own personality in that he is the Spirit and not the Son, still he is not alien to him. For he is called the Spirit of Truth, and the Truth is Christ. Hence in like manner he proceeds from him, just as he proceeds from God the Father."[56]

(20) But perhaps it is still asked: Since the Spirit proceeds from the Father and from the Son, why does that very Son say that he proceeds from the Father? Why is it that he did not say, "He proceeds from the Father and from me," but said rather, "The Spirit who proceeds from the Father"? Why do we think that he did this except that he is accustomed to refer even that which is his own to him from whom he is? The Son, indeed, is from the Father, and from him to whom he owes his being as God, he also has the property that the Holy Spirit also proceeds from him. And so elsewhere he says, "My teaching is not my own, but of him who sent me."[57] If, therefore, it is here clearly known that it is his teaching, which nevertheless he said is not his own but his Father's, how much more should it be understood there that the Holy Spirit proceeds from him, when he said, "He proceeds from the Father," so as in no wise to say, "He does not proceed from me"? That statement also, which he makes on another occasion, is similar to this, "He who believes in me does not believe in me, but in him who sent me."[58] What does he mean when he says, "He who believes in me does not believe in me"? How does one believe in him and not believe in him? How is one to understand something so contrary, something so much in opposition to itself through contradictory words as "He who believes in me does not believe in me, but in him who sent me," unless it is understood in this way, "He who believes in me" does not believe in what he sees, so that our hope is not placed in a creature, but in him who took on a creature. He said this in order to make known to us mortals that he is one with the Father and to cleanse the human hearts for the contemplation of him together with his Father. So, when he says, "My doctrine is not my own," he

---

56. Cf. Ryan, *Sources* no. 281, citing Smaragdus, *Libellus* 238 (MGH Concil. 2.1.238.25).

57. John 7.16.   58. John 12.44.

generates no little fog in the minds, unless the orderly use of reason is able to distinguish the physical from the spiritual. He did not say, "This teaching is not my own," but "my teaching is not my own." That very [doctrine] which he called his own he also called not his own. Now how could this be true, unless in one respect he calls it his own, and in another calls it not his own? In that he is God, it is his; in that he is a servant, it is not his. Thus, when he says, "[It is] not my own, but of him who sent me," he directs the insight of our mind to the Word itself that was hidden in the flesh, so it may know that he is at the same time one with the Father. For the teaching of the Father is the Father's Word, who is his only Son. Therefore, in saying, "My teaching is not my own," it must be understood as if he is saying, "I am not from myself, but from him who sent me."

(21) And so when he states his teaching, which at the same time he declares together with the Father to be not his own but the Father's, why should we wonder at his saying that the Holy Spirit proceeds from the Father, from whom, indeed, the Son himself had the attribute that the Spirit should proceed also from him? Hence, when in the creed of the Council of Nicaea, to which we referred above, the Holy Spirit is said to proceed not just from the Father without any qualification, but with the added word, "properly"[59]—"and [we believe] in the Holy Spirit," it says, "who proceeds properly from the Father"—this "properly" is not referred to the Father in such a way that the Holy Spirit proceeds from him alone, but that from him is given to the Son the attribute that he proceeds also from him. Hence also Augustine says in his book *On the Blessed Trinity*, "It is not without reason that in this Trinity only the Son is called the Word of God, and that only the Holy Spirit is the Gift of God, and that only God the Father is he, of whom the Word was begotten, and from whom the Holy Spirit principally proceeds." And then he continues, "I have, therefore, added 'principally,' because the Holy Spirit is found to proceed also from the Son. Yet the Father also gave this to him, not as though he already existed and did not yet have it, but whatever he gave to the only-begotten Word, he gave

---

59. Ryan, *Sources* 128 no. 282, refers to Pseudo-Jerome, *Epistola* 17, c. 1 (PL 30.176D), as mentioned *supra* in n. 23.

by begetting him."[60] The faith should not, therefore, be disturbed when one hears that the Holy Spirit proceeds properly or principally from the Father, because this attribute is given by the Father to the Son that the Spirit proceeds from him, and from the Father he also proceeds by an ineffable and incomprehensible generation, as he, who is the Wisdom of the Father, says through Solomon, "I came forth from the mouth of the Most High."[61] And we read in the Gospel, "For I proceeded and came from God."[62] We must also carefully beware lest in saying that the Son has it from the Father that the Advocate proceeds from him, we should also believe that the Holy Spirit proceeds from the Father to the Son, and proceeds from the Son for our sanctification. Far be it that this should be believed, lest it appear, as it were, that the simple and incomprehensible divinity is arranged in various steps, since Scripture says, "You must not ascend to my altar by steps."[63]

(22) Indeed, it must be believed without any doubt that the Holy Spirit proceeds simultaneously from both, even though the Father gave this property to the Son, that just as he proceeds from himself, the Spirit should proceed also from him. For the Holy Spirit is a certain ineffable communion of the Father and the Son, and it seems, therefore, that his name is appropriate, because this term certainly fits both the Father and the Son. For the Holy Spirit is properly given a name according to that which the Father and the Son are jointly called, since both the Father is spirit and the Son is spirit, the Father holy and the Son holy. And just as his name applies without distinction to both, so he proceeds simultaneously from both.

(23) I could gather still further texts from the Scriptures, nor would it be impossible to use [other] outstanding defenders of the Catholic faith along with their arguments in support of my contention. But since we are forbidden by law to plant a grove of trees near the altar,[64] I have no intention of hiding the fruits of

---

60. Ryan, *Sources* 128f. no. 283, citing Augustine, *De trinitate* 15.17 (CC 50A, 503–504). This text is not in Smaragdus; Damian could have cited it directly from Augustine.

61. Sir 24.5.

63. Exod 20.26.

62. John 8.42.

64. Cf. Judg 6.25–26.

the Spirit under the thick foliage of garrulous speech. Therefore may Your Holiness, venerable father, even though fully
and lavishly refreshed by the food of God's word, hunger more
and more for the truth, and in the meantime not despise this
meager appetizer from a poor little man, so that afterwards you
may enjoy the delights of a royal banquet from the hands of
our lord pope, as though through the prophet Habakkuk,[65] or
even through an angel.

65. Cf. Dan 14.31–38.

LETTER 92

Peter Damian to the hermit Adam. Requested by his confrere to discourse upon events before creation, upon what will happen to the world after the Last Judgment, and upon the Judgment itself, Damian admits his ignorance. He agrees, however, that meditation on these subjects is good for the soul and proceeds to write about the reign of Antichrist. Damian presents the fifteen signs that will occur on the fifteen days preceding the Last Judgment (taken from Pseudo-Bede and Haimo of Auxerre). He advises Adam to apply the lessons to be learned from meditation on the end of the world to his own spiritual life, judging himself now, so that he will not be in need of judgment before the last tribunal. This letter escaped inclusion in all major manuscripts of the eleventh century but is found in twenty later manuscripts that paid special attention to Damian's discussion of the last days. A new conclusion, not printed in Migne's *Patrologia Latina* and found in only three manuscripts, has been added here.

(*ca.* 1062)[1]

O HIS MOST BELOVED brother Adam,[2] the monk Peter the sinner offers humble servitude in the Lord.

(2) Dearest brother, in questioning me on what took place before the creation of the world, on what will happen to the world after the Judgment yet to come, and in ingeniously asking about the Judgment itself, you are indeed behaving devoutly and prudently, but you draw me into the unknown and compel me to teach what I have not yet learned. Clearly, you are inquiring about something I do not know; you are searching for information in a matter of which I am ignorant. For Isaiah also says, "Proclaim to me things of before and those that are to be in the very end, and I will say that you are gods,"[3] obviously wishing

1. The dating follows Lucchesi, *Vita* 2.153.
2. It appears likely that the Adam referred to in *Letter* 109 as a model of penitential heroism is the same as the present addressee.
3. Isa 41.22–23. See also Sabatier 2.584, where this text is similarly cited in Jerome, *Epistola* 18A, c. 7 (CSEL 54.83).

to state that no one can explain what took place before the world or what will happen afterwards. Yet it is profitable to inquire, even though the subject absolutely defies explanation. For the human mind by nature is not able to remain unoccupied by thoughts. It either exerts itself in serious matters or delights in the frivolous; and while thinking about useful things, it is protected from the invasion of attacking thoughts. Nor does depravity find an opportunity of whispering into its ear where the mind, intent on what is useful, keeps close counsel with sober thoughts. Therefore, it is worthwhile and highly useful to meditate on the shortness of passing time when compared with unbroken eternity. For if we should wish to compare that immeasurable span of time in which God existed before the beginning of this world, and that in which he will continue to exist after the end of the same world, with the short amount of time that stretches from the beginning of the world until its end, by comparison it would amount to less than if you would throw a handful of water into the sea or if you would try to compare the length of a cubit with the total size of the earth. For both the vastness of the sea and the size of the earth are finite, just as a handful of water or the length of a cubit, though the former are greater, while the latter are incomparably smaller. And so, finite things can more easily be compared with finite, than things that have an end with those that cannot be concluded by an end. For since God is the "Alpha and Omega, the beginning and the end,"[4] and as he always existed without beginning, so he can have no end. But it is known that from its beginning at the creation this world has not yet completed seven thousand years.[5] And who knows how short will be the span of time until God judges the world? How therefore can seven thousand, or even ten thousand years[6] be compared to the unending essence of God, which could have neither beginning nor end?

(3) And thus, as we analyze this and similar topics in ever

4. Rev 22.13.

5. For these seven thousand years as the age of the world, see Reindel, *Briefe* 3.15, n. 3, which gives extensive citation of sources and literature.

6. This extension is interesting in terms of the evolutionary progress of the world, and in the process goes beyond its sources.

watchful meditation, as we turn these things over in our thoughts with precision, no small advantage accrues to our mind, since, while it meditates on things eternal, it clearly sees how much temporal things are to be despised. And so, as the rational mind thinks through these matters, it comes to the notion that it too will not pass away with time, but will survive without end. It considers, moreover, that it possesses such a nature, that of necessity it will either enjoy perpetual reward or be tormented by eternal suffering. Therefore, no little benefit derives from diligently analyzing these things and taking careful precautions for the date of Judgment. On this day, the one for whom it has turned out in his favor will once and for all no longer fall down, while the one for whom the matter has gone awry will not get up again. For the information you seek on the day of Judgment and on the Antichrist, you should read St. Augustine's work *On the City of God*,[7] St. Jerome's *Explanation of the Prophet Daniel*,[8] and also the *Apocalypse* with its commentaries,[9] in which you will surely find sufficient discussion of this subject. For as, in the first place, the authentic works of Scripture indicate, and afterwards the additional writings of the expositors make clear, Antichrist[10] will reign for three and a half years. After Elijah and Enoch have been killed by him, St. Michael the archangel will slay Antichrist and most of his members.[11] This is not opposed to what the Apostle says, "The Lord Jesus will slay him with the breath of his mouth and destroy him by the radiance of his coming."[12] For whether Christ kills him directly or uses an angelic agent, it is by him principally that the ancient pest is destroyed, by whose might and power he is overcome. Moreover, as is conveyed by learned

---

7. See FOTC, vols. 8, 14, 24.   8. Jerome, *In Danielem.*

9. For pre-Damian commentaries on the Apocalypse, see Reindel, *Briefe* 3.17, n. 7.

10. For a general treatment of the Antichrist, see E. Lohmeyer, "Antichrist," *Reallexikon für Antike und Christentum* 1 (1950) 450–457; B. McGinn, *Visions of the End: Apocalyptic Traditions in the MA* (Records of Civilization. Sources and Studies 96, 1979).

11. On the length of Antichrist's rule, see Victorinus of Pettau, *Commentarii in Apocalypsin*, ed. J. Haussleiter, CSEL 49 (1916) 12–153, esp. 114; Haimo of Auxerre, *In epistola prima ad Thessalonicenses*, c. 5 (PL 117.773C–774A); and other sources cited by Reindel, *Briefe* 3.17, n. 9.

12. 2 Thess 2.8.

men, the Lord will kill him on the Mount of Olives, seated on his
throne in his tent, on the very spot from which he ascended triumphantly into heaven as his apostles looked on.[13] And thus Isaiah says, "On the holy mountain the Lord will cast down the face
of the ruler of darkness, and him who rules all peoples."[14] Of him
also Daniel says, "He will utter words against the Most High and
will wear down the saints of the Most High. He will think that he
can alter times and laws, and they will be delivered into his hand
for a time and times and half a time."[15] From this we conclude
that Antichrist will reign for three and a half years. For *time* is a
year, and *times* are two years.[16] Therefore, he is to reign for three
and a half years. Then he has to be killed by the sword of God's
fury so that the tyrant will be completely ruined and every creature will submit to the true King. And so, the same Daniel says,
"He will take his seat unto judgment, that his sovereignty may be
taken away, crushed, and abolished forever. The kingdom, however, and the power and the greatness of the kingdom, which is
beneath[17] the heavens will be granted to the people of the saints
of the Most High, whose kingdom is everlasting, and all kings
will serve him and obey."[18]

(4) Then, after the death of Antichrist, forty-five days will remain until the coming of Jesus Christ,[19] during which persecution will come to an end and there will be great peace and tranquillity, so that within this space of time those just ones who had
wavered under the strain of persecution may do penance, and
the servants of the devil may relax in the security of idleness and
inactivity. For, as in the days of Noah,[20] they will plant and build,
attend banquets, contract marriages—and while they are intent
upon the pursuit of frivolous vanity, sudden destruction will

13. For patristic references, see Reindel, *Briefe* 3.18, n. 11.

14. Isa 25.7. For this variant from the Vulgate, cf. Jerome, *In Danielem* 4.11,
ed. F. Glorie, CC 75A (1964) 935.

15. Dan 7.25.

16. Cf. Jerome, *In Danielem* 2.7, 849.

17. For the variant *supra* see Reindel, *Briefe* 3.19, n. 15.

18. Dan 7.26–27.

19. These times and events are found also in Jerome, Bede, and Haimo, *Ad
Thess.* 1.5 (PL 117.773D); see Reindel, *Briefe* 3.19, n. 16.

20. Cf. Matt 24.37–38.

come upon them. To your further questions as to whether this world would first be destroyed by fire, and then afterwards the Judgment would take place, it has been determined by the clear opinion of most commentators that the Judgment precedes and the conflagration of the world follows.[21] For when the Judgment has been finished, fire will suddenly erupt and occupy so much of the airspace as was filled by the rising waters of the great flood. This fire will burn the earth and the dense part of the air, and will thus purify the elect. But since I collected some of the evidence of the Scriptures on the day of Judgment in the letter which I wrote to the Countess Blanche,[22] and on this theme so much is also found in the expositors of the Sacred Word that it cannot be abridged within the limits of a letter, I direct you to their overflowing streams as I advise you to avoid dried-up rills and rather drink of the fountains of Israel.

(5) And yet, I do not think it superfluous to insert here in his very own words what I have learned to be reported by blessed Jerome[23] about the fifteen signs that will occur on the same number of days preceding the day of Judgment. But just as I do not quite accept these words as authoritative, so too I do not completely deny their credibility. This matter, therefore, just as it has come down to us, has been inserted into this hand without distinction, so that from their writings it may become known also to the ancient peoples of the Hebrews, for whom the terror of divine judgment has increased. He says:[24]

21. For patristic opinion, see Reindel, *Briefe* 3.20, n.17.

22. See *Letter* 66. This reference provides evidence for the authenticity of the present letter.

23. Not found in the authentic writings of Jerome; see R. E. Lerner, "Refreshment of the Saints," *Traditio* 32 (1976) 103, n. 20.

24. On the ascription of this portion of Damian's letter to Jerome, then to Pseudo-Jerome, and eventually to Pseudo-Bede, see W. W. Heist, *The Fifteen Signs Before Doomsday* (East Lansing, Michigan, 1952) 25; with a wealth of literature, Heist identifies Damian's source as Pseudo-Bede (PL 94.555B-D). The two lists of fifteen signs do not agree in detail, but there is enough similarity to suggest dependence, or mutual dependence on some earlier text. Heist, *Signs* 125, 130, doubts the presence of an English line of MS tradition for this legend, lying between Pseudo-Bede and Damian, but sees the two families of MSS as direct progenitors of later versions, reaching down to Thomas Aquinas and into Irish, German, and Old-French narratives. See also Reindel, *Briefe* 3.20–22, n. 20.

Sign of the first day: All the seas will be raised up to a height of fifteen cubits above the highest mountains. They will not damage the land, but will stand like sea walls.

Sign of the second day: All the seas sink to the uttermost depths, so that they can hardly be seen by human eyes.

Sign of the third day: All the seas will be restored to their ancient state, just as they had been created from the beginning.

Sign of the fourth day: All the beasts and all that moves in the waters of the sea will be brought together and lifted above the massive ocean as if they were in a great contention, bellowing and roaring at one another; men will not know what they are saying or what they are thinking, but only God knows, for whom all things live to render service."

These four signs pertain to the sea, and the three that follow to the lower and upper air.

Sign of the fifth day: All the birds of the heavens will gather in the plains, each kind in its own group. These birds will be conversing and pleading with one another, neither eating nor drinking, fearing the coming of the Judge.

Sign of the sixth day: Streams of fire will well up across the face of the heavens, running their course from sunset to dawn.

Sign of the seventh day: All the stars, wandering and stationary, will display fiery tails, as we see in comets, a sign for the world and its inhabitants.

Sign of the eighth day: A great earthquake will occur, so that no man can stand, or any animal, but all will be laid flat on the ground.

Sign of the ninth day: All stones, great and small, will be broken into four parts, and each will strike against the other, and no man, but only God, will understand that sound.

Sign of the tenth day: All the trees of the forests and all the blades of grass will be streaming with a bloody dew.

Sign of the eleventh day: All the mountains and hills and all man-made structures previously built will be reduced to dust.

Sign of the twelfth day: All the animals of the earth will come from the forests and the mountains down to the plains, roaring and bellowing, neither eating nor drinking.

Sign of the thirteenth day: All graves from sunrise to sunset will open, and the dead will rise up as far as the mouth of the grave.

Sign of the fourteenth day: The whole human race that was still to be found will quickly leave the abodes and places in which they will be, neither understanding nor speaking, but running to and fro like madmen.

Sign of the fifteenth day: All men still alive will die, in order to rise

again with the dead who had passed away long before. The end, that is,
day of Judgment.[25]

Since, therefore, the ancient period has passed through seven
ages, but in the eighth age the time of the Gospel unfolds,[26] and
since from seven and eight the total of fifteen is obtained, it was
indeed fitting that the same number of signs that go to make up
time, should bring both times to an end. But the option of believing or not believing these things we put at the reader's discretion, or, rather, we leave it to the knowledge of almighty God,
to whom all things are evident.

(6) You then, venerable brother, meditate carefully on these
and similar matters. Never cease exerting on them the natural
talents of your mind, so that as you turn them over within your
conscience, intent on that which is serious, you may shut out the
foolishness of empty thoughts. Now empty thoughts issue from
coldness of heart, that is, when the soul grows lukewarm in its
love for the true bridegroom and, as it were, runs after other
lovers through other figments of thought. For as soon as it dis-
entangles itself and leaves the embrace of its Redeemer, in its
false freedom it wanders about with vagrant steps through the
enticements of titillating thoughts, that, as the prophet says,[27] it
may sprawl like an unchaste prostitute under every shady tree,
and, stretched out, subject its body to every passer-by. Then the
unhappy soul is at once cold and unsettled, because while it, in
growing cold, is not attached to the love of its Creator, it is
snatched up, as in a gusting wind, by the force of attacking vices.
And so, the prophet says, "The food of the serpent is his dust."[28]
And David says, "Wicked men are not like this; no, they are like
dust that the wind kicks up from the face of the earth."[29]

---

25. The following text was not edited in Gaetani nor in its reprint by Migne,
but by Giuseppe Luca Pasini, *Codices manuscripti bibliothecae Regiae Taurinensis* 2
(1749) 40–41, and by Mittarelli-Costadoni, *Annales Camaldulenses* 9.9–10, following a MS of Turin. See later edition from *Cod. Vat. Pal. lat.* 300 by J. Leclercq,
Revue bénédictine 67 (1957) 165–168.

26. On the meaning of seven and eight in this context, see Gregory I,
Moralia 35.8.17 (CC 143B, 1784f.).

27. Cf. Jer 2.20.   28. Isa 65.25.
29. Ps 1.4.

(7) So then, my dear friend, be what you are called, that in very fact you may visibly express the mystery contained in your name. "Adam," to be sure, means "red earth."[30] And indeed Ecclesiastes says, "Generations pass away and generations come, but the earth stands forever."[31] And in the Canticle the beloved says to his spouse, "Your lips are like a scarlet headband, and your words are sweet. Your cheeks are like a section of pomegranate."[32] Thus "earth" denotes the stability of constancy, while "red" indicates the ardor of charity. Speaking boldly, I will say that no one but Adam enters the kingdom of heaven, and only he who contains in himself the hidden mystery of his name can hope to join the company of the elect. Therefore, be "earth," so that standing firm with a fixed weight, you may not be blown away by the breeze of attacking temptations. You should also be "red," that your mind may always grow warm at the love of its Redeemer. Be "earth," that an abundant spiritual harvest may spring from you; be "red," so that the fire of heavenly desire may ignite the altar of your soul. Be "earth," that by the safeguard of humility you may always keep yourself down in the lowest place, as befits worthless mud; be "red," nevertheless, so that, by coming to a boil yourself, you may enkindle whomever you can to yearn for the things of heaven. Be "earth," that you may not establish within yourself the foundation of a wavering faith; be "red," so that the structure of attached virtues may be built up on the foundation of charity, that there may be in you, as the Apostle says, "faith that works through love."[33]

(8) Thus, you should set before yourself the day of Judgment as something grand and fearful, toward which the total span of time is geared, and to which all the pages of Scripture render service, which the mind, no matter how brilliant, cannot comprehend as it is, nor any speech of the human tongue explain. May your mind, pierced through by the continual dread of this event, never be able to delight in the enticements of the flesh, nor be weakened by any adversity from maintaining the steady

---

30. Jerome, *Nom. hebr.* 2.17 (CC 72.60).
31. Eccl 1.4.   32. Cant 4.3.
33. Gal 5.6.

pace of an arduous way of life. Thus, let it fear the imminent day of Judgment, that you may not have to fear when it is upon you; that, as you prudently examine yourself in your own judgment, you may appear before the tribunal of the eternal Judge, not to be judged anew, but as one already judged and purified in the process; and that because through confession you have stood in the presence of the Judge, you may not be compelled to undergo the severe examination of the Judgment, but with the judges and senators of the land,[34] as a judge yourself you may joyfully be conducted into glory. Amen.

34. Cf. Prov 31.23.

LETTER 93

Peter Damian to one of his two sisters. At her request, he discusses the events of the period prior to the Last Judgment, especially the reign of Antichrist, and the fifteen days preceding the Judgment, along with the marvels that will occur on these days. This letter is a shorter version of *Letter* 92, sent to the hermit Adam, but the text is somewhat altered, reflecting either the three MSS in which it is found or changes made by Damian himself.

(*ca.* 1062)[1]

O HIS SWEETEST and most illustrious sister,[2] the monk Peter the sinner offers humble servitude in the Lord.

(2) Dearest sister, in asking me to make known to you what took place before the creation of the world, what will happen to the world after the Judgment yet to come, and in ingeniously asking about the Judgment itself, you are indeed behaving devoutly and prudently, but you draw me into the unknown and compel me to teach what I have not yet learned. Clearly, you are inquiring about something I do not know; you are searching for information in a matter of which I am ignorant. For Isaiah also says, "Proclaim to me things of before and those that are to be in the very end, and I will say that you are gods,"[3] obviously wishing to state that no one can explain what took place before the world, or what will happen afterwards. Yet it is profitable to inquire, even though the subject absolutely defies explanation. For the human mind by nature is not able to remain unoccupied by thoughts. It either exerts itself in serious matters or delights in the frivolous; and while thinking about useful things, it is protected from the invasion of attacking thoughts. Nor does de-

1. For dating, see Lucchesi, *Vita* 2.157.
2. According to Lucchesi, *Vita* 2.157, Damian refers here to his sister, Rodelinda. On her, see *Letter* 94, n. 1.
3. Isa 41.22–23.

pravity find an opportunity of whispering into its ear where the mind, intent on what is useful, keeps close counsel with sober thoughts. Therefore, it is worthwhile and highly useful to meditate on the shortness of passing time when compared with an unbroken eternity. For if we should wish to compare that immeasurable span of time in which God existed before the beginning of this world, and that in which he will continue to exist after the end of the same world, with the short amount of time that stretches from the beginning of the world till its end, by comparison it would amount to less than if you would throw a handful of water into the sea or if you would try to compare the length of a cubit with the total size of the earth. For both the vastness of the sea and the size of the earth are finite, just as a handful of water or the length of a cubit, though the former are greater, while the latter are incomparably smaller. And so, finite things can more easily be compared with finite, than things that have an end with those that cannot be concluded by an end. For since God is the "Alpha and Omega, the beginning and the end,"[4] and as he always existed without beginning, so he can have no end. But it is known that from its beginning at the creation this world has not yet completed seven thousand years. And who knows how short will be the span of time until God judges the world? How therefore can seven thousand, or even ten thousand years be compared to the unending and eternal divinity, which could have neither beginning nor end?

(3) And thus, as we analyze this and similar topics in ever watchful meditation, as we turn these things over in our thoughts with precision, no small advantage accrues to our mind, since, while it meditates on things eternal, it clearly sees how much temporal things are to be despised. And so, as the rational mind thinks through these matters, it comes to the notion that it too will not pass away with time, but will survive without end. It considers, moreover, that it possesses such a nature, that of necessity it will either enjoy perpetual reward or be tormented by eternal suffering. Therefore, no little benefit derives from diligently analyzing these things and taking careful precautions for the date

4. Rev 22.13.

of Judgment. On this day, the one for whom it has turned out in his favor will once and for all no longer fall down, while the one for whom the matter has gone awry will not get up again. For the information you seek on the day of Judgment and on the Antichrist, you should read St. Augustine's work *On the City of God,* St. Jerome's *Explanation of the Prophet Daniel,* and also the *Apocalypse* with its commentaries, in which you will surely find sufficient discussion of this subject.[5] For as, in the first place, the authentic works of Scripture indicate, and afterwards the additional writings of the expositors make clear,[6] Antichrist will reign for three and a half years. After Elijah and Enoch have been killed by him, St. Michael the archangel will slay Antichrist and most of his members. This is not opposed to what the Apostle says, "The Lord Jesus will slay him with the breath of his mouth and will destroy him by the radiance of his coming."[7] For whether Christ kills him directly or uses an angelic agent, it is by him principally that the ancient pest is destroyed, by whose might and power he is overcome. Moreover, as is conveyed by learned men, the Lord will kill him on the Mount of Olives, seated on his throne in his tent, on the very spot from which he ascended triumphantly into heaven as his apostles looked on. And thus Isaiah says, "On the holy mountain the Lord will cast down the face of the ruler of darkness, and him who rules all peoples."[8] Of him also Daniel says, "He will utter words against the Most High and will wear down the saints of the Most High. He will think that he can alter times and laws, and they will be delivered into his hand for a time and times and half a time."[9] From this we conclude that Antichrist will reign for three and a half years. For *time* is a year, and *times* are two years. Therefore, he is to reign for three and a

5. Damian presumes that his sister was able to read the letter in hand, as well as the writings of Augustine and Jerome, to which he alludes. This is exceptional for women in the eleventh century. Apart from the fact that Rodelinda and her sister Sufficia were both widows (cf. *Letter* 94), and that Rodelinda had been a second mother to him (cf. *Letter* 149 Ad Agnetem, ed. Wilmart, *Une lettre* 144), we know nothing further of Damian's sisters.

6. Here Damian uses Haimo of Auxerre, *In epistola prima ad Thess.,* c. 5 (PL 117.773C-774A).

7. 2 Thess 2.8.   8. Isa 25.7.

9. Dan 7.25.

half years. Then he has to be killed by the sword of God's fury
so that the tyrant will be completely ruined and every creature
will submit to the true King. And so, the same Daniel says, "Judgment will take its seat, that his sovereignty may be taken away,
crushed, and abolished forever. The kingdom and power and
greatness of the kingdom, which is above the heavens, will be
granted to the people of the saints of the Most High, whose kingdom is everlasting, and all kings will serve him and obey."[10]

(4) Then, after the death of Antichrist, forty-five days will remain until the coming of Christ,[11] during which persecution will
come to an end and there will be great peace and tranquillity, so
that within this space of time those just ones who had wavered
under the strain of persecution may do penance, and the servants of the devil may relax in the security of idleness and inactivity. For, as in the days of Noah,[12] they will plant and build, attend banquets, contract marriages—and while they are intent
upon the pursuit of frivolous vanity, sudden destruction will
come upon them. To your further questions as to whether this
world would first be destroyed by fire and then afterwards the
Judgment would take place, it has been determined by the clear
opinion of most commentators that the Judgment precedes and
the conflagration of the world follows. For when the Judgment
has been finished, fire will suddenly erupt and occupy the airspace to as high as the waters rose when the great flood covered
over or washed [the earth]. This fire will burn the earth and the
dense part of the air, and will thus purify the elect. But since I collected some of the evidence of the Scriptures on the day of Judgment in the letter which I wrote to the Countess Blanche,[13] and
on this theme so much is also found in the expositors of the Sacred Word that it cannot be abridged within the limits of a letter,
I direct you to their overflowing streams, as I advise you to avoid
the dried-up rills and rather drink of the fountains of Israel.

(5) And yet, I do not think it superfluous to insert here in his

10. Dan 7.26–27.
11. See Haimo, *Expositio in epistolas ad Thessalonicenses* c. 5 (PL 117.773D).
12. Cf. Matt 24.37–38.
13. Cf. Damian, *Letter* 66. This reference provides evidence for the authenticity of the present letter.

very own words what I have learned to be reported by blessed Jerome[14] about the fifteen signs that will occur on the same number of days preceding the day of Judgment. But just as I do not quite accept these words as authoritative, so too I do not completely deny their credibility. This matter, therefore, just as it has come down to us, has been inserted into this hand without distinction, so that from their writings it may become known also to the ancient peoples of the Hebrews, for whom the terror of divine judgment has increased. He says:[15]

Sign of the first day: All the seas will be raised up to a height of fifteen cubits above the highest mountains. They will not damage the land, but will stand like sea walls.

Sign of the second day: All the seas will sink to the uttermost depths, so that they can hardly be seen by human eyes.

Sign of the third day: All the seas will be restored to their ancient state, just as they had been created from the beginning.

Sign of the fourth day: All the beasts and all that moves in the waters of the sea will be brought together and lifted above the massive ocean, as if they were in a great contention, bellowing and roaring at one another; men are not knowing what they are saying or what they are thinking, but only God knows, for whom all things live to render service.

These four signs pertain to the sea, and the three that follow to the lower and upper air.

Sign of the fifth day: All the birds of the heavens will gather in the plains, each kind in its own group. These birds will be conversing and pleading with one another, neither eating nor drinking, fearing the coming of the Judge.

Sign of the sixth day: Flashes[16] of fire will well up across the face of the heavens, running their course from sunset to dawn.

Sign of the seventh day: Stars, wandering and stationary, will display fiery tails, as we see in comets, a sign for the world and its inhabitants.

Sign of the eighth day: A great earthquake will occur, so that no man can stand, or any animal, but all will be laid flat on the ground.

Sign of the ninth day: All stones, great and small, will be broken into

14. Not found in the authentic writings of Jerome. See *Letter* 92, n. 22.

15. See W. W. Heist, *The Fifteen Signs Before Doomsday* (East Lansing, Michigan, 1952) 25; Reindel, *Briefe* 3.20–22, n. 20.

16. I have followed the variant reading *fulmina* rather than *flumina*. See Reindel, *Briefe* 3.30, line 18, variant 's.'

four parts, and each will strike against the other, and no man, but only God, will understand that sound.

Sign of the tenth day: All the trees of the forests and all the blades of grass will be streaming with a bloody dew.

Sign of the eleventh day: All the mountains and hills and all man-made structures previously built will be reduced to dust.

Sign of the twelfth day: All the animals of the earth will come from the forests and the mountains down to the plains, roaring and bellowing, neither eating nor drinking.

Sign of the thirteenth day: All graves from sunrise to sunset will open, and the dead will rise up as far as the mouth of the grave.

Sign of the fourteenth day: The whole human race that was still to be found will quickly leave the abodes and places in which they will be, neither understanding nor speaking, but running to and fro like madmen.

Sign of the fifteenth day: All men still alive will die, and will rise again with the dead who had passed away long before.

LETTER 94

Peter Damian to his sisters, Rodelinda and Sufficia. In a long fraternal letter to his two widowed sisters, he advises them to persevere in both bodily and spiritual chastity, to be patient in adversity, and diligent in constant
prayer. He further exhorts them to frequent confession, to kindness toward those who wrong them, and to generosity toward the poor. He warns
them against substituting the accumulation of worldly goods for the loss
of their deceased husbands, encouraging them in their advancing years
to turn away from the world and to concentrate on things eternal. He asks
for their prayers in exchange for his spiritual advice.

(1062–1063)[1]

O MY DEAREST sisters in Christ, Rodelinda[2] and Sufficia,[3]
the monk Peter the sinner sends the deep affection of a
brother.

(2) I render many thanks to divine providence, as I learn
from the news that has spread abroad, that you are of like mind
in eagerly practicing the spiritual virtues, even though you are
still subjected to various afflictions in the world. It is well-known,
of course, that in the normal pattern of higher justice the invisible Judge in this life instructs by inflicting temporal distress on
those to whom he is disposed to grant the rights of an everlasting
inheritance. With heavy blows he chastises like slaves those
whom, already in his carefully hidden decision, he has pledged
to receive as legitimate children for the inheritance of his patrimony as their own possession. For if anyone, while leading an upright life, overflows with successes, he would rightly experience
fear in his heart lest, while seeing his good deeds rewarded with
temporal wealth, they be repaid, perhaps, with something less,

---

1. Dating follows Lucchesi, *Vita* no. 183.
2. In *Letter* 149 (ed. Wilmart, *Une lettre* 144), Damian says of his older sister,
Rodelinda, that "she nurtured me as a second mother."
3. Of Sufficia we have no further information.

or with nothing at all in eternity. But he who performs good works and is worn down by tribulations can now rightly rejoice in the certainty that he will be given, as a reward for his labors, a good measure, pressed down and shaken together.[4] For he discovers that afterwards in our homeland, the sum of his accrued interest has grown to the degree that in this life he failed to receive even the payment of a momentary well-being. And so it is said by blessed James, "My brothers, whenever you fall into various trials, count yourself possessed of every joy."[5] And to this point also Solomon says, "For whomever he loves the Lord reproves, and he chastises every son whom he receives."[6]

(3) It is not without justification, therefore, that he rejoices who, firmly established on the path of a holy way of life, as he considers himself to be surrounded with avenging lashes, has no doubt of having been adopted into the company of God's children. Only this must be avoided with anxious thought, that among the works of righteousness themselves, to which indeed a reward is owed, we should intermingle also some disordered things, be they very small, for which at least temporal punishment would be inflicted. Hence Peter says, "Let none of you suffer as a murderer or thief or slanderer or covetor of others' things."[7] Whoever, therefore, covets the things of another or abuses anyone with slanderous words does not deserve a reward for his suffering, because he suffers rightly.

(4) Now you, most beloved sisters, since by professing continence as widows after your marriage bond was dissolved, you have not only entered into union with an immortal spouse, but with application of marvelous fervor have decided to suppress, even to crucify, all incentives to the enticement of the flesh, restrain yourselves from inflicting harm on anyone, and patiently bear injury done to you by others. So that, because our Redeemer both did no evils and yet bore his cross, even now the pledge of union with that same heavenly Spouse may be apparent in you, so long as your life is in accord with his way. Even though you are unable, as virgins, to follow the Lamb wherever

---

4. Cf. Luke 6.38. 5. Jas 1.2.
6. Prov 3.12; Heb 12.6.
7. 1 Pet 4.15; for variant from the Vulgate, cf. Sabatier 3.954.

he went,[8] it would suffice for you to imitate him through the path of patience, who, indeed, through his death passed over to the resurrection of life.

(5) And lest long-lasting annoyances perhaps become tedious for you, set Anna in the Gospel before yourself as a model for your widowhood. After she had enjoyed the company of her husband for seven years, as Scripture attests without doubt,[9] she had now as a widow reached the age of eighty-four. Did she, who had received such a drawn out and aged time for living, by remaining in idle conversation or by living in luxury, temper the difficulties arising from the stooped condition of old age? For after mentioning her many years of continence, the evangelist at once adds, "Because she never left the temple, but worshipped day and night, fasting and praying."[10] What, I ask, would this woman do, were she to read the Apostle's exhortations, "Pray without ceasing,"[11] and especially if she were to hear the Lord himself calling us to persevere in constant prayer?[12] Moreover, because she fulfilled the Gospel before she could have learned of it, she was found worthy to recognize the Lord by prophetic inspiration, and, so to speak, having become an evangelist, to announce his presence. For as it is read, "Coming up at that hour, she was confessing the Lord and talking about him to all who were awaiting the redemption of Jerusalem."[13]

(6) And so, earnestly impress this outstanding widow on your mind as you would a seal, that you may be worthy of winning the reward of true widowhood. Always keep in mind the words of the Apostle when he said, "One who is truly a widow, however, and left alone, has hoped in the Lord and persisted in prayer night and day."[14] But you do not need to hear what follows, for with the grace of God you are taking care with energetic foresight. "But [a widow] given over to pleasures, though she lives, is [already] dead."[15]

8. Cf. Rev 14.4.   9. Cf. Luke 2.36–38.
10. Luke 2.37.   11. 1 Thess 5.17.
12. Cf. Luke 18.1.   13. Luke 2.38.
14. 1 Tim 5.5; for variant from the Vulgate, see Sabatier 3.874, where Augustine is cited as the source.
15. 1 Tim 5.6; Sabatier 3.874.

(7) Surely, if wives of any sort with the greatest longing try to please their mortal husbands,[16] how much more carefully and with what greater attention to detail ought holy widows contrive to make up the appearance of their inner being that they might be able to appear beautiful in the sight of their invisible spouse? For as the same Apostle says, "The unmarried woman has concern for the Lord's business, to be holy in body and in spirit; but the married woman has concern for worldly things, as to how she might please her husband."[17] A married woman is concerned about not in any way displeasing her husband who will die in a few years; with how much more concern must a widow strive to please the heavenly spouse who will reign forever? A married woman strives so that her figure, adorned with jewels, might be alluring to her husband; how much more effort must a widow expend so as to glow in the sight of God, adorned with holy virtues as if with sparkling pearls? The former struggles that her countenance might seem attractive, that no offending blemish might steal up on her beauty; how much more carefully must a holy widow take precautions that her soul be not soiled by the filth of implacable hatred or of base concupiscence?

(8) Lastly, impress this securely upon your minds, and consider this in untiring meditation, when it is said, "That she be holy in body and in spirit." For of what benefit is chastity of the body, of what benefit is chastisement or affliction of the flesh, if purity and cleanness of heart be wanting? "Blessed," indeed, "are the pure of heart, for they shall see God."[18] And so Jeremiah, using Jerusalem as a type, says to the soul that thinks harmful thoughts, "Wash your heart of malice, Jerusalem, so that you may become saved; how long will harmful thoughts remain in you?"[19] I have certainly learned and have sufficiently—and more than sufficiently—experienced, that the farther you retreat from the occupations of the world or from secular contacts, the more trouble you have struggling with the bothersome din of attacking thoughts. This is especially the case, since what is said prophetically through a mystery, is fulfilled in you, "An un-

---

16. Cf. 1 Cor 7.34.   17. 1 Cor 7.34.
18. Matt 5.8.   19. Jer 4.14.

just brother has supplanted me, and every friend has fraudu-
lently attacked me."[20]

(9) Wherefore, if among the bounteous fields of good works
that you never cease to cultivate, certain briars of prickling
thoughts should perhaps be growing from that root of your afflictions, at once take up the hoe of salutary confession and self-
correction, and tear out at the roots this poisonous growth from
the soil of your heart. In this matter, the divine voice commanded well through the prophet, saying, "Break up your fallow
ground, and do not sow among thorns."[21] What he means by
these earlier words, he at once explains when he adds, "Be cir-
cumcised to the service of the Lord, and remove the foreskins of
your hearts, men of Judah and dwellers in Jerusalem."[22] Those,
indeed, break up fallow ground, who still frequently harrow the
field of their hearts with the ploughshare of pious confession,
even though it had previously been plowed. And, sad to say, the
growth of carnal desire, since once dug out it never ceases to
sprout and grow again, must always be cut away with the hoe of
self-correction and repentance. Once the fallow ground is broken, we do not sow among thorns, because, by frequent harrow-
ing with the ploughshare of confession and correction, we cut
away the thorny undergrowth of thoughts, so that we may scatter
the seeds of virtuous living onto the neatly prepared soil of the
heart.

(10) It is specifically the men of Judah and the dwellers in
Jerusalem who are given this command to carry out, so that they
especially may be stirred to wage war against the desires within
them, since, having turned their back on the disruptions of the
world, they are firmly established in the confession of truth and
they focus continually on a vision of the highest peace. And this
most aptly applies to you also, who by burning with a desire for
God which is enkindled in the depths of your mind, endure the
evils of a savage world, since you have not loved the allurements
of the enticer. And since the clever schemer was unable to incite
you to pay back those who had done you harm, you must espe-

20. Jer 9.4.   21. Jer 4.3.
22. Jer 4.4.

cially beware lest he succeed in getting you to hate them even in secret. And because, after fighting with you for many years, with God standing at your side on the battlefield of action, he was forced to lose, you must make sure that he does not gain access to the home of your thoughts because you were not on your guard. When the hands are outwardly clean through innocence, he will scheme to show before the eyes of God a heart that has been polluted through hatred. Thus God speaks by the prophet to those who carry out the ceremonies of the Law, "Who asked for these things from your hands? Your hands are filled with blood."[23] This he addressed to those whose heart he saw to be full of malice.

(11) Therefore, my dearest sisters, since your life is considered so holy, so upright, and so disciplined, that, as far as good works are concerned, it seems to have no need of my advice, nevertheless, that there might still be room for me to write something for your edification, I approach the innermost recesses of your mind, where, the more outstanding one becomes in practicing virtue, the more astute one must be in guarding against temptation. For, the very thing which was made an occasion of victory, our sly enemy often transforms into a subject for battle. To this may be added that almighty God himself dwells in the minds of the elect. For even though we must believe that he dwells also in chaste bodies, as the Apostle says, "Your body is a temple of the indwelling Holy Spirit whom you have received from God,"[24] his special seat, nevertheless, is attributed to the mind, which presides over the subject body with a certain authority of direction. And as the same Apostle says, "The Holy Spirit dwells in our hearts through faith."[25] Of course, just as the soul gives life to the members of the body, it too subsists in having been given life by God. Thus, if you wish to construct in your minds a chamber worthy of God, energetically strive to clear from your minds every kindling of hostility and hatred, and every stain of malice.

23. Isa 1.12, 15.
24. 1 Cor 6.19; see Sabatier 3.676 for variant.
25. Eph 3.17. Here Damian substitutes "Holy Spirit" for "Christ" of the Vulgate.

(12) When one is expecting to have the king as a guest, what good is it to decorate all the entrance halls of the house with various embossed panels, to hang linen drapery from the fretted ceiling, to see that everything that greets the eye is neat and tidy, only to have him enter the bedroom for rest and, finding it utterly filthy, to become completely horrified? Therefore, since you guard your bodies in holy purity through the vehemence of tireless prayer, through almost daily fasting, and through the resplendence of matronly chastity, constantly hold forth a strict concern toward your thoughts also, so that, as you are constructing in your mind a chamber for the heavenly Spouse, you may not permit anything there to be foul, anything disarranged which might offend his eyes. For, true light does not dwell in the darkness of hatred, and the Prince of Peace does not seek quarters in an unpacified mind.

(13) You are indeed not unaware that certain women who live according to the flesh grind up in their teeth various kinds of spices and juices, that they might more delightfully please their husbands with the charm of emitting a fragrance. Your tongue and lips should never be unoccupied with the praise of God, but always roll around [on them] the psalms and other prayers, as if you were chewing spices, so that you might offer up in the sight of God an odor of sweetness that will not go unrewarded.

(14) It is also no secret to you that, when girls growing up at home with their parents begin to come of age and to approach the benefits of marriage, knowing that the estate of their father is reserved mostly for his male heirs,[26] they acquire purses or other kinds of pouches, so that whatever they can scrape together here and there, they carefully stuff into these bags. This is done so that when they enter their bridal chambers, the richer a supply of accumulated wealth accompanies them from their father's house, the less ashamed they will have to be before strangers.

(15) So now, you who hurry along with the strides of firm hope to heavenly nuptuals, store away no small part of your

26. For bibliographic handling of this statement, see Reindel, *Briefe* 3.36, n. 13.

goods in a safe place, that you need not pass over to your immortal Spouse with any embarrassment. But the pouch in which these things are stored away most securely is the pocket of the poor, the support of those in need. This, indeed, is a safe place of deposit that, with absolutely no loss, will return whatever it has received. Do not, therefore, leave everything to those who remain behind, and fail to provide for yourselves who will soon depart this life. But if there is little at hand, and if the poverty of your estate constrains you, he who valued the widow's mite above all the offerings of the rich,[27] will not be ungrateful in receiving your small gift or pittance into the treasury of his consideration. But if that too is lacking, which I hardly believe, it would suffice for you to offer pious tears, deep groanings, and lofty sighs. Even more, whatever you know, whatever you are capable of, whatever you live for, whatever it is that you aspire to, place it all on the altar of your devotion, and thus offer yourselves to God as a sacrifice which is greater than all holocausts.

(16) Abhor conversations with people of the world, and avoid looking at carnal things. Your door should not give access to everyone. Until you know why they have come, entry should be denied to some. Judith also should be a holy model for your life and an instruction in widowed continence. Sacred Scripture gives testimony about her in these words, "She had a secret chamber erected on the upper stories of her house; she spent her time closed away there along with her handmaidens. Wearing sackcloth over her loins, she fasted every day of her life except sabbaths, new moons, and feasts of the house of Israel."[28]

(17) One must consider how much praise this widow deserves, as she burned with so intense a fire of divine love. Not content, moreover, with the limits of the widowed state, she had progressed to such a point in holy religion that she became a hermitess not simply by herself, but along with her handmaidens. Of her ordinary home she made a cloister, and, in a heavily populated town, ingenious love found solitude. With how many earthly endowments of prosperity did she abound! These were

---

27. Cf. Luke 21.1–4.
28. Jdt 8.5–6.

certainly enticing enough to attract to her a second marriage with a suitor. For, as sacred history relates, "she was exceedingly attractive to behold, to whom her husband had left much wealth, a plentiful household, and landholdings filled with herds of cattle and flocks of sheep."[29] And what was still more important than all of this, it is also said that "she was everywhere renowned, because she feared God very much, nor was there anyone who could speak an ill word about her."[30] But when would she ever have occasion to meet suitors, since there was not easy access for anyone to speak to her handmaidens? How would she concern herself with fashion, whose limbs were constantly worn down by sackcloth? Or would she perhaps be preoccupied with lavish banquets, whom daily abstinence was wasting away?

(18) But perhaps you object to all this, that it is easy for her to practice virtue, since she abounded on all sides with so many advantages of wealth. But for those who are not permitted to live as they choose, how will it be to their liking to lead a life of virtue? It is certainly easy for us to refrain from things that have been offered, but it is generally our habit to covet eagerly what has been taken away. To put it plainly, offering something of one's own accord is a joy, but when one is compelled to do so, it befogs the wavering will.

(19) But go ahead and find an excuse in the fact that you do not have the abundance of wealthy Judith. Can you be unaware that Ruth, the impoverished little Moabite, suffered exile, disasters, hunger, thirst, the endurance of unbearable labors?[31] Have you ever, for the sake of preserving the integrity of your most chaste widowhood, been reduced to such poverty as she, who gleaned the grain that was left behind by the reapers, and, without any man's help, indeed, without any help at all, she used a rod and pounded out what she had gleaned? She, indeed, from whom a progeny of such great kings was going to emerge, seemed to be delivered over to servile works like vile chattel. Yet, weighed down and hemmed in by so many difficulties, she did not abandon the spiritual virtues. She patiently carried the bur-

29. Jdt 8.7.   30. Jdt 8.8.
31. Ruth 1.

den which weighed down on her, of living without resources, but considered it unbecoming to fall below the height of nobility deep within herself, who for instance was worthy to become the great-grandmother of David. She showed proper respect for her mother-in-law, maintained the chastity of a wife, remained faithful to her deceased husband, left her parents and a homeland given over to idolatry, and went over to the cult of the true God as a noble convert, without having received any formal teaching.[32]

(20) So here we see Judith casting off the goods by which she was propped up in life, and Ruth embracing the hardships by which she was weighed down. Both were certainly of one mind, though they were in different circumstances. Both pleased the one God, and not without merit, since the latter did not succumb to adversities, while the former did not abandon herself to riches, forgetful of her own well-being. The one put up with her abundant riches, while the other rejoiced in what she had to bear. Each could doubtless say about the vicissitudes of worldly instability, "Just as his darkness, so too is his light."[33] And while one was content with her first marriage, and the other was prepared to enter upon a second, even though Ruth married again, she did not desert her disposition to chastity, because the continence of widowhood was changed into conjugal purity, not out of desire for carnal enticement, but rather because God ordained it so.

(21) And what should I recall about the most blessed Mother of God, who did not possess an abundance of earthly goods, and endured the bitterness of a most intense sorrow? To her, of course, it was foretold, "A sword shall pierce your soul."[34] For if almighty God considered the advantages of this life to be of great value, surely he would never have permitted this unique and perpetual virgin, from whom he deigned to be incarnated, to be afflicted with sorrows. Wherefore, "You also," according to the statement of blessed Peter, "arm yourselves with the same thinking,"[35] and conquer through patience the evils of the world,

---

32. Ruth 2.11.
34. Luke 2.35.

33. Ps 138.12.
35. 1 Pet 4.1.

which, as you certainly are not unaware, all the elect endured from the very beginning of the human race. Whence the Apostle says, "It is fitting to pass through many tribulations to enter the kingdom of God."[36]

(22) Truly, it is not beyond belief that if this life were to soften and thereby become pleasant for you, it would slow you down somewhat from racing toward the object of heavenly desire. And your mind would grow cold toward God to the extent that it found rest in the warmth of temporal possessions. Therefore, it is God's plan to permit you to be tossed about on the high seas of this life by storms whirling all around, as by violent gusts of raging winds, so that your mind might turn more eagerly to desiring the things above, since down below it does not find a pleasant resting place. For Hagar, bolstered by successes, became puffed up against her mistress; but later, when she had been afflicted, and was wandering about in the wilderness as an exile, she received the address of an angel promising joyful things.[37] When Rachel struggled under the misfortune of sterility, she showed the reverence of fitting worship to the true God.[38] But after she merited the gift of fertility when Joseph was born, she stole the idol from Laban her father.[39] If, in answer to your petition, a wave of prosperity should arise and lift you up onto its heights, it would either draw in the wreckage of some sin, or at least draw your minds far from the shore of interior peace, with happiness flowing far away.

(23) Hence I exhort and earnestly admonish you not to be found ungrateful—far be it—for divine benefits, but always properly thank God, who steers you. By removing from you the opportunity of sinning, he deprives you, as it were, of poisonous foods, that he may carry you forth to the strength of eternal immunity. He surrounds you with harsher lashes and teaches you with blows, so that, by filing away and polishing his pearls now, he may afterwards set them in the edifice of his heavenly temple without the clanging of ax and hammer or without the noise of any iron implement whatsoever.[40]

---

36. Acts 14.21.
37. Cf. Gen 16.4–10.
38. Cf. Gen 30.1.
39. Cf. Gen 30.22–25, 31.19.
40. Cf. 1 Kgs 6.7.

(24) Therefore, my dearest sisters, when, from the whirlwinds of this world, a storm rages more wildly and bursts down on you, when you suffer severe setbacks from those who oppose you, seek refuge at once in prayer, have recourse to weeping and lament, and quickly seek the cool refreshment of tears, away from the heat of those who persecute you. When your soul is unable to find a secure abode outside itself, let it turn inward and there seek rest apart from the disturbance of every earthly distraction. Nor should your inability to weep keep you from persevering in prayer, especially if at the beginning of your effort tears will not flow. For it is of the very nature of fasting, we know, something which you are accustomed to practice, that as it produces great success, it sometimes provokes us and lessens our ability to weep. That anger is incited through fasting, is also clear from the words of Isaiah, who says, "For your fasting leads only to wrangling and strife and dealing vicious blows with the fist."[41]

(25) That tears are dried up by long fasting, is also the opinion of Josephus, who in telling about the vengeance wrought on Jerusalem and the Lord's persecutors by the emperors, Vespasian and Titus, mentioned the following among the various kinds of avenging punishment, "Nor did they practice customary mourning and weeping for the dead, because hunger made this totally impossible, and the dryness brought on by their need left no liquid for tears with anyone."[42] So, when you are physically unable to evoke visible tears, it will suffice to deplore your sins within the secret recesses of a contrite heart. There you should take note of the darkness of your acknowledged guilt, and admitting that what you suffer is your due, pass judgment on it after proper examination. For light gains strength amid darkness, and Venus which in the daytime cannot be detected by the eye, at night shines with its own splendor. Therefore, if we wish to have the true light rise in our hearts, we should not pretend to be the light, but truly acknowledge the darkness of our sin; and then whatever we suffer will seem insignificant to us, because we judge that the punishment we deserve should be much more severe.

41. Isa 58.4.
42. Flavius Josephus, *De Bello Iudaico* 5.515 (Loeb Classical Library, *Josephus* 3.360–361). The Latin text used by Damian, however, could not be identified.

(26) It should be noted that, just as those who are blind hear more sharply, as if a vigorous sense of perception that is lost in one member is transferred with greater acuity to the other, so too it is that some who have disdained luxuries are more greatly consumed with avarice. And while human concupiscence is restrained in its search for sexual pleasure, the appetite reaches out with greater vigor in acquiring wealth. In your case, may the love of riches grow cold together with your desire for marriage, so that your generosity in helping the poor may grow more active, and not burn, never to be extinguished, to satisfy the avaricious. God forbid that in your heart money should replace the love of your husband, but rather that a spiritual feast delight your hearts in exchange for bodily pleasure, that is to say, constant meditation on the word of God, the psalms, wholesome thoughts, the frequent practice of good works, preparation for death, the hope of future life, and similar matters on which the soul is profitably nourished and has its fill, in fact as at a heavenly banquet.

(27) But now, since I have prolonged my conversation with you in all charity, breaking all the rules that govern letter writing, I am, so to speak, sending you a brief, and have not been very brief about it. For as I seek to promote your edification rather than my own elegance of style, by speaking too much I have not observed the proper norms of speech. Finally, you will show me no small favor if you make every effort to be perfect in the practice of the holy virtues. For as I have no doubt that Lazarus was restored to life at the prayers of his faithful sisters,[43] I have every confidence that through your merits if, as I believe, they were deserving, I too will be absolved from my sins and restored to innocence of life. May almighty God, the zealous lover of souls, lead me by your prayers on the way to virtue, and by my exhortations guide you to still greater deeds. Praised be the name of the Lord.

43. Cf. John 11.19–32.

LETTER 95

Peter Damian to Desiderius, the abbot of Monte Cassino. He attempts to provoke his friend to answer his letters by presuming, as one less wise, to teach his more learned friend a few spiritual lessons. He advises the abbot to disregard his virtues and concentrate on his faults; to accept correction from others; not to overlook, but to reprimand the failings of his subjects, and that face to face; to practice fasting and frequently to celebrate the sacrifice of the Mass.

(1063, or somewhat earlier)[1]

O THE MOST REVEREND ABBOT, Desiderius,[2] the monk Peter the sinner sends greetings in the Lord.

(2) Sacred history relates that Absalom summoned Joab, the commander of the troops, by sending a messenger, but he refused to come. When he sent for him a second time and the latter obstinately and firmly declined, Absalom promptly sent his men to Joab's barley field that was ready for the harvest, and set fire to it.[3] At that, Joab came to Absalom to demand an explanation from him; but the latter was pleased that with such favors he had succeeded in having him come, namely, that what he had not achieved by his requests he brought about by his damaging action.

(3) Venerable brother, I have written to you, not twice but frequently;[4] and to this very day I have been unable to extract one single iota that you saw fit to write in return. Indeed, you promised to send me a scribe, who would copy on parchment at your expense at least those items which I especially wrote to you. But you failed completely to answer by letter and to send the

1. Dating follows Lucchesi, *Vita* no. 161.
2. On Desiderius, see *Letter* 82, n. 2.
3. 2 Sam 14.29–31.
4. In this time frame Damian wrote and sent to Desiderius *Letters* 82, 86, and 90; see Lucchesi, *Vita* no. 161.

scribe as you yourself had pledged to do.[5] Now the first of these was under the obligation of charity, while the other was required by truth, since you were bound to carry it out. So what shall I do? Since I am unable to rouse you from your sleep by pushing or pinching you, I will sting you, and thus at least will succeed in getting you awake. And so, like a teacher, I will take the rod of instruction to you, and as I would to an inferior or a student, presume to call to your attention those things which are perhaps better known to you than to me. And let this be my sting, that I should wish to teach one more learned than myself. Perhaps aroused in view of this pain you will now be wide awake, so that in failing to act out of charity, you will at least take revenge on him who injured you. And thus, as you see me having fun in exciting you, the younger brothers may doubtless think of me as seriously advising you.

(4) And now to the point. Do not as very many do, my brother, pay too much attention to the virtue you may possess and thus neglect passing judgment on the vices that you have disregarded. But imitate the example of the peacock which naturally acts quite differently. It has its ugly feet, like those of a chicken, always in view, but displays the spectacular beauty of its tail behind it. In its feet it sees something gross that it may despise, but ignores its tail that might cause it to be admired. Before its eyes is that which causes humiliation, but on the back it carries that for which it can strut before all other birds. You too should hide that which is virtuous within you, but never fail to view and judge what might be sinful and in need of correction.

(5) Do not resent zealous fraternal reproof, but accept it joyfully and use it as an antidote that will surely cure the inner sickness of the soul. Call to mind, moreover, what Solomon said, "Open reproof is better than love concealed. The blows a friend gives are well meant, but the kisses of any enemy are perfidious."[6] And elsewhere he says, "A man who is stubborn after much re-

---

5. In consequence, *Letters* 82, 90, 95, 102, 106, 119, and 159, all written to Desiderius, are not found in the Monte Cassino MSS 358 and 359 (C1, C2). In one case, *Letter* 90, the text must be reconstructed from MS Vat. lat. 4930 (V5), which contains the *Collectanea* of John of Lodi.

6. Prov 27.5.

proof will suddenly be destroyed; and health shall not follow him."[7] Also take note of this further advice of his, "Conceal your faults, and you will not be directed; confess and give them up, and you will find mercy."[8] And again, "He who loves correction loves wisdom; but he who hates reproof is a fool."[9] Glass, indeed, because it allows one to see clearly through it and reveals what it contains, seems to be more outstanding than all metals, except that when it is struck, it easily breaks. But because it at once goes to pieces when struck a single blow, a pound's worth of glass is hardly equal to three quarters of a pound of silver. A purple rose appears to be more brilliant than cloth dyed red; but because it cannot bear handling, it is valued as rubbish ready for the fire.

(6) Moreover, because you are the abbot of your venerable monastery, do not fail to take note of failings. As soon as they appear, correct them, so that like Phinehas your zeal may promote you to the ranks of the eternal priesthood,[10] and like Eli, sudden punishment may not strike you as you meanly yawn in slothful inactivity.[11] And so Solomon says, "Do not withold discipline from a boy; take the stick to him, and save him from death. If you take the stick to him yourself, you will preserve him from the jaws of hell."[12] But be careful not to become hardhearted in applying discipline excessively, and allow unbridled zeal to turn into anger, lest by removing the stains of guilt, you break the fragile vessel. Hence Solomon says, "Never make friends with an angry man nor keep company with a bad-tempered one; be careful not to learn his ways, or you will find yourself caught in a trap."[13] And again, "Better to live alone in the desert than with a nagging and ill-tempered wife."[14] Some, to be sure, when because of the kindling of their impatience they recoil from showing affection for their brothers—something that Paul and Barnabas did as they parted company because of the disciple Mark[15]—alter the evidence in their own defense. But what the Apostle did was not the result of vicious discord, but of the decision of divine provi-

---

7. Prov 29.1.
9. Prov 12.1.
11. 1 Sam 4.18.
13. Prov 22.24–25.
15. Cf. Acts 15.39.

8. Prov 28.13.
10. Cf. Num 25.11–13.
12. Prov 23.13–14.
14. Prov 21.19.

dence, so that these holy apostles in spreading the faith like grains of wheat, might reap a more plentiful harvest, far apart from one another where the breeze of dissension had blown them.

(7) Never disparage those who are absent, but properly confront them as the situation warrants. And so we read in the book of Proverbs, "Keep your mouth from wicked speech and your lips from detraction."[16] And in Ecclesiastes, "If a snake quietly bites you, it is just as if someone secretly disparages you."[17] And the wise man also says, "Curses on the gossiper and the hypocrite! For they have been the ruin of many peaceable men."[18] But to the one who hears he says, "Hedge in your ears by thorns, and do not listen to a wicked tongue, and set up gates for your mouth and hours for your ears."[19] We are commanded to hedge in our ears by thorns against a wicked tongue, that by the sting of our prickly response we might restrain those who engage in detraction.

(8) Love fasting, so that by afflicting your body with deprivation, your soul may be fed with a wealth of heavenly grace. The serpent that used the weapon of food to subvert the man who was eating,[20] now by force of sobriety falls victim to him who fasts. As those who have diligently investigated the nature of things tell us, a serpent will suddenly die if it tastes the spittle of a man who is fasting.[21] If such is the power of fasting over this animal that physically crawls along the ground, how much greater will be its effect on the dragon that slithers along invisibly? But to be still more effective in destroying this serpent, make every effort at frequently offering the salutary sacrifice of the Mass, so that as it beholds your lips reddened with the blood of Christ, it will be seized with terror, at once slink away, and not dare to come closer to the mystery by which it was taken captive. Thus, as it grows weaker, it will be overcome and, as far as you are concerned, will hide away forever in its maleficent lair.

---

16. Prov 4.24. 17. Eccl 10.11.
18. Sir 28.15.
19. Sir 28.28; for this variant from the Vulgate, cf. Sabatier 2.465.
20. Cf. Gen 3.5.
21. Cf. Pliny, *Naturalis historia* 28.7.35; *Bestiarius* 3.53 (PL 177.103B).

(9) But now I will silence my pen because I blame myself for my daring presumption, and like one who has just set fire to the harvest, I take flight lest I be caught destroying the crops in the fruitful field, when my only intention was to burn the briars and the wild underbrush.

LETTER 96

Peter Damian to Pope Alexander II. He replies to the pope who by letter had requested a letter from him, noting that in the midst of his contemplation he should not forget to write now and then. Damian complains that his attempts at solitude are seriously disturbed by the violence endemic to his region. He then describes the moral decay of the times, summing up his view by stating that "these days the whole world is nothing but gluttony, avarice, and sex." The pope, he hopes, by virtue of his office will reform and punish the evildoers. Satisfied that the burden of episcopal service in the county of Ostia has been lifted from his shoulders, he asks to be relieved of all episcopal duty. A few exhortatory verses on the Apostolic See bring the letter to a close.

(Lent 1063)[1]

O SIR ALEXANDER,[2] bishop of the highest see, the monk Peter the sinner offers his service.

(2) When the letter[3] from your holiness arrived, brought by some ill-tempered priest, I received it with joy, kissed it as I opened it, and eagerly read it with great haste. But since the burden of office weighing on you is so great, that it would have sufficed had you directed someone under your authority to write a few lines, I find in it such flowery eloquence, such pleasant words filled with paternal grace and not, I should say, with masterful command, that what was sent to a poor little person like me would have been worthy of his royal majesty himself.

(3) Yet I find two matters in your letter that, I must confess, cause me to blush. For you said, if not in these words, that because of my constant efforts at practicing contemplation, I should not put off occasionally writing to you. Seeing that you

1. Dating follows Lucchesi, *Vita* no. 167f.
2. On Alexander II, see Damian, *Letter* 65, n. 12; Reindel, *Briefe* 2.231, n. 18. Damian also addressed to him *Letters* 98, 107, 108, 109, 122, 140, 164, and 167, and in his name wrote *Letter* 84 to the people of Milan.
3. The letters of Pope Alexander II to Damian have not survived.

heartily agree with me, venerable father, in laying aside my episcopal burden, I indeed enjoy the leisure to engage in contemplation and writing, but am not able to breathe easily because of
the difficulties and troublesome affairs that stand in my way.
However, as I restrict myself to the confines of my cell, it is as if I
live in a safe harbor or at a lonely post on the shore. But of what
good is that to me? For while I am here in apparent security,
eager to partake of the peace of quiet leisure, the blasts of a savage world strike at me, and a flood of overwhelming affairs violently swells in on me. I am buffeted by the dashing waves of personal damage, disturbed by the wrongful loss of lands and of any
profit that might emerge from them, and I must say with the
prophet, "I hoped for peace, and find nothing good; for a time
of healing, and all is disaster."[4]

(4) In the meantime, there are always those who demand advice for the welfare of their souls, and in addition, which is still
more difficult, they attempt to extract an episcopal decision
from one who is no longer a bishop. Thus, in fleeing the episco-
pacy I cannot avoid being a bishop, and grow weary of the episcopal burden after abandoning the dignity of the episcopal
throne.[5] And thus hemmed in by these worries, I keep trying to
practice contemplation. I strive, but at once grow weary; I never
reach the heights of contemplation and never break forth in
tears of compunction. A soul that is darkened by worldly affairs
tries in vain to lift itself up to the summit of contemplation, but
because of secular concerns it is weighted down, as it were, by
heaps of heavy stones. Just as shoe leather, after it has been satu-
rated by muddy water, cannot be greased, thus unless the soul of
man has been sucked dry of the moisture of worldly cares, it will
not receive the grace of heavenly bounty. A dry skin absorbs oil,
but when moist it repels it. The human heart also, so long as it is
swollen with the moisture of secular affairs, will not allow the oil
of interior grace to enter. Hence we read that the law was given
on Mount Horeb,[6] which has the meaning of "dryness."[7] The

---

4. Jer 14.19.
5. See also *infra*, ch. 23; and in general on this topic, see Damian, *Letters* 57
and 71.
6. Cf. Exod 20.1–25.
7. Cf. Jerome, *Nom. hebr.* 14.18 (CC 72.77).

soul, therefore, that is lifted up above earthly things by the love of what is spiritual,[8] is the mountain on which the blameless law of God, which undoubtedly is charity, is divinely promulgated. And this mountain is truly Horeb, which is called dryness, from which the moisture of all vice has been boiled away, and by the rays of the sun of justice all rheum of licentiousness and carnal pleasure has been dried up. Thus it was that at Solomon's command Hiram cast the vessels of the temple in clay-filled soil that would absorb the water.[9]

(5) Now among these vessels is that which yearns to be filled with rain from heaven, when it says, "My soul is athirst for you like land without water."[10] And so, burning with desire, it calls out, "My soul thirsts for the living God. When shall I come to God and appear in his presence?"[11] And of these vessels we read in the third book of Kings that "in the plain of the Jordan the king cast them in clay-filled soil between Succoth and Zarethan."[12] "Succoth" may be translated as "tabernacles,"[13] while "Zarethan" has the meaning "those in trouble," or "those who destroy or cause affliction."[14] What else should be understood by "Succoth," which we said has the meaning "tabernacles," if not holy men who say, "here we have no permanent home, but we are seekers after the city that is to come"?[15] And to this point Peter also says, "I know that very soon I shall not lodge in this body."[16] And what should we make of the word "Zarethan," which we said means "those in trouble," except to say that it signifies the persecution of wicked men who cause us trouble? These men are destroyers and people who cause distress, for as they try to demolish and destroy the structure of our faith or of our good works, they afflict us with pressing calamities and injury, which are hard to bear. And so, the vessels of the temple, that is, all the elect, are cast in the plain

---

8. Cf. Ps 18.6–7.   9. Cf. 1 Kgs 7.40–45.

10. Ps 142.6.

11. Ps 41.3; cf. Sabatier 2.85 for this variant from the Vulgate and for models of Damian's usage in Ambrose, Augustine, and Cassiodorus.

12. 1 Kgs 7.46.

13. Jerome, *Nom. hebr.* 14.29 (CC 72.77).

14. Jerome, *Nom. hebr.* 43.11 (CC 72.112).

15. Heb 13.14.

16. 2 Pet 1.14; for this variant, see *Beuroner Vetus Latina* 26.1.199, with the usage of Bede (PL 93.10A).

of the Jordan, that is, in the lowliness of baptism between Succoth and Zarethan, that is, between the just and the wicked, so
that the model of good men may be set before them as an example of an upright life for their imitation, while the persecution of the wicked serves to increase their merits. Indeed, "as the
work of a potter is tested in the furnace, so good men are tried
by suffering."[17] Thus the temple vessels are cast in arid soil, since
the soul of man is not fit to receive the gift of heavenly grace unless it is first drained of all the moisture of carnal desire. A heart
that is dry produces a clear and harmonious sound, but one that
is moist lacks resonance. A drum will sound dull if water gets to
it, and it becomes damp. Thus the moisture of carnal pleasure
must be extracted from a man's soul if its prayers are to resound
in the ears of almighty God.

(6) For just as a blind man exposes himself to the rays of the
sun and tries in vain to see, attempting to open the hollow sock-
ets of the eye and the empty eyelids, but never beholds the splendor that comes down from it, so too is it useless for one to search
for the light of contemplation who lost the keenness of his soul
by immersing himself in the life of the world. For if someone unknown breaks into the king's chamber, and like one of the family tries to wait on him, the king will not speak to him because he
does not value his company as someone he previously came to
know. And so, we unhappy and miserable men, and this I say also
of others like me, we often spend long hours alone in the narrow
confines of our cells, trembling in the presence of the sun of
God's majesty, but because our sins are an obstacle in its path, we
never deserve a single spark of interior illumination or the grace
of compunction.

(7) Thus, indeed, we are seen, as it were, standing in the presence of the King, but since he does not recognize us as leading
a virtuous life, we are unable to enjoy the pleasure of intimate
discourse with him. But oh how sweet as honey it is, when the
Lord delights in his servant and the servant in his Lord! Hence
the psalmist says, "May my praise be pleasing to him, for I will rejoice in the Lord."[18] How miserable I am, for though the will to

17. Sir 27.6.
18. Ps 103.34; cf. Sabatier 2.205.

do good is present, I am unable to carry through.[19] For I find nothing worthwhile in my body, and while I long for this goodness and yearn for it with all my heart, I never succeed in achieving it because my sins hold me back. The guilt of a worthless life is an obstacle in my way, and external affairs do not allow me to see the glory of this interior light. And this very disturbance caused by earthly involvement, which obscures the sharpness of my mind, keeping it from contemplative insight, deprives me also of the ability to write. To this I might add that, even though I were able to dictate a few things, I have no scribe to copy them in book hand.[20] But why do I complain about the lack of a copyist, since there is no one free to transcribe what I write, nor even quickly to read it through? Almost all heads of churches whose duty it is to supervise ecclesiastical matter, are involved in such a daily whirl of worldly events, that while they are distinguishable from laymen by their lack of beard,[21] they do not differ from them in their duties; they do not meditate on the words of sacred Scripture, but are busy with legal statutes and litigation in court. The judicial tribunals and the royal courts are not large enough for the crush of bishops, since they spew forth crowds of clerics and monks, complaining about the lack of space. The cloisters are empty, the books of the Gospels remain closed, and affairs of state are on the lips of men who belong to the estate of the Church.[22]

(8) But would that we were content only with legal disputes and decrees. Rather we take up arms, engage in battle with naked swords, and contrary to the rule of our estate, fight not

19. Cf. Rom 7.18.

20. On this reference to the last phase of his letter-writing technique, see Reindel, *Studien* 1.54f.

21. It may be noted from this observation, that in the eleventh century and perhaps earlier, bishops and other clerics in the Western church did not wear beards. Cf. DuCange 1.567 with reference to Gregory VII, *Register* 8.10.529. Cf. also Michael Cerularius, who c. 1054 was aware of the unbearded clerics of the West, and accused them of being women. The iconography of Damian is therefore usually incorrect, since from the 15th century onward he is generally depicted as a bearded man. But see the tempera painting of 1430–1440 in the Galleria dell'accademia in Ravenna (G. Lucchesi, *Studi su San Pier Damiani*, Faenza, 1961, 194–195), and the statue of Damian in the church in Rott am Inn (Bavaria) by Ignaz Günther, which are properly beardless.

22. Cf. Gaudenzi, *Svolgimento* 123, n. 2.

with words but with steel. To us the Apostle says, "The sword of the spirit is the Word of God,"[23] but in reality distress of such enormous pressure weights upon the Church, that it seems to be surrounded by the forces of the Babylonian army, and that Jerusalem with all its inhabitants appears to be under siege. Lay princes usurp the rights of the Church, subvert its provisions, invade its possessions, and then brag that they carry off the means of supporting the poor as if they were enemy spoils. These very lords, moreover, plunder one another's property, one trying to surpass the other, and finding themselves living in the same world, fight with one another because they are unable to prevail alone. Then they set fire to the thatched roofs of the farmers, and shamelessly pour out the venom of their fury on unarmed serfs, since they find it impossible so to attack their enemies. Thus, what the prophet sang is literally fulfilled, "When the wicked man grows proud, he sets fire to the homes of the poor."[24]

(9) In all of this, a serpent's poison is a nobler thing than man's cruelty. For the serpent flees from a naked man, but goes on the attack to bite one who is clothed.[25] And so, a brave and noble warrior avoids an unarmed man, but attacks one who comes at him with sword unsheathed. Also the hawk will not plunder in a wide area surrounding its nesting place,[26] nobly bypassing easy prey that lies close at hand, but hunts farther afield where he must work harder for his victory. But these princes attack unarmed people, and while their enemies get out of their way, they lash out at those who do no harm. Moreover, when one is first to invade, the other at once attacks and is not satisfied to reply with an eye for an eye, as the Law suggests,[27] but returns injury with interest. Indeed, retaliation which is described by Cicero's law,[28] is unknown in our days, and self-restraint in practicing vengeance, that was formerly observed by pagans under the Empire, is now ignored, despite the Gospel's terrible warning to

---

23. Eph 6.17.   24. Ps 10.2.
25. Cf. Frugoni, *Letteratura* 45f.; Damian, *Letter* 86.48–53, especially 51.
26. See Damian, *Letter* 86.60.   27. Cf. Exod 21.24.
28. Cf. Tertullian, *De anima* 37, ed. J. H. Waszink, CC 2 (1954) 839; Augustine, *De civitate Dei* 21.11 (CSEL 40.539).

practice foregiveness.[29] Therefore, in return for a beating with rods they will use the bullwhip, for the lash the mace, for words iron, for a pole the sword. They blush at not exceeding another's injury, and find it below their dignity to cause equal pain. They strive to appear as conquerors and terrorists, and with a passion seek after trophies of their victory. And so, as one is roused to anger, the other is provoked to frenzy; madness begets madness and fury induces fury.

(10) For it is known from experience, that if a rabid dog by chance bits a man, the dog's madness is at once, and with such force, transferred into the man's bowels, that quickly young dogs are produced in his bladder. This is proved by clear evidence, that if someone is bitten by a dog and drinks crickets,[30] a kind of fly, shredded into water, he at once, but not without experiencing great pain, dispels the pups along with the urine. And surely we should not reject what is deemed a marvel, namely, that young ones are born from dried up teeth in which, indeed, no semen is to be found; for what nature cannot easily do by means of the male organ, it produces by the fertility of teeth, but in a different way. And perhaps it is not wholly mysterious, that by this animal, called the cricket, poison is discharged that is generated by the rabies in the dog. It is called a charmer or a preacher in sacred Scripture, since it is said in the psalm, "Like the deaf asp which stops its ears and will not listen to the sound of the charmers, and the spells that are muttered by the wizard."[31] And elsewhere we read of the preacher who is spiritually impaired, "Who will heal the charmer when he is bitten by the snake?"[32] And in Proverbs, "Like vinegar in soda, so is the minstrel to the hardhearted."[33] Therefore, just as the poison of rabid fury is dispelled by crickets, so is malicious anger calmed by the exhortation of a holy preacher.

(11) But now let us get back to what we were discussing. With the world in flames because of this and similar madness, torn to

29. Cf. Matt 18.35.

30. For this interpretation of the word *cantalena*, see Reindel, *Briefe* 3.52, n. 16.

31. Ps 57.5–6; cf. Sabatier 2.115 for this variant from the Vulgate.

32. Sir 12.13.   33. Prov 25.20.

pieces by its citizens everywhere fighting with one another, its violence strikes also at us who have been divorced from such things and dulls our spirit, keeping us from writing and from interior contemplation. Add to this, that even though perhaps there is someone still writing, as I said above, no one is at hand who can transcribe, no one finally who will at least hurriedly read it through.

(12) For when the storm comes on with its furious winds, and the hurricane whips the waves to mountainous heights, the sea appears more calm where it is deepest, but along the coast it is so wild that ships trying to land begin to break up. Consequently, oarsmen will avoid areas that are near the coast as they would the treacherous Syrtian promontory,[34] and head for deeper waters which are calmer. Thus too, as this age approaches its end, the earth's ferment boils up near its coast, rouses itself to heights of confusion and pride, and while in former times it was seemingly peaceful where the sea was deep, now as the world nears its end it is wildly disturbed, and anyone trying to land can scarcely avoid shipwreck. This violence and confusion are born of lust, and contrary to nature, distress is begotten of voluptuousness. And so Solomon says, "It is a sorry business that God has given men to busy themselves with. I have seen all the deeds that are done under the sun; they are all vanity and distress for the spirit."[35] All those who strive to acquire the things that will afford them pleasure are necessarily compelled to suffer affliction of spirit; and since others stand in the way of what we seek, we can achieve that which delights us only with great effort. Hence Solomon says again, "And when I turned and reviewed all my handiwork, and all the labor at which I sweated in vain, I saw that everything was vanity and affliction of spirit."[36] But this very suffering delights hard and reprobate men, for they take pleasure not only in sweet luxuries, but also in the pungent flavor of heavy exertion. Consequently, the Israelites, enticed by the urgency of their gluttony, complained not only that they no longer enjoyed the fleshpots and the delicious fish, but also that they no

34. Cf. Isidore, *Etymologies* 13.18.6.   35. Eccl 1.13–14.
36. Eccl 2.11.

longer had leeks and onions and garlic.[37] Now while these vegetables with their sharp taste burn your mouth, they also bring
tears to your eyes. Do not those men long for the sharp taste of
onions and garlic, who abandon the delicious food they have at
home, who turn up their nose at the delightfully rich gravy
which the waiter gladly brings them, and enduring the frightful
brush and the steep slopes of the mountains, hunt with their
spears for wild-flavored meat of the chase; and disdain the food
brought from the storeroom and go fowling for scurrying birds
by sending up their hawks? When they might normally enjoy
peace and quiet, they consider it a pleasant diversion to exert
themselves in riding or sueing at law. The leisure of rest they consider as something flabby; they say it is base and dull and dissolute. And that is just what the Israelites said, "Our spirit is dry.
There is nothing wherever we look except this manna."[38] And
elsewhere they complained, "There is neither food nor water.
We are heartily sick of this miserable fare."[39] Now food is considered of no consequence if it is not associated with hard and
heavy work. For by work people are relaxed, but are tired out by
leisure.

(13) Indeed, we might do well to observe how small is that
part of the body which nothing in the world can satisfy, and which
craves for the costliest of earthly things. For since the other bodily members seem to be dull and irrational, there is one area of
the body, measuring scarcely two feet, whose appetite nothing
can sate. All human desire reaches from the eyes to the genital
organs. It is by the necessity of nature contained in this small
space, but it is not restricted by the laws of this natural limitation.
It embraces all things external, and while it emerges from one
tiny source, it is not content with a few small matters, but grasps
at everything, yearning to be fed by them and to enjoy them
to the full. The eyes feast on every beauty, the ears are attune
to ringing and harmonious sounds or to the flattery of pretty
words. The nose perceives the scent of perfume, the mouth delights in tasty food, the heart is busy with most secret thoughts,

37. Cf. Num 11.4–5.   38. Num 11.6.
39. Num 21.5.

the tongue pours forth speech, and what the heart considers, the mouth proclaims as its interpreter. "For the words that the mouth utters come from the overflowing of the heart."[40] The genital organs, moreover, are more passionately excited to sexual intercourse the more abundantly the stomach is filled with masses of food and drink. Gluttony, indeed, is a kind of leech which has two daughters, namely, drunkenness and lust, of which Solomon says, "The leech has two daughters; 'Give,' says one, and 'Give,' says the other."[41] Obviously, the more immoderately one eats, the more eager, of course, is one to drink. And while the amount of food one eats cooks in the boiling caldron of the stomach, it requires frequent drafts to replenish it. And when the stomach swells with food and drink, it follows that, employing alternate channels, one must evacuate into the latrine and ejaculate semen from the private parts. As grape-skins are removed from the wine in the wine press, so is excrement separated from the semen in the groin. Therefore, this leech, which is gluttony, has two daughters, drunkenness and lust; and since this one disease experiences pleasure in conception, it necessarily gives birth to twin offspring. And they both shout, "Give, give," for since both are insatiable, they are both violently demanding.

(14) And so this area of man's anatomy, from the private parts to the eyes, destroys the whole man, and totally undermines the dignity of his natural excellence. For in man's unhappy condition, from these vents of the senses that which is conducive to his salvation flows away, and that which leads to his damnation gains admittance. In a few words the apostle John explained it all, when he said, "Everything this world affords is lust of the flesh, enticement for the eyes, and the pride of life."[42] Lust of the flesh refers to bodily pleasure, enticement for the eyes involves the beauty of visible things, and the pride of life includes the heights of worldly honor and prestige. We know that the first man was tempted by all of these, as Scripture asserts, "The woman saw that the fruit of the tree was good to eat;"[43] here we have lust of the flesh. And then it continues, "It was pleasing to the eye and de-

40. Matt 12.34.　　　　　41. Prov 30.15.
42. 1 John 2.16.　　　　　43. Gen 3.6.

lightful to look at";[44] here was pride of the eyes. For to be haughty with the eye involves everyone who takes pleasure in the things which God forbids. But pride of life was present, when the same woman gladly listened to the serpent as it said, "You will be like gods, knowing both good and evil."[45]

(15) Thus in our day the whole world is nothing but gluttony, avarice, and sex. And as once the world was divided into three parts,[46] so that together it was subject to three rulers, so now, sad to say, the human race like slaves bends its neck to these three vices, and willingly obeys the laws of the same number of tyrants. "For all," as Scripture says, "high and low, are out to practice avarice."[47] And what shall I say of gluttony, since the rich never know hunger, never expect to experience need? Unless they frequently vent their fat bellies at both ends, they must fear the embarrassment of noisily breaking wind, and so good health consists in having an unobstructed bowel. They guzzle till their faces are fiery red and, if good taste did not forbid, one would say that they do not eat, but rather lick up their food.

(16) And so, while punishing the body is frowned upon by almost all penitents, the vigorous application of the canons in assigning penance is weakened beyond repair. Wherefore, we must either completely abandon the penitentials, or stop commuting the penance to a money payment.[48] What layman can endure fasting for three days or for a week if he is ordered to do so? He will either say that he has stomach trouble, or complain that he is suffering pain in the spleen or bladder, or allege that he has difficulty with his feeble lungs and can hardly breathe. On the one hand, he pleads no end of family obligations, and on the other, pretends that he is overburdened with supervising the help. What more need I say? Laymen pile up a bewildering show of arguments, they act like Proteus[49] and take on various monstrous forms, and simulate every kind of disease to avoid weakness from fasting which they especially fear.

---

44. Gen 3.6.   45. Gen 3.5.
46. Cf. Isidore, *Etymologies* 14.2.1.   47. Jer 6.13.
48. Cf. Ryan, *Sources* no. 180. Damian here opposes the use of money fines in place of canonical penance; but see his *Letter* 45.8.
49. Cf. Jerome, *Adversus Jovinianum* 2.21 (PL 23.315B).

(17) And while subject to the clamoring of gluttony rather than the requirements of nature, whether they wish it or not, they unleash the fetters of lust. The stomach and the sexual organs are closely related, and when the former is intemperately satisfied, the latter is quickly aroused to shameful action. Food is indeed a lure to lust, and it transmits to the sexual organs the excess of its own juices brought on by immoderate intake. These humors, when they accumulate, itch and titillate, and more urgently demand to be released in intercourse. And so it happens that many men in practicing intercourse in marriage as the law permits, are totally undisciplined in granting the marriage right, nor do they use moderation in sleeping with their wives, since they are uninterested in bearing children, but are urged to satisfy their innate pleasure. I would certainly not call such men husbands but rather seducers, not spouses but rather illicit lovers. They place no time limits on their profligate use of coitus, and what is disgusting to say, do not even refrain from their wives during pregnancy, and never blush in violating the rule of chastity that even dumb animals observe when their mates are pregnant.

(18) Observe, O man, and see whether the dog goes after the bitch after she has conceived. Look at the cow or certainly at the mare, and notice whether the bulls or stallions bother them after they are with young. Obviously, they forego the pleasure of intercourse when they sense that they are unable to produce offspring. Therefore, since bulls and dogs and other kinds of animal show such regard for their young, it is men alone, whose teacher was born of the Virgin, who have no fear of destroying and killing their little ones, made in the image of God, just so that they can satisfy their lust. This is the reason why many women practice abortion before their term is complete, or certainly why they discover means of mutilating or damaging the tiny and still fragile limbs of these little ones.[50] And thus, as they

50. Here we have one of the few references, perhaps the only explicit one, in Damian's letters, to the practices of abortion. And to the horror of post-modern feminists he puts the blame on "the many women who practice abortion," charging them "with being murderers before they became parents." This discussion and its context are important evidence from the Central Middle Ages, reflecting the constant opposition of the Church to abortion from the Council of Elvira (ca. 302) to the present.

are impelled by their incentives to lust, they are first murderers before they become parents; and what is most perilous, as they ascribe these actions to the defect of sinful nature, they fail to acknowledge that they themselves are guilty of such heinous crimes.

(19) And what is more, at times they know this quite well; for while they benefit from what other people are ignorant of, they keep silent and do not confess this sin to the priests. The barrus, which is also called the elephant, is said to have such regard for the beauty of chastity and so hates the obscenity of lust, that when compelled to have intercourse to propagate the species, turns its head away, and thus, as if forced by a command of nature, shows that it is acting unwillingly and is ashamed of what it does.[51] Clearly, every animal engages in coitus only to have offspring, while man alone gives birth only to have coitus. For animals, therefore, giving birth is the purpose of intercourse, while for men the purpose of giving birth is intercourse. Vultures give birth by not violating one another through coitus.[52] Bees feed the offspring of those that come after them, and thus remain virginal.[53] In this way, creatures that lack reason imitate the Son of the Virgin, while men, for whom he was born, delight in wallowing in lust.[54]

(20) Now who spreads seed on top of seed? Who would think of plowing up a field clothed in the beauty of growing crops? A man first begins to plow when the field is empty, and then follows with the sowing that will grow into a crop; otherwise, if seed follows seed, he will not harvest a plentiful yield, not, I would say, because of his double effort but not even as a result of one of them. Therefore, O weak and effeminate man, take note of what you are doing. Be aware that you are dust and ashes, that what you are pursuing as you burn with the fires of passion, namely, as you embrace a woman's body, should be seen as the worms, the filth, and the intolerable stench it will shortly become, so that

51. Cf. Pliny, *Naturalis historia* 8.5.13; Isidore, *Etymologies* 12.2.4 and 16.5.19; *Physiologus lat.* Y 20.117–119.
52. Isidore, *Etymologies* 12.7.12.
53. For patristic references to this statement, cf. Reindel, *Briefe* 3.59, n. 29.
54. Cf. Frugoni, *Letteratura* 39.

this cautious reflection on future corruption may cause you to reject the disguise of theatrical beauty. The good judgment of a wise man will see not only what pleases the eyes, but also the truth that lies hidden within. For all the pleasure that wives now afford their husbands they will also necessarily give to other men if, as is customary, they should marry again, or even a third time, after their husband's death. After he is gone, they are not faithful to him, but seeking to provide pleasure for their later husbands, they shamelessly blush at even hearing the name of their former spouses, with shame spread all over their faces.

(21) I once knew a man who was killed trying to avenge an injury done to his wife; and then, as it was reported, she entered a second marriage before the year was up. So in abandoning God, let husbands go on trusting in their wives. After loving them extravagantly, they often discover that through them they are bequeathing their property not only to strangers but even to their enemies. I might also add that, if a woman is unfaithful to her husband, as news of this spreads from mouth to mouth through the whole village, it is only the husband who is unaware; and while he is the first to suffer this disgrace on his house, he is almost the last to learn of it.

(22) Therefore, the incentive to lust enkindles avarice and provides the fuel for covetousness. For since there is little doubt that a luxurious style can be enjoyed only at great expense, unless an abundance of comfort is at hand it cannot provide sensual pleasure. But just as those who prove to be slaves to this world strive to burden themselves with earthly goods, so, on the other hand, the soul that yearns for the things of heaven is proud to be divested of them.

(23) Oh, what a joy, what a pleasant message it was that brought me the news that you had taken from me the episcopal county[55] of Ostia and had given it to another! As the messenger from Rome made known to me what had happened, he acted in my presence as if he were accusing you for what you did, apparently siding with me and feeling sorry at my loss; yet in thinking that he was putting the blame on you, he unwittingly praised you.

---

55. The Latin word used here is *comitatus*; see also Lucchesi, *Vita* no. 113, 105f.

At first I seemed to be taking the news badly; but as I began to experience the good fortune that was mine, I was unable, even superficially, to feign sadness. Besides, I beg the good God that you not put off filling the see as soon as possible, and that you take from my hands the barren plow that worked this deserted coast. There is no one today, wishing to follow the path of purity and innocence, who would want to carry the burden of ruling a diocese, especially since almost all men are rushing headlong on the dangerous path of vice, and like wild horses are galloping without restraint through the plains in search of pleasure. And what else do we see amid so much evil and crime, but that the way is now open for Antichrist[56] who is soon to come, and that he may proceed with no obstacle to his wickedness? For as the Apostle says, "The secret power of wickedness is already at work."[57] Indeed, the world borrows light from darkness, since now its end is near. And it seems that dusk is wavering between day and night, as the light of virtue is failing and the night of vice is upon us.

(24) This truly is what was meant as Scripture reported of Abraham, "Then, as the sun was going down," it said, "a trance came over Abram and great fear and darkness came over him."[58] Now, the setting of the sun means the downfall of the world, and the great fear and darkness signify the blackness of vice and crime which daily spread like the plague because of the violent depravity of reprobate men. And so the text shortly after continues, "And when the sun went down it became dark and gloomy and there appeared a smoking brazier."[59] Now, as smoke comes forth from the fire of a smoldering brazier, so the dark vapors of all vice and crime are born in the furnace of flaming avarice, as the Apostle says, "Avarice is the root of all evil."[60] And this takes place as the day comes to a close, that is, as the end of the world draws near. Thus a smoking brazier produces darkness as black as night, because the furnace of avarice which glows in the hearts of wicked men, like a plague covers the earth with the heavy smog of depravity. Does it not blind the mind of unhappy

56. On the coming of the Antichrist, see Damian, *Letter* 92.
57. 2 Thess 2.7.   58. Gen 15.12.
59. Gen 15.17.
60. 1 Tim 6.10; cf. Sabatier, 3.878 for this variant form the Vulgate and its patristic antecedents.

men, depriving them of faith, and extinguishing in their hearts the light of all virtue? Consequently, after the Apostle had made the statement cited above, he at once added, "There are some who in searching after it," namely avarice, "have wandered from the faith and have involved themselves in much grief."[61] They involve themselves in much grief when, because of temporal gain, they recoil from one another with implacable hatred. And often, as they go to war over physical things, they physically lose their lives. But those who strive only for the things of heaven obtain pleasure instead of pain, because they delight in living together in fraternal charity. This is why Abraham, when offering sacrifice as the sun was going down, arranged the field animals in separate parts, but did not cut the birds into pieces. Hence Scripture says, "He brought him all these, halved the animals down the middle and placed each piece opposite its corresponding piece, but he did not halve the birds."[62] Now the field animals were placed opposite their corresponding pieces, because all worldly men violently oppose their neighbors with quarrels and arguments, or certainly burn with secret hatred against them. On the other hand, those who lift themselves on high on the wings of heavenly desire, in offering themselves as a sacrifice to God, do not refuse to be bound by mutual charity.

(25) In my letter to you, venerable father, I lament the madness of this violent world which I am daily forced to bear and to hate. Nor do I fear to be known as the plaintiff as I expose the crimes of these culprits, since correcting their evil deeds holds the first place in all that I do. For he cannot be accused of slander who takes pains to lay bare the guilt of the erring, who is able to correct what has been rashly undertaken. Now these are the words of Elijah, "The people of Israel have torn down your altars, O Lord, and put your prophets to death with the sword, and I alone am left."[63] And the Lord replied, "But I have left for myself seven thousand in Israel, all who have not bent their knee to Baal."[64] Now as the prophet said that he alone was left, but was contradicted by the

---

61. 1 Tim 6.10.
62. Gen 15.10.
63. 1 Kgs 19.14; for variants, see Sabatier 1.586.
64. 1 Kgs 19.18; cf. Sabatier 1.586.

Lord who replied that seven thousand remained, Elijah cannot be accused of lying, because as he glowed with the fire of heavenly zeal, he said what he thought was true. Therefore, if Elijah did not sin because he was excessive in his accusations, prompted by zeal and not by hatred, should I be charged with audacity in making known a few crimes among so many, especially to him whose chief prerogative it is to correct? Thus, it was my duty to bring these matters to your attention, in whatever way it could be done; it remains for you to curb them insofar as you are able. You must, therefore, get busy and carry out this task at once, so that at the terrible judgment of the highest Shepherd, like Elijah, your deeply rooted burning zeal will excuse you, or like Peter, which is more glorious, an abundant harvest of the flock committed to your care will adorn you. Please do not be surprised, I beg you, that this letter is composed in an unpolished style; for as my hand hurries at its task of writing, there is Cadalus,[65] on the one hand, breathing fire like a terrible dragon, and on the other, a poisonous throng of serpents, hissing as they leave their holes. And since I am unable to crush them with charms, I am prepared to cut off their scaly heads with the sword. But because the synod is at hand, I submit the following pedestrian verses:

> He who would wish to secure a vigorous See
> Apostolic,
> Let him be sure to maintain equal weight for
> the rigors of justice.
> He cannot hope to preserve the scales of the
> law in true balance,
> If he should bow to applause or let prospect
> of gain be his motive.
> He for whom purse strings are loosed, and ill-
> gotten gold is his bounty
> As a pauper his fate it will be to have lost
> his soul void of justice.
> Rome guards the portals on high, in its hands
> are the reins of earth's power:
> Those who would yearn after more will find
> only hell as their portion.[66]

65. On Cadalus, see Damian, *Letters* 88 and 89.
66. Cf. Reindel, *Briefe* 3.64, n. 39.

LETTER 97

Peter Damian to the cardinal bishops. Returning to Fonte Avellana after strenuously fighting for the rights of the Holy See against the interloper Cadalus, he advises his fellow cardinal bishops to combat avarice, the all-pervading clerical evil of the times and the root of all evils. His deep concern for spiritual renewal in the episcopate prompted him to note that, as in the case of Cadalus, greed was the corrupting cause of the Church's ills. Ostentatious attire and vain, glorious ornamentation were the symptoms of an evil that gnawed at the vitality of the Church, and especially that of the bishops. Both justice and the reforming vigor of papal synods themselves were in danger of perversion if the cardinals, the senate of the Church, did not oppose the evil of avarice.

(Shortly before the Easter synod of May 1063)[1]

O THE CARDINAL BISHOPS of the Apostolic See,[2] the monk Peter the sinner sends greetings in the Lord.

(2) Just as words serve to disclose one's ideas to those who are present, so to those who are absent a letter is the instrument of one's words. And as a man learns the arts of war in combat that later they may be taught in times of peace, thus as one afterwards teaches at leisure, one acts with greater caution in battle. In the struggles of the Apostolic See in which you are still unanimously engaged, I was also once your comrade-in-arms.[3] But now that I am retired from service and live in the peace of the monastery, I am free to teach what I have learned.

(3) Among all the forces of vice that rage around us, and amid the dense storms of missiles raining down on us like hailstones, you should be especially wary of avarice, always protecting yourselves with your shield against the arrows it unleashes.

1. Dating follows Lucchesi, *Vita* 2.159. But see Schmidt, *Alexander II* 187.

2. He also addressed the cardinals in general in *Letter* 48. Cf. Maccarrone, *La teologia* 71, n. 179.

3. On Damian's appointment as cardinal, cf. Cacciamani, *La nomina* 193 and Lucchesi, *Vita* no. 111.

This vice rushes headlong toward its objective, to inflict a lethal wound on miserable men; in the beginning, however, it seeks to blind, not the eye, but the heart. And so the wise man says, "Hospitality and presents blind the eyes of judges; as though mute in the mouth it turns aside their criticisms."[4] For men who are still advancing in rank it furnishes with bribes, and through them attacks and blinds the hearts of those who acquire the position of giving advice in high places. Of such the Lord complains through Isaiah when he says, "Your very rulers are unfaithful, confederate with thieves; every one of them loves a bribe, retribution follows."[5] But someone may reply, "I ask for nothing, but if something is freely offered, I will not refuse it." Here we are not speaking of those who are looking for bribes, but only of those who love them. Thus it is not improper to call them confederates of thieves, because in accepting secret gifts, they dread to be apprehended by their fellow-ministers and associates, like one who has committed theft. We should note that Scripture says, "retribution follows," because even though these paid with their gifts for the assistance they required, they will not escape the stain of guilt, because as they receive punishment for accepting bribes, they lose the fruits of eternal reward. And shortly after, the Lord says of such men, "Enough! I shall be consoled over my foes and take vengeance from my enemies."[6]

(4) Now, we read that the sons of Samuel were guilty of no other crime except that they loved bribes; and because they failed to follow the example of their father's unsullied life, they lost their position as leaders of the people of Israel, which they could never recover. And it should be noted that when Scripture says of them, "They stooped to avarice and took bribes," it at once added, "They perverted justice."[7] The two things are indeed closely related and joined; after accepting a bribe, justice is perverted because the judge has been corrupted. But what a good reputation Samuel had in respect to bribes when he said, "To this very day I have been your leader since I was a child. Here I am. Lay your complaints against me in the presence of the Lord and of his

4. Sir 20.31.   5. Isa 1.23.
6. Isa 1.24.   7. 1 Sam 8.3.

anointed king. Whose ox have I taken, whose ass have I taken? Whom have I wronged? Whom have I oppressed? From whom have I taken a bribe? If I have done so, I will denounce it today and make restitution to you."[8] In the Law, moreover, it was commanded, "You shall not accept bribes, which make even the discerning man blind and bring the just man to give a crooked answer."[9] And in Deuteronomy we find approximately the same, "You shall not show favor, nor shall you accept a bribe; for bribery blinds the eyes of the wise and changes the words of the just."[10] And how opposed to accepting bribes Abraham was as he rebuked Melchizedek,[11] the king of Sodom, "I lift my hand and swear by the Lord, God Most High, to whom heaven and earth belong, not a thread of a shoestring will I accept of anything that is yours."[12] Moreover, how clean was Moses of receiving bribes, as he called on the Lord who knows all things to be his witness, "You know that I have never taken from them so much as a single ass; I have done no wrong to any of them."[13] When someone is eager to receive bribes, it follows that when as a judge he acquits a person who has given him a bribe, he wrongs the one who gave him nothing. And so Isaiah says, "Woe to you who for a bribe acquit the guilty and deny justice to those in the right."[14] And immediately he threatens such as these with the punishment they deserve, as he adds, "So, as a tongue of fire licks up the stubble and the heat of the flame burns it up, their root will be like ash, and their shoots will rise up like dust."[15] Elsewhere the same prophet complains of such men when he says, "Each of them has gone off down his own path, each to his avarice, from the highest to the lowliest."[16] It is clear, then, that avarice provokes against itself the anger of almighty God and always troubles with delusive thoughts the heart that accommodates it. Wherefore, he complains about an avaricious people when he says, "I was angry over the wickedness of their avarice; I smote them, and I

---

8. 1 Sam 12.2–3.   9. Exod 23.8.
10. Deut 16.19.
11. Damian here confused Melchizedek, king of Salem, with Bera, king of Sodom. All major MSS concur in this reading.
12. Gen 14.22–23.   13. Num 16.15.
14. Isa 5.23.   15. Isa 5.24.
16. Isa 56.11.

withdrew, and I became angry. But they wandered off in the way of their heart."[17]

(5) Hardly any festering wound causes a more intolerable stench for the nose of God than the excrement that is avarice. And every greedy man who receives profit from money that defiles him, turns a palatial hall into a latrine where he accumulates a heap of dung. To this point Ezekiel says, "They shall fling their silver into the streets and cast aside their gold like filth; their silver and their gold will be powerless to save them on the day of the Lord's fury."[18] And elsewhere it is written, "Woe betide him who continues to heap up wealth that is not his and weighs himself down with heavy mud."[19] For an avaricious man to weigh himself down with heavy mud is to accumulate worldly gain under the burden of sin. And the prophet Habakkuk also says, "Woe betide the man who gathers up wicked avarice for his house, to build his nest on a height, thinking to save himself in evil times."[20] Moreover, just as there is never enough wood for a fire, so by gathering money one does not abate the ardor of avarice. But as the flames rise higher when fed with fuel, so also when wealth is piled up, avarice grows stronger. And so Ecclesiastes says, "The man who loves money can never have enough, and the man who is in love with riches will receive no fruits from them."[21] He would enjoy fruits from these if he had wished to distribute them wisely and not loved them so. But because he loves to keep them for himself, he will be left without fruit. And then the text continues, "When riches multiply, so do those who live off them."[22] And what good are they to their owner unless he can have them always in sight? And of this the same Solomon says, "A man hoards wealth to his own hurt, and then that wealth is lost in a most severe affliction, and the owner's son left with nothing."[23] And to show how unfaithful riches are to him who owns them, he continues right away, "As he came naked from his mother's womb, so will he return, and all his toil will produce nothing that he can

---

17. Isa 57.17.   18. Ezek 7.19.
19. Hab 2.6.   20. Hab 2.9.
21. Eccl 5.9.
22. Eccl 5.10; cf. Sabatier 2.362 citing Jerome, *Commentarius in Ecclesiasten* 5.9 (CC 72.294).
23. Eccl 5.12–13.

take with him. This indeed is a miserable infirmity: exactly as he came, so will he go; and what profit does he get when his labor is for the wind all the days of his life?"[24] And so forth.

(6) Do we perhaps amass wealth that we might buy up land and possessions? But what good is it to extend the boundaries of our property, since this cannot drive away worry from our life? Hence the wise man says, "Do not be intent upon wicked possessions and say, 'I have a sufficient life.' They will do you no good when the day of punishment arrives."[25] For Isaiah also says, "Shame on you! You who add house to house and join field to field, until not an acre remains. Will you dwell all alone in the land?"[26] It is as if he were actually saying, "How far will you extend your holdings, you who are unable to live in a common world without neighbors? You indeed crowd in upon those who live nearby and are your neighbors, but you will always find someone against whom you can carry on your expansion. And so it is written, "One who is in a hurry to grow rich will not go unpunished."[27] And elsewhere it is said, "Nothing is more abominable than a greedy man. Dust and ashes, what have you to be proud of? There is nothing more wicked than the love of money."[28] This is certainly a hard and most fearful statement. For if there is nothing more abominable or more wicked than a greedy man, he is therefore no better than a murderer, he is not preferred to those who practice incest, he is on a par with heretics, and is put in the same class with idolaters. And so the Apostle says, "Greed is nothing less than idolatry."[29] Therefore, even though a man be pure and temperate, involved in feeding the poor, and dedicated to practicing hospitality; even though he may fast, meditate long hours, and chant the psalms day and night: if he is an avaricious person, he loses all this, so that among all criminals no one worse than him can be found. And so it was said above, "Nothing is more abominable than a greedy man, there is nothing more wicked than the love of money." Hence, what good is it not to commit murder or adultery, not to

---

24. Eccl 5.14–16.   25. Sir 5.1.
26. Isa 5.8.   27. Prov 28.10.
28. Sir 10.9–10.
29. Col 3.5; cf. Sabatier 3.838 for patristic antecedents.

steal or perjure oneself, and to be wholly on guard against every crime? For, so long as you do not rid yourself of avarice, there is nothing more abominable, nothing worse than you.

(7) So, let a greedy man do what he will. He may build churches or engage in preaching; he may act as a peace-maker or strengthen the wavering in the truth of the Catholic faith; he may be devoted in celebrating Mass every day and keep aloof from secular affairs. But so long as he does not put out the fire of avarice within him, his every flower of virtue is burned away, and no one more criminal than he can be found. Now, after Scripture stated that nothing is so abominable as a greedy man, lest anyone have the slightest doubt about what was meant by the word "greedy," it took pains to add, "Nothing is more wicked than the love of money." Therefore, to be avaricious is nothing else but loving money. He loves the money he has made, and also loves the money still to be made. Avarice is indeed a two-headed serpent that is accustomed to strike with both, and with both to inject its harmful venom, either in seeking to acquire what belongs to another, or in greedily enjoying what it already possesses. Surely, it was written of him who swallows with both mouths of this serpent, "To no purpose does a covetous and greedy man have material possessions. What use is gold to a miser? He unjustly hoards for other men and others will live in luxury on his riches."[30]

(8) There are those, moreover, whose total desire is to acquire what belongs to others, but cannot spend it fast enough after it is theirs. And there are those who do not avidly long to own other people's goods, but hoard what they own as if they were guarding the temple of Ceres.[31] But worst of all are those who both are shameless in their pursuit of what belongs to others, and with selfish tenacity protect what is already theirs. They are worse than the dragons of Babylon which, although they are said to guard a vast hoard of gold and silver, do not strive to deprive others of their property, but content with what is theirs, do not seek what belongs to others.[32] Moreover, why should I amass riches

---

30. Sir 14.3–4.

31. Cf. Horace, *Carmina* 3.2.26.

32. Cf. Sextus Pompeius Festus, *De verborum significatu quae supersunt cum Pauli epitome*, ed. W. M. Lindsay (1913) 59 (dragons), 8 (gold).

which no one brought with him when he came into this world, and which cannot accompany him when he leaves? To this point the Apostle says, "We brought nothing into the world; undoubtedly we cannot take anything away with us, but if we have food and covering we may rest content. Those who want to be rich fall into the temptation and snare of the devil and many useless and harmful desires which plunge men into ruin and perdition. The love of money is the root of all evil things, and there are some who in reaching for it have wandered from the faith and have enrolled themselves among many sorrows."[33]

(9) Why should one wonder over what we stated above, that there is nothing more abominable than a greedy man, since it is said that the love of money is the root of all evil things? Because it is the root of all evil things, it follows that the avaricious man is guilty of all evil things, for by having their roots in the field of his heart he cannot avoid their poisonous growth. Nor dare we pass over lightly what was also said, "And there are those who in reaching for it have wandered from the faith."[34] This was just what the Savior's traitor did. To obtain a small sum of money he sold the Creator of all things, and for love of filthy lucre betrayed the Author of life. Balaam, son of Beor, acted in a similar way. As he sought to acquire the money offered him, he turned his back on God and gave advice leading to the destruction of the people of Israel.[35] Some have indeed claimed[36]—and their authority should not be rejected—that Balaam is to be identified with Elihu, the Buzite of the family of Buz, who was the second son of Nachor, Abraham's brother.[37] In the book of blessed Job, this same Elihu is said to have been Job's friend,[38] since he was a prophet and possessed the grace of divine revelation. But it is said that after succumbing to the vice of avarice he ceased being a prophet and became a soothsayer, and then engaged in magic.

33. 1 Tim 6.7–10.   34. 1 Tim 6.10.
35. Cf. Num 22.5.

36. Here Damian is reporting the opinion of Pseudo-Jerome, *Commentarium in librum Job* 32 (PL 26.764 A–C), where both Balaam's descent from Abraham's brother, Nachor, and his identification with Elihu in Job 32.2 are claimed. It is noteworthy that Damian did not attribute this opinion to Jerome; cf. Cornelius a Lapide, *Commentaria in scripturam sacram* 2 (1877) 312.

37. See also Gen 22.20–24.   38. Cf. Job 32.2.

So, what good can come from avarice, which by depriving men of their faith, changes a prophet into a magician and causes one to fall from the heights of apostolic rank into the depths of hell? Did not Gehazi stray from the faith when, by accepting silver offered by Naaman, he thought that his master was not with him in spirit? But Elisha said, "Was I not with you in spirit when the man turned back from his chariot to meet you?"[39] Here we should carefully ponder that if he who benefited from the power of the prophet was afflicted with leprosy, how dare one sell the judicial opinion of the pope? "You have accepted the money and the clothing," Elisha said, "so that you may buy olive-trees and vineyards, sheep and oxen, slaves and slave-girls; but the disease of Naaman will fasten on you and on your descendants forever."[40]

(10) Now there are two originators of the heresy of simony, one in the Old Testament and the other in the New. They also practice these two types of simony, namely, selling and buying. Gehazi it was who sold the gift of the Holy Spirit,[41] while Simon the Magician tried to buy it.[42] Nor should he alone be called a simonist who gives or receives a price for administering sacred orders, but also he who betrays a synod or sells a bishop's legal decision. But perhaps someone might say, "Therefore he too incurs the guilt of simony who offers something for the synodal decision handed down in his favor." But I would not agree with this, because Naaman did not commit a sin in offering a gift to the deceitful servant out of gratitude to his master who healed him. It is one thing for a person to seek justice for his cause, and quite another to purchase a canonical decision which is under the guidance of the Holy Spirit.[43] And how in conscience can we accept a gift for passing a judicial sentence, when he to whom we offer this valuable service may be pleading justly or unjustly? If justice is on his side, we are undoubtedly selling the truth; but if his case is unjust, we rashly and impudently fight against the

---

39. 2 Kgs 5.26.
40. 2 Kgs 5.26–27.
41. Cf. 2 Kgs 5.22–23.
42. Cf. Acts 8.18. On the two types of simony, cf. H.-J. Horn, "Giezi und Simonie," *Jahrbuch für Antike und Christentum* 8/9 (1965–1966) 189–202.
43. Ryan, *Sources* 118 no. 251 cites the *Rescriptum beati papae Damasi Aurelio archiepiscopo* (Hinschius 21), and his own comments at no. 194 and no. 248.

truth which is Christ. And for this reason it is commanded in the Law, "You shall justly pursue what is just."[44] He indeed unjustly pursues what is just, if in the defense of justice he is not motivated by the practice of virtue, but by love of temporal gain. For he is rightly said to pursue unjustly what is just, if he has no fear of selling the justice he pretends to dispense. Yet, he demonstrates that he is justly following what is just, if in proclaiming justice he seeks nothing but justice alone.

(11) And indeed there are some who either before administering ordination, or before the case under consideration is decided, agree to no reward for their service. Later, however, they make demands as if they were dealing with debtors and harshly persist in being paid. Such men should have no doubt that they have incurred the guilt of Gehazi who at once went back to Naaman after the latter had been cured, and dared to demand money for the gift of the Holy Spirit.[45] And as he was struck down with nothing less than leprosy which was the cause of removing people from the camp, such men likewise contract not just some light guilt, but the guilt of the very crime of Gehazi which denies them the sacraments of the Church.

(12) When I was still performing the honorable office of a bishop,[46] I saw one of our brother bishops, whose name I will suppress but whose sin I will tell you about, who so skipped about and grew in importance that, when the time appointed for a synod drew near, you would think we were ready to harvest the grain or gather the grapes.[47] He busied himself in taking bribes, for the reaping of which he did not sharpen a sickle, but the scythe of his eloquence, employing fraudulent tactics just as the pseudo-apostles were said to have done, raking in money here and there and stuffing it in their purses which were already overflowing. But if anyone should be angry with me for handling my fellow-bishop so harshly, let him reprove John and Matthew, who while proclaiming the truth in their sacred narratives,

---

44. Deut 16.20.   45. Cf. 2 Kgs 5.26–27.

46. Here he refers to the bishoprics of Ostia and Gubbio; cf. Damian, *Letter* 57, n. 7, where the inference is unclear.

47. He is probably hinting at the approaching synod of May 1063; cf. Schmale, *Synoden* 311ff.

showed up their co-apostle as a sacrilegious money-grubber and a traitor.[48]

(13) But our ancient enemy often deceives those who hope for this kind of profit by not at all giving them what he promised. Just as the fowler lures the hawk to eat a piece of meat, but just as it has the meat in its claws, he takes it away and ties its feet with a leather thong; so too the devil at first promises wealth, but afterwards withdraws it and only catches us in the snare of sin. In the same way, he who eagerly looks about for bribes, is like the mouse that while busy gnawing at the bait is choked by the noose. The celebrated Fabricius cleverly avoided this trap when Pyrrhus, the king of Epirus, was at war with the Roman Republic. Learning that the former was a poor man, Pyrrhus began to solicit him, promising him a quarter of his kingdom if he would come over to his side. But Fabricius flatly turned him down, and by his action continued to live as a poor man, more illustrious than the king.[49] A Christian who is avaricious should pay heed to this account, should be ashamed of his own paganism, and should blush at seeing this pagan's Gospel-like principles. And often a gift is accepted with the understanding that if the donor is found to be culpable, he will not profit from this departure from justice. This is easier said than done. For if we should accuse the donor after we have accepted his gifts, the words often melt in our mouth, we begin to stammer, and our tongue is obstructed as if it were ashamed to move. Indeed, a conscience burdened with accepting bribes weakens the force of our judgment and curbs our freedom of speech. Even though high-minded judgment is not totally destroyed, the authority of the judicial process is lessened.

(14) Still there are some who take care not to accept an offered gift while the case is under consideration; but once the action is complete, they will not refuse when something is offered with no strings attached. But in certain situations it often happens that what they thought had been accepted gratis, they are

---

48. Cf. John 12.4–6, 13.2, 19.11; Matt 26.21–25, 47–50; 27.3–10.
49. On C. Fabricius Luscinus, cf. Eutropius, *Breviarium* 12 (MGH Auct ant. 2.32–34).

now forced to offset in other cases, and the danger of flood they had hoped to have left behind them, they unexpectedly find ready to engulf them. It is, therefore, safe and sound advice which the prophet gives us, "We should shake off every bribe,"[50] and we should keep ourselves truly free to help or harm, so that we will not plead in court under the pressure of money, but act in the service of unfettered justice. If one, perhaps, should complain about the inadequacy of his personal resources, he should pay close attention to what was written; "Many have fallen into sin because of their poverty and a money-grubber turns a blind eye."[51]

(15) Therefore, if those involved in the judicial process who suffer personal poverty are at fault, those who know that they are even in need of food; if, I say, even those sin who make every effort to acquire the necessities and not what is merely superfluous; what kind of judgment will await those who scramble to get more than enough and to hoard all kinds of precious metal and clothes that will be the food of moths? The apostle James gives such men this terrible warning, "Now a word to you who have great possessions. Weep and wail over the miserable fate descending on you."[52] Having said this, he at once gives the reason, "Your riches have rotted; your fine clothes are moth-eaten; your silver and gold have rusted away, and their very rust will be evidence against you and consume your flesh like fire. You have piled up wrath against you in an age that is near its close."[53]

(16) Those, moreover, who are in this class, do not complain about their poverty so that they may support their natural needs with the props of necessary things, but that their plates might be piled high with food that savors of spices from India, that their wine, flavored with honey, might sparkle in crystal glasses. Clearly, they seek to accumulate wealth that they might at once decorate their chambers with elaborate and marvelously woven draperies, whatever their provenance, and thus disguise the walls of the house from the eyes of their attentive guests, as they would

---

50. Isa 33.15. But, as usual, Damian is somewhat lax in citing the Vulgate, allowing the translator the same latitude.

51. Sir 27.1.   52. Jas 5.1.

53. Jas 5.2–3.

a dead body prepared for burial. They often cover the chairs with fabric embroidered with prodigious figures, and hang coverings on the ceilings that nothing might fall to the floor and scatter the crowd of their dependents. Some, to be sure, reverently attend to their lord and watch for his every nod, should he perhaps beckon, keeping a sharp eye on him as if they were closely investigating the stars. Others, like Martha, are busy with much service, running here and there like restless swallows.[54] Amid all this mad display of ambition, why do they search for wall tapestries to be placed behind the seating, which cannot be seen by their lords? They suffer this heavy expense for decor, even though the eye cannot see the back of the head or the neck. And how useful is this kind of wealth which serves no other purpose than to display its beauty, but cannot be viewed to the satisfaction of its owner? It serves only to please the eyes of strangers, since it does not face him to whom it belongs, but hangs behind his back.

(17) Not totally unlike this, I think, is also that other mad practice of adorning the bed with such precious hanging that it exceeds the ornamentation of the altar of any saint or even of the very apostles themselves. How absurd it appears to be more careful in decking out the bed where corruptible flesh takes its rest, than the altar of the cross on which the sacrifice of the Lord's body is offered. By so acting, the bishops who were formerly commendable for their moderation, have become gluttons in their ostentatious display of wealth. Royal purple, because it is uniform in color, is belittled; but coverings dyed in various shades are considered the proper adornment for their high bed.[55] And since our domestic cats offend the eye, they delight in furs brought in from overseas because they are more costly. They despise the wool of sheep and lambs and search for ermine, sable, marten, and fox. The former are spoken of with honor in sacred Scripture, and figuratively bespeak either the Church or the person of the Savior, "My sheep," he says, "hear

---

54. Cf. Luke 10.38–41.

55. According to the scholion of Gaetani (PL 145.512ff.) Damian here gives evidence that at this period the cardinals were attired in purple. See also Schramm, *Herrschaftszeichen* 57, 715.

my voice,"[56] and "Look, there is the Lamb of God, it is he who takes away the sins of the world."[57] About the latter, however, Scripture either has nothing to say, and considers them unworthy of mention, or, if there is a word about them, they are referred to in a pejorative way. And so, there is the statement, "Foxes have their holes, but the Son of man has nowhere to lay his head."[58] Note that Christ did not lie down with foxes, but the Christian sleeps under fox fur. He turns his back on animals bearing the name of the Redeemer of the world, and uses as his adornment those which symbolize the damned. But these wealthy bishops suffer no small obstruction. For while they cover themselves with fancy and elaborate quilts, the poor devils cannot sleep with watchful eyes.

(18) We must, therefore, envy Regulus, formerly the Roman consul, whom the Carthaginians mutilated by cutting off his eyelids because he persisted in his loyalty to the Republic.[59] And, in fact, what good purpose is served by this beautiful decor if it cannot be seen? Or, indeed, of what value is this splendid variety if it does not delight the sensibility of the beholder? For this outstanding type of wealth is such, that when used it cannot be seen, and when seen serves no useful purpose. It is disgusting to talk about the rest of these ridiculous vanities, which should not be seen but deplored, and it is tiresome to enumerate so many extravagant examples of ambition and colossal madness: papal vestments sparkling with gems and cloth of gold, spoils from various lands, imperial horses which while prancing with nimble steps and arching necks, by their unbroken liveliness tire their riders tugging at the reins. I will say nothing of the rings set with enormous pearls, and will pass over their crosiers, not just conspicuous for their gold and gems, but actually buried in them.

(19) To tell the truth, I cannot recall ever having seen pontifical crosiers so completely covered and splendidly wrought in this radiant metal, as those carried by the bishops of Ascoli and

56. John 10.3, a variant of the Vulgate.
57. John 1.29; for variant see Sabatier 3.390.
58. Matt 8.20; Luke 9.58.
59. For Marcus Atilius Regulus, cf. Orosius, *Historiarum adversus paganos libri septem* 4.10.1 (ed. A. Lippold 1.302).

Trani. Both were deposed, the one in the region of Puglia with Nicholas presiding,[60] the other at the church of the Lateran before Alexander, both Roman pontiffs, of course.[61] Nor did it do them any good that bishops were using wooden crosiers that had been gilded, since the worth of a bishop is not enhanced by the splendor of his vestments but by the quality of his spiritual virtues; and it is not brilliant pearls or gems that are becoming to a bishop, but his golden moral life. For just as a bishop's sincere humility makes God his friend, and his other good deeds procure God's favor, so too arrogance and vain ambition provoke God's indignation and wrath against him and fight against the good he had perhaps previously achieved. And so the Lord says through Isaiah, "Should I not be angry over these things? On the mountaintop you have gone up to offer sacrifices."[62] A bishop goes up to the mountaintop when he assumes an attitude of disdainful pride by his haughty use of adulterous finery.

(20) And since the soul of a bishop, like a bride, is joined to Christ by the bond of spiritual marriage, if he so fosters external elegance that he fails to enrich himself interiorly, how can he bring an adulterer to his husband's bed? And so the word of God hastens to add, "Because in my presence you have stripped off your clothes and have taken an adulterer."[63] Oh, how bitter the pain if, while the husband is present, one should bring in an adulterer and use his very bed to lie with a sinful rival! And he goes on to say, "You have enlarged your bed and made bargains with them and openly enjoyed sleeping with them."[64] And not forgetting to mention adornment or other delights, he then adds, "You applied royal ointments and added still more perfumes."[65] But after rebuking the arrogance of the proud and of those living in luxury, he then consoles the heart of the humble and of those who suffer for their own good. "Sweep away," he says, "all that blocks my people's path. Thus speaks the high and

60. The deposition of the bishop of Trani took place at the Council of Melfi (1059) under Nicholas II; cf. JL 4407; Ryan, *Sources* no. 252.

61. This Roman council under Alexander II is unknown; see Schmidt, *Alexander II* 187–195; Reindel, *Briefe* 3.77–78, nos. 25, 26.

62. Isa 57.6–7.   63. Isa 57.8.

64. Isa 57.8.   65. Isa 57.9.

exalted Lord who lives forever: I dwell in a high and holy place with him who is broken and humble in spirit, to revive the spirit of the humble, to revive the heart of the broken."[66]

(21) Finally, the heart of a bishop should be the temple of God, the sanctuary of Christ, and certainly not, as we read, a den of thieves or a hiding place of contaminating money.[67] For every soul will be valued in the judgment of God for what is desired in its thoughts. Should it dwell on fornication or adultery, it becomes a bawdy house inhabited by whores. Should it think about spilling blood and think of hatred, it becomes a field for raging warriors. If one should fix his thoughts on delicate foods and sumptuous banquets, how else does he appear in the sight of God but as a pot or caldron in which food is cooked? If he engages in controversy and lawsuits, what else is seen but a court or a judge's tribunal? And so when the Lord said to Ezekiel, "Go in and see the vile abominations they practice here," he at once added, "So I went in and saw figures of reptiles, beasts, and vermin, and all the idols of the Israelites, carved round the walls."[68] For whatever is mulled over in the mind appears as carvings on the wall. And our mind holds the pictures of those things which it carefully meditates, and paints them as so many images in action insofar as it thinks about them as either unprofitable or useful. It is as if someone first views the shining stars, and then turns his eyes to look into a latrine; now he marvels at the brilliance of glittering gold, and later he sees the flaking surface of rusting iron. Thus it is with the human mind. As it thinks about base and worldly things, it undoubtedly sees the earth; but when considering holy things, when it meditates on that which is divine and heavenly, it deservedly beholds heaven, the temple and sanctuary of God.

(22) The Roman Church, moreover, which is the see of the apostles, should imitate the ancient assembly of the Romans.[69] Just as formerly that earthly senate conducted all its discussions and directed and carefully exercised its common effort to sub-

66. Isa 57.14–15.   67. Cf. Matt 21.13.
68. Ezek 8.9–10.
69. Cf. Schramm, *Kaiser* 1.225; Laqua 326 ff.

due the whole non-Roman world to its authority, so now the custodians of the Apostolic See who are the spiritual senators of the universal Church, must earnestly engage in the exclusive effort to win the human race for the dominion of Christ, the true emperor. And as formerly the Roman consuls brought back trophies of victory from various parts of the world after defeating their enemies, so must these now free the captured souls of men from the land of the devil. They must always long for those honors of victory, those triumphs, so that they rejoice in snatching away the spoils of perishing souls from the ancient robber and take them back as signs of victory to Christ, their king.

(23) David, moreover, typified this fight when he, as victor, gained the community of Rabbah. For "Rabbah" has the meaning of "multitude" or "great,"[70] which quite conveniently is understood to signify all of this world.[71] Thus David gained the community of Rabbah, when Christ brought the great and abundant multitude of this world under his laws. But David took away the crown from the head of this king, and, as Scripture testifies, put it upon himself. Christ, the true David, fulfilled this, when he snatched away the wise ones of the world with whom the devil in a certain way had adorned himself, and changed them into a diadem for his own beauty and glory. The multitude of the faithful, moreover, is called a crown not only of Christ, but also of the teacher by whose preaching they are converted. Paul speaks thus to the Philippians, "Therefore, my beloved brethren, my joy and my crown, continue to stay firm in the Lord."[72] The spoils, in fact, are taken from Rabbah, when all the sincere and faithful ones are converted from this world to the service of almighty God.

(24) I call upon you, O holy bishops, you especially who must be spoilers of this kind, daily making every effort to rescue the souls of men from the hands of that reprobate who holds them, and carry them back as triumphant spoils to David, your king. Nor does it suffice when someone snatched from the devil is converted to God by your loving devotion, unless also his hard heart

---

70. Cf. Jerome, *Nom. hebr.* 23.6 (CC 72.87).
71. Cf. 2 Sam 12.29–30.   72. Phil 4.1.

is fragmented by the repeated hammering of holy preaching. And so Jeremiah says, "Do not my words scorch like fire, says the Lord? Are they not like a hammer that splinters rock?"[73] The Lord's words are truly like fire, because they expel the cold and bring warmth to the heart. They are a hammer, since they soften the hardness of obstinacy and stubbornness. Therefore sacred history aptly adds, "He also took its inhabitants and kept them under guard, drove iron carts over them, cut them to pieces with knives, and transported them like bricks."[74] What is meant by iron carts, which are indeed some kind of conveyance, if not the powerful and impregnable chariot of the holy evangelists, by which we must understand the total message of divine Scripture? For, as we have already said elsewhere, iron indeed is a base metal, but it overcomes all others. As iron is superior to all metals, so too the teaching of the Gospel is recognized as softening the hardest hearts. And what is meant by driving iron carts over people who were taken prisoner, if it does not intend to say that it is like threshing the field of men's souls with the wheels of sacred Scripture, that in them God's word might trample the soil of opposing vices, making it smooth and level to receive the seeds of the heavenly commandments? And what is the significance of cutting them to pieces with knives, if not through preaching to open the conscience of sinful men to belief in God's word? Of this word the Apostle says, "The sword of the spirit which is the word of God."[75] For then, as it were, is man cut to pieces by spiritual knives, when he is cut open by the sword of God's word to lay bare the infection in his soul. Why is it said that they were carted away like bricks, if not to state that they are bricks made of clay and then baked? For a sinner becomes like brick when by hearing the word of God proclaimed he receives the warmth of the Holy Spirit, and is truly made humble, recognizing that he is but earth and clay. Thus it is that one who alters his life and repents, becomes like brick; when he is humbled by realizing that he is as fragile as clay and, as it were, grows fire red and glows with the love of God, so that, after counting himself to

73. Jer 23.29.   74. 2 Sam 12.31.
75. Eph 6.17.

be but earthly dust, he enkindles his heart to give thanks to God who invited him to return. And so "Adam" may be interpreted to mean " the red earth,"[76] so that from the name of our first parent one may learn to know what he was originally made of, or what he actually is.

(25) Like bishops of the Church, like holy pontiffs, they must therefore strive to win such victories, and not grow soft from lavishly served banquets or from wanton indulgence in pleasure. For from the beginning of the world, for almost sixteen-hundred years, the human race lived without drinking wine or eating meat,[77] and still no one of whom Scripture speaks ever wasted away through weakness until he died.

(26) And now let me conclude with a brief epilogue what I have written at some length above, and by performing the function of a whetstone, while I myself may not cut, I might make ever more sharp the edge of the blade that another will use. Let us uproot avarice from our heart, a vice clearly condemned by all concurring evidence of Scripture, and buried with Achan, son of Carmi,[78] under the same number of stones as there are statements by the Fathers. We should be pleased never to accept a bribe, lest, which God forbid, we be expelled from episcopal ranks by the secret procedure of our judge, like the sons of Samuel who for this crime lost the judicial office they had attained.[79] We must never put a synod up for sale, nor set a price on a synodal decision, so as not to appear to sell the Holy Spirit, the source of authority at a sacred council.[80] Be done with pursuing worldly display, modest in your use of splendid and novel attire, and temperate in your consumption of food and drink. Let our money pass into the hands of the poor. Let that which through avarice made our purses bulge, be dispensed with compassion until they are empty. Winning souls should be our treasure and our wealth, and we should amass talents of virtue in the coffers of our heart. And on this altar we should primarily offer

---

76. Cf. Jerome, *Nom. hebr.* 2.17 (CC 72.60).
77. Cf. Bultot, *Pierre Damien* 132, n. 330, citing only Damian.
78. Cf. Josh 7.25–26.   79. Cf. 1 Sam 4.17.
80. Cf. *Rescriptum beati papae Damasi Aurelio archiepiscopo*: Ryan, *Sources* nos. 194, 248, 251, 254.

our sacrifice, so that having used up the oblations round about us, we may at length immolate ourselves as living victims for God. By so doing, we shall be seen as priests in the eyes of men and rightfully carry out the functions of true priests in the sight of the hidden Judge.

LETTER 98

Peter Damian to Pope Alexander II. In a reforming mood, relative to the eleventh-century phenomenon of the rapid spread of canonical living, Damian requests Alexander to legislate further in this matter. Besides promoting the reforming objectives of the common life for all canons, whose primary function it was to perform the liturgy in the cathedral, he further demanded that the canons return to the apostolic life, which required personal poverty in addition to communal ownership. Against the arguments of the canons, Damian cites evidence from Augustine, Jerome, and Julianus Pomerius (Pseudo-Prosper), in addition to the *Institutio canonicorum*, issued by the Council of Aachen in 816.

(After the Easter synod of 1063)[1]

O THE BLESSED POPE, Sir Alexander,[2] the monk Peter the sinner offers his service.

(2) According to my limited way of thinking, venerable father, there is no evil perpetrated by the human race that is so pernicious a crime as the defense of depravity. To this point David says, "Turn not my heart to evil words, to offer excuses for my sins."[3] Offending God, to be sure, deserves his wrath, but excuses provoke him to vengeance. Now this vice, proceeding as it does from the very roots of mankind, spreads daily and never ceases to grow like branches sprouting from a tree. For when Adam was asked why he had eaten of the forbidden fruit, he replied, "The woman you gave me for a companion, she gave me fruit from the tree and I ate it."[4] Also the woman, when asked why she had done this, answered, "The serpent tricked me, and I ate."[5] It was as if both of them turned this sin back upon the Creator and attacked him who had reprimanded them, saying,

---

1. Dating follows Lucchesi, *Vita* no. 170.
2. See *Letter* 96, n. 2. On the problem here addressed see also *Letter* 39 to the clerics of Fano; cf. also Laudage, *Priesterbild* 190, n. 98.
3. Ps 140.4.   4. Gen 3.12.
5. Gen 3.13.

"Without a doubt the guilt for this action must be charged to you and not to us, since you united man and wife and decided that the serpent should live with men in paradise." Both of them acted like the first boy who ever went to school, who replied to the Lord when asked about Abel, "Am I my brother's keeper?"[6]

(3) David surely avoided this sin when he said, "Let no flood carry me away, no abyss swallow me up, nor may the mouth of the well close over me."[7] Now, when a man sins, he falls, as it were, into a well; but when he defends his sins, the mouth of the well closes over him so that he may not escape. And so, a man falls into the well when he sins, but closes the mouth of the well when he makes excuses. Moreover, heresy is born from this defense or excuse of crime, for heresy may be defined as "choice."[8] And when a person makes his choice and then tries to defend it, he abandons the path of truth, and led down the steep ways of perverse teaching, he necessarily falls into heresy. But there is this difference between a sinner and a heretic: the sinner is he who commits a fault, but a heretic is one who defends his sin by false doctrine. But since we have the holy apostles and other apostolic men as our teachers, we must not follow our own opinion in choosing, nor obstinately and willfully defend what once we have chosen to do, but place irrevocable faith only in those teachings that have been settled by approved doctors of the Church.[9]

(4) I have prefaced these remarks, because I am grieved over certain holy brothers living under the rule of the canons, who have dared to express themselves with such unbridled liberty, that not only do they claim the right to own money, but audaciously assert that this right belongs to them by authority of their rule.[10] To credibly refute them, I could indeed assemble many texts from both the Old and the New Testament, if our Fathers

6. Gen 4.9.   7. Ps 68.16.
8. Cf. Jerome, *Commentariorum in epistolam ad Titum liber unus,* c. 3 (PL 26.597B).
9. See Miccoli, "Ecclesiae primitivae forma," 476, n. 14; also *idem, Chiesa Gregoriana* 260, n. 86.
10. On the identification of this "regular authority" with the *Institutio canonicorum* (Council of Aachen, 816: MGH Conc. 2.1.308–421), see Laqua, *Traditionen* 91; Ryan, *Sources* no. 211 and nos. 217ff. See also Reindel, *Briefe* 3.85, no. 5.

and doctors of the Church who preceded us had said nothing on this topic.[11] But it is superfluous for me to break up the earth there with my poor little hoe, when such energetic cultivators of the land of the living are found to have furrowed the soil with the sharp plow of their words.

(5) But first of all, let Augustine come forward as a witness, and tell us by the most evident authority of his experience whether a canon is allowed to own property. In his sermon, entitled *On the Clerical Life*,[12] he says, "Your charity is aware that I said to my brothers who are living with me, that whoever owns anything should either sell it and bestow the money on the poor, or give it as a gift, or make it common property. Let him be satisfied with the Church through which God supports us. And I have allowed this to be put off till Epiphany, on account of those who have either not yet divided their goods among their brethren, or have indeed apportioned what they had among their brothers, but have not yet disposed of their property because they were not of age. Thereafter, they may do what they will, so long as they live poorly with me, and together we depend on the mercy of God. But if they are unwilling and are vigorously opposed, I have certainly decided, as you know, that I would not ordain any cleric unless he wished to remain with me; but if he wished to withdraw from his purpose, it would be proper for me to remove him from the clerical state because he would be abandoning his promise and his membership in this holy association to which he had agreed. But now in your presence and in the sight of God I alter my position: Those who wish to own property, and for whom God and his Church do not suffice, should remain where they will and where they can; I will not deprive them of the clerical state, but will have nothing to do with hypocrites. It is indeed evil to be like that, it is evil to fall from one's resolve, but it is worse to pretend such a purpose. Note that I say 'he falls,' if he abandons his membership in the common life he has already assumed, a state which is praised in the Acts of the Apos-

---

11. Cf. C. Dereine, *Problème de la vie commune* 291f.

12. The text here cited is from Augustine, *Sermones* 355 and 356, ed. C. Lambot, *Sancti Aurelii Augustini Hipponensis episcopi sermones selecti duodeviginti* (*Stromata patristica et mediaevalia* 1, 1950) 123–143.

tles;[13] he falls from something good that he has done, he falls from his holy profession. Let him heed the Judge, not me, but God." And a bit further on he says, "He who wishes to stay with me, if he is prepared to be supported by God through his Church, to have nothing of his own, but either to donate it to the poor, or to make it common property, let him remain with me; he who does not wish this should be free to do so, but let him consider whether he is able to possess eternal happiness."[14]

(6) In the second sermon of this same work he also says, "Whoever lives like a hypocrite, whoever is discovered owning personal property, I shall not thereafter permit him to make a will, but shall remove him from the clerical register. Let him appeal against me to a thousand councils, let him proceed against me where he will, and be certainly where he can. The Lord help me, for where I am bishop, he cannot be a cleric."[15]

(7) Perhaps I have been somewhat excessive in extending the quotation from this blessed doctor. But I should very much like to have him believed, for in no way does his statement differ from what I have been saying. For from these words of the holy man it is evident that a cleric who possesses money cannot belong to Christ, or be his heir, or have God as his inheritance. But I say this not of all clerics, but particularly of those who are enrolled under the title of canon and live together in common. For since God is to be their portion, they are forbidden to own earthly things. Accordingly the Lord himself spoke to Aaron in Deuteronomy when he said, "You shall have no patrimony in their land, no holdings among them; I am your holding in Israel, I am your patrimony."[16]

(8) But if in forbidding money to clerics the authority of such a doctor alone should perhaps not yet suffice, we ought not to fail to note also what blessed Jerome has to say on this topic. Among other things, this is what he wrote to Bishop Eliodorus, "Be careful, my brother, you are not permitted to have any of the

---

13. Cf. Acts 4.32.

14. Augustine, *Sermo* 355 c. 6 (see *supra* n. 12) 129, l. 22−130, l. 16 and 131, ll. 10−14.

15. Augustine, *Sermo* 356 c. 14 (see *supra* n. 12) 141, l. 30−142, l. 4.

16. Num 18.20.

things that belong to you. 'None of you,' says the Lord, 'can be a disciple of mine without parting with all his possession.'[17] Why are you such a fearful Christian? Look to Peter who abandoned his net,[18] and to the tax collector getting up from his booth,[19] both at once becoming apostles. 'The Son of man has nowhere to lay his head,'[20] and you have an abundance of porticoes and enormous amounts of space under your roofs. Do you look to the world for your inheritance? If so, you cannot be a co-heir of Christ. And somewhat farther on, listen to the Lord saying, 'If you wish to be perfect, go, sell all your possessions, and give to the poor, and come, follow me.'[21] But you promised that you would be perfect. For after giving up service in the world and emasculating yourself for the sake of the kingdom of heaven,[22] what else was that but following the life of perfection? Now, the perfect servant of Christ has nothing besides Christ; or, if he has anything other than Christ, he is not perfect; and if he is not perfect when previously he had promised God that he would be perfect, he lied. 'A lying tongue destroys the soul.'[23]

(9) "And now to conclude: if you are perfect, why do you wish to have your father's property? If you are not perfect, you have deceived God. With the voice of God the Gospel announces, 'You cannot serve two masters,'[24] and will any Christian dare to tell a lie by serving the Lord and money? The Lord often exclaimed, 'If anyone wishes to be a follower of mine, he must leave self behind; he must take up his cross and come with me.'[25] And when weighted down with gold, I think that I am following Christ?"[26]

(10) Also when writing to the priest Nepotianus, after saying many other things, he continued, "A cleric, therefore, who serves the Church of Christ, must first bear out the meaning of that word, and having set forth the definition of the name, he must strive to be what it says. For if the Greek word *kleros* has the mean-

---

17. Luke 14.33.   18. Cf. Matt 4.22.
19. Cf. Matt 9.9.   20. Matt 8.20; Luke 9.58.
21. Matt 19.21.   22. Cf. Matt 19.12.
23. Wis 1.11; for variant, see Jerome, *Epistola* 14.5 (CSEL 54.51f.).
24. Matt 6.24.   25. Matt 16.24.
26. Cf. Jerome, *Epistola* 14.6 (CSEL 54.53f.)

ing *sors* in Latin, clerics are therefore so called because they are the Lord's portion, or because the Lord himself is their portion, that is, the clerics' inheritance. And because he is either the Lord's portion, or has the Lord as his portion, he must so live to demonstrate that he has the Lord as his possession and that he is possessed by the Lord. He who possesses the Lord and says with the prophet, 'The Lord is my portion,'[27] can own nothing except the Lord. But if he owns anything else besides the Lord, the Lord will not be his portion. For example, if he owns gold or silver or property or various furniture, along with these possessions the Lord will not deign to be his portion. But if I am the Lord's portion and a share of his inheritance; if I am not to receive patrimony among the other tribes, but like the Levite and the priest live on tithes,[28] serving at the altar I am sustained by offerings at the altar; having food and clothing, with these I shall be satisfied,[29] and as one who is naked I will follow after the naked cross."[30]

(11) In forbidding clerics the ownership of money, also blessed Prosper made this statement, "Where divided ownership exists there can be no unity of purpose."[31] Thus in condemning and totally abolishing the canons' money, I have introduced not just ordinary teachers, but three irresistible doctors to bolster my position, so that all facts may be duly established on the evidence of two or three witnesses.[32]

(12) But when I bring up these arguments against them, they promptly show me the book containing their Rule, cite the authority of their Rule which grants them the right of private property, and complain that they are the victims of prejudice. Now, I do not fundamentally object to this Rule, nor do I accept it as authoritative without further ado. I approve of it insofar

27. Ps 72.26.
28. Num 18.21–23.
29. Cf. 1 Tim 6.8.
30. *Institutio canonicorum*, c. 94 (MGH Conc. 2.1.370, 12–23); Jerome, *Epistola* 52.5 (CSEL 54.421f.).
31. Ryan, *Sources* no. 216 identified this Ps.-Prosper as Julianus Pomerius, *De vita contemplativa* 2.17 (PL 59.462C). He is frequently cited in the *Institutio canonicorum*, but not in this instance.
32. Matt 18.16.

as it agrees with the holy doctors of the Church, but reject and make little of it when it does not concur with their authentic decrees.[33]

(13) But now let their Rule be brought forward, and in just one page let us decide whether in its entirety it should indiscriminately be accepted, or only in part, and that, cautiously and with suspicion. This, indeed, is found in one of its summaries, "The decision of the holy Fathers teaches that clerics must not strive after wealth, nor are they allowed, contrary to their obligation, to accept things that belong to the churches. Those who serve the Church and have things for which there is no need, or who willingly receive or demand them, are living in a most worldly manner. It is certainly improper for the faithful and fruitful devotion of clerics to despise an eternal reward to gain worldly payment, so that they are to be held accountable for what they receive, and they increase their own sins by the sins of others. Therefore, it is necessary and indeed useful for clerics to avoid danger to themselves in accepting ecclesiastical property. Hence, they must not accept or demand more than is needed of things that are their own or belong to the Church, that is, they may accept food and drink and clothing, and with these they should be satisfied, lest in receiving more, they incur the grave sin of oppressing the poor, and that they not take the substance from which the poor man is to live."[34] In these words, therefore, where the Rule declares that clerics must be content with food, drink, and clothing, it agrees with what I have been saying, and with the authority of the whole Church.

(14) But what follows thereafter, seems to be absolutely absurd, improper, and frivolous, "Yet those," it says, "who are neither personally well off nor have their wherewithal from the Church, and are of great use to the Church, may receive food and clothing and part of the alms from the canonical congregation." This is added because in Prosper's work it says of such as these, "Clerics who are poor from choice or from birth, shall receive the necessaries of life by living in the community."[35] So first

---

33. See Ryan, *Sources* no. 217.
34. *Instit. can.*, c. 120 (MGH Conc. 2.1.399f.); cf. Ryan, *Sources* no. 218.
35. Cf. Ryan, *Sources* no. 219; *Instit. can.*, c. 120 (MGH Conc. 2.1.400, 4–8).

it grants food and clothing, and then allows them to participate in the alms; the former, to be sure, to supply the necessaries of life, the latter to stuff their purses. The former is given to support bodily life, the latter to provide food for eternal death.

(15) We must look a bit more closely at these ominous and insidious words, at this disgraceful and confused kind of talk. For when first of all it is said that along with food and vesture clerics may also receive part of the alms, it seems to give the reason for all of this, since in the work of Prosper such matters are discussed when he says, "Clerics who are poor by choice or from birth, shall receive the necessaries of life by living in the community."

(16) Tell us, you who try to improve on Ciceronian eloquence, tell us you new Demosthenes, because Prosper states that clerics should receive the necessaries of life, does he also prescribe that besides food and clothing each is to receive part of the alms? According to your interpretation, is receiving the necessaries of life the same as sharing the alms after being supplied with food and clothing? How glad the clerics are to do this, those who take you at your word and are overjoyed to embrace such heavy and unbearable pronouncements in your law! And indeed, what you decree is most heavy and unbearable, since from the largest to the smallest, that is, even if there is a little boy living with you who is two or three years old, you ply with five measures of wine and four of bread, so that he is stuffed not just to the point of vomiting, but with enough to disembowel him. And to crown your practice of the virtue of discretion, you prescribe that, even if one eats only once a day, this amount of bread and wine is not to be lessened,[36] so that according to your practice of sobriety, the restrictions on eating are so relaxed, that the clerics are constrained not only to belch, but their bellies and bowels are compelled to break wind. Certainly, aside from several opinions of the holy Fathers that are found in this little book, just as for the most part the style of writing is quite abominable, so also in most sentences the erroneous meaning is in need of correction.[37] For

---

36. *Instit. can.*, c. 121 (MGH Conc. 2.1.400); *ibid.*, c. 122: *De mensura cibi et potus*; cf. Ryan, *Sources* no. 220. Obviously, for effect, Damian uses the highest quantity allowed by the Rule.

37. Cf. Ryan, *Sources* no. 221. It seems questionable that by "this little book" Damian meant only the *Institutio canonicorum*.

the author was unable to find what he should write about, and was incapable of writing even if he discovered certain absurdities. Those who by their irritating way of life, oppose the discipline of the Church, must love these flowers of eloquence.

(17) Now, since the holy Fathers do not disagree in condemning clerical income, but with one mind and one voice concur in strictly forbidding and absolutely denying money to clerics, let us go to the source from which they drew their opinions, and return to the very origins of this rushing stream. And although it would be improper to dispute the opinion of such men, we should not fear to approach their teachers, that is, those of our masters, so that we too may deserve to be instructed by them from whom also our teachers learned. By so doing, as the source from which the pure water sprang is made available, the audacity of abusive and defiling indiscretion may be refuted. It is therefore an obvious fact that the Rule of the canons originated from the norms of apostolic life, and if any spiritual community is to maintain discipline and good order, it must somehow imitate the early days of the infant Church.[38]

(18) So, let us hear of the customs and manner of living the Church observed under the apostles, as it was accepting the faith. "The whole body of believers," says Luke, "was united in heart and soul. Not one of them claimed any of his possessions as his own, but everything was held in common."[39] Notice that where differences over property did not exist, unity of purpose was maintained, that is, where income was not distributed, good will among many temperaments was fused into common charity. For where property is not held in common, there is also no united purpose; and where individual ownership of goods exists, individuals are at odds. But if everything is held collectively, various personalities come together in one accord, because there is nothing over which they are forced to quarrel. Therefore, if a cleric attempts to have his own income, he is not following in the footsteps of the apostles, because he will not be of one mind and one heart with his brothers. Since Judas was able to have money and to control the purse,[40] he could not main-

---

38. See Fonseca, *Le canoniche* 347.
39. Acts 4.32.   40. Cf. John 12.6.

tain harmony and good relations with the apostles. Hence, concerning their norms in these matters, we read in their Acts that "all who had property in land or houses sold it, brought the proceeds of the sale, and laid the money at the feet of the apostles."[41] And then the Acts continued, "It was then distributed to any who stood in need."[42]

(19) Now tell us, O cleric, as you claim permission to hoard money for yourself and usurp the right of owning property, reply, I beg you, who owns the goods from which you claim you are entitled to have your own income? Do they belong to you, or to the Church? But if you are permitted to keep your own money, how have you laid it at the feet of the apostles? If what you are hoarding belongs to the Church, why did you hold in contempt that which belonged to you? Moreover, if you retained some of your own property, listen to the terrible rebuke the apostle hurls at you, "How was it," he asked, "that Satan so possessed your mind that you lied to the Holy Spirit, and kept back part of the price of the land? While it remained, did it not remain yours? When it was turned into money, was it not still at your own disposal? What made you think of doing this thing? You have lied not to men but to God."[43] But if you are trying not to retain your own property but to distribute what belongs to the Church, the goods, that is, that you and your brothers hold in common, then tell him, Master Jesus, tell my brother to give me a part of this inheritance.

(20) You should further note that the evangelist prefaced his remarks with the words, "A person in the crowd said to him."[44] So you should ask Jesus, not as a levite or as a cleric, but as a layman, just one of the crowd, to tell your brother to divide the family property with you. And then he will at once answer you, "My good man, who set me over you to judge or arbitrate?"[45] To which he will add, "Beware! Be on your guard against greed of every kind, for even when a man has more than enough, his wealth does not give him life."[46] So, do you wish to divide the property? If so, you will not have Jesus as a judge or arbiter, but rather as the

---

41. Acts 4.34–35.   42. Acts 4.35.
43. Acts 5.3–4.   44. Luke 12.13.
45. Luke 12.14.   46. Luke 12.15.

avenger of schismatic disruption. "He who is not with me," he says, "is against me, and he who does not gather with me, scatters."[47] Moreover, if you are permitted to have money, there is none better than your own. But if you own what formerly was yours, what did you bequeath to the community when you entered the religious life? What is more, by returning to your own vomit,[48] and deserting the plow as you keep looking back, you will no longer be fit for the kingdom of God.[49] But if you are allowed to hoard the goods of the Church, you are seen as one amassing wealth, not as turning your back on it, so that your purpose is the pursuit of money rather than the religious life, and that you are not interested in reaching the heights of sanctity, but rather in accumulating heaps of gold. Or will Christ grant to clerics what he did not allow the apostles? For when he sent them on mission, as Mark says, he instructed them to take nothing for the journey beyond a stick: no pack, no bread, no money in their belts;[50] but as a purse for you and your money I would say that a belt would not suffice; you would need a chest. And since the Apostle says that greed is nothing less than idolatry,[51] how can you honor Christ when you venerate money as your idol? "What does justice have to do with wickedness? Can light consort with darkness? Can Christ agree with Belial, or a believer join hands with an unbeliever? Can there be a compact between the temple of God and the idols [of the heathen]?"[52]

(21) Obviously, since contrary to the Rule of your order you secretly amass money and put your trust in the uncertainty of wealth, while you should be pinning your hopes on God alone— for where your treasure is, there without doubt your heart is also[53]—you should no longer rightly be called a worshiper of Christ but a worshiper of money. And as the Lord says of the Levites, "I am their inheritance,"[54] you should respond as you chant, "The Lord is all that I have."[55] Certainly, if you observe your Rule, if you despise and abominate money, you shall be

---

47. Luke 11.23.
49. Cf. Luke 9.62.
51. Cf. Col 3.5.
53. Cf. Matt 6.21.
55. Ps 118.57.

48. Cf. Prov 26.11; 2 Pet 2.22.
50. Cf. Mark 6.8.
52. 2 Cor 6.14–16.
54. Ezek 44.28.

God's inheritance and God will be yours. But this whole sacred matter is made adulterous, when an unfortunate cleric becomes a slave of money, when he gives his entire attention to serving it as if it were God. He, indeed, is possessed by the money that is his, and by overriding avarice is compelled to rivet his heart on it and care for it with constant devotion. Shall I, therefore expel Christ from the treasury of my heart, and in his place store my hoard of money? Certainly, Christ is such a noble currency that he will utterly despise any association with wealth, and will not permit himself to be involved with filthy lucre. And so, if Christ is to fill the purse of your heart, remove from it every last coin so that Christ may imprint his sign upon your soul,[56] and that the paltry double drachma, bearing the head of Caesar, may disappear.

(22) Finally, private ownership causes clerics to disdain the rule of their bishop, desert the true freedom of self-discipline or obedience, and shamefully allow themselves to surrender disgracefully to the things of this world. To this point the Lord said to Moses, "Bring forward the tribe of Levi and appoint them to serve Aaron the priest and to minister to him. They shall be in attendance on him and watch carefully over whatever pertains to the worship of the whole community before the Tent of the Presence. They shall be in charge of all the equipment in the Tent of the Presence, attending to its service. You shall assign the Levites to Aaron and his sons as especially dedicated to him out of all the Israelites."[57] Now, who would doubt that Aaron and his sons functioned as bishops, and who is not aware that the tribe of Levi prefigured the ranks of clerics? So, the Levites are especially dedicated to Aaron and his sons, chosen from all the Israelites, when the clerical order is taken from the entire Christian people to administer divine worship in the Church, and are ordained to assist and serve their bishops. But whoever is a slave of money, finds only disgust in the Church's liturgy.

(23) Nor should we fail to say a word about the statement that follows immediately, "I take the Levites for myself," says the Lord,

56. Cf. Matt 22.21.
57. Num 3.6–10.

"out of all the Israelites as a substitute for the eldest male child of every woman in Israel; the Levites shall be mine."[58] This was said to show clearly that the clerical order belongs to almighty God, just as God himself is the special inheritance of the clerics. What folly it is, what madness for him to look for comfort to the things of this world and to despise God who is given to him as his portion. If God does not suffice for his inheritance, he does not know at all what will satisfy him, because insane greed has made him blind.

(24) In violating his calling out of love for money, undoubtedly such a man is unworthy of preferment in the Church. Hence also Solomon says, "Like one who puts a stone on the cairn of Mercury is he who bestows honor on a fool."[59] Now, since among the pagans Mercury was known as the god of the purse or of money,[60] the cairn of Mercury is a heap or hoard of coins. And because the mintage mark is pressed on the coin, what else is understood by a heap of coins but an assembly of clerics living by their Rule and bearing the mark of true sanctity? And what do we mean by stone, if not the obdurate, stolid and insensible mind of him who, while not believing with certain faith that God exists, places all that he hopes for in some earthly possessions? Of him the prophet says, "The impious fool said in his heart, 'There is no God.' "[61] But such a fool is honored when someone dedicated not to God but to money is promoted to high ecclesiastical office. As a pile of coins is caused to fall apart if a stone is placed on top of it, so too, by the advancement of an unworthy or insensitive pastor, the closed rank of those who live by the Rule, and of clerics obedient to the law of charity is destroyed. It is oppressed by the shadow of an evil pastor, and like a stack of heavenly coins, it is broken down by the weight of an infernal stone.

(25) A senseless fool must therefore be denied a place of dignity in the Church, lest the assembly of holy clerics, like spiritual

---

58. Num 3.12.   59. Prov 26.8.

60. The god of good luck and commerce, Mercury is frequently represented carrying a purse, his iconographic attribute; cf. *Oxford Latin Dictionary*, ed. P. G. W. Glare (Oxford, 1982) 1102.

61. Ps 13.1.

coins, be ruined. Just before the statement of Solomon I cited above, he said of the fool, "He who sends a fool to bear his message is lame of foot and imbibes wickedness."[62] What else might be construed from these words but that we must not entrust the office of preaching to one who is worldly wise, and is therefore a fool? For of holy preachers it is said, "How welcome are the feet of the messengers of peace and of good news!"[63] Therefore, when any administrator of the church advances worthy and suitable men to orders, he walks as it were with feet unimpaired. With them he goes about spreading the word, and what he is unable to achieve by himself, he is assured of efficiently carrying out through them. But if he should presume to ordain worldly and wicked men, he walks on the feet of a cripple. He is also said to imbibe wickedness, because by sending a fool to bring the message of God's word, and against the advice of the Apostle, is over-hasty in laying on hands in ordination,[64] he participates in the sin of others.

(26) However, if he is prudent in his speech, but does not bring his actions into accord with what he says, he can rightly be called a cripple on the road of the spirit. And so quite aptly Solomon continued, "Just as it is useless for a cripple to have handsome legs, so a proverb is unseemly in the mouth of a stupid man."[65] Indeed, one walks on handsome legs if his speech is clear and brilliant. But if his studied words are not accompanied by good works, he seems to be moving the well-shaped legs of his words without making progress. He appears to have legs that are pleasing to the eye but useless for walking, if while hindered by gouty vices, he stumbles like a poor cripple as he urges others to walk along with ease. A parable on the lips of these stupid men is unseemly, because while they sound like spiritual men but live by the flesh, their life does not agree with what they are saying. Acceptable preaching does not acquit those whose words are proper, but whose lives do not conform; rather their guilty conscience violently reproaches them. Hence fittingly the point is made again, "Like a thorn that pierces a drunkard's hand is a

62. Prov 26.6.
64. Cf. 1 Tim 5.22.

63. Rom 10.15; cf. Isa 52.7.
65. Prov 26.7.

proverb in a stupid man's mouth."[66] There is surely a thorn in the hand of a drunkard when stinging reproach is born in the soul of him who is intoxicated with the love of the present life. In the mouth of a stupid man a proverb is like a thorn, because as they say one thing and do another, their mind seems to harbor a contradiction, and is obviously pierced by a sharp thorn. Certainly there is a thorn piercing the conscience of one whose life is evil but whose words are sound, since what he says openly causes him to suffer inner wounds from the sting of shame and fear.

(27) And now getting back to addressing those with whom we began, a cleric who is the prisoner of love for money, is totally unfit to be a minister of the Gospel. In addition to what I said above, there is also the example given us by the apostles. For after Scripture first stated, "The whole body of believers was united in heart and soul," and at once continued, "not one of them claimed any of his possessions as his own, but everything was held in common," it immediately said, "The apostles bore witness with great power to the resurrection of our Lord Jesus Christ, and great was the grace in all of them;" and then added, "for they had never a needy person among them."[67]

(28) But what does the author of this sacred history mean to say when, in speaking of the attitude of the apostles and of the common life, he suddenly interrupted his discourse, and altering his style, as it were, proceeded to tell how constant they were in their preaching, "And the apostles bore witness with great power to the resurrection"?[68] Why did he insert something else into the narrative which, once begun, he should have continued and brought to conclusion, except that he obviously wished to show that only those are fit to undertake the office of preaching who gain no profit from earthly goods, and while personally having nothing, own everything in common? "For while being penniless, we own the whole world."[69] They, indeed, who are not impeded by earthly things are ready to defend the Lord's cause on the field of battle. Because they have divested themselves of all things, and are equipped only with the arms of virtue and fight

66. Prov 26.9.   67. Acts 4.32–34.
68. Acts 4.33.   69. 2 Cor 6.10.

with the sword of the spirit against the forces of vice, they are fitting warriors to sever the necks of the opposing foe. Those, however, are unprepared for battle and easily surrender, who are not content with common property but attempt to burden themselves with personal wealth. Hence, in Deuteronomy it is said of those who go into battle, "Any man who has planted a vineyard and has not made it common property from which all can be supported, shall go back home, or he may die in battle and another man use it."[70]

(29) But now, venerable father, I have said enough as I extended my inelegant remarks far beyond measure. Yet, that my words may be worthwhile in suppressing the rebellion of these disobedient clerics, these worshipers of money, I would like to see your holy apostolic office vigorously intervene.

70. Deut 20.6.

LETTER 99

Peter Damian to Archbishop Anno of Cologne. This letter was occasioned by the schism of Antipope Honorius II (Cadalus of Parma). Damian requests the archbishop of Cologne to curb the madness of Cadalus and work vigorously for the freedom of the Apostolic See. Using remarkably relevant Old Testament symbolism, he calls on Anno, the forceful tutor of young Herny IV and guarantor of his throne, to demonstrate similar energy in restoring order to the *Sacerdotium*. His plea that Anno use his good offices to convoke a general council won for Damian the severest rebuke from Hildebrand, his "holy Satan."

(June 1063)[1]

O SIR ANNO,[2] the most reverend archbishop, the monk Peter the sinner sends the homage of his proper service. (2) Since I am presently on the road,[3] I am unable with my own hands to give proper attention to the niceties of style, and because of the constant motion of the horses, to be of service to you as is becoming. But although clear speech is preferable to mumbling, when necessity demands, it is at times better to mumble than to remain absolutely dumb. Venerable father, when I recall your diligence and effort, the noble faith and prudence of the priest Jehoiada keeps running through my mind.[4] As you well know, sacred history relates now when Athaliah, the

1. Dating follows Lucchesi, *Vita* no. 176.
2. For a thorough treatment of Anno, see Jenal, *Anno II* (cf. Bibliography).
3. This letter is a well-remembered piece of Damian's writing; cf. Meyer von Knonau, *Heinrich IV* 1, 318ff. and 361f.; Maria Ludovica Arduini, "Kirchengeschichtliche Probleme im 11.Jh. Das Verhältnis Kölns zu Rom zur Zeit Annos II.," *Rev. bénéd.* 92 (1982) 141–148. This letter was written while Damian was on his mission to Cluny (early summer to 27 October 1063). See Lucchesi, *Vita* no. 173. It is reported in the *Iter Gallicum* (MGH SS 30/2, 1034–1046), written possibly in Besançon.
4. Cf. 2 Kgs 11.1–18. According to Jenal, *Anno II* 192ff., the mention of Jehoiada shows that the abduction of the young king (April 1062) had already taken place.

wife of Jehoram, learned that her son Ahaziah, the king of Israel, was dead, she cruelly began a purge of the entire royal stock, and this savage Bellona[5] attempted to do away with all the posterity of David's house.[6] But the noble priest Jehoiada, by a pious trick that deserves great praise, secretly carried away Joash, the son of Ahaziah, and kept him hidden in the confines of the Temple for six years,[7] afterwards handing over to him his royal rights. He strengthened him to reign over the people of Israel according to the custom of his forebears.

(3) And then, as if these deeds were not enough for this outstanding priest, after establishing the king on the throne, he turned his attention to the welfare of the priesthood or of the temple, and together with the king engaged in ordering and directing the way of life of his fellow bishops. He ordained that the buildings of the temple be brought into good repair and published various orders that pertained to the bishops. He was aware that each dignity is in need of the services of the other; that while the priesthood is protected by the defenses of the realm, the latter is supported by the sanctity of the priestly office.

(4) But why do I pursue these events in sacred Scripture except that in you I see the re-enactment of these events in our time? Venerable father, you have saved the boy who was left to your care, you have brought order to the kingdom, you have guaranteed for your ward the imperial rights of his father.[8] Your excellence, moreover, has reached out his hand to the priesthood in that you labored to sever the scaly neck of the "beast of Parma"[9] with the sword of evangelical rigor and to reinstate the bishop of the Apostolic See on the throne of his dignity. But once the work has begun, unless you give it the finishing touch and use the opportunities that still remain, the holy edifice to which you have set your hand is in danger of collapsing. For the

5. The goddess of war, sister of Mars.

6. Cf. 2 Chr 22.10–12, 23.1–19.

7. In 1063 when this letter was written, it was the seventh year since Anno had taken custody of the boy, King Henry IV.

8. How aware Damian might have been of the role of Adalbert of Bremen in the imperial government at this time, is not clear. See the *Regesta Imperii* 3.2.3.1 (1984) nos. 287 and 290.

9. On Cadalus of Parma in this time frame, see Peter Damian, *Letter* 100, n. 4.

infamous Cadalus, the disturber of Holy Church, the subverter of apostolic discipline, the enemy of man's salvation;[10] he, I say, who is the root of sin,[11] the herald of the devil, the apostle of Antichrist, the arrow drawn from the quiver of Satan, the rod of Assyria,[12] son of Belial,[13] the son of perdition[14] "who claims to be so much greater than all that men call 'god,' so much greater than anything that is worshipped,"[15] still breathes fire like some hideous dragon, with the filth of his poisoned money causes a stench in the nostrils of men, and by the wind of his perfidy like a new chief of heretics disturbs the faltering faith of many.

(5) As the make-believe fables of old[16] have Jupiter come down into Danae's womb in the form of a shower of gold, so he too with gold sought from the sacrilegious debasement of his church attempts an adulterous rape of the Apostolic See, and like some unfaithful wanton burns with fiery passion to violate the Roman Church.

(6) Therefore, venerable father, to make certain that your holy efforts bear fruit, and that the good name of the Roman Church be not degraded in the opinion of the people by this remnant of a burned out firebrand,[17] or rather by this foul member of the devil, and that now, which God forbid, the Christian people be permanently in error, it is necessary that your excellence make every effort that a general council[18] be held as soon as possible to remove the thorns of this pernicious error in which the sorry world now finds itself enmeshed. I would gladly travel, moreover, if the occasion presented itself, to speak with your holiness, so that a live exchange of words, which my absence makes impossible, might enhance the advice I have sent to

10. Cf. Phil 3.18.

11. Cf. 1 Macc 1.11.

12. Cf. Isa 10.5.

13. Cf. 1 Sam 2.12, 25.17.

14. John 17.12.

15. 2 Thess 2.3–4.

16. Cf. Horace, *Carm.* 3.16.1; Ovid, *Met.* 4.611 and 4.698; Isidore, *Etymologies* 8.11.35–36. For more detail, see A. Hermann, "Danae," *Reallexikon für Antike und Christentum* 3 (1957) 567–571.

17. Cf. Isa 7.4.

18. By sending his nephew Burchard of Halberstadt (*Regesta Imperii* 3.2.3.1 [1984] no. 335), Hildebrand who had hopes of defeating the antipope with the aid of the Normans, had no intentions of becoming indebted to the German court. Consequently, for his efforts Damian seems to have returned to Fonte Avellana in disfavor. See his *Letter* 107, *infra*.

you. But since perhaps I did not deserve such favor, I ask, I beseech, and in all humility I suggest that in your good judgment you strive to wipe out this pestiferous Cadalus who will not stop his raging. By your effort may the Christian religion earn the right to peaceful existence, so that while the Empire and the Church enjoy through your good offices the peace we all desire, he who is the Author of both authorities may grant you the reward of eternal peace which you deserve.

(7) But since my horse is ready, and my companions have all set out, I now turn away from my letter and set my feet to the stirrup.

LETTER 100

Peter Damian to the monks of Cluny. This letter was the first he sent to Cluny after his return to Fonte Avellana from a three-month mission as papal legate. He had won a decision in favor of the abbey in its jurisdictional dispute with Drogo, the bishop of Mâcon. Damian speaks of a dangerous trip through the Alps, made still more hazardous by armed forces supporting the antipope Honorius II (Cadalus of Parma). He praises the life and work of the Cluniacs, confirming his admiration with numerous references to Scripture. He concludes the letter by calling down God's blessing upon them with a unique liturgical formula and imparting his own episcopal blessing.

(November 1063)[1]

O THE TRULY HOLY BRETHREN of the monastery of Cluny, worthy of angelic honor, the monk Peter the sinner sends his constant servitude in the Lord.

(2) I would like you to know, my dearest friends, that, as I was returning home from my visit with you,[2] I felt great sadness and frustration. Many dark thoughts and impatience caused me to languish and lose heart. Indeed, as I recalled having been enticed like a boy with an egg, and thus bound by caressing words as with purple or delicately blue folds of the softest silk, in having been promised one thing with words but experiencing something altogether different in reality, I seethed in my heart, and must admit that those who had then strayed from the truth caused me more than ordinary displeasure. For, to mention only one instance which should suffice to illustrate the others, I was assured that by 1 August I would have returned home. But, after

1. The dating follows Lucchesi, *Vita* no. 180.
2. There is an account of Damian's journey to Cluny, written by one of his travel companions: *De Gallica Petri Damiani profectione et eius ultramontano itinere*, MGH SS 30.2 (1926) 1034–1046 (=*Iter Gallicum*). See in general Roth, *Petrus Damiani* 7.2, 49ff. (see bibliography), with a very detailed account of this event; Dressler, *Petrus Damiani* 75ff.; Lucchesi, *Vita* 2.42ff.

almost three months had been wasted, I travelled with as much speed as I could muster—and still barely reached the heights of Fonte Avellana from where I had set out, by 27 October.[3]

(3) And so, as I forded many streams swollen by torrential rain, climbed through rocky overhangs in the snow-filled Alps, and, what was worse, always had to be on guard against the massed ambushes inspired by the fury of Cadalus,[4] my resolve suffered through a heavy storm, so to speak, of internal conflict. And, though this resolve remained strong and never flinched in determining not to repay evil for evil, no matter how I tried, I could not entirely forget the harm that I had suffered.

(4) But, after I arrived at my cell, and what is more, after I had entered into myself, having been shut outside before, my over-heated heart at once cooled off; the grumbling of contentious strife was put to rest; excitement, noise, and anger were suddenly left aside; and all the bitterness I had experienced was by God's help turned sweet. For, like an obstinate plaintiff brought up to the judge's tribunal, I did not dare continue the useless complaint before the majesty of my sober little cell.

(5) I was like a listless person entering a marvelously scented room. Before I had taken any medicine, my illness left me and I recovered. Indeed, as soon as I walked through the door of my cell, and had not yet opened a book—what a joy it was to be there—I discovered that I was well and unharmed, with all the wounds of my spirit healed. And so, at the sight of the sacred books, which were still unopened before me, even before I had swallowed the medicine, I imbibed health while still only smelling the aroma of its fragrant spices.

(6) Wherefore, not only do I forgive the injury inflicted by your holy abbot,[5] who caused me so much trouble, but, be-

3. On the return to Fonte Avellana on 27 October 1063, instead of on 1 August, cf. *Iter Gallicum* c. 20, 1046; Dressler, *Petrus Damiani* 82.
4. Earlier Damian had opposed Cadalus in two letters (88 and 89), and in *Letter* 99 to Anno of Cologne, asked that he use his best efforts to call a General Council. Damian thus had reason to be concerned about the supporters of the antipope. Cadalus himself was safe in Rome from September/October 1063 to May 1064; see Borino, *Censio* 395ff. and 408.
5. The abbot Hugh (1049–1109); cf. Noreen Hunt, *Cluny under Saint Hugh 1049–1109* (1967). Damian sent several letters to Hugh, *Letters* 103, 113, and 125.

cause of your regard for me, I even restore to him the prerogatives of our earlier friendship. For, as we beg that our sins be forgiven us by God, not absolutely, but as we forgive others,[6] while asking for God's grace together with the remission of our sins, it is proper that we should totally restore to our enemies the full status of our previous friendship after pardoning their offense.

(7) Just as it is undoubtedly a sin not to be mindful of God's commandments, so it is no small virtue not to be mindful of an injury that was done us. I should, moreover, also be grateful to one who burdened me with so much distress, since, by arrangement of the one who brings forth good results from the evil we must endure, I happened to get better acquainted with all of you through his offense.

(8) And at this I am especially happy, that my effort brought you relief and quiet security, that my inconvenience won pleasant days after the anxious times you had endured.[7] I have thus participated in your good works, and, even if I have not followed in your footsteps of holy living, I still assisted you that you might lead holy lives.

(9) It was thus that Obadiah, the steward of Ahab's household, hid the prophets fleeing from the sword of Jezebel, putting them in caves, fifty by fifty,[8] and for his part gloriously earned the gift of a prophetic spirit afterwards.[9] And now he supplies the Church with a banquet of spiritual food by earlier having brought bread and water to those who were starving. Thus too, after serving his master with faithful dedication, Elisha inherited a double share of his power to work wonders.[10] So also Rahab, because she concealed the spies of Israel from the face of an enraged tyrant, herself escaped from the sword at the fall of Jericho. And this Gentile prostitute was taken into the company of

6. Cf. Matt 6.15; Luke 11.4.

7. The struggle between Hugh of Cluny and bishop Drogo of Mâcon ended favorably for Cluny; see the acts of the synod of Chalon-sur-Saône of 1063 (Mansi 19.1025); Hefele-Leclercq, *Histoire* 4.1231ff.

8. Cf. 1 Kgs 18.12–13.

9. Damian here seems to identify the Obadiah of 1 Kings with Obadiah, the minor prophet.

10. Cf. 2 Kgs 2.9–15.

the Israelites because she had provided support for the safe escape of their emissaries.[11]

(10) I also hope that I participated in the merits of your holy life, since I removed the burden of the diocese of Mâcon,[12] which the bishop of that see tried to impose on you, and, as I am convinced, protected myself, because of you, from the snares of the devil, in that I snatched from the hands of those clerics the club of Hercules[13] with which they threatened you. And I struck him down like Benob, who was about to kill David, and I resisted him so that the lamp of Israel might not be extinguished.[14]

(11) Thinking back, moreover, on your strict and totally occupied order of the day, I consider it to be not the result of human invention, but something devised by the Holy Spirit. For such was the extent of your continuous effort to observe the Rule, especially your constant participation at Mass and in choir, that, even in the great heat of June and July, when the days are longest,[15] there was hardly half an hour throughout the day in which the brethren were unoccupied and permitted to engage in conversation.[16]

(12) The purpose of this practice of constant work was provided, I think, by the Rule's great solicitude and foresight, that it might curb the frailty of the lax and weaker brothers, and might almost totally remove the occasion for sin. Even if they wanted to, the brethren could scarcely sin at all, except in thought. And thus all of this was done with the shortcomings of the frailer brothers in mind, so that, in performing this constant round of duties, the total amount of time, both day and night, was occupied.

(13) Now even almighty God himself saw fit to use this device for human salvation when he issued so many commands to the people wandering in the desert:[17] namely, that the elaborate and intricate tabernacle should be built, that various sacrifices should

---

11. Cf. Josh 2.1–21.

12. On the diocese of Mâcon, see H. Leclercq, "Mâcon," DACL 10.1 (1931) 747–753.

13. Cf. Ovid, *Met.* 9.114 and 9.236; Seutonius, *De vita Caesarum* 6.53.

14. Cf. 2 Sam 21.16.   15. Cf. Isidore, *Etymologies* 3.71.20.

16. Cf. *Iter Gallicum* c. 13, 1042; see also Reindel, *Briefe* 3.105, n. 10.

17. Cf. Exod 34–36.

be offered to him with much ceremony and ritual, and that the regimen of the camp, both for residents and aliens, should be carried out with meticulous and symbolic variety. This was done so that, by their constant occupation with these matters, this carnal people would not relapse into idolatry.

(14) Indeed, since the Israelites did not rely on weaving, did not practice the art of working with leather, did not depend on agriculture, and had no need to provide for future necessity through their own efforts, they had to be kept busy with many tasks laid down for them at God's command, so that, as they performed these chores with great effort, they would never have leisure to engage in sacrilegious practices.

(15) No wonder that even the Pharaoh himself tried to employ this same plan when he said, "You have free time, and that is why you talk about going to offer sacrifice to the Lord."[18] And Moses himself stated that this people did not have an earthly thing to do besides carrying out the commands of the law. He said to them, "The Lord fed you on manna, which neither you nor your fathers before you had known, to teach you that human beings do not live on bread alone but by every word that comes from the mouth of the Lord."[19] And then he continued, "The clothes by which you were covered did not wear out, nor did your feet swell all these forty years, so that you might take this lesson to heart: that the Lord your God was disciplining you as a father disciplines his son to keep the commandments of the Lord your God, to walk in his ways, and to fear him."[20]

(16) In this citation we should pay special attention to the words, "He fed you on manna to teach you that human beings do not live on bread alone but by every word that comes from the mouth of the Lord." Here it is perfectly clear that this manna with which they were physically fed meant the nourishment of the Word of God, by which we are now restored in our soul. And one has to take note of what we read about this manna in the book of Exodus, "When the Israelites had seen this, they said to

18. Exod 5.17.
19. Deut 8.3; for these variants from the Vulgate, see *Biblia sacra* 3.399; cf. also Matt 4.4; Luke 4.4.
20. Deut 8.4–6.

one another, 'Manhu?' which means, 'What is this?' "[21] These therefore truly eat manna, that is 'What is this?' who when they read or hear, readily inquire about the mystery of the Word of God. They certainly go right under the cover of the literal chaff and take out the sweet kernels of the spiritual understanding. Certainly this "What is this?" truly feeds the one who readily remains in a constant inquiry into sacred Scripture. For as if it were some question we also eat the "What is this?" with the eagerly longing mouth of our heart when we carefully pursue and penetrate the mysteries of the Scriptures, when we minutely ruminate upon the sumptous foods of the heavenly communication.

(17) And how well does the monastic lifestyle correspond with the people of Israel, because from wherever these were then fed in the desert, we are now feasting in the cloister. For what is the desert except that it signifies what is separated from a human dwelling place? And what is the cloister except being cut off from all activity of worldly business? And as the light of fire shone among the shadows of the night for those wandering about in the desert areas, so also are the ones who abide in the spiritual cloister often illuminated by the rays of the heavenly light, which drive away the shadows of bodily passions and bedew them with the splendor of most profound contemplation.

(18) We must, therefore, flee the world which begets darkness and seek seclusion, where the true light breaks through as once it did in the wilderness. We must totally reject all friendship with the world, for, since it produces dark shadows in those who always foster such relationships, it extinguishes the light in those who agree with it and obey its commands. And, what is more, we must constantly wage implacable war against the world, because it destroys the sight of its friends.

(19) This is what we learn from the account in sacred history furnished us in the book of Kings, for, when Nahash the Ammonite went up to take Jabesh-Gilead with his forces, the men of Jabesh said to Nahash with one voice, " 'Come to terms with us and we shall be your subjects.' Nahash answered them, 'On one condition only shall I come to terms with you: that I gouge out

---

21. Exod 16.15. See also Jerome, *Nom. hebr.* (CC 72.142, 157, and 160).

your right eyes and bring disgrace on all Israel.' The elders of Jabesh then said, 'Give us seven days to send messengers throughout Israel and then, if no one relieves us, we shall surrender to you.' "[22] When Saul heard this, he assembled a great army, went into battle, massacred numerous Ammonites, and won a glorious victory.

(20) What should we understand by the proud king, Nahash the Ammonite, if not the world in rebellion against its Creator, or its prince, the devil? For of him it is said that "he is king over all the children of pride."[23] And, since "Nahash" in translation means "the serpent,"[24] he properly signifies that poisonous and slimy snake. And how should we interpret Jabesh, an Israelite city, except to say that it prefigures the Christian soul trying to see God by the practice of contemplation? And, since "Jabesh" means "dried out" or "dryness,"[25] we are correct in saying that Jabesh represents the soul that rejects the richness of heavenly grace and dries up in the heat of carnal desire.

(21) When the soul abandons the eagerly-awaited dew of God's gift, it becomes dry, while, in former times, by receiving the dew, it grew strong because of its health-giving moisture, as the Lord says through Isaiah, "I will pour down rain on a thirsty land, showers on the dry ground."[26] But Nahash would come to terms with Jabesh only on condition that he could gouge out their right eyes, because anyone who succumbs to the evil suggestions of the ancient enemy, or becomes tangled up in the restless affairs of this world, by disgracefully allying himself with this haughty king, as it were, loses his right eye, that is, the light of contemplation.[27]

(22) And thus disgrace comes upon Israel, because, as one descends from the heights of contemplation to pursue earthly or unclean affairs, he will necessarily be tormented in the Church by detraction and shameful abuse. Then they begged him for a

---

22. 1 Sam 11.1–3. 23. Job 41.25.
24. Jerome, *Nom. hebr.* 39.16 (CC 72.108).
25. Jerome, *Nom. hebr.* 33.2 (CC 72.100).
26. Isa 44.3.
27. Cf. J. Leclercq, "Contemplation et vie contemplative du VIe au XIIe siècle," *Dictionnaire de spiritualité* 2 (1953) 1929–1948, esp. 1942f.

truce of seven days. And, since we read that on the seventh day
God rested after his work of creation,[28] what should be understood by the number seven if not a period of respite? The disobedient Saul ignored this number when Samuel commanded
him to wait for him for this amount of time, "Wait seven days
until I join you; then I will tell you what to do."[29] But, since this
reprobate man refused to accept this spiritual respite, an evil
spirit seized and tormented him.

(23) And so, the city of Jabesh was free of this wicked king for
seven days, since any soul that the world, at the devil's suggestion, tries to entice to join it, and tries to blind with the darkness
of secular affairs, will keep the eye of contemplation unimpaired
only if it resists with all its powers and stands firm in its resolve
to remain at rest. Our Redeemer rescues such a soul from the
temptation that it endures when he sees it quietly at rest in the
severity of the solitary life. Therefore was it there written: "The
next day," it says, "Saul drew up his men in three columns; they
forced their way right into the enemy camp during the morning
watch and massacred the Ammonites until the day grew hot."[30]
Who is meant by Saul, who was called the Lord's anointed,[31] if
not he who is the true king of Israel, the Mediator between God
and men?[32] What should we understand by his drawing up of the
troops in three columns but that there are three principal virtues
within the soul, namely, faith, hope, and charity?[33] When the
combatants are drawn up in three columns, we win victory in the
struggle, because, with Christ as our leader, these three virtues
will conquer every temptation of the devil.

(24) Nor do we lack mystery in the number of fighting men
which Scripture mentions. "There were three hundred thousand
sons of Israel," it says, "and thirty thousand of Judah."[34] Now the
number one thousand and the number ten, since they are perfect numbers,[35] signify the perfection of the saints, while the
numbers three hundred and thirty, since they derive from the

28. Cf. Gen 2.12.   29. 1 Sam 10.8.
30. 1 Sam 11.11.   31. Cf. 1 Sam 12.3, 24.7.
32. Cf. 1 Tim 2.5.   33. Cf. 1 Cor 13.13.
34. 1 Sam 11.8.
35. On 10 and 100 as perfect numbers, see Meyer, *Zahlenallegorese* 142ff.

number three, point to the divine Trinity.[36] What should be understood by three hundred thousand or thirty thousand combatants if not the holy doctors of the Church, who were orthodox in the faith and performed religious deeds to perfection? With these men, Saul defeated the hostile forces of King Nahash, which means that Christ with the doctors of his Church triumphed over the crafty machinations of the ancient serpent. For, when their injunctions or examples are carefully obeyed, listless hearts overcome by dangerous tepidity again grow fervent, and they are inspired to cut down the forces of attacking vices with the brandished sword, as it were, of the spirit.

(25) And so it was that the fighting men of Israel and Judah said to the messengers who had come to them, "Tell the men of Jabesh-Gilead, 'Safety will be yours tomorrow by the time the sun is hot.' "[37] For, as soon as the mind that has become lukewarm through sloth, but is turning back into itself and grows fervent with desire for its Creator, when it abandons the sluggishness of negligence and thaws out its previous icy insensibility at the fire of holy love, then, as the sun growing hot, it wins a victory over its enemies, and the besieged city is freed from the forces of a proud king. Therefore was it written of Abraham, "The Lord appeared to him in the valley of Mamre in the heat of the day."[38] And it was also said of Lot, "The sun had risen over the land as Lot entered Zoar."[39]

(26) Rightly, therefore, do we despise friendly relations with the world or its ruler and disdain likewise any agreement for making alliances with them, lest in joining forces with darkness we be deprived of the light. It should be noted, moreover, that the wicked king did not insist that both eyes of his enemies be gouged, but only one, that he might bring them as a disgrace upon Israel, because the evil enemy often deprives a reprobate who has joined his cause of the stronger part of his holiness and illustrious deeds. He leaves by some ingenious device of his cunning only the lesser, so that what has been taken away from him

36. On 30 and 300 as symbols of the Trinity, see Meyer, *Zahlenallegorese* 117f.
37. 1 Sam 11.9.   38. Gen 18.1.
39. Gen 19.23.

might be the occasion of his ruin as well, and that [the person] might be lost in presuming to be reassured by what remains intact and not having recourse to penance as a sinner. But, from the very remains of the holiness he has lost, on which the sinner leans as on a cane, he is abused and disgraced by those who know that he has fallen. And thus the loss of his good works becomes the instrument that leads rightfully to his shame.

(27) Not unlike this situation was that which happened to the envoys sent by David when Nahash died and was succeeded by his son: "'I shall keep up,'" he said, "'the same loyal friendship with Hanun, son of Nahash, as his father showed me.' David therefore sent a message through his servants to console him over the death of his father."[40] But, to report this long narrative in a few words, "Hanun took David's servants, shaved off half their beards, cut off half their garments up to the buttocks, and dismissed them."[41]

(28) What is meant by Hanun but the evil spirit? And what can be understood by the beard, which is proper to men, but the strength of sacred virtues? And also, how should we interpret the garments except to say that they are the clothing of holiness, of which the psalmist says, "Let your priests be clothed with justice"?[42] So Hanun shaved off half the beards of those who came asking for friendly diplomatic relations, because the ancient enemy impairs the virility of the formerly brave warrior. But, after shaving his beard, he also cuts off his garments, for, as soon as the evil spirit deprives a man of his inner resolution, he then also divests him of the outward dignity he gained by his outstanding way of life. For what is meant by cutting off a man's garments up to the buttocks if not to expose his nakedness by removing the covering of justice, revealing the baseness of his obscene and unmentionable deed.

(29) So let Sir Stephan[43] take note of this, he who some time ago left your holy community to have friendly relations with the

---

40. 2 Sam 10.2.　　　　　　　41. 2 Sam 10.4.
42. Ps 131.9.

43. Sir Stephen seems to be the strange Cardinal Stephen of St. Chrysogonus, whom Damian included among the recipients of his *Letter* 49; see Reindel, *Briefe* 2.62–63, n. 1.

king of the Ammonites, and who now wanders about the streets of Rome like one whose beard was shaved and whose clothes were cut short, not without shame to David. Let also those take heed who still yearn perhaps to go out in public, lest, while eagerly giving free rein to their eyes in taking in every foolish sight, they put out their right eye, that is, their ability to practice interior contemplation.

(30) Nor must their gluttony, like that of the carnal Israelites, lust after leeks and onions and garlic.[44] The strong pungency of these vegetables irritates the eyes and causes them to water. For, since living in the world is associated with much tension and anxiety, and is plagued by frequent disturbance and great labors, those to whom it promises a happy life it often brings to tears.

(31) Certainly, for those who enjoy working, holy solitude provides its own exertion. And so the Lord said to Moses, "Go and tell them to return to their tents, but you yourself stand here beside me, and I will set forth to you all the commandments, the ceremonies, and the judgments."[45] While others were pleasantly resting in their carnal tents, the servant of God was ordered not to sit but to stand with the Lord, that the farther he was removed from worldly labors, the more fervent he would be in holy solitude for devoting himself with all his strength to serving God.

(32) But now, coming back to my own situation, I prostrate myself at your holy feet, so that, as all of you promised me when I was with you, you will offer the support of your constant prayer to me who am submerged in the yawning depths of my sins. For, even though I was unable to live in your midst, I have at least brought peace to your house. As we know, Barzillai, the Gileadite from Rogelim, brought supplies to David when he was fleeing from Absalom.[46] After his victory, when the king invited him to come to Jerusalem to retire in his household, he would not do so, but offered him his son instead. "Please let me go back as your servant," he said, "and end my days in my own city and be buried near the grave of my father. Here is your servant Chimham; let him cross over with your majesty. Do with him whatever you think

---

44. Cf. Num 11.5.   45. Deut 5.30–31.
46. Cf. 2 Sam 17.27–29.

best."[47] Not unlike Barzillai, I too assisted you when you were under hostile attack, but when God granted you success I returned home, saying to you monks of Cluny what Paul remarked to the Colossians, "For though absent in body, I am with you in spirit, and rejoice to see your orderly array."[48] And so, as the old man offered his son to the king, so I too commend my own soul into your hands, and ask that it be fed at the table of your prayers. For, since God's law commands us to return good for evil, how much more does it expect us to render good things for good? And why should we wonder that human nature performs this obligation from a self-imposed law, since at times even dumb animals do this, even though they are not subject to laws?

(33) As I learned from the report of one of my brethren, certain Venetian merchants were in difficulty at sea and were hard at work at the oars. When they had landed, they saw something dreadful and amazing on the sand, a prodigy not far from the water's edge, a lion, as it appeared, snared by the coils of a huge dragon. As this beast was forcibly dragging the prey to its den, the poor lion resisted with all the strength it could muster. At length, the weaker the lion became in its desperate struggle, the more eager the dragon was to win by ensnaring him in its grasp from which there was no escape. But the tradesmen, quickly coming upon the scene, felt sorry for the unlucky lion, drew their swords without fear and killed the dragon, allowing the lion, now freed from the jaws of death, to go off. But the lion that might be called the noblest of beast,[49] showed its gratitude to those who had saved its life, and for the time they stayed in the area, daily brought them the pelt of an animal it had captured.

(34) So why should we be surprised when holy men, instructed in the law of God, after experiencing the good offices of charity, in return show their gratitude, since even a dumb animal can be observed doing the same? And this story can also be made to apply to you. Not without good reason you might be said to be the lion. You are so asleep to the world, that ever watchful you always have your eyes fixed on God and chant in unison with the

47. 2 Sam 19.37.   48. Col 2.5.
49. Cf. Prov 30.30.

bride, "I sleep but my heart is awake."[50] "You shall step on asp and cobra, you shall tread safely on the lion and the dragon."[51] Like the lion, moreover, you are confident and not afraid, and will not turn tail at the attack of evil that opposes you.[52] And then there was Michal who placed a hide at the head of David's bed, and by that means he escaped from the swords of King Saul.[53] Almighty God clothed our first parents in tunics made of skin,[54] which symbolically meant that they would die as a result of the sin they had committed. And so, since through my efforts you were freed from the toils of the dragon,[55] present me with a pelt as a token of your gratitude, and by your prayers request for me life-giving mortification so that the world may never again entice me, and if some time to live still remains for me, it may be spent in gaining merit toward eternal salvation. Yet although the Apostle says that "beyond all dispute the lesser is always blessed by the greater,"[56] still, because charity compels me, I cannot withhold my blessing.[57]

(35) May almighty God protect you from all the attacks of vile Satan, and wash away all contamination of body and soul. Amen. May he extinguish in you the embers of consuming vice, and cause you to flourish with the beauty of virtue. Amen. Through the intercession of his apostles, Peter and Paul, may he absolve you from all sin, and make you reign forever as fellow-citizens with him and his saints. Amen.

(36) May the blessing of almighty God, Father, Son, and Holy Spirit descend and remain upon you. Amen.

50. Cant 5.2.

51. Ps 90.13.

52. Cf. Prov 30.30.

53. Cf. 1 Sam 19.13.

54. Cf. Gen 3.21.

55. Damian is here, perhaps, playing on the name, Drogo, the bishop of Mâcon, from whose attacks he delivered the Cluniacs.

56. Heb 7.7.

57. Dressler, *Petrus Damiani* 76, n. 34, conjectured that the following paragraph was a later addition, since at this point the letter concludes in *MS Paris, BNL nov. acq. 1578*, 16th cent. But I have disregarded this evidence since it is too recent.

LETTER 101

Peter Damian to Wido, the archbishop of Milan. Contrary to his custom of refusing gifts (e.g., at Milan in 1059 and at Cluny in 1063), he accepts the gift of two stoles from Wido. Reluctant to receive these tokens of friendship, he nevertheless acquiesces with promises of prayer for his benefactor, offered by all his communities.

(November 1063)[1]

O SIR WIDO, the most reverend archbishop of Milan, the monk Peter the sinner sends the devotion of his most faithful service.

(2) Your holiness should know, venerable father, that it grieved me very much and my heart, so to say, gave me great pain because I did not spare your generous and bounteous liberality. As if I were already enjoying the future resurrection, you have decided to invest me with two stoles.[2] Overwhelmed by your authority, I have offered no resistance, did not withdraw my hand, but forgetful of the natural inflexibility of the servants

---

1. Dating follows Reindel, *Briefe* 3.115, n. (*Datierung*). After much hesitation and mind-changing among the scholars (Gaetani, Neukirch, and Lucchesi), who have undertaken to date and assign an addressee to this letter, Prof. Reindel (*Briefe* 3.115–116, n.1) made the difficult decision to name Wido, archbishop of Milan, and not Archbishop Hugh of Besançon. He follows the evidence of *MS Ch 2*, an eleventh century MS in the Chigi collection of the Vatican Library, rejecting other eleventh-century MSS (C1 and V1), which use the symbol V, easily read as U, instead of W found in Ch 2, and omit the adjective *Mediolanensis* found only in Ch 2. Otherwise, Hugh (Ugo) given the MS evidence, would have been a most proper choice. Damian had visited him on his return from Cluny (cf. *Letter* 111), calling him "a venerable and most eloquent man" (cf. *Iter Gallicum* c. 17, 1044). Most impressive to Damian was Hugh's school, which appeared to him as a "heavenly Athens." That Damian would accept a gift of two stoles from such a man, is not to be wondered at. In the light of the evidence, the choice between Wido and Hugh might be called a toss-up, with the latter more warmly recommended by the tenor of the letter, read with *Letter* 111. And yet, I find it difficult to reject Reindel's choice.

2. Cf. Rev 7.13.

of God, I easily accepted all your gifts. But as I now call this to mind, my guilty conscience disapproves, I am filled with shame and blush at my own private rebuke, just as if I were being censured by others.

(3) Nor is this beside the point. For if King David suffered reproach of conscience, as Scripture attests, because he stealthily cut off only the fringe of Saul's cloak,[3] what about me who extorted from my lord not just a part of a cape, but entire garments, and precious ones at that, and under the pretext of not giving but receiving charity, as I clothed myself, I robbed from another? Indeed, if I were truly a priest, I would strive to be attired in justice rather than in ornaments of the weaver's art. Amid such thoughts, however, as I stand for questioning before the tribunal of my own mind and straightforwardly investigate myself with severe self-inspection, this is my plea, and I stand by it firmly, that at that time several gifts were offered to me that I did not accept, but quickly returned to those who had sent them.[4] And so I can perhaps infer that the same charity that prompted my lord to grant his gift, persuaded his servant to accept what was granted.

(4) But as I recall the manner in which you gave this gift, I am reminded of the statement of Zechariah, "Now Jesus was wearing filthy clothes as he stood before the angel. And the angel turned and said to those in attendance on him, 'Take off his filthy clothes.' "[5] Then, as Scripture goes on to say, they put clean garments on him. Happy will be the day when we celebrate this change of clothing, and the body of Jesus, which is the Church, after divesting itself of all the filth of mourning and sorrow, will put on the glorious garments of blessed immortality, as the psalmist sang with joy at the dedication of his house, "You have turned my laments into gladness, you have stripped off my sackcloth and clothed me with joy that I might sing psalms and give you glory."[6]

(5) But why do I speak of such things? It is enough for me to

3. Cf. 1 Sam 24.5–6.
4. Gifts received by him in Milan (*Letter* 76) and at Cluny (*Iter Gallicum* c. 20, 1046) were returned by Damian.
5. Zech 3.3–4.   6. Ps 29.12–13.

say, venerable father, that you have become for me the angel of the Lord, who for love of Jesus removed my filthy clothes, and in me adorned him in priestly attire. For these gifts, however, I am not at all ungrateful and have repaid this exchange, in that I have inscribed your name in many hermitages and monasteries, not only in those that belong to our congregation, but in others as well that are distant from us, and with the humble effort of my devotion I have recommended you to the prayers of my brothers.

LETTER 102

Peter Damian to the Abbot Desiderius and the monks of Monte Cassino. While in Rome on synodal business, and after completing the report on his mission to Cluny, Damian was in a storytelling mood as he wrote to his friends at Monte Cassino. This letter is replete with marvelous tales, some of which deal with miraculous happenings relating to the Holy Eucharist. It is interesting to note his repeated efforts to verify these *exempla*.

(After a synod during the winter of 1063–1064)[1]

 O SIR DESIDERIUS, the abbot of this venerable community, and to the other holy brethren,[2] the monk Peter the sinner sends the submission of his most dedicated service. (2) As the warmth of my affection for you glows in my heart, unable to be extinguished, not permitting me to grow lukewarm in my memory of you, something recently came to mind that prompted me to send you a letter. For, as I was so preoccupied in thinking about you that in imagination I was as if physically present in the midst of your holy and angelic community of brothers, I suddenly remembered, among many other things, the letter of inquiry you sent,[3] to which, however, I have not replied because of the urgency of synodal business.[4] And, if I recall correctly, this was the subject that was contained in your letter. A certain jealous woman, having a husband whom she suspected of adulterous relations, sought advice from a neighbor woman on how she might win him back and cause him to be satisfied with his own marriage. Now this wicked woman, obviously

---

1. Dating follows Lucchesi, *Vita* no. 181.

2. On Desiderius, see *Letter* 82, n. 2. See also Herbert Bloch, *Monte Cassino in the Middle Ages* 1 (1986) 40–110.

3. It was not customary at the time archivally to preserve the letters received. Yet the subject of the letter was so bizarre that Damian had not forgotten it.

4. The reference is unclear, but may refer to the synod of Chalon-sur-Saône, held in 1063 over the case of Cluny v. the Bishop of Mâcon. Lucchesi's reference to a winter synod of 1063 cannot be verified.

deserving of punishment in the flames of hell, on the poisonous advice of the ancient serpent, urged her to perform the sacrilegious act of receiving the Body of the Lord as if she were going to communion, but cleverly preserving it, later to have her husband drink it down with certain magic potions. Yet the host was taken from her by a priest who placed it in a small corporal where it was to be reserved until something could be done. In the meantime, however, the host gave rise to a miracle which caused no inconsiderable amazement. For one half of this particle of the Lord's Body was found turned into flesh, while the other half had not changed its appearance as bread. This, then, if my memory serves me well, was the case you proposed, and you asked what this happening might forebode. Since it is not necessary to dwell too long on this matter, I shall promptly write a few lines and give you my opinion.

(3) Almighty God changed this Most Holy Sacrament into the appearance of flesh in order to impeach the disbelief of this wicked woman, while at the same time demonstrating the obvious truth of the Body of the Lord. By so doing, that which she previously believed to be ordinary bread—as it appeared to be—she would see under the appearance of true flesh, and thus she would condemn by her judgment the sacrilegious audacity of the crime she had attempted. The fact that half of the appearance remained, however, served to furnish clearer evidence that, as you saw in one and the same substance the appearance of bread on one side and flesh on the other, you would recognize without separation the reality both of true flesh and of true bread, since it is at once the very "bread that came down from heaven"[5] and at the same time the very flesh that proceeded from the substance of the Virgin's womb.

(4) Similarly, your neighbor of blessed memory, the bishop of Amalfi[6] whose name I do not know, often declared under oath to

5. John 6.59.
6. This might be a reference to the archbishop Peter of Amalfi, who in 1054 was in Constantinople with Cardinal Humbert of Silva Candida, and with Frederick of Lorraine, the future Pope Stephen IX. But given the unusual circumstances of this mission to the Byzantine emperor and the singular nature of the story, it is difficult to imagine that Damian had forgotten the name.

Stephen,[7] the Roman pontiff, in my presence, that on one occasion, as he was about to say Mass at the table of the Lord, he wavered in his belief about the sacrament of the Lord's Body. Just as he was in the act of breaking the Sacred Host, completely red and perfect flesh appeared in his hands so that it covered his fingers with blood, and thus for the bishop removed even the slightest doubt. Here we should note what a horrible danger it is to handle this awesome Sacrament with unworthy hands. But what do we say about the sacraments themselves when at times we see such terrible punishment meted out to those who offend even against the vessels in which they are kept?

(5) You were certainly well acquainted with Arnaldus, the bishop of the diocese of Arezzo.[8] Martin the hermit,[9] a man who was held in great esteem and enjoyed an outstanding reputation, told me of him, that he had taken a golden chalice from one of the monasteries under his jurisdiction, and, because he was in certain financial difficulties, he sold it. On this chalice a devout woman of the nobility, who had dedicated it to the saints, had a curse engraved as a precaution against anyone who would steal it. In the meantime, it happened that a certain brother, weighed down by sleep, saw a lake that was seething from extreme heat, giving off a stench of pitch and sulphur amid clouds of foul smoke. Around the lake, certain extremely horrible men—like Ethiopians[10]—were mounted on horses that were likewise black, but as high as towers. In the lake, moreover, were countless monstrous forms of cruel torturers, which were seen inflicting various types of horrible torment on the damned. Then it happened that he saw the bishop Arnaldus among them as well. Two horrible Ethiopians were keeping him immersed neck deep in the waters, which were boiling over as a result of the excessive heat.

---

7. Stephen IX (2 August 1057–27 March 1058).

8. On Bishop Arnaldus of Arezzo, see Schwarz, *Bistümer* 201.

9. Perhaps the reference is to Martin Storacus, one of his community; see *Letter* 44.9–11.

10. Damian here, as on several other occasions in his letters, betrays a prejudice against black Ethiopians. He refers to them in *Letters* 72.52 (see n. 72), 106 (cf. Reindel, *Briefe* 3.172, n. 12), and 109 (cf. Reindel, *Briefe* 3.217, line 12f.). Whether Damian was unique in this regard, or merely reflected an attitude of his times, is unclear.

One of them was seen to have an iron pan in his hands, the other a golden chalice. The first used the pan to fill the chalice with water, while the second continuously held the chalice to the bishop's lips, making him drink to the last drop. And so it went on interminably, the torturers emptying the cup into his open mouth, and the bishop constantly being compelled to drink. In the midst of all this, the bishop asked, "Why are you doing this?" and the one who was pouring replied, "Because of the chalice of the holy Trinity which you stole."

(6) But why need I continue? The bishop heared about this vision and called on him to restore the chalice to the monastery. It was suggested by his friends, however, that he promise to return it, but perhaps not commit himself. And so, while the matter was put off, and, what is more, as he paid little heed to his salvation, divine judgment did not fall asleep on him. For, as blessed Peter says of those who are avaricious and deal with deceptive words, "But the judgment long decreed for them does not grow idle; their perdition does not sleep."[11] And so, one day when it was almost nine o'clock in the morning, he ordered his chair to be placed on the quay of the castle where he was, that he might take the warmth of the rising sun and ward off what was left of the morning chill. And, while the household servants and body guards stood about the seated man, and while he exchanged witty pleasantries with them in a secure, happy, and joking disposition, he suddenly experienced an unexpected pain in his head that pierced like a sword, causing him to cry out, "I am dying, I am dying!" After he had been carried to bed by his attendants, he received the sacrament of holy communion and soon breathed his last.

(7) Therefore, let everyone beware selling equipment used for ministry in the church, or making light about the utterance of a curse, lest he be caught in the snare of some hidden judgment as he apparently goes securely on his way. Oh, how utterly miserable and unhappy is man's estate! Certainly, even though negligence and inactivity surprised the aforementioned bishop, he otherwise behaved astutely, cleverly, and cautiously. He was

11. 2 Pet 2.3.

possessed of such fluency in speech that, though he experienced no hindrance in his words, he could rightly be said to speak with uncircumcised lips.[12] But, since the Apostle says, "Prudence of the flesh spells death, but prudence of the spirit means life and peace,"[13] how does one profit from being skilled in the prudence of this world, from having an intuitive understanding that comprehends secret things right away, or from using clever wiles like Proteus and changing into various monstrous forms?[14]

(8) And, while I am on the subject, I am reminded of the former Bishop Tedaldus,[15] the predecessor of the man we have been discussing, who had this to say as he was preaching from the pulpit to the assembly on the feast of blessed Donatus.[16] "In the region of Lombardy," he said, "where I was born, there was a man possessed of a dissimulating nature and of the keenest subtlety. He was duplicitous, charming in speech, learned in the art of contriving and fabricating falsehood, and very astute in coming up with schemes tailored to the occasion. Never did he swim against the stream, but, from whatever direction the winds of this world were blowing,[17] he would promptly clothe himself in just the right mantle of cunning and deception. But then it happened that in a dream a certain brother saw him after he had died. There was a fiery lake, which, steaming, belching forth flames, and crackling with balls of fire, brought terror and horror to the hearts of those who saw it. Fierce and enormous dragons appeared to be infesting this lake, and various kinds of serpents crept here and there along its shores. Now the man of whom we have been speaking was confined in this pool of hissing flames. He tried, indeed, to escape, but, because these ani-

12. Cf. Exod 6.12, 30.   13. Rom 8.6.
14. A sea-god in the service of Neptune, who often changed his form; cf. Ovid, *Met.* 8.731; 2.9; *Liber monstrorum*, ed. F. Porsia (1976) 188f.
15. Tedaldus was the son of the Margrave Tedaldus, of the house of Canossa, installed in his see in 1022/23; cf. Schwartz, *Bistümer* 200.
16. Second bishop of Arezzo (4th century); patron of the city; feast 7 August. Damian wrote his *Sermon* 38 (Lucchesi, *Sermones* 232–239) in his honor, as well as two hymns (see Lokrantz, *L'opera* nos. 20 and 21, 109ff.), and referred to him in two further poems, no. 35 (p. 122) and no. 51 (p. 135). The monastery of S. Donato di Pulpiano belongs to the Congregation of the Holy Cross, Fonte Avellana.
17. Cf. Juvenal, *Saturae* 4.89.

mals were blocking his efforts, he despaired of finding a way out. As soon as he tried to get away on one side, there was a serpent waiting for him. He sought to break through on the other side, and there also another beast, with open jaws, blocked his path. He tried path after path of escape, but, because these creatures were bearing down, no course of escape was open. Moreover, since Truth itself says, "Whatever measure you deal out to others will be dealt back to you,"[18] this happened to him because of the just judgment of God. For, even as he was able to escape every snare in this world by the deceptions of carnal trickery, so afterwards—quite the reverse—no amount of genius afforded him an escape from the torture he was then enduring. To be sure, if he had applied to observing God's commands the wisdom that had served his deceptions, he would not be roasting, surrounded by savage snakes, but instead would be celebrating amid the ranks of the blessed."

(9) An event also took place in our region, one that should not be passed over in silence, having to do with a certain man who was wise in the ways of the flesh. A leading citizen of Fano, Hugh by name, during the night of Good Friday, which precedes the Lord's burial on Holy Saturday, with weapons and armed men entered the church during divine services and violently seized a man whom he thoroughly hated and cruelly clapped him in chains. Because he dared to do this unprecedented thing, almighty God condemned him to an unprecedented punishment. For, while he was completely sane as far as I could judge, everyone avoided him, despised him, and reproached him as one who was crazy, without honor, and out of his mind. Like the complaint of blessed Job,[19] his wife shuddered at his very breath, his daughter-in-law ranted at him as if he were a raving maniac, and his son would not allow him to take part in meals or conversation. His servants looked the other way, and his friends made fun of him. His vassals, knights, relatives, and friends, even the bishop of the city, and, to list them all briefly, the entire clergy and people for almost twelve years thought him

18. Matt 7.2; Mark 4.24.
19. Cf. Job 19.17.

to be out of his mind and insane, and they would have nothing
to do with him as if he were possessed by the devil. Moreover,
even though he was wealthy and his home was luxurious, it was
strewn with tattered and unwashed clothes, his hair was un-
kempt, his head stank from constant sweating, and his whole
body was filthy because of long periods of neglect.

(10) Now, when he learned that I was around, he made an effort to see me, told me of the ills he was undergoing, soberly
complained of his family, and, as far as I could gather from his
words, spoke quite rationally. And then I met with his son, and
also with the bishop and with many people of the town, and I
carefully asked them what they observed in him that was disordered, or crazy, or foolish, through which they judged him to be
mad. From these I could learn nothing, not even a word that
pointed to certainty, except that all agreed in stating that he was
insane. And when I asked, "How do you know, and what evidence do you have that he is out of his mind?" they found nothing else to say except to reiterate, "He's crazy." To me this seemed
to be a profound and astonishing judgment of almighty God,
that a wise and knowledgeable man, who was known to have
acted deliberately like a maniac, should, though wise and knowledgeable, be punished by being considered deranged, and that
he who, of his own accord, became mad should, against his will,
be judged by everyone to be mentally imbalanced.

(11) Rightly, and against his will, is one judged to be mad if
he voluntarily undertakes to act like a madman. For, if he were
truly out of his mind, he would be less miserable than if, out of
touch with himself, he were unaware of the evil that he suffered.
Therefore, he who is not conscious of his surroundings is not
like one who has died in this world,[20] but like one who is dead in
hell and continually dying and never ceasing to experience that
death. With the exception of the terrible judgment at the end
of the world, at this time also almighty God punishes not only
cruel deeds, but—quite rightly—proud or sacrilegious words
as well.

(12) Certainly he avenged the action of Belshazzar who un-

20. Cf. Ps 142.3

worthily handled the sacred vessels while he was drunk,[21] nor did he allow the bombastic and arrogant words spoken by Nebuchadnezzar to go unpunished. "Is this not Babylon the great," he said, "which I have built as a royal residence in the strength of my power and in the honor of my majesty?"[22] And then, as the prophet reported, "while the words were still on the king's lips, a voice came down from heaven, 'You address these words to yourself, King Nebuchadnezzar. The kingdom will pass from you. You will be banished from the society of men and you will live with the wild beasts.' "[23] The Lord, moreover, punished Zedekiah, the king of Judah,[24] because by his wicked deeds he despised the laws of God. He also took vengeance on Hananiah the prophet, not because of the evil he had done, but because he told lies. Jeremiah said to him, "The Lord has not sent you, and you have led this nation to trust in falsehood. These, therefore, are the words of the Lord, 'Beware, I shall remove you from the face of the earth; you will die within the year.' "[25]

(13) It happened in recent times also that there was a certain cleric in the kingdom of Burgundy who was so extremely proud and arrogant that, not only did he live the secular life of a layman, but contrary to his state, was a terror in combat. Moreover, after he had despoiled the celebrated church of St. Maurice[26] of many of its holdings and kept them for his own, a certain powerful man opposed him, claiming with great resentment and threats that they belonged to him. At length, after both had agreed, the day for the battle was fixed, and from all around great numbers of fierce troops clashed. Now that powerful man, the second one I mentioned, sent an envoy to the enemy camp so that he might carefully observe their battle equipment and quickly inform him of what he had seen. It just so happened [right when the envoy arrived] that the cleric, along with his supporters who were about to enter combat, was hearing Mass. When it came time for the Gospel, at the end of which was read, "Everyone who exalts himself will be humbled; and whoever

21. Cf. Dan 5.30–31.   22. Dan 4.27.
23. Dan 4.28–29.   24. 2 Chr 36.15–17.
25. Jer 28.15–16.
26. Saint Maurice d'Agaune in Upper Burgundy; cf. Reindel, *Briefe* 3.126, n. 16.

humbles himself will be exalted,"[27] the cleric impudently shouted these sacrilegious words, "This statement is not true," he said, "for if I had humbly bowed to my opponents, I would today not have so many possessions and so many vassals." When the envoy returned to his lord, he faithfully reported not only what he had observed of the enemy's battle preparations, but also what he had heard the proud cleric saying. Then [this lord] praised God, and was in good spirits, exhorting his men to the hope that they would undoubtedly be victorious.

(14) And so, as the troops on both sides massed into wedged shapes against one another and went into action, might against might, dropping a dense forest of spears, they attacked with swords, hacking away at human bodies. Now the cleric had a mare that he mounted to carry him into battle, a beast of such speed and strength that no other horse or mule, it seemed to him, could surpass it for combat. By chance, or rather, at God's disposition, it happened that on the previous night the animal had gotten out of its stall, and finding a heap of salt, it had eaten quite a bit of it. Therefore, as the cleric was drawn up in battle array and came to a stream to engage in combat with the enemy, his mount was overcome by thirst because of the large amount of salt she had swallowed, violently tore the bridle from the hand of her rider, brought it entirely under her own control, and with that plunged its head into the water and gulped it down. But, since the cleric was struggling with the animal, using the hand that held his shield, he was forced to expose his face to the enemy weapons, when suddenly, like a bolt of lightning a sword pierced him through the mouth, and thus this wicked man lost his life.

(15) How fitting it was that he should be punished in that part of his body by which he had spewed forth the black bile of his blasphemy against the Lord! And since of such men the prophet says, "Children of human beings, their teeth are spears and arrows, and their tongues sharp swords,"[28] he who brandished his tongue and teeth like a sword to be wielded against God rightly paid the penalty of a physical sword thrust through

27. Luke 14.11.
28. Ps 56.5; cf. Sabatier 2.114.

these same parts of the body. Indeed, what the Lord says in the Gospel happened to him, that "a tower fell on eighteen people at Siloam and killed them."[29] Whom does this tower mystically signify but the one of whom the psalmist sings, "You have rescued me and become my hope, a tower of strength from the enemy's face"?[30] For, with regard to this explanation, the name Siloam also fits, since Siloam has the meaning "one sent,"[31] undoubtedly referring to the one who says, "He who sent me is present with me."[32] And it was at Siloam[33] that the man blind from birth received his sight from the one who said, "I have come into the world as light."[34] Elsewhere he speaks about the fall of this tower using the figure of a stone, "Any man who falls on this stone will be dashed to pieces; but if it falls on a man, it will crush him."[35] A man falls on this tower or on this stone and is dashed to pieces when he sins because of some frailty; but it falls on him and crushes him when he proudly blasphemes. And thus the tower at Siloam fell upon this cleric and crushed him as his blasphemy deserved.

(16) And why should we wonder that grave sins bring torment to us, since God's keen judgment does not allow even slight sins to go unpunished? And what, moreover, is novel about his condemnation of the sacrilege of evil speech, since he even abominates prayers in his honor unless they are offered properly? Now, what I am about to write, I learned from the report of that prudent and religious man, Adraldus,[36] who presides as abbot over the monastery of Breme, who said that it was also to be found in writing. "A cleric of the diocese of Cologne," he said, "was crossing a ford in the river, when suddenly blessed Severin,[37] who had recently been the bishop of that see, took hold of his reins and

---

29. Luke 13.4.   30. Ps 60.3–4.
31. Cf. Jerome, *Nom. hebr.* 50.25 (CC 72.122).
32. John 8.29.   33. Cf. John 8.7.
34. John 12.46.   35. Matt 21.44.

36. On Adraldus, see A. Clerval, "Adralde," DHGE 1 (1922) 594ff. Damian informs us in his *Vita sancti Odilonis* (PL 144.928BC), that Adraldus was a student of Odilo. He also accompanied Damian on his legation into Gaul (*Iter Gallicum* c.11, 1041). Adraldus is further mentioned in Damian's *Letters* 110 and 114.

37. There is no known bishop Severin of Cologne in the eleventh century, but the name occurs as of a bishop in the second half of the 4th century.

forced him to stop. When he turned about in astonishment and marveled why such an outstanding and celebrated man should be detaining him, the latter said, 'Give me your hand so that you can learn what had happened to me, not just by sound but also by touch.' And when the bishop took his hand and forced it into the water, it became so hot that the flesh about his hand began to loosen and the bones of his fingers were almost bare. The cleric said to him, 'Since your name is held in such benediction among us, and your renown is proclaimed in song by the entire Church, why are you forced to stay in this pestiferous pool and, sad to say, tortured in this heat?' The holy bishop replied, 'There was nothing else for which I had to atone but this, that while at the court and deeply involved in the imperial council, I did not recite the hours of the divine office at their proper time. By saying them all together each morning, I had the whole day free to devote to the overwhelming affairs of my position. And so, for neglecting the hours, I am now tortured in this heat. But let us together humbly beg the goodness of almighty God to restore your hand to its former healthy state.' After this had happened, he said, 'Go, my son, and beg our brothers, the clerics and other spiritual men of the Church, to offer their prayers for me, to help the needy, and participate in the sacrifice of the Mass. For when all this has been done, I will surely soon be freed from the bonds of this punishment and will happily join the band of the blessed who await me.' "

(17) Certainly, this story must cause us great anxiety, for since such intolerable punishment in purgatory[38] oppressed this holy man who was guilty of only one fault, woe to me and to others like me! What sort of sentence must we hear, since we are burdened with so many sins?

(18) Therefore, the official prayers of the Church must be recited at separate times, and they must be said with great exactness out of fear and reverence for God, lest as we pray we adul-

38. One of several references to purgatory in Damian's letters. He is, perhaps, the first to use the word as a substantive. The word is not reported in Blaise, *Lexicon* as a noun used in patristic literature. It is instructive to note that the liturgical introduction of All Souls' Day by Odilo of Cluny, whose biography Damian wrote, certainly increased the spread of the idea of purgatory. See the *Statutum s. Odilonis de defunctis* (PL 142.1037f.).

terate the fruit of the spirit with the slothfulness of the flesh. For what good is achieved by giving praise to God, if through inactivity and neglect we defile our offering by foul thoughts? The Gospel text, moreover, points to this blend of good and evil, where it says, "For at the very time," when the Lord was teaching, "there were some people present who told him about the Galileans whose blood Pilate had mixed with their sacrifices."[39] Now, since the name "Pilate" may be taken to mean "the mouth of the blacksmith,"[40] what else should we see in him but the devil who is always ready to deal men crushing blows? And so, also the prophet says that he holds a rod over the shoulders of men, "You have overcome by putting the rod to his shoulders, as on the day of Midian's defeat."[41] What does blood signify except sins? And what sacrifices except good deeds that are acceptable to God? Thus, Pilate was said to have mixed the blood of the Galileans with their sacrifices, because the evil spirit either pollutes our prayers with bad thoughts, or spoils our good works by the contamination of some sin, so that blood might defile the sacrifice while the obstacle of sin debases the victim of our virtuous deeds offered to God. And so it was written, that as Abraham devoutly offered God a sacrifice of animals and birds, "birds of prey swooped down on the carcasses, and Abraham scared them away."[42] What do these birds represent, if not the wicked spirits that fly through the air? And thus, we are careful to keep the birds away from our sacrifice when we protect the offering of our deeds from the evil spirits that try to defile them.

(19) Now the same Adraldus whom I mentioned before, told me the following as we were traveling together in the kingdom of Burgundy.[43] "In this very region through which we are now passing," he said, "something happened that will not be out of place for me to tell you. There was a certain brother from our monastery"—undoubtedly from the monastery of Cluny—"who at one time was traveling through this area, a pious man of upright life. Unexpectedly, he met a long-haired man coming

---

39. Luke 13.1.

40. Cf. Jerome, *Nom. hebr.* 50.25 (CC 72.141).

41. Isa 9.4.   42. Gen 15.11.

43. Cf. *supra*, no. 36.

along, apparently returning from a pilgrimage to Jerusalem,[44] who was carrying a palm in his hand. As the pilgrim and the monk met, and were about to pass one another, the former said, 'It is neither profitable nor conducive to salvation to recite Compline[45] in bed.' When the brother heard these words, he was astonished, and quickly looking back over his shoulder, could no longer see the pilgrim. For as soon as he had spoken, he completely disappeared. When the monk came to his senses, he remembered that last evening as he was exhausted from his journey, and was resting his tired limbs in bed, he had said his Compline. Whether this had been an angel, or actually a man, as it seemed, I think we must leave to God's decision."

(20) Also, in this hermitage of Fonte Avellana, where I am now living, there was once a prior named John,[46] who because of certain lingering infirmities always appeared thin and emaciated. Worn out by his bodily weakness, he often recited Compline while lying in bed. Now in the neighborhood there happened to be a man possessed by the devil, who shamelessly divulged many secret and impure deeds that people had committed. When this same John was trying to expel the devil, and was harassing him with the various procedures of exorcism, the devil said, "So you are the one who daily mumbles his Compline under his quilt, and now like a saint do you wish to drive me out and free the man who shelters me from my power over him?" When the brother heard this he was ashamed, for he was aware that the charge was true, even though it came from the father of lies.

(21) There was also another hermit, named John of Anso,[47] who used every means to exorcise this devil, and repeatedly adjured him in the name of God. At which the devil said, "Have you forgotten what I did to you last night? If it has not escaped your memory, you will certainly recall that after I had disguised myself

44. A long beard was characteristic of pilgrims.

45. The concluding or night prayer of the Divine Office.

46. See Mittarelli-Costadoni, *Annales Camaldulenses* 2.44 for a list of the first four priors, the third of whom was John, in office ca. 1009.

47. For Anson, a village near the Etsch river, province of Verona, see Granata, *Montecassino* 263, n. 20; see also Mittarelli-Costadoni, *Annales Camaldulenses* 2.271.

as a wild boar of the forest, you pursued me as the hunter is wont to do. But after appearing as a wild boar, I suddenly took the form of a beautiful woman, and running up to give you a kiss that you might pollute yourself, I was gloriously successful." If, therefore, the evil spirit can congratulate himself on triumphing over a brother who sins because of his vivid dreams, how much more will he dance for joy over those who sin by adultery or incest? And so, almighty God often passes terrible judgment even in this life, and still miserable men will not stop repeating sins for which they will be punished.

(22) I am reminded of Robert, the French king,[48] the grandfather of Philip, the present successor to his father on the throne, who married a close relative from whom he had a son whose neck and head had all the appearance of a goose. For good measure, almost all the bishops of France unanimously excommunicated them, namely, the man and his wife. At this decision of the bishops, the people everywhere were so filled with terror, that no one would have anything to do with them, except two servant lads who stayed to provide their necessary food. But even these young men considered all the tableware from which the king ate or drank as loathsome, and threw it into the fire. At length, under such pressure, the king followed the good advice of his council, dissolved his incestuous relationship, and was legally married.

(23) And then there was Otto, the king of the Germans, and later chosen emperor of the Romans, who married Adelheid, the queen of Italy, his godmother.[49] His son, the saintly bishop of the church of Mainz, earnestly began to censure him and to condemn him publicly for this shameful and ghastly marriage.[50] Becoming violently angry, his father ordered his arrest. He was at once put in jail where he spent almost a year, but his dreadful chains did not cause him to hold his censorious tongue. Then as

---

48. For literature on King Robert, see Reindel, *Briefe* 3.132, n. 29.

49. On the relationship between Otto I and Adelheid, see Hroswitha of Gandersheim, *Gesta Ottonis*, ed. P. von Winterfeld, MGH SS Rer. Germ. 34 (1902) 222f. For further sources and literature, cf. Reindel, *Briefe* 3.133, n. 31.

50. The sources, cited by Reindel, *Briefe* 3.133, n. 32, do not mention this matter as the cause of the ruptured relations between Otto and his son, William.

the Lenten fast began, his father ordered him to be released from prison, but he refused to leave before he had finished the psalter that he was writing in letters of gold. Nevertheless, burning with the zeal of his episcopal authority, he did not stop his accusations, and after a brief period publicly excommunicated his father.

(24) What a bishop he was, worthy of his royal ancestry, who in the service of God did not recognize the imperial dignity or consider his affection for his father! Placing all paternal and royal authority in God alone, he judged this man who resisted God's law as if he were a total stranger. And then he said to his father, "You may think that I treated you insolently, and that you are the victim of prejudice. But know this beforehand, on the sacred day of Pentecost we shall both be standing before God, and there this contest between us will be aired in a court of justice. There it will become perfectly clear which one of us has been following the rules of equity, and who has been opposing the laws of God." And so it happened that on the very day of this most holy feast, as he predicted, as the emperor, clothed in his imperial garb, was assisting at the solemn Mass, surrounded by a great number of bishops and a host of dignitaries, suddenly the judgment of God came upon him, and they found that he was dead. The bishop, however, had already passed away.[51] And so, he who had refused to be judged by men for his incestuous marriage, was forced to be brought before the tribunal of the eternal Judge; and he who would not consent to listen to a bishop who was his subject, was unable to avoid the terrible majesty that overwhelmed him.

(25) I am writing these and many other things, venerable father, not without great fear and anxiety lest my source had strayed from the narrow path of naked truth, or lest I had failed properly to remember what had been reported to me. Therefore, as my conscience will witness, I have tried to make notes of what was told me, the better to recall them, not with the inten-

---

51. The events and dates are garbled: Otto I died on 7 May 973 in Memleben as he attended Vespers. Damian correctly foredates William's death on 2 March 968.

tion of deceiving, but for the purpose of edification. If, however, my memory has proved false in these matters, and what is more, in whatever way I fail out of human weakness before I am released from this flesh, may God's goodness cause me to remember your prayers for me, and permit me properly to lament my sins, lest while I am still alive something for which I should be sorry remain hidden, that might stand against me when I am dying.

(26) This year, in fact, as the abbot of Cluny[52] brought me to his monastery, there was a certain old brother lying in the infirmary, his whole body terribly swollen. When he became aware that the abbot was present, he seemed pleased and began praying for God's mercy. "O Lord," he said, "from whom nothing is hidden, I beg that if there is any fault in me which I have not yet confessed, in your mercy let me recall it and rightly confess it to my abbot while he is here, so that I might receive absolution from him who before all others has the right to judge me." After he had said this, a voice spoke to him in these or similar words, "Yes, indeed, there is still something that you have not yet confessed." Since he had heard only the voice, but was unaware where it came from, he continued praying, "Tell me clearly, Lord, what it is, so that after I have confessed, I may correct what I have done wrong." And then, as he had asked, the same voice specifically told him of a certain sin which he at once remembered having committed, and which the abbot, on hearing his confession, quickly absolved. A few days later the old man died peacefully in the Lord.

(27) Not so was the death of a cleric of whom Hugh, the same abbot of the monastery of Cluny, told me in this trustworthy report. "A certain religious bishop," he said, "was on a trip, and coming to the bank of a river he halted, and because he was tired, thought he would catch his breath. As he peacefully rested there, he heard a voice coming from the channel of the river, clearly saying, 'The time has come, but the man has not yet arrived.' Upon hearing these words, the bishop became alarmed, and considering that this event contained no little mystery, was

52. Hugh of Cluny. See *Letter* 100, n. 5.

prepared to see something out of the ordinary. But as he looked about and carefully waited, thinking over all the possibilities, suddenly a cleric briskly rode up, spurred on his horse, and promptly tried to cross the river. The bishop, however, alerted his men to block the path of the newcomer and stop him from going any farther. But when he alertly moved toward the river and tried to cross it without delay, and the bishop's men violently opposed him and forced him to stop, he said, 'Get away, I tell you, let me go. Get back by order of the king. This is something that cannot be put off. It is secret business of the king and requires instant attention.' But why go into further detail? The holy bishop held him by force, and with night coming on, compelled him to stay. But how miserable and deplorable is the human condition that can more easily bring evil upon itself when it is not there, than avoid it when it is present! While the bishop and his attendants were sound asleep, the courier found a basin of water in his lodging in which he ducked his head, and in this way became his own executioner and took his own life. And so, as one man secretly, but by the severe judgment of God, met bodily death, the other through his goodness escaped death for both soul and body."

(28) Now, what I am about to tell you, I often heard from the account of the same abbot of Cluny and from the lips of him to whom it happened. There was a certain young man in the region of Aquitaine who, together with other young people his age, was discussing their spiritual well-being. After deliberating for a while they at length agreed and unanimously made a pact among themselves to leave the pleasures of this world and together enter a monastic order. But as the matter was still not settled and was postponed, and the flow of events underwent many changes, the young man did not remain firm in his proposal. But I will spare you all the details. At length he changed his mind and made preparations to marry. When in the course of time his attitude had gradually erased the memory of his sacred promise, and under the pretext of marriage had stimulated him to eagerly satisfy his lust for carnal pleasure, by the ever watchful goodness of God he suddenly became ill, and was shortly after on his deathbed.

(29) And so, while the servants and relatives were discussing his burial as if he were already dead, as he was lying there, seemingly, a lifeless corpse, with not the slightest indication that he was still breathing, suddenly two fierce and savage looking Ethiopians,[53] as it appeared to him, came at him like roaring lions, brutally took hold of him and violently tugged at his body. Then they tied his feet and arms with stout ropes, and one following the other, they hauled him out like a young goat hanging from a carrying-pole. What pain and torture he suffered, what a variety of things he saw and heard as they towed him through many towns, would take too long not only to put into writing but even to listen to his telling about it in a few simple words. It will here suffice to say, that as they carried him through obscure and darkened areas, suddenly blessed Peter the apostle appeared in shining garments, snatched him from the shoulders of his bearers, and untied the ropes that held him. When their victim had thus been seized, the Ethiopians left, howling and gnashing their teeth, complaining and sobbing that they had been wronged.

(30) Then the blessed apostle took the young man along to the monastery of Cluny, left him at the gate, and told him to wait there till he returned. "I am going into my monastery for a visit," he said, "taking a look around to see what is going on, and after I have inspected everything, I will then come back to you."

(31) But as soon as the young man was alone, the Ethiopians returned with quite cruel and violent behaviour. They seized him not only by hand and foot, but also by the genitals, and thus trussed him up causing him extreme pain. Like a sparrow in the beak of a hawk, or like a dove plucked clean by the talons of an eagle, so was this miserable man grabbed by these reprobate spirits, carried in a horizontal position, suspended by his genitals, and taken away like a rich prize they had recovered after it was lost. But then blessed Peter appeared in a radiant light and in terrifying splendor, and striking like lightning, snatched their prey as if impelled by a violent wind, and fiercely beat those evil robbers with the keys he held in his hand. Thereupon he took him home, reunited soul and body, and restored both to health.

53. See *supra*, n. 10.

When the young man had promptly recovered, he disposed of his house without delay, and proceeding to the monastery of Cluny, received the monastic habit with exemplary devotion. So it was that this fugitive from the service of God, taught from on high by the scourge administered by his Father, was freed from the cruel hands of the spoiler, and the errant sheep was called back to the hut of its own shepherd.

(32) But now it is time for my pen to be quiet and to put an end to its writing, lest it exceed epistolary conciseness and breach the rules of brevity. And if you should find it to your liking, you might inscribe this distich in the refectory, under the feet of the apostles:

Fiery tongues then appeared to inflame the assembled apostles,
Like a bounteous voice from on high, they now grow to produce divers
  language.[54]

54. Petrus Damiani, *Ubi Spiritus Sanctus descendit super apostolos* (ed. M. Lokrantz, *L'opera* no. L, 61).

LETTER 103

Peter Damian to Hugh, the abbot of Cluny. In exchange for his services to Cluny on the occasion of his dangerous trip through the Alps on their behalf, Damian extracted from Hugh the written promise to offer a perpetual memorial on the anniversary of his death, and to feed and clothe a poor man in perpetuity. Fearing that the promise might be forgotten, he reminds Hugh to be true to his word, and to include in these suffrages all the other houses subject to his jurisdiction. His epigram on this subject (Lokrantz, no. XCVII) may well have been included in this letter.

(End of 1063 or early 1064)[1]

TO SIR HUGH, the abbot of estimable holiness,[2] the monk Peter the sinner, his servant whatever it is worth.

(2) When a person looks for one thing and finds something quite different, the searcher's purpose is not fulfilled. It was Paul who complained that when he asked that Satan's messenger be taken from him, the sharp physical pain was not removed, as he had urged, but he was reminded that God's grace was all that he needed.[3] Moses, too, prayed to the Lord who spoke to him, asking him to appear to him face to face, but his prayer was not answered.[4] But on another occasion, when the Lord said that he would make a great nation spring from him, if he so wished, he heard him say, "Now, let me alone to vent my anger upon this people, so that I might put an end to them and make a great nation spring from you."[5] To this Moses unrestrainedly replied, "If you will forgive them this sin, forgive. But if not, blot out my name from the book which you have written."[6] In one case, therefore, that which Moses did not want, God's liberality freely gave him; but in another case, what he eagerly begged for, God would in no way grant. In his petition, however,

---

1. Dating follows Lucchesi, *Vita* no. 180.
2. On Hugh of Cluny, see *Letter* 100, n. 5.
3. Cf. 2 Cor 12.9. 4. Cf. Exod 33.18–23.
5. Exod 32.10. 6. Exod 32.31–32.

142

Solomon was the more fortunate of the two, in that along with
the docile spirit he requested, he received both glory and wealth
for which he did not ask. For God said to him, "Therefore I
grant your request; I give you a heart so wise and so understanding that there has been none like you before your time nor will
be after you. I give you furthermore those things for which you
did not ask, such wealth and honor as no king before your time
can match."[7]

(3) The reason for prefacing these remarks, however, I will
now briefly explain. In your holy prudence, venerable father,
you are certainly aware, that as I was already experiencing the infirmities of old age, and because of my body's lack of strength, I
had begun to totter with uncertain steps, yet at your command I
took my life in my own hands, so to speak, and climbed the
craggy Alps, covered with summer snows, and went into the interior of Gaul, quite near the ocean,[8] for the benefit of your esteemed monastery. In compensation for this great effort I especially beg that since you and your incomparably holy community
have promised me in writing always to keep alive the memory of
the anniversary of my death, and through all succeeding ages to
commend me to the dread Judge by your pious prayers for the
dead. To this solemn promise was added that on my behalf you
would in perpetuity support one poor man with food and clothing. This is the fruit of my labor, the reward for my effort, this is
my retaliation.

(4) But while your liberality has rewarded me with such bounteous and precious gifts, I have reason to fear that once the task
was finished and a certain amount of earthly compensation had
been paid, I would be deprived of this blessed gift of your
prayers. For after a day's wage has been given for a day's work,
there is nothing more that a worker can hope for, unless perhaps, like Solomon, it should be my lot to obtain both what he

7. 1 Kgs 3.12–13.
8. He may have thought that Cluny lay near the Mediterranean Sea, or, because of his long trip, made more difficult by his infirmities, was deceived in
placing it near the Atlantic. In any event, his knowledge of the geography of
France, to him a *terra incognita*, was uncertain. For his journey to Cluny, see *Letter* 100, n. 2. At best, he went as far as Limoges in Hugh's interest, still some 120
miles from the coast.

asked for, and to receive besides that which he had not re-quested.[9] While satisfied with the first, however, I would never be pleased with the other; and as I earnestly request the gift of your holy prayers, and eagerly long for it with all my heart, I make light of any earthly benefit, no matter how expensive or difficult to bestow. Even though your charity be both so total and so perfect that it abundantly provides both with no less liberality to those it judges to be its friends, for me the one will suffice, and I do not request the other. Indeed, an unfortunate suspicion lurks at the back of my head, that while worldly rewards are offered to me, the spiritual remuneration will somehow be diminished. For on the scales by which I judge, the farthing of your holy prayers weighs more than a talent of gold or a heap of glittering gems. In fact, it is that gold which I seek, that which I firmly hope will be given to me, of which it was written, "The elders held golden bowls full of incense, the prayers of the saints."[10] I prefer this gold to all the wealth that one can hope to obtain, this I eagerly embrace, and by comparison belittle all the goods one may search for on earth.

(5) Wherefore, venerable father, I appeal to your kind charity that the protocol containing your solemn promise, written for the holy monastery of Cluny, also be sent in writing to the other houses that are subject of your authority.[11] Once again I humbly call attention to your goodness, and in tears prostrate myself and embrace your holy feet, that what you saw fit to promise me by issuing this memorial document, should at your command be copied in the other monasteries that are under your jurisdiction. But if the rustic style of my petition should not prove effective, may the Holy Spirit, who dwells in the recesses of your heart, lovingly inspire you to grant my prayers. Just as I have no doubt that I would offer my body to cruel torments for you, so through your intercession may God's mercy see fit to free my soul from the pains of hell, and by the memorial written in your hand may I deserve to be enrolled in the company of the saints.

---

9. Cf. Wis 7.11.   10. Rev 5.8.

11. While the necrologies of Cluny for this period have not survived, Damian's name does appear in the necrology of Bernold of Constance; cf. Dressler, *Petrus Damiani* 83, n. 375, and Damian, *Letter* 113.

LETTER 104

Peter Damian to the empress Agnes. Some years after the death of her husband, Henry III, on 5 October 1056, Agnes forsook her imperial estate and entered the religious life. She came to Italy, staying for a year (1062–1063) in the monastery of Fruttuaria, where Damian visited her. Probably in the spring of 1063 Agnes came to Rome, and there in St. Peter's Damian heard her general confession. Later in the same year she was again in Rome to celebrate Christmas, and again Damian had a chance to talk with her. Upon his return to Fonte Avellana in January 1064, he wrote to her, recalling these events, and counseling her to continue in her new way of life. He seemed to hope that this letter would be widely circulated, and that its readers would be edified by the example of an empress embracing the monastic vocation, disdaining her former wealth, engaging in a life of prayer, and exchanging her deceased imperial husband for the King of heaven. Lest she reconsider her choice, he used a remarkable display of detail to demonstrate the unhappy end of many great men and women in Roman history who excessively loved the pleasures of the world. He begged her to persevere in her new role as the spouse of the Redeemer. An interesting sidelight of this letter is his reference to two lunar eclipses, one in 1056, the other in early April 1062, two years before his present letter.

(1063–1065)[1]

O THE EMPRESS AGNES,[2] hedged round by the shield of God's favor,[3] the monk Peter the sinner sends his service. (2) The Queen of Sheba came to Jerusalem to listen to the wisdom of Solomon;[4] the empress Agnes traveled to Rome to

1. The dating of this letter, written after the empress Agnes had traveled to Rome, depends on the length of her stay in that city. Various dates in 1063 and 1064 have been assigned by research in this matter. A review of the data appears in Struve, *Romreise* (1985) 3, n. 15, where the author opted for 1065.

2. On Agnes and Damian, see Bulst-Thiele, *Agnes* 87ff. and 104ff. See also Wilmart, *Une lettre* 128, 134. Damian also wrote *Letters* 71, 124, 130, 144, and 149 to Agnes.

3. Cf. Ps 5.13.

4. Cf. 1 Kgs 10.1; 2 Chr 9.1. See also Struve, *Romreise* 19, n. 95, where he refers to a poem, written by a monk, Arnulf, comparing Henry III to Solomon and Agnes to the Queen of Sheba.

learn the foolishness of the Fisherman. For as Paul says, "Since the world failed to find God by its wisdom, he chose to save those who have faith by the folly of the Gospel."[5] As sacred history reports, the former arrived with a large retinue and great riches, with camels laden with spices, gold in great quantity, and precious stones.[6] But the latter with her relative, Ermensinde,[7] both equally aglow with the ardor of the Holy Spirit, came to the sepulcher like Mary Magdalen and the other Mary,[8] not to anoint with aromatic oil the body of Jesus, but to wash his feet with their tears. They were not seeking among the dead for one who was alive, but in adoration they followed in the footsteps of him who had risen from the dead. The earthly Solomon resolved the knotty problems and mysterious puzzles of the Queen of Sheba, but our queen had nothing to loosen but the fetters of her sins.[9] For Solomon was the figure of Christ,[10] and like some image or prophecy represented the figure of our Savior. It was said of him that "he uttered three thousand proverbs, and his songs numbered five thousand." And then the text went on to say that "he discoursed of trees, from the cedar of Lebanon down to the hyssop that grows out of the wall, of beasts and birds, of reptiles and fishes."[11]

(3) No one who carefully examines the matter, can doubt that all of this is in keeping with our Redeemer. He, indeed, proclaimed three thousand parables, when in discussing the mystic deeds of the Fathers who preceded him, the allegorical utterances of the prophets, or also the shining pages of the Gospel he explained almost all of them under the guise of symbols, thus

5. 1 Cor 1.21.   6. Cf. 1 Kgs 10.2.
7. Ermensinde was the sister-in-law of Agnes, who in 1050 had married Peter William VII, the duke of Aquitaine and the count of Poitou. After his death in 1058 she vowed never to marry again. Damian wrote Letter 136 to her and also referred to her in Letter 124.
8. Cf. Matt 28.1; Mark 16.1.
9. Struve, Romreise 21, n. 101, and others, see in this statement a reference to the guilt of Agnes in taking part in the illegal promotion of Cadalus to the papacy.
10. On Solomon as a figure of Christ, see Schramm, Staatslehre 127–130. A letter ascribed to Damian on the possibility of Solomon's salvation, was considered spurious by this edition on the basis of MS ascription and style.
11. 1 Kgs 4.32–33. Cf. Biblia sacra 6.96 for variants from the Vulgate.

seemingly reaching the number of three thousand parables in his sermons. And so Matthew says in the Gospel, "In all his teaching to the crowds Jesus spoke in parables; in fact, he never spoke to them without using parables."[12] His songs also came to five thousand, because the choir of virgins, who are spoken of in terms of five,[13] always sing a new song before his throne, as John relates in the Apocalypse.[14] Or, we may use the same number because of the five wounds the Lord bore in his body,[15] which proclaim his glorious victory throughout the world, and by which his unique victory won for him the glory of everlasting praise.

(4) And thus, when it is said in Canticles, "Rise up, my darling, my fairest, come away, my dove that hides in holes in the cliffs and in crannies on the high ledges," the text continues, "Let me see your face, let me hear your voice, for your voice is pleasant."[16] Now, while not going into detail, but handling these words only briefly and in passing, it will suffice to say that since the rock is Christ, the holes in the cliff are undoubtedly the wounds in the Lord's body. But when the voice of the bride is asked to speak to the groom from the holes in the cliff, what else is meant here but that each soul, or the entire holy Church should give praise to the five wounds in the same number of hymns? Thus, as it were, by singing the same number of hymns, the Christian soul will not forget the wounds that were borne for it, and will dedicate all its bodily senses to him whom it beholds bearing these wounds on its behalf. Truly, the wounds in our five senses were healed by the five wounds in the Lord's body.

(5) Now Solomon was said to have discoursed of trees, from the cedar of Lebanon down to the hyssop that grows out of the wall. To this I will have to give a spiritual interpretation, since the literal meaning can hardly make sense. For hyssop is never seen growing from walls, but rather has its habitat in craggy moun-

---

12. Matt 13.34.   13. Cf. Matt 25.1–2.
14. Cf. Rev 14.3.
15. On honoring the number five as a symbol of Christ's wounds, see Gougaud, *Dévotions* 74–128.
16. Cant. 2.13–14; for variants from the Vulgate, see *Biblia sacra* 11.183 citing Bede, *In cantica canticorum allegorica expositio* 3 (PL 91.1111CD, 1113, and 1114A).

tains.[17] And so, the wall is our mortal condition which, like the obstacle of a house that stands in the way, hinders us from the contemplation of our Creator and compels us to turn our attention to things below. "A perishable body weighs down the soul, and its frame of clay burdens the mind so full of thoughts."[18] Consequently, hyssop grows from this wall because it springs from the weakness of our mortality, which must always be cut away with the knife of penance. For we use hyssop to purge the bowels, an apt figure of the confession of sins.[19]

(6) Our Solomon, therefore, "discoursed of trees," that is, of men rooted in the woodland of a fertile Church. "From the cedar of Lebanon, down to the hyssop which grew from the wall,"[20] that is, from the great saints, clothed in the splendor of justice, down to sinners and fallen men, converted at length to bewail their sins through penance. And then the text continues, "He spoke of beasts," namely of Catholic men who were the helpers of the saints. "And of birds," that is, of men lifted up to heaven by their holy desires. "And of reptiles and fish," that is, of those who crawl along the earth on the belly of their concupiscence, and who wander at large through the stream of worldly affairs. It is also said that "Solomon's wisdom surpassed the wisdom of all the men of the East and all of Egypt,"[21] because our Redeemer exceeded the understanding of angels and men. "He had forty thousand cavalry horses and twelve thousand horsemen."[22] What was prefigured by the number four but the team of the four evangelists? And what did the number twelve represent if not the senate of the apostles? Indeed, on the doctrine of the Gospels and of the apostles the Lord rode through the whole world. "Ten thousand were God's chariots, thousands upon thousands rejoiced when the Lord came in them to Sinai, the holy mountain."[23] For since "Sinai" may be taken to mean "commandment,"[24] it is clear that the Lord will ride only in those who observe his heavenly commands.

17. Cf. Isidore, *Etymologies* 43.9.39.　　18. Wis 9.15.
19. Cf. Isidore, *Etymologies* 17.9.39.　　20. 1 Kgs 4.33.
21. 1 Kgs 4.30.　　22. 1 Kgs 4.26.
23. Ps 67.18.
24. Cf. Jerome, *Nom. hebr.* 81.17 (CC 72.161).

(7) It must be noted, however, that just as the kingdom of David who had to endure so much distress, is a figure of the Lord still at work during his mortal life, so the incomparable glory of the reign of Solomon prefigured the same Lord ruling in the majesty of his Father's glory after the end of the world.[25] And so, in the book cited above, it says that "there was no silver, and it was reckoned of no value in the days of Solomon."[26] But how can this be taken literally, so that one might believe that in Solomon's time there was no silver at all, and thus had completely disappeared from the earth, or that it had not the slightest value? For, as was said, if it was of no value, a thousand talents of silver could not buy even a single egg. But how foolish and absurd it would be to believe this, is shown by the text and what it goes on to say. For after stating, "There was no silver, and it was reckoned of no value in the days of Solomon," it continues, "The king had a fleet of merchantmen at sea with Hiram's fleet; once every three years this fleet visited Tharsis and came home, bringing gold and silver."[27] Why should his fleet carry this metal through such dangerous waters if it was totally worthless? And shortly thereafter the text says that "vessels of gold and silver were brought to him."[28] And following that it was stated that "chariots were imported from Egypt for six hundred shekels of silver each, and horses for a hundred and fifty."[29]

(8) Therefore, silver was not worthless if horse-drawn vehicles could be bought with it. So, by silver was meant the brilliance of the Church's teaching, of which it is said, "The words of the Lord are pure as silver."[30] But we will consider the silver of this holy teaching, if I might put it so, as having no value, nor shall we have any further use for it once we have been brought from this calamitous age into the kingdom of the true Solomon. For then we shall not need the words of a teacher when we shall see face to face the King of glory in his splendor, whom we used to hear speaking through the lips of the preacher. This the Lord prom-

25. On David as the figure of the earthly ruler, see E. H. Kantorowicz, *The King's Two Bodies. A Study in Mediaeval Political Theology* (1957) 77, 81ff.

26. 1 Kgs 10.21.   27. 1 Kgs 10.21–22.

28. 1 Kgs 10.25.   29. 1 Kgs 10.29.

30. Ps 11.7.

ised by the prophet when he said, "No one will say: Know the Lord; all of them, high and low alike, shall know me, says the Lord."[31]

(9) But perhaps someone will claim that I am violently distorting the words of Scripture to my own purposes, stating that what Solomon seems to be saying of himself, in all cases pertains in a special way to the Savior. But let him who so objects tell me, how these words, apparently spoken of himself, can be applied to Solomon, "God gave me a true understanding of things as they are: a knowledge of the structure of the world and the operation of the elements; the beginning and end of epochs and their middle course; the alternating solstices and the changes of men; the cycles of the year and the constellations of the stars; the natures of living creatures and the behavior of wild beasts; the violent force of winds and the thoughts of men. I learned it all, things hidden and unforeseen."[32] Now to pass over for a moment all other matters, how could Solomon have known the thoughts of men, since in another text he himself said to God, "You alone know the hearts of all men"?[33] And who, moreover, learned all things hidden and unforeseen except our Redeemer, "in whose heart lie hidden all treasures of wisdom and knowledge"?[34] It was he, to be sure, who learned through his humanity what he naturally knew through his divinity.[35]

(10) And thus, O queen, you have recently come to this Solomon, not like the Queen of Sheba with chariots and horses and elephants, but rather with tears, sighs, and lamentation. Therefore, you are the true Queen of Sheba. "Sheba" may be said to mean "lowly situated or in the plain."[36] And "in the plain" is an apt description. For you might come down into the field of battle that you might engage in hand to hand combat, and standing bravely for the army of Christ, you valiantly fight the enemy. You have come, I say, not that he might solve for you your doubts and mysterious riddles, but to open the door of the heavenly king-

---

31. Jer 31.34.   32. Wis 7.17–21.
33. 2 Chr 6.30.   34. Col 2.3.
35. See Cantin, *Sciences séculières* 567.
36. Cf. Jerome, *Nom. hebr.* 66.29 (CC 72.143), s.v. Arabes. Isidore, *Etymologies* 9.2.18 identifies Sheba as Arabia.

dom through the good offices of the simple bearer of the keys. With humility you have come to him who was lowly, in poverty to him who was poor, and like the roughshod and unlettered shepherds, you have come to adore the child crying in a manger.[37]

(11) To have seen you and those of your company at that moment was a marvelous spectacle to behold, and an edifying example of imitating the Savior. Your garments were gray and were made of wool. The animal you rode—I will not call it a horse, but rather a mule or a pony—was hardly larger than a listless donkey. You exchanged your crown for a veil, purple for sackcloth, and your hand, soft as a dove, which was accustomed to bear the scepter, was now rough from carrying a psalter. Indeed, because "all the glory of the daughter of kings is from within,"[38] the beauty of sparkling jewels and the elegance of attire, glittering with gold, have now gone into hiding, and the inner comeliness of the bride is resplendent only in the eyes of the hidden beholder. And the groom will say to her, "You are beautiful, my dearest, beautiful without a fault."[39] And again, "You are beautiful, my dearest, sweet and lovely."[40] Your delicate neck, from which formerly hung a necklace with golden trinkets and gleaming pearls, is now irritated by the neckline of your woolen dress. Hence the attendants of the heavenly groom flatter you and say, "We will make you braided plaits of gold set with beads of silver."[41] And again the groom will say, "Hurry down from the heights of Senir to be crowned, from Amana's top and Hermon's, from the lion's lairs, and the hills the leopards haunt."[42] Now Amana is said to be a mountain in Cilicia, which by many is called the Taurus.[43] Senir and Hermon are mountains in the land of Judah where lions and leopards were thought to live.[44]

(12) By these mountains we are to understand kings and princes and various powerful men of this world, who like mountains rise up in their pride and make their home with evil spirits that are like leopards and lions. From these mountains, there-

37. Cf. Luke 2.16.
38. Ps 44.14.
39. Cant 4.7.
40. Cant 6.3.
41. Cant 1.10.
42. Cant 4.8.
43. Cf. Isidore, *Etymologies* 14.8.3.
44. Cf. Hrabanus Maurus, *De universo* 10.1 (PL 111.359D).

fore, you will be crowned, for however many princes and powerful men of the world are converted to God by your example, to
that degree will you accumulate the rewards of eternal glory. Not
only will you be crowned, moreover, but as the prophet attests,
you will be that very crown, "You will be a glorious crown in the
Lord's hand, a kingly diadem in the hand of your God."[45]

(13) My queen, you have lost your husband, and after his
death declined marrying again or being engaged to any other
suitor, unless he were superior in dignity to the exalted status of
your former husband. What, therefore, were you to do? Your
husband had been the emperor, he was at the very peak of royal
power, and what was unique in human experience, he ruled as
monarch of the Roman world. And so, since he was so preeminent because of his exalted position, you could find no one in
the world who was superior to him. And since nowhere on earth
could you find a suitable husband, one who appealed to you, you
violently rushed to embrace the Spouse of heaven. I say violently,
for "the kingdom of heaven has been subjected to violence, and
violent men are seizing it."[46]

(14) Blessed be this pride, blessed this self-exaltation, worthy
of all possible praise, which by despising the bonds of earthly
marriage entered into glorious espousals with the eternal King.
An earthly husband, indeed, breaches the mysteries of virginity,
but the Spouse of heaven at once and without difficulty restores
virginal beauty, even when he is associated with those who have
lost it. This he does that they may divest themselves of the defiling squalor they have contracted, and like shrubs that have become dry, their leaves may once again be green in all their pris-
tine beauty. Besides, when a girl about to be married is provided
with an earthly husband,[47] she at once attempts to collect money
from all her relatives and friends, and whatever she can acquire,
she promptly stuffs into purses or chests that can be made secure. This she does, so that the greater her baggage when she
comes to her husband, the more pretentious she will appear and
the more ardent will be his love for her.

---

45. Isa 62.3.   46. Matt 11.12.
47. Cf. Bultot, *Pierre Damien* 106.

(15) But you, on the contrary, as you contracted marriage with your heavenly Spouse, gave away what had been collected in the royal treasury, and disbursed your gleaming pearls along with your gold and silver. Your tapestries done in purple, or rather in cloth of gold, hang from ceilings in the churches, and your royal ornaments serve the sacred altars. You spared nothing, so to speak, and only that was not given to the poor or to churches which was not your own property. You disposed of everything, you threw it all away that you might come to your heavenly Spouse's embrace completely unencumbered, even naked, I might say.

(16) Now, I make these things known, venerable empress, not on your account, since you, I fear, will be quite offended by my words, but rather that wherever your outstanding virtue is proclaimed, it may provide great edification for those who read of it.[48] For where such high estate has been cast off out of love for one's Creator, what neck will not relax the rigid tension with which pride had endowed it? What pompous attitude will not suddenly be deflated when it sees a ruler clothed with so much glory, now become as despicable as a slave? Who, moreover, will fear the loss of possessions that will pass away, when he beholds the voluntary poverty of a woman whom just a few years ago he saw ruling so many kingdoms? Or who will be horrified by rough attire, when he sees her royal majesty prefer cheap cloth to that woven with gold or to other kingly display?

(17) I come now to the table and, so to speak, to the starvation rations of your overflowing abundance. What is it like, I ask, to have heavily laden platters of food and splendid servings of meat everywhere on the tables before you, and not at times even to taste the fat of the meat; to have this fare in your hands, and never to let it pass your lips? Or what is more, only with the greatest precaution even to taste bread or other food indifferently prepared? Therefore, you often complained to me that you could hardly control the urge to eat or at times to indulge immoderately in the meal that was set before you. And so, you often

48. Here we have a clear example of either an "open letter," or of a piece made public after her death (†1077) to edify all who read it.

wept and lamented, and were deeply disturbed. You deplored this situation, because no matter how disciplined you were and exerted every precaution, you were never completely able to control your nature. But just as then, too, I was not silent, I must say, O queen, that your fasting is of many kinds. Off and on we abstain from food, but you have given up the purple, you refrain from using the crown and from all the magnificent display of imperial glory. To abstain from these things from which, indeed, one's earthly disposition derives pleasure and nourishment, is also undoubtedly fasting. For, as Scripture relates, if simple water that David poured out upon the ground was considered a sacrifice,[49] how greatly will one be rewarded by God for despising material things and worldly recognition?

(18) How severe was the abstinence and how praiseworthy for a young girl, accustomed to married life, to refrain from embracing her husband! Is this not also great fasting abnormally to deprive yourself of certain things becoming to your dignity, while in others you were attended with great honor, and now content with domestic trifles, to avoid the public eye and continually to devote yourself to prayer and psalmody? For as formerly you lived like Susanna with your husband,[50] you have now become like Anna after losing her husband.[51] And while then you blamelessly observed conjugal chastity, now with the daughter of Phanuel, which means the "temple of God," you never leave the church.

(19) And so it was, that through the good offices of the venerable Rainaldus, the bishop of Como, you asked me whether it was allowed to recite psalms while engaged in relieving nature on the toilet.[52] To which I replied in words that at that moment occurred to me, that almighty God visited blessed Job while he was seated on a dungheap,[53] and that the blessed martyr Agnes, for whom you were named, discovered both an angel and the

---

49. Cf. 2 Sam 23.15–17. 50. Cf. Dan 13.1–2.
51. Cf. Luke 2.36–37.

52. It seems clear that he is speaking of the "bathroom," and that the *debitum naturale* in the Latin text does not refer to the marriage act, as Lucchesi (*Vita* 2, no. 185) had conjectured. Moreover, the reference to Job and to the martyr Agnes are not appropriate to the latter explanation. See also Reindel, *Briefe* 3.150, n. 37.

53. Cf. Job 2.8.

garments supplied by him in common and filthy places in a brothel. For the Apostle tells us to pray everywhere, when he says, "It is my desire that men pray everywhere, lifting up their hands with pure intention, excluding angry or quarrelsome thoughts,"[54] even though it is generally better in such a place to pray mentally than to put your prayers into words. Even though this subject should properly be passed over in silence and not disclosed for popular discussion, still I will speak of it, that to my readers it may clearly be known how great was your love for God, that even for a short moment you would not refrain from praying to him. What will those say to that, who make of the church, not an oratory but a parlor, not a chapel but a meeting place, and by so doing engage in secular discourse in a house that was built only for the purpose of abstaining from all worldly affairs?

(20) But that those who come in great numbers to the basilica of the apostles may for their welfare imitate the example of your holy devotion, I will say that you had me be seated at the tomb of St. Peter before the sacred altar, and with much sorrow and bitter tears you began confessing what you had done from the tender age of five when you had hardly been weaned.[55] And just as if the blessed apostle were physically present there, you faithfully divulged every little thing that in your life could arouse your senses, everything that was untoward in thought, and everything unnecessary, moreover, that could steal into your speech. And when you were finished, I found it proper to impose no greater penance than that I should only repeat these words of divine commands, "Do what you are doing, work at the task you have undertaken,"[56] or the word that was sent by the angel to the men of Thyatira, "On you I will impose no further burden. Only hold fast to what you have."[57] For as God is my witness, I did not prescribe one day of fasting or any similar penance, but com-

---

54. 1 Tim 2.8.

55. Agnes made a general confession. But how could he write of these matters—even to her—without endangering the secrecy of confession? Did he ever send this letter to Agnes, or was it meant only for later "publication"? See Struve, *Romreise* 20; Bulst-Thiele, *Agnes* 105.

56. A proverb used by the Romans; see Gregory I, *Dialogi* 4.58 (Sources chrétiennes 265, vol. 3, 194).

57. Rev 2.24–25.

manded that you should only persevere in the holy deeds that you had begun.

(21) Would that such grief and tears might be forthcoming in confession from murderers and those guilty of various crimes, that the soul consumed by fear and transfixed by bitter sorrow might complain in like manner. Would that hearts harboring a bad conscience might sob in the same way, as here she lamented over every worthless thought and imagination, every foolish trifle from her childhood. Let those who come in their devotion to honor the bodies of the saints be challenged by this example. Here, then let them discharge the ill effects of their own sins as if they were toxic humors and diseases, those who through their efforts at true confession drink of the antidote of salutary penance, the better to be rid of them. Here let them resolve to receive the baptism of penance, and after being immersed in it by the sentence of the priestly office, let them put off the garments of their former human condition, that now they may live as new men who have emerged from the old.

(22) And now, my lady, since I have no doubt that you are the bride of my Redeemer, I do not blush to call you my lady. As I say, my lady, stand fast and persevere, be totally on fire with love of him to whom, through the hands of priests and of the poor, you have daily given everything, so that the prescriptions of the Law may rightly happen to you. For it says that, if one should perhaps fall in love with a woman captured in war and should wish to make her his wife, he must first shave her head, pare her nails, discard the clothes she had on when captured, and then lawfully marry her, making her a freeborn Israelite.[58] They have already begun to cut your hair and pare your nails, and to discard the clothes that covered you, for everything in your wardrobe that was beautiful, everything precious among your belongings that externally surrounded or adorned you, was daily disposed of in charitable works.

(23) Now it remains for you to come to the intimate delight of your bridegroom, to that sweet union where two hearts are like one. "He who links himself with the Lord is spiritually one

58. Cf. Deut 21.11–13.

with him,"[59] namely, that he may pour the essence of divine love into your innermost being, and ignite the secret recesses of your heart at the flame of his own sweetness, unknown to this poor world and to every soul attached to earthly things, that you might fervently cry out in the words of Canticles, "The throat of my beloved is sweetness itself, wholly desirable;"[60] that he in turn may gladly reply, "Your lips drop sweetness like the honeycomb, my bride, honey and milk are under your tongue, and your dress has the scent of incense."[61] Nor should you be disturbed if bad times perhaps afflict you; for this will happen, so that he who secretly disposes may attract you to this sweetness. For when a mother wishes to wean her son, she often puts something bitter on her breasts, so that when the youngster rejects that which makes him shudder, he may be forced to turn to food that will nourish him. Therefore, the king of Egypt was permitted to beat and oppress the people of Israel that they might be incited to travel more quickly to the promised land.

(24) But now turning to another subject, since by vicarious retaliation you hate the world and in turn are rejected as one whom it hates, has not the world been turned into bitterness for those kings who delighted in it and whom it flattered with captious deceit, so that today one may return victorious over the enemy, preceded by glorious and triumphant banners, and tomorrow be pierced by the enemy's sword as he flees in ignominy? The very day, for example, on which Belshazzar drunkenly dared to defile the vessels from the temple of the Lord at the lips of his concubines, he fell to the swords of the Medes when Darius won his victory.[62] Galba, the Roman emperor, ruled for only four months and died, struck down by the sword in the Roman forum. I will say nothing of Nero and will ignore Otho who, as the history of the Roman state tells us, died at their own hands.[63] Was not Vitellius slain by the commanders of Vespasian? And was not Pertinax killed by the Praetorian guard? Macrinus, Antoninus, Alexander, Philip, Gallienus, did not all these emper-

---

59. 1 Cor 6.17.   60. Cant 5.16.
61. Cant 4.11.   62. Cf. Dan 5.1–4, 30–31.

63. For these later Roman emperors, Damian is possibly citing at random from Eusebius, Eutropius, or Aurelius Victor.

ors die by the sword in battle? Domitian, moreover, was struck down by a conspiracy of his own men. As he made camp on the Tigris, Probus was suddenly killed by lightning from heaven.

(25) But if one should wish to be more fully informed on these matters, he should consult the histories of Roman antiquities about each of them, and there he will clearly see how few of the emperors died a natural death. Gordian and Philip, Decius, Gallus, Volusianus, Gallienus, Quintilius, Aurelian, Numerian, Licinius, Constans, Constantine the Younger, Julian the Apostate, Valens, Gratian, Valentinian the Younger, John; and also Valentinian the third, Majorianus, Anthemius, and Nepos—were not all these rulers of the Roman empire either assassinated in time of peace in a rebellion of their own men, or killed in battle by the sword of their enemies? But for some of them, how did they profit from enjoying a longer life in this world? For to omit all the details, the emperor Valerianus, while engaged in battle in Mesopotamia with Sapor, the king of the Persians, was defeated, promptly captured, and placed in chains under constant guard. As history relates, he grew old in slavery among the Parthians, and so long as he lived was subjected to the ignominious punishment of having the king of that province place his foot upon his neck as he bent over, and thus proudly mount his horse.[64]

(26) And who is there that fortune does not influence, with dramatic variety now changing bad times into good and then good times into bad? Indeed, what glory and good repute among his people did Hannibal not enjoy, when at Cannae he defeated Aemilius Paulus and so many men of the Roman army, and when at length three measures of golden rings, taken from the hands of the Roman cavalry, senators, and infantry, were sent to Carthage?[65] He also captured many cities in Italy, so that the citizens of Rome decided to leave Italy, completely despairing of the state of the collapsing empire. But how this success was changed into its very opposite, when his brother Mago was captured by Scipio at Cartagena in Spain, when the head of another

64. See Eutropius, *Breviarium* 9.7, 152 and Paulus Diaconus, *Historia Romana* 9.7, 152, esp. 127.
65. Cf. Eutropius 3.11 (MGH Auct. ant. 2.54).

brother, Hasdrubal, was cut off with a sword and thrown into Hannibal's camp, and when at length he himself, after futilely trying to flee, in this necessity was compelled to die by poison at his own hand?

(27) What an ill-fated change in fortune was the lot of the famous Pompey who, after so many triumphs and outstanding victories achieved in various parts of the world, and after defeating twenty-two kings in the East, was cut down by the sword of the despicable Achillas? Caesar, too, who was so set on winning, that the whole western world could not satisfy his ambition, for whom the troublesome and proud ocean, I might say, stood in his way like an obstacle contesting his advance, whose bloody swords could not be sated by the slaughter of countless nations, fell victim in the curia to the blades of the senators, by which he died, suffering twenty-two wounds.[66]

(28) And were women found to be immune to the wheel of fortune[67] in this deceptive world? Cleopatra, to be sure, was the magnificent ruler of all Egypt, which kingdom was said to contain one hundred thousand villages. And then it happened that Anthony, who held both the East and Asia, divorced the sister of the emperor Augustus and married Cleopatra under misfortunate forebodings.[68] But what an end was in store for this glorious and magnificent couple? Anthony, we know, was defeated by the emperor in the naval battle at Actium, fled to Egypt, and when the situation became desperate, committed suicide. Cleopatra, on the other hand, forced by similar necessity, of her own accord took refuge in the splendid tomb of her husband, held an asp to her breast, and died as it sucked her blood and she contracted its poison.[69] Semiramis, too, how much slaughter she caused, and how many kingdoms she subdued after the death of her husband, and how finally she died, all of this the ancient annals relate.[70]

66. Cf. Eutropius 6.25 (MGH Auct. ant. 2.112), where the number of wounds amounts to twenty-three.

67. On the wheel of fortune, see Cicero, In L. Calpurnium Pisonem oratio 10.22; Boethius, Philosophiae consolatio 2.2, ed. L. Bieler (CC 94 [1957] 20).

68. Cf. Eutropius, Breviarium 7.6 (MGH Auct. ant. 2.116).

69. Cf. Eutropius, Breviarium (Iordanis ad 1.17) 7.7 (MGH Auct. ant. 22.116−117).

70. For this queen of Assyria, cf. Iustinus, Epitoma historiarum Philippicarum Pompei Trogi 1.1.10−2.13.

(29) Since, therefore, the false happiness of this world is subject to so many calamities; since temporal power is affected by such changing conditions, and the state of affairs is thrown into confusion like the constant deviation one witnesses on the stage, what sensible person would not hold back from things so frivolous and fleeting? For lest I forget to refer to events that are well known to you, what glory attended Pope Victor[71] and your husband, the emperor Henry,[72] both of holy memory, when both were in good health and held in high esteem, with the moon bathing the earth in all its tranquil splendor. But suddenly an eclipse occurred, the moon began to wane, and exchanged its mirror-like golden-red brilliance for not just some obscure pallor, but rather for complete darkness. As would become evident from what followed, this event was a portent of the approaching death of both rulers. For both died that same year.[73]

(30) But that afterwards—and this happened almost two years ago—the moon was turned into blood, because, as Scripture says, blood signifies sins. "My God, deliver me from blood,"[74] to my way of thinking, this prefigured nothing else but the holy Church stained with the bloody crimes of Cadalus.[75] Countless times he was condemned for distributing vast sums of money among the people, trying to buy the Roman Church, and through avarice turned the hearts of men into the likeness of brass as though he were changing them into blood. And thus, when destructive men continuously have the rusty appearance of this metal, the brilliance of the Church seems to be turned into blood. For what the heart desires, causes it to assume that object's appearance in the sight of God. But more about this later.

71. Pope Victor II died on 28 September 1057.
72. Emperor Henry III died on 5 October 1056.
73. For literature detailing medieval eclipses, see Reindel, *Briefe* 3.156, nn. 60–61. But, as Damian maintains, Victor and Henry did not die in the same year.
74. Ps 50.16.
75. For this reference to Cadalus as represented by the second eclipse of the moon, see Reindel, *Briefe* 3.156–157, nn. 61–63. Damian attaches significance to the ruddy coloration of the moon on the second occasion by referring it to Cadalus' blood lust or to the color of the money Cadalus lavishly distributed.

(31) And now to return to the subject from which I digressed: all men, whether they be powerful or in want, all have the same origin and all will have the same end. Between these two limits, however, there is a certain difference of lifestyle, in that some take pride in being perceived as great, while others bewail their poverty. Yet this diversity of human life is ended by the momentary nature of time, so that distinguished men will no longer enjoy their good fortune, and the lowly will quickly escape from the misfortunes of their mean estate. Therefore, as to our beginning and to our end, these, as I said above, we cannot alter, for we all alike who share mortality will possess them without distinction. But listen to what the wise man says in the book of Wisdom, "I too am a mortal man like all the rest, descended from the first man, who was made of dust, and in my mother's womb I was wrought into flesh during a ten-month space, compacted in blood from the seed of her husband and the pleasure that is joined with sleep. When I was born, I breathed the common air and was laid on the earth that all men tread; and the first sound I uttered, as all do, was a cry; they wrapped me up and nursed me and cared for me. No king begins life in any other way." And then he promptly adds, "for all come into life by a single path, and by a single path go out again."[76]

(32) If, therefore, we pay close attention to the single path by which life comes and by which it leaves again, the variety that lies between will necessarily be despised as if it were a passing fancy and a fleeting dream. And the statement made above, "During a ten-month space I was compacted in blood from the seed of her husband and the pleasure that was joined with sleep," if it will not be untoward to take careful note, what person upon hearing this will be able to remain haughty and arrogant? And who will not constantly be reminded of his rottenness, when he thinks of his vile origin, saying to himself, "What do you have to be proud of, dust and ashes?"[77] And that after his death he will first be the food of worms, and then dust? Therefore, a proud man should be embarrassed, and whoever observes that between birth and

76. Wis 7.1–6.
77. Sir 10.9.

death he is bound by the laws of a nature common to us all, will stop boasting of his uniquely glorious condition.

(33) Now you, venerable lady, who have risen from the banquet of earthly pride to the high estate of true humility, remain steadfastly at this summit, persevere in that land of the living which once you attained through hope, so that you may never again fall back into the morass of a secular life. For while formerly you were the wife of the earthly emperor, now by the dowry of your holy profession you have become the bride of our Redeemer. Therefore, surrender yourself to him with true humility of heart, so unite yourself with him in the bonds of fervent love, that you might join in singing with that mystic bride, "I met my true love; I seized him and would not let him go."[78] And further, "My beloved will lie on my breast."[79] And since the heart of man lies hidden beneath the breast, may the constant love of your spouse never depart from the depths of your heart. And as now your holy soul is joined with him in love, may it never be snatched from his sweet embrace, so that in you the prophecy of Isaiah may be solemnly fulfilled, "And your God will rejoice over you as a bridegroom rejoices over the bride."[80]

78. Cant 3.4.   79. Cant 1.12.
80. Isa 62.5.

LETTER 105

Peter Damian to Bonizo, the former abbot of St. Peter in Perugia. He congratulates the abbot for having renounced his prelacy to become a hermit in Damian's Congregation of the Holy Cross. With biting irony he tells of his admiration for certain newly elected abbots: how in one day they learn what for ten years as subjects had escaped them; how serious of mien they are, how imperious in voice, how sharp in reprimand, how prompt to judge. They seem not to have been only recently elected, but to have been born an abbot. Bonizo can now lay aside the worldly cares his office required, his involvement in military affairs and building projects, and can concentrate on the spiritual life. He warns against the temptation to reconsider his decision, and prays that the abbot will stand firm. In return for this lengthy epistolary concern, Damian asks for Bonizo's prayers.

(Somewhat after January 1064)[1]

O THE MOST ASCETIC ABBOT, Sir Bonizo,[2] the monk Peter the sinner sends all due respect and service.

(2) Dear father, I give proper thanks to God, the author of all good things, who through his Spirit taught you to lay aside the withered staff of empty honor and to hasten with quickened steps to provide for the care of your own soul. Now you have become my abbot after you ceased being in command of others. You have been freed from the yoke of various services, and by God's mercy have been restored to genuine liberty. For, of necessity you were the slave of worldly men, and also the slave of the monks. The former you served lest they do harm to your monastery; but the latter that they might not conspire to become a roadblock to your efforts. Indeed, you feared the former who might steal the property of the house of God, and the latter lest they contrive to form a seditious clique against you. And while

---

1. Dating follows Lucchesi, *Vita* no. 184.
2. On the high probability that this letter was addressed to Abbot Bonizo of St. Peter in Perugia, cf. Reindel, *Briefe* 3.159, n.1.

one head was subject to so many masters, the unhappy soul, as it were, was held captive by multiple chains, preventing it from following in the footsteps of its Creator.

(3) Tell me, father, I pray you, as an expert tell me, who in this iron age can govern a monastery without endangering his life, and what is more, who can be an abbot and a monk at the same time? For as soon as one becomes an abbot, he ceases being a monk. To strive for the office of abbot seems to be nothing short of laying aside the unbearable burden of being a monk, and lest one seem to be an apostate, he tries to hide under the false colors of authority. And thus, that he might hide his sin, he searches for the artifice of higher office. He covers himself with the defective skin of pastoral care, that he might hide the infection of a perverse mind under the unadulterated filth of a polluted man. To such, surely, the statement in the Gospel aptly applies, "Alas for you," it says, "you are like tombs covered with whitewash; they look well from outside, but inside they are full of dead men's bones and all kinds of filth."[3]

(4) A monk is advised to die to the world, but how does an abbot fulfill this injunction when he is overwhelmed by so many disturbing areas and is implicated in so many perplexing secular affairs? He spends the day in discussing and handling various matters, and half the night in giving advice. He has no time to recite Compline with the community and always says Prime before the sun has risen. And when the whole community is observing silence, he is never among them with unsullied lips. Nor is his tongue then prepared to speak of heavenly things, since it was first debauched by such lengthy and involved discourse on earthly things.

(5) Moreover, since a monk is commanded to possess nothing in this world, to desire absolutely nothing, what monastic qualities do we find in that abbot whom we see belching flames like Mount Etna,[4] on fire with avarice, extending the boundaries of his lands, eager to collect money here and there, and striving with every fiber of his being to acquire that which belongs to oth-

3. Matt 23.27.
4. Cf. Isidore, *Etymologies* 14.3.46, 14.6.32 and 14.8.14.

ers? To him, whatever exists is nothing, unless he tries to get that too which he does not have. For him the monastery becomes a hostel, for he spends each day on horseback. Gauntlets, spurs, crops, cruppers, and other equipment used for riding are never left lying about and falling to pieces, while priestly attire used in the service of the holy altar is often found to be motheaten. Where can we find offices or tribunals in which abbots are not present? Which courts or princely chambers are not ransacked by the ironclad staves of abbots? Abbots are forever crossing the threshold of princes, and their complaints and arguments importune the ears of kings. Armed camps do not escape them, but you will often see cowled heads scattered among the pressing crowd of helmeted men in armor, present under the guise of negotiating peace

(6) If you wish to know what is going on in the courts of public law, do not inquire in judicial quarters, but rather in lodgings where abbots are staying. Whatever is happening in the world should be sought from them as from instructors in secular affairs. But since the Lord says, "Keep a watch on yourselves; do not let your minds be dulled by dissipation and drunkenness and worldly cares";[5] and again, "No one can serve two masters,"[6] with which the Apostle agrees when he exclaims, "A soldier on active duty for God will not let himself be involved in civilian affairs; he must be wholly at his commanding officer's disposal,"[7] what else can we think of him who is so fully attuned to earthly news and still voluntarily seeks to govern a monastery, but that he is now tired of fighting for Christ and loathes any further service? And since he refuses to carry on his tender shoulders the yoke of Christ, which is indeed easy to bear,[8] he no longer aspires to join him at his banquet. In the words of Truth itself, this refreshment is promised to those who do not grow weary under this light load: "Come to me," he says, "all you whose work is hard and whose load is heavy, and I will give you relief."[9]

(7) Furthermore, anyone who wishes to leave the service be-

---

5. Luke 21.34.
6. Matt 6.24; Luke 16.13.
7. 2 Tim 2.4.
8. Cf. Matt 11.30.
9. Matt 11.28.

fore going into battle, does not deserve to have citizenship in the heavenly fatherland. And he for whom the fight is too heavy will never be able to receive the crown of victory. This is especially true of him who, while avoiding the burdens of military service, ambitiously seeks to command the military operation. For while in the eyes of men he appears to be a leader in battle, he is rated by the hidden Judge as a faithless deserter. To avoid the danger of fighting, he pretends to carry the standard in place of the commander, but in fact he actually takes to flight. And he who in a company of knights could not even bring up the rear, by his desire to lead, is now viewed as the commander in the first wing of the army. This unhappy man fails to remember what the Holy Spirit so terrifyingly proclaims through the words of St. Benedict, "He who assumes the office of directing souls, should be prepared to render an account of his actions."[10] And again, "The abbot should know that he must give an account to God, the just Judge, for all his decisions."[11] And in another text he also says, "Let the abbot be aware that whatever the father of the family may find that is less proper in the sheep, redounds to the fault of the shepherd."[12] Whoever, then, should wish to be a judge of souls, must be aware of the stern and severe judgment that awaits him. For as Scripture says, "Strict justice will fall on those in high office."[13]

(8) One thing, moreover, that I observe in newly elected abbots greatly astounds me. This man who for ten years or more lived under the authority of another, was never able to learn how to be a perfect monk; but now on the very day he becomes abbot, he appears so like one in authority, and presents such a majestic figure, that you might say he was not just recently elected but was born an abbot. His face becomes suddenly stern, his voice imperious. He is sharp in correcting, prompt in reaching a decision, and if he gives offense, he is totally unaware that he should apologize. He refuses to be seated in anything but an octagonal chair, so constructed that it appears to be a curule chair for senators in the curia.[14] At his whim he orders some-

---

10. *Benedicti regula* c. 2.37, 28.   11. *Benedicti regula* c. 3.11, 31.

12. *Benedicti regula* c. 2.7, 22.   13. Wis 6.6.

14. Cf. Isidore, *Etymologies* 20.11. For *octogona* in the Latin text, see DuCange 8.27, s.v. *octachorum*.

thing to be done; others he decisively forbids, binds, looses, promotes, removes. And in all of this, he never seeks counsel of us younger monks, but self-sufficiently disposes as if he were the seat of autocratic power. To those, indeed, who are submissive and devoted to him he grants his favor; but he breathes fiery revenge on those who oppose him, acting rather like a secular prince than a humble minister of the Church. He turns up his nose at eating with us at the common table, so that it is necessary for the cooks to prepare many special dishes that will satisfy him alone. Ordinary food taken from the common pot that serves the brothers, he considers unworthy of the tender digestion of a delicate man. Recently having left the dormitory, he cannot sleep unless he has a private room all to himself. Although he is a young man, enjoying good health, he is unable to walk without a staff on which he can lean for support.

(9) And so, in these and many other matters which would take too long to pursue, he so quickly became a master, that in the whole scope of administration, like some ancient Father, he never seems to err. How learnedly, how imperiously he can teach everything as if endowed with some majestic authority, while for years as a subject he was never wise enough to obey his own teachers. I should describe the art of ruling as a discipline that is easily learned; for it is so quickly learned that anyone, even if he is incompetent in other matters, as soon as he takes it up, is regarded as a most expert master. And that one may more quickly grasp the subject, not only does it become at once self evident, but it totally wipes out from its student's mind the art of obeying, which is quite foreign to it. Many things, therefore, threaten the rulers of monasteries, because of which they either fail of their own accord, lured on by their very unrestrained immunity, or they blunder, even unwillingly, under pressure of the disturbances around them.

(10) Granted, moreover, that no secular annoyance afflicts them, and that everywhere the storm of the flood of earthly affairs quiets down, who can endure the evils of internal strife or even the irksomeness of the monks? Who can satisfy so many and such varied wills? Who can live with such differing and strange types of action? They, indeed, decide that their abbot

should lead a spiritual life, but force him to spend the whole day involved in secular affairs, lest ecclesiastical property be lost, and the house of God, which heaven forbid, begin to decline from its sound condition. They consider it more tolerable that all regular discipline should go to ruin because of the abbot's absence, than that the monastery's well-being and usefulness to the Church be impaired. If the abbot corrects offenders' sins and strictly punishes them, he is damned; if he acts leniently with them, he is thought to lack zeal for God's cause. If at times he remains silent, it is said that when the shepherd holds his tongue, the wolf attacks the flock.

(11) And if I may speak a bit more freely, how dare the abbot command others to observe silence when he is continuously chattering away himself? When he is fasting, they say he is looking for a pat on the back, and when the father eats pork, he is perceived as a step-father giving food to a stranger. Should he wear splendid attire, he is said to indulge in ostentatious display; but if he is satisfied with clothes that are poor or tattered, it is said that he brings shame on the monastery. If he preaches too long, the monks are disgusted and hold him in contempt, saying that his sermon puts them to sleep and does not promote edification. Should his words be brief, they say that since he did not make an effort to fill his own flask, he cannot provide for others. And a fountain that dries up along its course does not allow water to gush forth from the pipe.

(12) There is one thing which the monks consider highly in their abbot, and for which they give him highest marks, namely, if he is able to hold his own among the powerful of this world, if at will he can harm or help others, if he does not freeze while speaking in a crowd or in promoting his own interests. This is why in our day the monks wish no one to be their superior, unless he is of powerful and noble stature, and is distinguished because of the bloodline of his ancestors. Even though he be holy and outstanding for possessing every virtue, if he lacks these other natural qualities, and is even thought to be another Anthony, in everyone's opinion he would be considered unworthy of election. In addition, they will not permit anyone to be their abbot unless he comes from their own community. For if he is an

outsider, and were even endowed with the power of working miracles, he need not aspire to this high office.

(13) Indeed, the monks are fearful of ever giving the office to
strangers, and become alarmed should anyone presume to correct the slightest practice to which they were long accustomed,
lest, which God forbid, he teach them to mortify themselves, or
out of pure superstition compel them to fast; lest he teach them
to love poverty or command them to do something new, and
what would perhaps be still more intolerable for all, force them
to give up their own will. Thus, obviously, they prefer one of their
own, someone worthy of guarding a herd of swine, rather than
one who comes from outside their monastery, but is accomplished in holiness and in leading a religious life.

(14) In our day, to be sure, that abbot is praised and judged
worthy of the honor bestowed on him, if he is able to enlarge the
monastery's landed estate, to erect pretentious buildings, to amass
earthly goods, and to supply his monks, not only with the things
they need but also with what is superfluous. Moreover, if in caring
for such matters he neglects the cure of souls, the monks will say
that he should mercifully be forgiven this slight fault that counts
for little among so many other wonderful things he has done.
Each can surely provide for his own spiritual welfare, but not
everyone is able to perform such difficult and necessary tasks. In
this view, it is easy to forgive when one neglects such minor things,
so that he might occupy himself with more weighty matters.

(15) But if the abbot is remiss in attending to external things
and is preoccupied with the spiritual, the monks grumble and
protest, and everyone complains that the physical plant is going
to wrack and ruin. "Look," they say, "our holy monastery is falling
to pieces, our holdings are being diminished, and because of
one man's carelessness the welfare of the whole community is
left unattended. Let's do some accounting and tally it all up.
After this man unfortunately took office, for which he was not
prepared, what equipment and of what quality did he add to the
church, how many manorial holdings did he acquire? Where did
he extend the boundaries of our land? Clearly, if we look carefully into this matter, our monastery did not expand in his time,
but in many ways it has rather become smaller."

(16) Therefore, abbots are often under attack for having allowed these and similar calamities, and disturbed by the ill will of their subjects, can hardly lead a quiet life or devote themselves to the welfare of souls as their office requires. But as I speak of such matters that touch the evil lives of certain abbots or monks, no one should suspect that along with them I am attacking other upright and religious men. Indeed, I humbly kiss and embrace their feet, and in them, as is proper, pay my respects to Christ. Nor do I slander these other monks or blacken their reputation, but rather with brotherly compassion sympathize with them that their way of life should be considered so blameworthy. Quite clearly, by failing to reform their dissolute lives, not only are they a source of scandal to us, but also provide laymen an opportunity to disparage and hate the religious life.

(17) Therefore, my dear friend, you have acted laudably and with great prudence by laying aside the heavy burden of this fruitless effort, and with lightened shoulders have taken up a life of retirement and fruitful rest. Flesh and blood did not advise you, but rather from on high a merciful God inspired you. And so you are now free to devote greater care to your own salvation, secure from rendering a multiple account for the souls of others.

(18) But since the ancient enemy of the human race, who has a thousand ways of doing harm, never ceases afflicting the hearts of the servants of God, and does not allow them leisure from the many temptations he may devise, you would be well advised to devote more attention to your own welfare, since now you need no longer provide for the care of others. You have, indeed, changed your place of living, but not your enemy, and wherever you go, whether you wish it or not, you carry with you the burden of your own sinfulness. From this source it is certain that thorns and thistles will never cease to grow,[15] and you should be prepared to work tirelessly at uprooting them. There are no longer men who devise the means of piercing you with the arrows that fly from their tongues, but invisible enemies are at hand who never give up their fierce fight against you. The former, to be sure, are able to compose their senseless differences with you

15. Cf. Gen 3.18.

through easy reconciliation; but the latter can never enter into peaceful relations with men. The former knew only how to attack you with external weapons; but the latter savagely fight within the walls of your mind and do battle within the very city of your heart. And that this contest might appear even more dangerous, they find within your own flesh certain allies who are unfaithful to you, with whom they unite in strengthening their cause. Living in your midst is the traitor who causes your enemies to grow stronger. And when evil spirits begin their attack against us, monsters of vice join with them to engage us in fierce battle.

(19) Therefore, my dear friend, make every effort through a steady life of the spirit so to fight the enemy before you, that you are unable to see what is behind you. Always keep in mind what the Apostle says, "Forgetting what is behind me, and reaching out for that which lies ahead, I press toward the goal to win the prize which is God's call to the life above."[16] As Ezekiel said of those holy creatures, may your "feet be straight,"[17] that is, such as are able to proceed along the narrow path that once they took, that they may find it degrading to retrace their steps and return to the broader road they left behind. For, after laying aside the office of superior, some men are subjected to such surging temptations, that they can hardly endure the violent struggle within their own hearts. The evil spirits suggest to them the great and varied harvest of souls they might have won for God had they patiently remained in the office they formerly held. "For, by your advice," they say, "numerous people would have left the world to flock to the service of Christ, and even those who stayed behind would easily have reformed their evil ways. But inconstancy robbed you of these benefits, the vice of instability prevented them. Were you born only for your own welfare, so that your fellowmen could take no comfort from you, and that no fruit would be produced by you, as if you were a barren tree, and because of that, fit only for the fire?[18] The servant who hid his lord's talent in a handkerchief did not escape being sentenced to severe pun-

16. Phil 3.13–14.   17. Ezek 1.7.
18. Cf. Matt 7.19.

ishment.[19] And for that reason, he heedlessly ran the risk of damnation, when like a prudent man he thought he was providing for his future. You have squandered your reward on others, you have thrown away the opportunity of acquiring everlasting happiness."

(20) While mentioning all of this, they recall the goods of this world with which he was previously surrounded, they exaggerate the dire poverty in which he now unhappily finds himself. And that the battering ram of temptation may more forcibly strike the wall of his mind, they add, "Consider, therefore, how much better it is with God to have all good things, even those that are temporal, than without him to be in need of every resource that might sustain you. Because you did not fear God, in belittling and holding yourself in contempt, you should have acquired the temporal rewards of this life at least for your own use." At times also they secretly suggest a false love for those brothers to whose devoted service he was accustomed, at others they arouse no little anger against those who opposed him. He feels sorry for the former, because they complain of being deceived by him on whom they had pinned their hopes; and for the latter, because they brag that they had gone unpunished for their excessive presumption. He thinks that the former are distraught because of his degradation, but that the latter, like enemies, dance for joy over his misfortune. He imagines that the former are persecuted by their rivals out of hatred for him, while he is saddened that the latter are held in high esteem because of their arrogance.

(21) Evil spirits arouse these and many other fantastic thoughts in the minds of such men who never take precaution to protect themselves. And so it is, that we see some men at first fervently abandoning positions of authority, but afterwards, prompted by dangerous ambition, returning to the same vomit. Thus, surrounded by a dense cloud of various temptations, they either attain the objective they yearned for, or forsake their desire for a holy life which formerly incited them.

(22) But now, my dear friend, in your prudence as a brave warrior, buckle on the weapons of virtue, always be ready to en-

19. Cf. Luke 19.20.

gage in battle against the wiles of an ingenious enemy, despise the empty glory of this world, and have only contempt for the deceits of earthly happiness. When the world smiles on you, consider it a dream of a deluded imagination, and with all your strength burn with desire for the true joy of our heavenly fatherland. Whenever the battle grows fierce and disturbing temptations crowd in on you, let your soul gladly flee at once to this haven, there to rest delightfully as in some stronghold, that what the psalmist said may come to pass, "You will hide them under the cover of your presence from men who conspire against them; you keep them under your roof, safe from contentious men."[20] Putting behind you, therefore, all idleness and inactivity, wisely seek to practice every virtue and persevere steadfastly in what you have undertaken to do. Nor should you regret having left the monastery, but rather your conscience should accuse you for not bestirring yourself sooner, so that now by choosing for a time to be poor with Christ, you may enjoy with him immortal riches in the glory of his heavenly kingdom. And at the resurrection he will call you to take your place among those who were chosen abbot, since out of love for him in this life you removed yourself from the ranks of the abbots.

(23) So now, dear father, stirred by the pleasure of your affection, in attempting to write to you of many things, I have exceeded the norms of epistolary brevity. But I ask the Lord almighty that these crude and unskilled words may be of benefit to you, and that in return for them your holiness may not discontinue praying for me, your servant.

20. Ps 30.21.

LETTER 106

Peter Damian to Desiderius, the abbot of Monte Cassino. Warned by a messenger from Monte Cassino that if he did not visit that monastery he would not be remembered in the monks' suffrages after his death, Damian begs their indulgence and pleads his advanced years. A fifteen-day trip to the abbey would be too much for his strength. In his reply he stressed the value of prayer, especially to the Mother of God, and tells of many wonders wrought by her intercession. He points up the belief that prayers and the Eucharistic sacrifice are especially beneficial for the deceased. He cites examples from the saints, and even from the life of his brother Marinus, a layman, as related to him by another brother, Damianus. Finally, he still hopes that the Lord will permit him to visit the monastery and the tomb of St. Benedict.

(Lent 1064)[1]

O THE ARCHANGEL of monks, Desiderius,[2] the monk Peter the sinner sends his service.

(2) I could not have you unaware, venerable father, how sharp was the sword of sorrow that pierced me to the heart when young Guido, my servant, arrived to relate how you had threatened me. He reported that you had said, that unless I visited the monastery of Monte Cassino, which you so nobly rule, I would not enjoy the prayer of this holy house were I to die while you were still alive.[3] And when I recall these threats, they do not prick like needles, but rather like a lance or javelin they stab me to the quick since I am confined on all sides by double obstacles. For

1. Dating follows Lucchesi, *Vita* no. 187.

2. On Desiderius, see Damian's *Letter* 82, n. 2 and *Letter* 102, n. 2. On the stylistic art of this letter, see Lentini, *Prosa* 248ff. For an Italian translation, see Granata, *Monte Cassino* 231–249.

3. A letter of Desiderius to Damian is still extant, assuring the latter that he will be included in the suffrages of Monte Cassino. It is printed in the *Corollaria quaedam de vitae laude ac sanctitate B. Petri Damiani* no. 4 (PL 145.17D–18B); cf. Lucchesi, *Vita* no. 187. It is not clear, however, whether this letter was written before or after Damian's *Letter* 106. Cf. Dobmeier, *Montecassino* 172.

my advanced years make it likely that my death is imminent, and to be deprived of the prayers of so many holy men is no small danger. If I should travel, I have the awful fear of dying outside the monastery while I am on the way. For though death is uncertain where others are concerned, for old folks, to be sure, it is near at hand. And when in old age things no longer go well, it is a warning that life is about to end. Yet by not coming, I fear that if I remain here among the brothers with whom I presently live, I will lose the aid of a more numerous and incomparably holier community. Thus, as I stand between two dangers, I am unable to decide what I should do, since whichever I choose of the two, I will not escape the snare of dark suspicion.

(3) Here I am reminded that, as Grillius[4] said, Alexander dreamt so that he should not believe in dreams. Whenever Alexander chose an alternative, this brought the discussion to an end, so that what seemed correct to him would not be taken for a dream. For if he really believed in dreams, he lied in saying that his assertion was a dream that should not be believed. But if dreams were never to be believed, it follows that he too was not to be believed. Something like this is found in sacred Scripture, when it says, "I was out of my mind when I said, 'All men are liars.'"[5] To which one could reply, "If this is so, then you too are a liar, and the statement you make as a liar is also untrue. For if you are not a liar, the statement will not be true, because since you are truthful, not everybody is known to be a liar." And that sacred Scripture also not be open to calumny like the writings of the pagans, but may rather defend itself by its own authority, it should be noted that it first said, "I was out of my mind when I cried." Therefore, the author was out of his mind and forgot himself when pontificating about the human condition. It was as if he were saying, "I have reached this true conclusion about the deceitfulness of all men in that I myself was above all men. In that I am human, I too am a liar; but I am not a liar to the extent that, being out of my mind, I rose above men to contemplate the highest truth."

4. A fourth century grammarian. This citation, otherwise unknown, is not found in the fragments of his *Commentum in Ciceronis rhetorica.* Cf. Münscher, RE 7, 1876–1879; Schanz-Hosius 4.2, 263f.

5. Ps 115.11; cf. Sabatier 2.227.

(4) But since a journey of almost fifteen days separates us,[6] it would be in order that you should first experience what you ask an old man to do, since you are in the prime of life and enjoy excellent health. I may also add that you have an abundance of horses and are supplied with the services of crowds of attendants. It is said that Phalaris[7] provided an example of this norm, and after converting royal authority into tyranny, and savagely inflicting exquisite torture on various criminals, a certain craftsman built a brazen bull for him and made it so, that those condemned to death could be thrown into it after it was made red hot. The latter felt sure that Phalaris would be pleased with this barbarous device, since he considered him to be a master of inhuman cruelty, always eager to apply torture. This was especially the case, since when someone had been thrown into the beast and began to scream, the bull seemed to bellow through its nose and mouth. Then Phalaris rewarded his benefactor with a gift that he deserved. "My friend," he said, "I am indeed grateful for what you have given me, but it is my wish and unalterable command that you should be the first to experience what you have taught me." And so he was at once thrown into the bull, and was the first to suffer the torture he had taught him to apply to others. Thus, he who had previously built this penal labyrinth became the originator of this punishment. Therefore, you yourself should do what you command, and as a younger man should go to the older one to invite him to come to you. But now to speak seriously, if by such a long trip I could visit the tomb of our holy father Benedict, I would consider it no small additional reward.[8] And I am certain that if I should die in making this pilgrimage,

6. It took about 15 days to travel from Fonte Avellana to Monte Cassino at the rate of 20 miles a day. Cf. Lucchesi, *I viaggi* 91.

7. Phalaris, a tyrant of Agrigentum, *ca.* 570–554, besides being mentioned in several ancient sources, is also discussed in Orosius, *Adversus paganos* 1.20.1.84ff. An artisan named Persillus made for him a brazen bull in which the condemned were to be roasted alive. Cf. Th. Lenschau, RE 32.1649–1652.

8. Damian was of the opinion that the grave of St. Benedict—and of St. Scholastica—were at Monte Cassino. On this, cf. H. Leclercq, "Fleury-sur-Loire," DACL 5.2 (1923) 1709–1760, esp. 1715f.; P. Meyvaert, "Peter the Deacon and the Tomb of St. Benedict. A Re-examination of the Cassinese Tradition," *Revue bénédictine* 65 (1955) 3–70.

death would not increase my guilt, but would rather deprive him of the honor that is his due.[9]

(5) And so my hope has been fortified by what I heard only five days ago from that pious and prudent man, Stephen, the cardinal priest[10] of the Apostolic See. He told me that a certain vassal, a Burgundian by birth, devoutly went to pray at the church in the diocese of Annecy that bears the name of the blessed ever-virgin Mother of God, which is called le Puy (in Podio),[11] and having finished his prayers and fulfilled his devout mission, prepared to return home. Coming to a certain district where some monks lived in a daughter-house of a monastery, the name of which escapes me, he fainted, became ill and died. When the body was washed and as was the custom, lay in state wrapped in linen cloth, a pious group of the faithful spent the night in wake around his coffin.[12] It was almost dawn and daybreak was upon them, when the dead man suddenly sprang up, causing those who stood about to be overcome with shock and unbearable terror. Then the man cried out in a loud voice, and trembling with a horrible fear of punishment, began to beg the bystanders to pray earnestly and chant the psalms that by holy prayers they might put to flight the ruthless spirits of evil who everywhere seemed to infest the walls and rooms of the house.

(6) After prayers had been offered to God, and the devils had vanished like smoke blown away by the wind, the man's terror subsided, and taking courage now that he was safe, he publicly explained to all who were present what had secretly happened to him. "As I was leaving my body," he said, "two angels, splendidly garbed in white, suddenly appeared and began to take me with them to heaven. But then black swarms of demons, like a battalion of Ethiopians,[13] were all around me, and with sharp and con-

---

9. One might argue from this statement that Damian had never previously visited Monte Cassino. But see John of Lodi, *Vita* c. 20 (PL 144.141B).

10. On Stephen, see *Letter* 49, n. 2.

11. On Le Puy-en-Velay, cf. H. Leclercq, "Listes épiscopales," DACL 9.1 (1930) 1207–1536, esp. 1399–1402.

12. On this burial custom, see also Peter Damian, *Letter* 50, n. 92.

13. The reference to devils, appearing as black Ethiopians, goes back to biblical sources (cf. Jer 13.23 and Ps 73.14). Damian uses this figure elsewhere in his letters; cf. *Letters* 72, 102, and 109.

stant demand, wildly claimed that I belonged to them. 'This man is ours,' they said, 'he lived under our authority, and never once failed to obey our laws. For the law of the flesh always held the upper hand in him, but the law of the spirit he totally ignored.' In rebuttal the blessed angels replied, 'We do not deny,' they said, 'that he belonged to you while living on his estate. For one may not deny the truth. But since now he died in the service of our Lady, the queen of heaven, he shall never be subject to your impious rule because of failings during his lifetime, since he ended his days in such a holy manner. Nor can he be lost in the opinion of the eternal Judge, since he gave assistance to his mother.' To this the devils answered, 'Because without doubt,' they said, 'God is a just judge, he will not deprive us of what is ours, nor will he act against us with prejudice, since every form of injustice is unknown to him.'

(7) "But when the evil spirits tried to use force against the angels, and the latter, now recognizing the truth, resisted only lightly and not with all their might, they continuously promised me that help was on the way and warned that the Mother of God would soon be present. And while, on the one hand, the angels gave me moderate protection, and on the other, the devils furiously and grimly agitated to reclaim the man that belonged to them, suddenly a bright and radiant splendor, like a flash of lightning, illumined them, and to the utter surprise of all the Mother of God, the queen of heaven, appeared, reverently surrounded by ministering angels. Then the evil spirits, although at first terrified by the sight of such glory, causing them to shield their eyes from this excessive splendor, complained of the wrong that was being done them, and protested that the angels were using force to deprive them of their property, saying, 'If God is just, he will never free this wicked man from our grasp.' To these, on the other hand, the blessed Virgin replied, 'Even though, as you assert, this man belonged to you because of his wicked life, and lived badly according to his bodily desires, my most beloved and merciful Son and Lord will never allow him to be subject to your brutal treatment, because he was aware that the man died on a pilgrimage in my service, especially since he would have confessed his sins to the priests and with sorrow and contrition

received absolution, even though, because of his sudden death, he was unable to do so.'

(8) "At that, the evil spirits, as if dancing with joy over their victory, insultingly objected, 'Since you,' they said, 'are the mother of Truth and eternal Justice, can you be ignorant of the fact that he committed this heinous and bloody crime which he never made known to anyone in confession?' And then by name they shouted out the grave felony that I had committed. But the blessed Virgin, even though aware that these authors of lies had spoken the truth about this sin, discreetly remained silent for a moment, as if paying reverence to that truth. Then recovering her speech, she replied, 'Your objection is indeed true, but because with my merciful Lord and Son mercy normally supersedes justice, and the remission of sins is more pleasing to him than the punishment of sinners,'[14] and then turning to me, she said, 'return at once to your body. Confess this crime, with which the evil spirits have rightly charged you, to a priest among the monks who live in this little house close by, and on the authority of my command ask them to take upon themselves the penance that will be imposed on you, and to apply it to your absolution, for you are soon to die. After you have done this, return to me without delay. For I will not leave here and will wait till you get back.'" After he had related all this just as it happened, and in their charity the holy monks had accepted the penance imposed on him, and had demonstrated their obedience to the holy Virgin, the man happily died as if he were falling asleep. And thus, by his death he proved the truth of what he had said while he was alive. And if I too should die while trying to visit you as a pilgrim, I feel sure that I shall always be protected by St. Benedict.

(9) The same Stephen, moreover, told me another story, but of this he was not so certain as of the one I reported above. "I remember hearing of a certain cleric," he said, "who was simple, good for nothing, flighty, and tactless. In addition, he seemed to have no talent for the religious life, no quality that reflected the gravity and decorum pertaining to canonical discipline. But

14. Cf. Jas 2.13.

among these dead ashes of a useless life, one tiny flame continued to burn. Daily he would go to the holy altar of the blessed Mother of God, and there reverently bowing his head, would recite this angelic and Gospel verse, 'Hail Mary, full of grace, the Lord is with thee, blessed art thou among women.'[15] When at length the new bishop heard about this simple man's foolishness, he considered it improper that this useless person should serve the Church, and took away the benefice that he had received from his esteemed predecessor. But when the cleric began to feel the pinch of poverty, and had no other income on which he could live, in the still of the night the loving Mother of God appeared to the bishop in his sleep, preceded by a man who carried a lighted torch in one hand and a rod in the other. At once the blessed Virgin ordered him to give the delinquent bishop a few blows with the rod he carried. 'Why,' she said, 'did you deprive my chaplain who daily prayed to me, of the Church's stipend that you yourself did not provide for him?' At that, the bishop woke up trembling, restored the benefice to the cleric and now was more inclined to honor him as a friend, while previously, perhaps, he thought that God had been unaware of him."

(10) Therefore, if this cleric was rewarded with food for his body just for having sung one prayerful verse, with what confidence can those who daily recite all the hours of the office to the blessed queen of the world[16] look forward to eternal refreshment? Consequently, it has been the beautiful practice in some churches to celebrate a special Mass in her honor each Saturday, unless, perhaps, some feast or feria in Lent should intervene.[17] Moreover, in hermitages or monasteries where we serve to the

15. Luke 1.28. Damian departs from the Vulgate by adding "Maria" after the "Ave." See A. A. De Marco, "Hail Mary," NCE 6 (1967) 898; Reindel, *Briefe* 3.174, n. 13.

16. An indirect reference to the Little Office of the B.V.M., which Damian reorganized, recommending its daily recitation, and caused to spread throughout Europe. See G. E. Schidel, "Little Office of the B.V.M.," NCE 8 (1967) 854f.; Reindel, *Briefe* 3.175, n. 14.

17. Cf. H. Schauerte, LThK 9 (1964) 303. Since the 8th century Mary was honored on Saturday, and since Alcuin's time a Mass, *De beata*, was composed to celebrate this day; cf. Reindel, *Briefe* 3.175, n. 15.

glory of Christ, there are three days each week on which we celebrate a special Mass in honor of the saints who are assigned to these days. And we do not undertake to do this rashly, but with good reason, because in the pious opinion of illustrious men and according to statements they have made, all the departed souls are at peace on Sundays, and are free from their sufferings, but on Mondays they return to the place of punishment in which they were confined.[18] And so it is, that particularly on this day we celebrate Mass in honor of the angels, to win their patronage and protection for the dead and for those who are about to die. Friday, moreover, is fittingly dedicated to the life-giving cross,[19] for on this day the Lord hung on the cross and gloriously shed his blood. On this day, all our brothers, in harmony with the whole body of monks, have added the custom of administering the discipline to one another in chapter to increase the prospects of their own salvation, and observe the day, moreover, in fasting on bread and water, assured that in so doing we truly participate in the cross, undoubtedly die together with Christ if we punish our flesh by undergoing the torture of fasting on the very day whereon he suffered.

(11) The brothers state, moreover, that since through the vagaries of almost five thousand years[20] the whole human race was burdened by the iron yoke of the devil, and especially on this day was triumphantly freed by this marvelous banner of the cross, it is indeed proper that on the day on which he broke the bonds of all ages, our flesh should pay some amount of tribute, by which it might rejoice at being freed from the shackles of its captivity. They also say that when the eternal Judge appears in glory at the last judgment, surrounded by hosts of angels; when all beings will be filled with terror at such majesty, suddenly the blessed cross will be borne in the arms of the angels and placed in view of all mortals, not now adorned with gold and gems, but by the power of God, made brighter than the sun and all the stars. With what sincere desire and unburdened conscience will one then

18. For this legend and its literature, see Damian, *Letter* 72, n. 30; Reindel, *Briefe* 2.335, n. 27.
19. Fonte Avellana was dedicated to the Holy Cross; cf. *It. Pont.* 4.92f.
20. For a discussion of the figure 5,000, see Reindel, *Briefe* 3.176, n. 18.

stand before the heavenly throne of this fiery tribunal, aware that he has paid due service to the life-giving cross, by which he was freed from the servitude of the devil.

(12) Because of these and other arguments the holy brothers have decided to fast on Friday, and thus they show that they too have been crucified with the Lord who hung on the cross. And what is so burdensome for a Christian to sacrifice one day of the week for the benefit of his soul, when medical dieting moves him to do the same to preserve the health of his body? For as one historical account attests, Caesar Augustus, in whose reign the Savior saw fit to be born of the Virgin,[21] on the advice of his doctors always abstained from food one day of the week, so that by lightening his body's burden, he might remain sound and healthy.[22] In honor of the holy cross they also celebrate Masses that day, that they might obtain the protection of the cross in times of necessity.

(13) Saturday, however, which may be said to mean "rest,"[23] on which day, as we read, God rested, quite aptly is dedicated to the blessed Virgin. On her Wisdom built his house,[24] and through the mystery of assuming our humanity rested in her as in a most sacred bed. For those, to be sure, who pay her rightful honor, she undoubtedly provides assistance and a safe defense.

(14) In this regard I will now give you a faithful account, if my memory has not deceived me, of what I learned from my brother Damian,[25] who was then arch-priest, and later became a monk. Another brother of mine, named Marinus, who was a layman but a man who lived a devout life,[26] fell seriously ill from a disease that affected his lungs and chest. One day toward dawn he suddenly began to grow expectant as if someone were coming, to smile with joy, and quickly sat up with a festive look on his face. He then began to speak with great fervor addressing those who

---

21. Cf. Luke 2.
22. Cf. Suetonius, *De vita Caesarum* 2.76.
23. Cf. Jerome, *Nom. hebr.* 75.26 (CC 72.154).
24. Cf. Prov 9.1.
25. He also wrote *Letter* 138 to his brother Damian; cf. John of Lodi, *Vita* c. 2 (PL 144.117B); see also Lucchesi, *Vita* no. 187.
26. Perhaps his nephew Marinus, a son of Damian's brother Marinus, to whom he wrote (*Letter* 132).

sat at his bedside, "Get up," he said, "get up and reverently pay your respects to my Lady." And then, altering his voice somewhat, he continued, "And how is it, my Lady, queen of heaven and earth, that you have seen fit to visit your poor servant? Bless me, my Lady, and do not let me enter the darkness, since you have honored me with the light of your presence." When he had finished speaking in this way, his brother Damianus, and also mine, returned from the church where he had just finished saying Matins to God, and asked how his sick brother was doing. But the latter said he was sure he was going to die, and then sharply complained about those who were seated there in the room. "What a shame it is, brother," he said, "that we have such ignorant, awkward, irreverent, and totally undisciplined domestics. And you, vigorous man, Bonizo,"—among the others was this rich merchant—"how can you sit there in the presence of the queen of heaven? The queen of the world makes her appearance, and you fail to rise? The mother of the eternal Ruler comes to us, and do you consider her presence something insignificant?" To this Bonizo replied, "You are delirious and say these silly things because you are out of your mind in your illness. Do you think there is any truth in what you say? To me, certainly, what you say seems worthless and makes no sense." At that my brother answered, "Are you not aware that this illness I have never affects the mind of those who suffer from it? Therefore, beyond all shadow of a doubt you should be assured that the blessed mother of our Redeemer, accompanied by the angels, visited me, showed me her serene and happy countenance, blessed me, and then at once departed."

(15) Shortly after he had died, a certain old priest named Severus, who had been his spiritual father, told how many years before, when Marinus was still strong and enjoyed good health, he had taken off his clothes, tied a rope around his neck, and offered himself as a slave before the altar of the blessed Mother of God. Then, like a wicked servant, he had himself beaten in the presence of his Lady, saying, "My glorious Lady, mirror of virginal chastity and example of every virtue, I have miserably and unhappily offended you by the obscene and foul use of my body, and have violated my bodily integrity of which you are the

mother and author. Now, therefore, the only remedy that is left for me, is to offer myself to you as your servant, and in a spirit of submission to yield my neck to your command. Subdue this rebel, accept this obstinate subject, and let not your loving mercy turn away from the sinner, since your undefiled virginity gave birth to the author of true mercy. And so now, as a token of my servitude, I offer you this little gift, and from now on, so long as I live, I will give you a fixed amount as my annual tribute." He then placed a sum of money at the foot of the altar, and thus assured of the mercy he had sought, he departed. Perhaps my brother did not tell this story of our brother in just this way, for although I have forgotten his exact words, as far as possible I have at least not departed from something like his narrative. May this statement of confession regarding his report and my telling of it be to my benefit, and so far as I have erred through ignorance, let it be my excuse in the sight of God.

(16) And now to join what is yet to come with what I said above, please, dear father, do not hold to the threats you have leveled at me. Do not withhold the medicine of your prayers from your sick son while he is alive, or after his death. Unhappily, moreover, while I am still living, I am not productive because of my sloth and inactivity. But if you are still alive after my death, I hope to receive support from your hands, so that the Masses you offer may provide a feast for my soul, and the sacrifice of your prayer may be life-giving food for me. And why should one wonder at the belief that the host at holy Mass is nourishment for the dead, since at times it is changed into food also for the living when they are in danger of death?

(17) For the venerable old man, a priest and monk named Peter, who had formerly lived as a religious for almost seventy years under the jurisdiction of the monastery of Nonantola, and today still leads an angelic life in this hermitage, often told me the story he had heard from the report of brothers coming from the region of Lake Como. He said[27] that certain stonecutters at

27. In relation to this story, see Giles Constable, "Manuscripts of Works by Peter the Venerable," *Studia Anselmiana* 40 (1956) 219–242, who claims that Damian's account is at the base of a similar narrative by Peter the Venerable; cf. Reindel, *Briefe* 3.179, n. 24.

Mount Chiavenna were quarrying a vein of rock in the earth, and coming out after completing their work, were preparing to return home. One of them, becoming aware that he had forgotten one of his tools, went down into the hollow cave in the mountain to recover what he had lost. Suddenly a large section of the cavern fell in behind him and he was trapped by the pile of rubble so that he could not get out. His fellow workers tried by repeated digging to recover the maimed and broken body of the dead man, but found that all their efforts were in vain. At length, worn out and giving up all hope, they went back to their families.

(18) Afterwards, when almost a year had elapsed, his friends and relatives moved by a certain feeling of affection for him, searched with greater care that they might recover his remains, or at least some trace of him. They went to the mountain with another group of miners, searched here and there, curiously looking for an entry through some hidden crevice. After the rubble had been removed with great effort, they kept on digging, and at length entered the excavation in the mountain. Suddenly they saw the man, whose dead body they had scarcely hoped to find, healthy and unharmed, and with songs of praise led him out as from the grave.

(19) When asked how he could have lived so long without food, he replied, "From the time I was imprisoned in this narrow cave, a little bird, somewhat like a dove, daily flew in here to me with a small piece of white bread in its beak. With this food I was so satisfied and refreshed, that I thought I was filled with royal, even heavenly delight. There was only one day my little waiter did not visit me in its usual way, and on that day an intolerable hunger tormented me." Every day, it seems, his wife had arranged that a Mass be offered for the welfare of his soul, but one day when there had been a heavy snow, she failed to visit the church. And so, as they discussed the matter, it became obvious to them that it was just the day on which he had suffered from hunger, that the sacrifice of the Mass had not been celebrated for him.

(20) Moreover, I do not think it right to remain silent about the tale that Atto, a citizen of Osimo[28] of blessed memory, a pru-

28. On Damian's relations with Osimo, cf. Lucchesi, *Vita* no. 40.

dent and honest man, told us while I was present. "There was a certain woman whose husband had died," he said, "and in her widowhood had great confidence in a certain priest, that he would obtain salvation for her husband. By her maid she brought him many fine gifts, and through her always begged him to remember her deceased one in his prayers. He found it easy to promise her that he would comply with her wishes, but being greedy and niggardly, never gave the maid anything to eat, not even of the food which she had brought. And so it was that she grew tired of her repeated visits to his house, and to herself complained of the priest's stinginess.

(21) "After some time had passed, one day the same lady, using the same maid who had brought her previous pious gifts, sent the priest a roasted chicken, some freshly baked bread, and a bottle of wine. As the girl on that occasion, too, was hungry as usual, and was all wrought up by her feelings against the priest, she looked about in all directions, cautiously went to a remote room in the house, sat down, served herself, and eagerly ate everything that she had brought. After the servant had had her fill of food and drink, with a happy heart she bowed her head to the ground, arose, stretched out her hands to heaven, and cried out in this prayer, 'Almighty God,' she said, 'you give food to all your creatures.[29] As you have nourished me with this bodily food, so in your mercy may the soul of my master this day be refreshed in paradise.'

(22) "When the servant had returned to her mistress and was asked what the priest had said, she replied that he had been grateful, and promised to pray for the deceased man. The next night the woman's husband came to her in a dream and thanked his wife for yesterday's gifts. And when she earnestly asked how things were going with him, whether he was suffering any punishment or enjoying any respite, he replied, 'Until yesterday everything went badly, and among other inconveniences in my sorry state, I was terribly hungry. But yesterday I had the splendid dinner that you had sent, and my hunger was completely satisfied, thanks to your generous supply of food.' And after these words he immediately disappeared.

29. Ps 135.25.

(23) "Then the woman woke up and began carefully to think about what her husband had said. She was greatly surprised that he had spoken of yesterday's meal he had received from her, since she had very frequently sent food to the priest. Therefore, after giving more thought to what her husband had told her, she became aware that all this was very mysterious. Then she called the maid and began to ask harshly what she had done with the food, and what the priest had said about it. But when the latter in great fright made up this story, and that, refused to tell the truth, and struggled through every kind of evasion and fabrication that made little sense, her lady did not believe a word she had said, and threatened her with severe punishment. At last, forced by necessity, the girl told what had really happened, that she had eaten what she had brought with her, and confessed that she had prayed for her master."

(24) And so, just as it happened, this event was soon on everybody's lips and quickly spread through the whole region. As is evident from the report of many people, alms given to the poor are more fruitful and of greater use than any offering made to priests who live unworthily, since the man who was dead did not know of the gift made to the priest, but experienced as a great feast what had been eaten by this poor little woman. Alms, indeed, do not allow the souls of men to enter into darkness, and by earthly gifts one may win the kingdom of heaven. Accordingly, some monasteries in our region have recently introduced the beautiful practice, among other things, that the abbot always entertains three poor men at his private table, and serves each of them the same amount of food that is apportioned to each of the monks. For since the Rule commands that the abbot always have guests at his table,[30] in this way the double precept is zealously fulfilled, that the abbot's table not be used for the great men of this world but for holy guests, and that he not fail to eat with the brethren.

(25) Therefore, that greater amounts of food be provided for the poor, a tenth[31] of all their produce in monasteries and her-

---

30. *Benedicti regula* c. 56.1, 144.
31. Cf. G. Constable, *Monastic Tithes from their Origins to the Twelfth Century* (Cambridge Studies in Medieval Life and Thought, N.S. 10, 1964) 231ff.

mitages is given, not only of their cattle, but also of their chickens and eggs. And recently they have introduced something new to be added to their devotion for the dead.[32] For their loved ones who have passed away, they observe the octave of their death each year, and pray for them not only on the day they died, but each year they remember them for eight days. And I suggest and humbly beg you to accept this new practice of those I have just mentioned, and not find it unworthy of you to follow the example of these lesser brethren. It is certainly better for teachers to learn from their students, than proudly to ignore what is proper. It is more creditable for a greater person to learn what he does not know, than to be ignorant of what he should know. What a glorious virtue is humility, by which a man truly becomes a student of the Savior! "Learn of me," he says, "for I am meek and humble of heart."[33] This is, indeed, the virtue by which an acceptable sacrifice is offered to God, by which the teacher demonstrates the constancy of his effort, and the student his dependence.

(26) From the brothers in the esteemed monastery of Cluny I happened to learn these two outstanding examples of holy humility, one of which will greatly benefit certain superiors, and the other will serve to edify the subjects. Marcuardus,[34] who had been the head of that monastery, appointed Maiolus to succeed him as abbot, and since he was advanced in years, went into retirement. He lived alone in a little house, set aside for the sick, and one day toward evening asked that some cheese be brought to him. The cellarer, busy as usual with his many duties, not only did not provide the cheese, but in harsh words even began to abuse his assistant. He complained of the oversupply of abbots, grousing that he could not put up with the trouble caused by so many masters. When the old man heard this, he was greatly scandalized, and because he had lost his sight, was deeply hurt by these remarks. For the more a blind man is cut off from the outside world, the more carefully he thinks about what he hears, and because he does not get out among others, the more deeply he feels the sting of suppressed anger. The next morning he or-

---

32. Cf. Reindel, *Briefe* 3.182, n. 28.   33. Matt 11.29.

34. Damian here mistakes Marcuard for Aymard. See Joan Evans, *Monastic Life at Cluny 910–1157* (1968) 15f.

dered his attendant to take him by the hand and lead him to the chapter. Upon arriving, he upbraided the abbot in these words, "Brother Maiolus," he said, "I did not make you my superior to persecute me, but chose you as a son who would have pity on his father, and not as a buyer who would domineer over his slave." And after saying many other such things, almost overcome by anger, he added, "Are you not, I ask, my monk?" And the other replied, "I am, and I declare that I was never more yours than I am now." Then Marcuardus said, "If you are my monk, at once vacate your chair and take the place that you had before." When Maiolus heard this, he got up immediately and took a lower place as he was commanded. Then, as if he were resuming his former office, Marcuardus sat down in the empty chair, reproached the cellarer with whom he was angry, sharply corrected him as he lay prostrate on the floor, and finally imposed a penance which seemed appropriate to him. After completing this rather lengthy court proceeding, he at once rose from his seat, ordered Maiolus to take the chair, and without saying a word, the latter obeyed.

(27) And so in this holy man we clearly see the virtue of true obedience and the mortification involved in monastic discipline. Truly, we observe both the dignity of imperial patience and the majesty of apostolic humility reigning in him. When commanded to lay aside the authority of his office, he did not resist, and when told to accept it once again, he patiently and humbly obeyed; and dead to himself in both regards, and bound by the ties of the highest obedience as he totally subjected himself to another's will, he allowed no personal desires to influence him. But since such humility could not remain sterile in this holy man, the root that had previously been watered by the dew of the Holy Spirit grew profusely and spread its fruit-bearing branches.

(28) And so, when on one occasion this man of God was about to travel to Rome, he told a certain brother to accompany him because, as he had been requested, he had decided to make him abbot in the monastery of St. Paul.[35] But the latter raised several objections, difficult to overcome, and after saying one thing and

---

35. See Guy Oury, "Ingenauld de St.-Julien de Tours, abbé de Saint-Paul-hors-les-Murs à Rome, 953(?)–960(?)," *Revue Mabillon* 58 (1970–1975) 177–180.

another, at length obstinately refused to obey. But Maiolus calmly
put up with the brother's disobedience, and leaving him behind,
took off as he had planned. While the brother, because of his disobedience, remained in the monastery, and the other brothers severely upbraided him and unanimously charged him with his
hardheaded obstinacy, he finally came to his senses, fought back
at his self-willed stubbornness, girded himself with the weapons of
holy obedience, and glowing with the ardor of God's grace,
quickly took off to catch up with the blessed man. But since the latter was unaware of all this, because he was already on his way, the
monk, huffing and puffing, quickened his pace to overtake him.
Soon he came to a certain river which the man of God had already
crossed, and sat down on the bank on his side of the stream.

(29) While the monk was still on the other side of the river,
since without a boat he could not cross over, seeing his master
standing there quite some distance away, all he could do was
throw himself on the ground and humbly lie there. And since it
was impossible to hear his cries for forgiveness, he let his whole
body do the shouting. When Maiolus saw this from where he
was, and immediately recognized what he was trying to say, he at
once instructed the boatman and had the monk brought over to
him. Directly, the man of God asked him why he had come, and
the other begged pardon for what had happened and promised
in the future to carry out whatever he would order him to do.
Then Maiolus said, "Are you sure you want to be forgiven?" And
when the other replied, "That is my wish," he at once replied,
"Then give this man a kiss." For it just happened that there was a
leper standing near by, whose skin had hideous welts. At once
the monk kissed him, and suddenly the man's body was healed
and the leprosy completely disappeared. Thus, holy obedience
found the reward of its humility, not only as it merited forgiveness for bringing himself to task, but it also provided a proof of
his outstanding virtue. And to him for whom pride could have
brought on the disaster of apostasy, humility provided the opportunity of displaying apostolic virtue.[36]

36. On Damian's use of "apostasy" in contrasting it with "apostolic," Lucchesi
(*Vita* no. 187) refers to the same usage in the *Papal Election Decree* (*Papstwahldekret*
107), heightening the likelihood that Damian was involved in its composition.

(30) I relate all of this, venerable father, fearing that either through my own forgetfulness, or by daring to depart from what I have heard, I have somewhat overstepped the bounds of truth. Therefore, I do not affirm that these stories are all true, but only state that they were brought to my attention in something like this guise.

(31) Indeed, whoever speaks of obedience must be especially careful not to incur the mark of rebellious disobedience. For the farther a story travels, the easier it is to mar its author's reputation. When something is stated that opposes the facts, one doubtless destroys the law which he proposes. Therefore, I beseech the author of obedience and humility that he see fit to protect me from this infamous reproach, and soon permit me to chant this verse of the prophet at the gates of Monte Cassino, "On this account on that day my people shall know my name; they shall know that it is I who speak; here I am."[37]

37. Isa 52.6.

LETTER 107

Peter Damian to Pope Alexander II, and to the archdeacon Hildebrand. The occasion for this letter was twofold: (1) He replies humbly to Alexander and sardonically to Hildebrand regarding their request for a copy of the letter he had sent to Anno of Cologne (*Letter* 99) the previous summer, requesting the archbishop to assemble a general council. (2) He pleads old age for not traveling again to Rome, promising, however, to go with them to Mantua to attend a council there. But in the end he does not go.

(Lent 1064)[1]

O FATHER AND SON, the pope and the archdeacon,[2] the monk Peter the sinner offers his service.

(2) I am sending[3] you the letter on account of which you have beaten me black and blue,[4] that you may see and clearly verify what it contained, and what I did to oppose you. But if I have sent any other letter to anyone in this area, or if, to my knowledge, even one iota has been added or in any way changed in this letter, and was not sent to you just as it was forwarded to the lord archbishop of Cologne,[5] may the leprosy of Naaman the Syrian overwhelm me,[6] or the blindness of Bar-Jesus darken the eyes in my head.[7] I call Jesus and his holy angels as my witness that I am not lying in giving you this explanation. And so, if I must die because of this letter, I offer my neck, pierce me with your dagger. As for the rest, I humbly beg my holy Satan[8]

1. Dating follows Lucchesi, *Vita* no. 180.
2. On Pope Alexander II, cf. *Letter* 96, n. 2; on Hildebrand see *Letter* 57, n. 13.
3. This would indicate that Damian had preserved copies of his letters. Cf. Reindel, *Studien* 1.55 and 6off.
4. Without the pope's knowledge, Damian had sent *Letter* 99 to Anno of Cologne, suggesting that he call a synod to reconcile the schism of Cadalus. Cf. *Letter* 99, n. 3; Schmidt, *Alexander II* 210ff.
5. On Anno of Cologne, see *Letter* 99, n. 2.
6. Cf. 2 Kgs 5.20, 27.
7. Cf. Acts 13.6–11.
8. On Damian's relationship with Hildebrand, see *Letter* 57, n. 13.

not to act so cruelly toward me, nor should his impressive pride beat me with such frequent blows, but at length having its fill, it should show pity for his servant. My livid shoulders have had enough of this, and bearing welts from this beating, my swollen back cannot withstand so many lashes. And hence the wise man says, "The lash of a whip raises welts, but the lash of a tongue breaks bones."[9] Therefore, have a heart, for it is high time that I too . . . .

(3) But now I will save my breath, I will hold my tongue, and although tardily, I still ask for mercy. In that you have ordered me to come to Rome to be with you, however, and then to go with you to Mantua,[10] the effort of both journeys seems to be most difficult and too great for my advanced years. Hence, I will not come to Rome, which would be of less benefit to you, but I think that making the trip to Mantua is more necessary for you. In sending me this holy message, however, each of you seems to have taken a different approach. One, it appears to me, is charming and friendly with a fatherly interest, while the other threatens terror and hostile attack. One of you, like the sun, bathes me in the warmth of his brilliant splendor, but the other, like the blustery northwind, blows up a violent storm.

(4) And so, I recall what used to be told in the fables.[11] It is said that as a certain traveler was on his way, clad in his mantle, the sun and Eurus, the eastwind, proposed to make him the subject of a contest, namely, to see which of them could the more easily force him to take off his coat. When it was agreed that he who won would be crowned with a laurel wreath, Eurus began to blow fiercely and set the clouds in motion. But the traveler held on to his cloak and wrapped it more securely about him that it would not be lost. When the disciple of Aeolus[12] was worn out by his effort and despaired of ever finishing the task he had begun, the golden sun began to show his face and bathe the earth in his

9. Sirach 28.21.

10. On the council of Mantua, see Hefele-Leclercq, *Histoire* 4.1234ff. Yet Damian did not attend this council, as *Letter* 108 indicates.

11. Cf. Avianus, *Fables IV* (Loeb Classical Library, *Minor Latin Poets*, tr. J. W. Duff and A. Duff [1982]) 688–689.

12. The god of the winds.

warming rays. Soon the traveler became dehydrated by the excessive heat, sweat pouring from his moisture laden body, and he threw off his coat so as to moderate the sweltering temperature. Therefore, he who had hardly moved a finger was the winner in the contest, not the one who had tried to succeed by his fury and overwhelming violence.

(5) But let me cite a more proper example from sacred Scripture. If Rehoboam had followed the advice of the elders,[13] and had spoken kindly to the people, all Israel would have been submissive to his rule. But because he was convinced of the pride of their elders, he separated ten tribes from them and thus reduced the mighty power of their kingdom. The rhinoceros, also, which by its nimble agility can make light of the savage jaws of the dogs that pursue it, has no fear of letting itself be captured with its head in the lap of an attractive virgin.[14]

(6) But since I gave you everything you wanted, why must I still suffer persecution? Certainly, the investigators of nature tell us—I do not know whether the hunters also agree with them—that the beaver[15] in taking stock of its natural qualities, is convinced that it is hunted only for its private parts, which, when cut off, serve a medicinal purpose. Therefore, quickly running to a protruding branch of a tree, it violently thrusts itself against it and castrates itself. Then after going some distance, the beaver stands on its two hind feet, looking at the hunter, and shows him that the testicles for which he is being pursued, are missing. Therefore, should more brutal satisfaction be required of a man than is demanded from dumb animals?

(7) But that this letter may not exceed epistolary brevity, I will await your coming into my area to complain further about this matter.

13. Cf. 1 Kgs 12.8–24; 2 Chr 10.6–19.
14. Cf. *Letter* 86, n. 135.   15. Cf. *Letter* 86, n. 43.

LETTER 108

Peter Damian to Pope Alexander II. Instead of going to the council at Mantua (31 May–1 June 1064), he stayed at Fonte Avellana, from where he sent this letter to Alexander, who returned to Rome via the Romagna. On some earlier occasion Alexander had asked for Damian's opinion on the intriguing questions why recent popes had reigned no more than four or five years, and to this Damian replies. Here, too, he displays a deep interest in the world's material and spiritual ecology, which he obviously attributes to the goodness of divine providence. This letter also contains a significant statement about angelology.

(June 1064)[1]

O SIR ALEXANDER, the bishop of the highest see,[2] the monk Peter the sinner offers his service.

(2) Since I hear, venerable father, that on your return from the council of Mantua[3] you are here in the neighborhood, I thought it proper to send you a literary gift by which you will be pleased. And as soon as your ship approached our shores, the good news greatly excited me to take to the road to meet you. Jacob, indeed, of whom Scripture says that "he led a settled life and stayed among the tents,"[4] was therefore convinced that his brother could be satisfied with earthly gifts because he knew that he loved only earthly things. I, too, who like Jacob simply stay at home, since I have no doubt that you are pleased more by spiritual things than by those of the flesh, am prepared to satisfy you with a spiritual gift. Wherefore, when David fled to get away from Absalom, Hushai the Archite, who returned to Jerusalem, was of greater use to him than Ittai, who was the only ally who did not desert David in his flight.[5] David also established the custom in

1. Dating follows Lucchesi, *Vita* no. 189.
2. See *Letter* 96, n. 2.
3. On this council, see *Letter* 107, n. 10.
4. Gen 25.27.　　　　　　　　5. Cf. 2 Sam 15.21–37.

Israel, that those who went into battle, and those who remained with the stores, should share alike in the spoils.[6] And Moses was a more powerful help to the people of Israel when he seemed to be idly praying at Rephidim, than Joshua, armed to the teeth, who went out to meet the attacking Amalekites. This is clearly stated in Scripture, when it says, "Whenever Moses raised his hands Israel had the advantage, but when he lowered them Amalek began to win."[7] But no gift is more properly bestowed than that requested by him to whom it is given.

(3) Some time ago, if my memory serves me right, you earnestly requested my opinion on why the bishop of the Apostolic See never lived very long, but died in a short space of time,[8] so that after blessed Peter the apostle, who presided for almost twenty-five years,[9] none of the Roman pontiffs afterwards equaled this time in office, and that hardly anyone elevated to this see in modern times exceeded four, or at most, five years. If one thinks about this, one begins to wonder at such a prodigious fact, if I may use that word, for to my knowledge, this postulate of a short life is found in no other church in the world. But insofar as mortals can perceive the secrets of divine providence, it seems to me that the plan of heavenly justice has so ordained, that the human race might stand in fear of death, and that it might clearly demonstrate in the case of this glorious office itself how much the grandeur of temporal life should be despised. As a result, while the most preeminent of men dies within the span of just a few years, everyone should be challenged to carefully await his own death, and that the tree of the human race as it considers how easily its topmost part has fallen, may shake in all its branches as it is struck by this fearsome wind.

(4) But perhaps someone will object: Why does not this same short life apply also to kings? For in the case of Octavian Augustus, in whose reign the Savior of the world was born of the Vir-

6. Cf. 1 Sam 30.24.
7. Exod 17.11.
8. On the general interpretation of this work, see Bultot, *Pierre Damien* 71ff.; G. Cacciamani, "De brevitate vitae pontificum Romanorum, et divina providentia," *Vita monastica* 26 (1972) 226–242.
9. On the 25-year pontificate of Peter, cf. *Liber pontificalis* c. 1.1, 118.

gin,[10] and of King David from whose line he deigned to come, the one held royal authority for fifty-six years,[11] and the other forty.[12] Following them, other princes of both states, even though their reigns were shorter, did not, however, rule for only a brief period after the example of the Roman pontiffs. To this one might easily reply, that while a pope presides over the whole world, the earthly authority of most kings is limited; since every emperor prostrates himself at the feet of the pope as the king of kings and the prince of emperors, he exceeds all living beings in honor and dignity.[13] Thus, when a king dies, only the kingdom which he heads is deprived of his leadership, but when the pontiff of the Apostolic See passes away, the whole world is orphaned by the loss of its common father. What does Africa know about the kings of Asia, or Ethiopia of the princes in the west? For since they are far removed from them, they are equally unaware of whether they live or die.

(5) This is yet another reason why the death of any king is not a terrifying event, for earthly princes who are the leaders of great throngs of people often die by the sword. Just to cite a few examples, Gaius,[14] Claudius, Nero, Galba, Otho, and Vitellius, all of these emperors held the principate in a continuous line, one after the other, and with the exception of Claudius, all were killed by the swords of their own men or by those of their enemies. Later also, as Roman history relates, Macrinus, Antoninus, Alexander, Maximinus, Gordianus, Decius, Gallus, and Volusianus, all succeeding one another in a continuous line, were cut down by the sword.

(6) Secular princes, therefore, because they are exposed to various deadly hazards, do not shock those who hear about their passing; but since the life of a pope comes to an end only from

10. Cf. Luke 2.1.

11. Cf. Bede, *Martyrologium, editio Coloniensis* (PL 94.1140B–1141A).

12. For David it is reckoned that at most he reigned 33 years; cf. Lawrence A. Sinclaire, "David," *Theologische Realenzyklopädie* 8 (1981) 378–384.

13. See Schramm, *Herrschaftszeichen* 714; S. F. Wemple, *Atto of Vercelli* (1979) 265.

14. The first reference is to Gaius (Caius) Caligula; for the other emperors here listed, Damian seems indebted to Eutropius, *Breviarium*, including wrongly only Antoninus, who died a natural death.

natural causes[15] his leaving this world is always noted with great excitement. Moreover, since earthly princes, as was said, live within a limited territory, there is no reason why their death should be broadcast to various parts of the world. But the pope, because he alone is the universal bishop[16] of all the churches, when he dies, the notice of his death is spread to all the kingdoms of the earth. And just as the sun, since there is only one, suddenly causes darkness throughout the whole world if it should go into eclipse, so also the pope, because he is unique in the world, when he departs this life, the news of his death reaches to distant realms. And in consequence, the passing of such a sublime and outstanding person is disturbing, and causes fear and trembling regarding the end of one's own life. Here we should note how much almighty God wishes the life of the Roman pontiff to provide edification to men, since he has also decreed that his death should serve the welfare of all nations. How great should be his effort to work for the well-being of souls during his life, since also his death provides the means of calling back the souls of men to their Creator, so that as he is aware that he is the father of the whole world, he must not grow weary in promoting eternal salvation for so many children.

(7) Here I should like to expand our view somewhat, and briefly explore the immense benefits that are granted to man by God. For by divine institution all the elements are at man's service, and not only heaven and earth, air and water, but everything that is in them concur in being useful to man. And first of all, as I have said, the four elements are at hand to serve him, because he is composed of them,[17] and then whatever they have, they extrinsically bring to him. In the moist earth the roots of

15. This statement would seem to contradict the late 11th century rumors concerning the violent deaths of popes Clement II (d. 9 October 1047) and Damasus II (d. 9 August 1048).

16. This clear assertion of the primacy of the pope, and the bold use of the title *universalis episcopus*, is perhaps the most precise formulation in contemporary literature. For this, and for Damian's awareness of the controversy over the use of this title by the patriarchs of Constantinople, see Ryan, *Sources* 103–105, no. 200; Schmidt, *Alexander II* 182, n. 236.

17. Cf. Isidore, *Etymologies* 4.5.3 and 11.1.16. Also Isidore, *De natura rerum* 9.1.207.

plants and trees proceed to grow, afterwards reaching their natural height for the benefit of men. The very grass in the meadows is converted into the flesh of animals, and men are fed on their meat. Animals, moreover, when they are alive, are made to support various human needs, namely, some provide transportation for those who ride them, others plow the fields for the seeds that will be consigned and brought to them, others not only produce a supply of milk, but as if they were subject to the teaching of the Gospel, share their two shirts,[18] as they cover us with their hides and fleece. But since epistolary brevity does not allow me to linger on individual facts, for which many volumes would hardly be able to tell the story, let it suffice to conclude with these words of the psalmist, "You have put everything under his feet: all sheep and oxen, all the wild beasts, the birds in the air and the fish in the sea, and all that moves along the paths of the ocean."[19]

(8) And among other things, it is something marvelous, that neither the flight of birds, the bravery of lions, the speed of tigers, nor the enormous height of elephants free them from the domination of man. The lion,[20] indeed, is so terrifying that when it roars, suddenly many animals that by their great speed could avoid his attack, grow weak and are frozen in their tracks. And still, the lion is captured by man and like a feeble cat is stuffed into a cage. Also, the tiger,[21] which in the Parthian language is called an arrow, in one stretch can cover ten miles, and in one day, from sunup to sundown is said to run around the whole world. Yet this beast, which travels with such incredible speed, at times does not evade the snares of the hunter. But as we must wonder that these animals are subject to man's power, even the smallest of them and those that are unclean prove useful to man's well-being. For what is more insignificant than a bug? But if a leech[22] takes one in its mouth, when it gets a whiff of its fumes, the leech at once spits it out, and by its application eases one who has difficulty in urinating. According

---

18. Cf. Luke 3.11.   19. Ps 8.8–9.
20. Ambrose, *Exameron* 6.3.14, ed. C. Schenkle, CSEL 32.1 (1897) 212.
21. Isidore, *Etymologies* 12.2.7.
22. Cf. Pliny, *Naturalis historia* 29.17.62 and 32.42.124.

to the Law,[23] is there anything more unclean than the vulture? And still, it contains as many medicinal remedies as there are parts to its body.[24] For a fact, I met a bishop who was then very old, and was said to have converted many thousands of pagans to the faith of Christ. He was telling the story, that while traveling through Ethiopia, he ate the flesh of a great dragon which, because of his hunger, was sweet to the taste. Thus the saying of the psalmist seems to be literally fulfilled, "You crushed the head of the great dragon, and gave it to the people of Ethiopia for food."[25]

(9) But while almighty God has subjected all things to man, this too is no less a marvel, that he also diversifies the seasons[26] for him, giving each a beautiful variety of qualities, namely, that first the winter snow covers the seeds that have been planted in the fields; then in the mild spring weather he causes the earth to give birth to various kinds of plants; next he lets the summer heat dry up the fields; and lastly, during the rainy fall he allows man to pick the grapes from the vines and ripe fruit from the trees. Nor does the almighty Creator collect the produce of trees and fields into one vast harvest, but he so disposes it that at different times various tasks are performed or various foods are eaten. For if all the fruit were ready to be enjoyed at the same time, the mass of produce would cause the consumers to loathe their very abundance, and by eating everything at once, would cause need in the midst of plenty. But as it is, the several harvests occur at various times, so that while one type is eaten, the other is maturing, and as some things are consumed and disappear, others soon ripen and take their place. Moreover, if the crops to be gathered should all pile up at the same time, they would overburden the farmers with work they could not bear; but since they are distributed over several periods of time, the harvest is not diminished and human labor is lightened. For Moses, too, reported to the Pharaoh that some of the crops came in early and that others matured later. After a hail-storm had hit Egypt he said, "The flax and barley were destroyed because the barley was

---

23. Cf. Lev 11.13–14; Deut 14.11–13.
24. Cf. Pliny, *Naturalis historia* 29.4.6; see also Cantin, *Sciences séculières* 556.
25. Ps 73.14.   26. Cf. Cantin, *Sciences séculières* 584.

in the ear and the flax in bud, but the wheat and spelt were not destroyed because they come later."[27] A little further on, speaking of the early fruit, he said, "All the vegetation was devoured and all the fruit of the trees that the hail had spared."[28]

(10) Therefore, since the seas and the rivers, the lakes and pools with their countless kinds of fish are forced to serve man alone, and also the air with its birds and showers, the earth with its animals and all its plants, these in the meantime I will set aside as minor, so that we might ponder more important things. So I will say nothing of the state of the world that is governed with such restraint, that air and fire, namely the two elements that are masculine,[29] are preeminent, while the other two, water and earth, which are feminine, hold a lesser position, and from this double marriage, as it were, is born everything that we observe proceeding from whatever original substance. Let me also pass over in silence, that the whole fabric of the heavens so marvelously serves the purposes of men, that it strives to proceed in a perpetual circular motion against the orbit of the seven planetary spheres, so that as they are rising, it continuously inclines toward its setting. Still, by its very magnitude, it attracts them to itself, forcing them to stay in their orbits throughout the zodiac for a period of time preordained for each. Consequently, in this struggle within the universe we perceive no small mystery of its spiritual import, if we consider the conflict that exists in man who is, indeed a lesser world.[30] For what does the sphere of the heavens, which includes the planets, represent, if not the human body that envelopes the rational soul? And indeed, the soul possesses, as it were, the seven planets, since it is filled with the same number of gifts of the Holy Spirit.

(11) And what is meant by the sphere inclining toward its setting, while the planets, on the other hand, harmoniously strive to rise, if not the fulfillment of what the Apostle says, "Our lower nature sets its desires against the spirit, while the spirit fights against it"?[31] Does he not complain that the sphere of the heav-

---

27. Exod 9.31–32.   28. Exod 10.15.

29. On the gender of the elements and the notion of the seven planets, cf. Reindel, *Briefe* 3.195, nn. 20, 22.

30. Cf. Bultot, *Pierre Damien* 78ff.   31. Gal 5.17.

ens seems to be in conflict with the planets when he laments the struggle between body and soul in these words, "I perceive that there is in my bodily members a different law, fighting against the law that my reason approves"?[32] And like the sphere attracting the planets in its wakes, he at once added, "Making me a prisoner under the law that is in my members, the law of sin."[33] And so, the seven planets tend to rise, while the rational soul under the impulse of the Holy Spirit strives to return to God who is the source of all things. The heavenly sphere, however, inclines towards its setting, when the flesh, by neglecting the things that are above, is borne down into the depths of sin. And thus it was written, "A perishable body weighs down the soul, and its frame of clay burdens the mind so full of thoughts."[34]

(12) But epistolary brevity does not allow me to pursue this subject any further. And what shall I say of this heavenly sphere so constantly turning in upon itself and not extending outward, that with the revolution of one of its hemispheres it is day, and with the revolution of the other, it is night? And it occurs in this fashion, that with one revolution of the whole heavenly sphere, it completes twenty-four hours which comprise one day followed by its night. In this fashion, as the heavens serve man, day is brightened by the rays of the sun, and night is illumined by varying light from the moon and the twinkling stars. But since this phenomenon can be physically observed, I will say nothing more, and now proceed to more important invisible things.

(13) He, moreover, who occupies himself with the words of the divine Scriptures, is not unaware that a great number of heavenly forces daily course through the world, reaching out to us a helping hand in our struggle. We read about them in Daniel, "Thousands upon thousands served him, and myriads upon myriads attended his presence."[35] Their purpose in serving God is to protect us from the attack of the evil spirits. Hence also Paul says, "They are ministrant spirits, sent out to serve, for the sake of those who are to inherit salvation."[36] Nor would human

---

32. Rom 7.23.　　　　　　　　　33. Rom 7.23.
34. Wis 9.15.
35. Dan 7.10. On this variant from the Vulgate, cf. Sabatier 2.871.
36. Heb. 1.14.

frailty be able to resist the cunning of such a sly and well-trained enemy unless angelic power repelled him from tempting the elect. Consequently, from the day of our baptism until our death, an angel is assigned to each of us to shield us from temptation as we fight bravely, and never stops providing assistance in the performance of good works.[37] I would cite examples of this, if I were not aware that through frequent repetition it is already well known.

(14) Let it be noted here, that the more graces God bestows on man, the greater is the offense he must suffer from man. God assigns angelic forces to watch over him, and by abandoning the splendid purity of virtue, unhappy man pollutes himself with the squalid filth of vice. For as he wallows in the muck of malodorous and obscene immorality; as he befouls himself with the dirt of worm-infested avarice; as again, like the rivers of Egypt, his murderous soul is turned into bloody hate; and finally, like one who falls into a cesspool, he is covered with the ordure of manifold wickedness: all this stench, this shameful and corrupting nausea our angel unwillingly and bravely bears, and does not refuse to obey, for he is bound by the law of God's command. In the sight of the angels, to be sure, nothing is filthy or obscene except vice and sin. And thus they are horrified by our depravity, and hate our uncleanness like a man forced to retch at the stench rising from a latrine. And so, before the tribunal of the eternal Judge our angel daily laments the wickedness of the man entrusted to him, and because he suffers grave injury, he calls attention to each of his wicked deeds.

(15) Now if a powerful king should wish to place his young son in the custody of one of his princes, and the boy, in an insane fury, befouls himself with spittle and with mucous that runs from his nose, or even in a wild frenzy throws himself into the fire, or wallows in the mud like a pig, will not the king immediately demand that the boy be returned and put an end to the services of the tutor? How much more credible it is that the angels in their

---

37. A clear statement of belief in a personal guardian angel, with a summary of angelology, reflecting biblical, patristic, and medieval teaching on angels. For fuller treatment, cf. Reindel, *Briefe* 3.197, n. 29; see also J. Michl, "Angels," NCE 1 (1967) 506–514, and associated articles.

high estate should glorify God who bestows all good things, because of the holy life of the saints, and in his sight condemn the crimes of wicked men by specifically enumerating them.

(16) To this we may add, that on the day of Judgment the angels will be witness to their wickedness, but if they had lived properly, they would have been their defenders. Therefore, it so happens that for those who perform evil deeds, the custody of the angels serves to bring on disaster, while for those who live upright lives it occasions their salvation, because the holy angels who have been assigned to help the just, tend to heighten the pains of hell for the damned. Those who live virtuously are indeed fortunate, for as the evil spirits implacably attack them, they are protected by the powerful assistance of the angels.

(17) Here we might also add, that these very spirits of evil are destined to serve our progress. For as we are tempted and do not fall, as we are assailed and still overcome, while, to be sure, our violent enemy attacks and does not overrun us, the amount of our future reward grows greater, and as it imposes on us the burden of combat, it supplies us with the means of victory.

(18) Note that as we hastily and lightly touch on all these matters, we find that everything harmoniously serves the utility of men: heaven, earth, and even hell. And possibly one might here accuse me of presumption, if the authentic evidence of Scripture were not at hand. But here is what Paul says to the Corinthians, "For though everything belongs to you—Paul, Apollos, and Cephas, this world, life and death, the present and the future, all of them belong to you—yet you belong to Christ, and Christ to God."[38] So then, everything truly belongs to man, if man himself is truly a man. For he who is really and truly a man, alone deserves to be called a man.

(19) Listen to what Solomon says, "For this is the end of the matter: we have heard it all. Fear God and obey his commands: there is not more to man than this."[39] Who, then, is the end of the matter, if not he of whom the Apostle says, "For Christ is the end of the Law as a way to justice for everyone who has faith?"[40]

---

38. 1 Cor 3.22–23.   39. Sir 12.13.
40. Rom 10.4.

Christ, indeed, is the end of the Law as a way to justice, because everything that the old or the new Law says doubtless refers to him. It is not idly observed that he is the way to justice, because the words of God's law make us just and cleanse the soul from filth, as Truth itself says to his disciples, "You have already been cleansed by the word that I spoke to you."[41] But to fear God means that we must despise and abominate all that God forbids. To observe his commands is to put into action all that he prescribes.

(20) Therefore, he fears God who is eager to avoid what he forbids. He observes his laws who earnestly fulfills what he commands. And so, fear God and carry out his laws: there is no more to man than this. It is as if he were saying specifically: He who is not careful to avoid forbidden things, he who fails to observe the commandments, since he is acting unreasonably, indeed bears the name "Man," but does not possess what is essentially human, because he does not truly use the power of the title that he bears. To be sure, he truly acts like a man who recognizes the Author of men;[42] otherwise, he who does not acknowledge this, will be rejected. Now if Scripture clearly describes what man is like without these qualities, when it says, "The stars are not innocent in God's eyes,"[43] how much more does this apply to man who is corrupt, mortal man who is only a worm? Hence, even Abraham when raised to the very heights of divine discourse, when uniquely rewarded with the grace of enjoying familiarity with God, was depressed by recalling his own lowliness, when he said, "May I presume to speak to my Lord, dust and ashes that I am?"[44]

(21) Now it is said that it is customary among the Greeks,[45] that when an emperor takes office, as soon as he is clothed in his imperial robes, and adorned with his glorious crown and scepter, and as he receives the obeisance of the nobility, followed by the plaudits of the chorus, a man comes forward and with one hand offers him a vessel filled with dust and bones of the dead, while holding in the other a candle wick made of flax, carefully

41. John 15.3.   42. Cf. 1 Cor 14.38.
43. Job 25.5.   44. Gen 18.27.
45. On the source of Damian's knowledge of these Byzantine customs, see Reindel, *Briefe* 3.199, n. 30.

combed and slightly broken by pendent figures, which is then ignited, and in the blink of an eye is quickly consumed. In the one symbol he should recognize what he is, and in the other be made aware of what he has. Indeed, in the ashes he realizes that he is but dust, and in the candle wick he can see how suddenly the earth will be consumed by fire on the day of Judgment.[46] Thus as he reflects that he and all that he has are so fleeting and unimportant, he will never become haughty after reaching the giddy heights of the imperial throne. And while never doubting that its occupant and all that he possesses are subject to a fate that is common to all, he who has risen to such grandeur will not pride himself on the dignity that seems to be his alone.

(22) Therefore, as man meditates on the beautiful order that rules over earth's affairs, as he sees that all things are given him for his use, he will not congratulate himself, but give thanks to his Creator. In his good judgment he should inhibit the enticing glory of this world by treading it under foot, acknowledge that the vitality of his body is but sterile dust, always hold the day of his death like a mirror before his eyes, and live in fear of the severe justice that will be meted out on the last day. Thus, as he now submits to the laws of his Creator, he who is so preeminent among all the creatures of this world, may also be truly exalted in the glory of heaven.

46. On this topic, see Damian, *Letters* 92 and 93.

LETTER 109

Peter Damian to Pope Alexander II. At the command of the pope, Damian in this letter wrote the life of Rodulphus, the bishop of Gubbio, and of Dominicus Loricatus. Both were hermits belonging to his congregation, and both lived exemplary lives deemed memorable by the pope. The author is obviously overawed by the ascetical virtuosity of Dominicus.

(July–August 1064)[1]

O THE BLESSED POPE, Sir Alexander,[2] the monk Peter the sinner offers his service.

(2) Your blessedness, venerable father, commanded me never to send letters to you that might contain something trifling, frivolous, or properly forgettable, which the reader promptly throws into the devouring fire after a hurried perusal.[3] But you stated that I should always write something for you that contributes to the edification of the readers and is deemed worthy of preservation among one's important papers. And so we should give thanks to the Father of Lights[4] who illumined the recesses of your heart with the fire of his love, that you might always seek comfort in the lives of the ancient Fathers; and besides, where they do not appear to be suitable, you do not fail to promote their writing.

(3) Recently, as I left you when visiting the city of Florence,[5] a messenger suddenly arrived and turned midday into darkness

1. Dating follows Lucchesi, *Vita s. Rodulphi* 171ff.; and *idem, Vita* 55ff., no. 53 and no. 190.

2. See Damian, *Letter* 96, n. 2. Before his elevation to the papacy, Anselm of Lucca accompanied Damian on the legation to Milan; see *Letter* 65. For a general discussion of their relationship, see Schmidt, *Alexander II* 179–187.

3. This remark throws light on the problem of the preservation of Damian's letters and of those received. Cf. Reindel, *Studien* 1.62.

4. Cf. Jas 1.17.

5. The pope had attended the council of Mantua, and afterwards travelled to Pomposa and Lucca. Damian accompanied him on his tour through the Romagna.

for me, giving me the very sad news that the bishop of Gubbio was dead.[6] If you remember, his life was such that it would truly edify those who heard of it. It would also serve to provide a model for virtuous living and of applying discipline for the correction of abuses. Now, about seven years ago, he and his mother and his two brothers, who were somewhat older than he, after first freeing their serfs, turned over to me his castle, impregnably fortified, with all the lands that belong to him, and entering the hermitage, made his religious profession.

(4) I then built a monastery on their lands,[7] and for this holy house that now normally supports itself, I greatly rejoice in the Lord. Living there with their mother and other brother, who is in poor health, Rodulphus, who was later consecrated a bishop, and his older brother, Peter, led such a severe and disciplined eremitical life that their reputation became something marvelous to those who heard of it, and their conduct made them outstanding among their confreres. And, indeed, if I were to relate of Peter everything that is at hand, this piece of parchment would hardly suffice, and there would still be much to say. But to speak briefly of at least one matter among many, while we were once having a discussion in chapter, debating the subject of our prescribed disciplinary practices, Peter, who was still a novice, used an improper word that he was accustomed to say as a layman. Acting as if I were quite angry, I then corrected him harshly, and after a lengthy reproof, as if I were passing sentence on one who had been subjected to inquisition, I ordered him to abstain from drinking wine for forty days. It was my intention only temporarily to put the fear of God in him and others for using improper speech, and then later to moderate the penalty and discreetly rescind it. But as it happened, I was preoccupied with various other matters, and since no one called this to my attention, after the prescribed number of days had elapsed, with a start I suddenly remembered and anxiously inquired what Peter had done about the penance that had been given him. And so, from what the brothers told me, I learned that the penance had

6. For a lengthy discussion of Rodulphus of Gubbio and the year of his death in 1064, cf. Reindel, *Briefe* 3.202–203, nn. 5–6.

7. San Bartolomeo di Camporeggiano; cf. *It. Pont.* 4.90f.

been fulfilled. I must admit that I was sorry for having imposed this sentence, but was happily surprised at this brother's great patience, that for only one heedlessly spoken word he had borne so long a penance, and that neither of his own accord nor through others had asked for its remission.

(5) But now let us get back to the bishop with whom we began. Although Peter was the older and always took the lead in difficult tasks and in observing an ascetical life, still when Rodulphus was promoted to the episcopal office, he did not fail to practice in his diocese what he had learned in the hermitage. He continued to torment his body by wearing his usual hair shirt, and was satisfied with the same poor and despicable garments. Since he was young, and often suffered from grave melancholy because of his passionate nature, he used to attach ropes to the rafters in his cell, and inserting his arms, chanted the psalms while thus suspended. He never ate fat or eggs or cheese. Mortified in the use of food that was placed before him, he practiced such frugality, that sitting at table was more a battle than a meal, and while outwardly seeming to eat, he was rather waging an inner war with gluttony. I often argued with him that at least during the cold winter weather he should put straw under his papyrus mat, or at night sleep in his clothes. He would lay naked on a bare board, satisfied with wearing only his undershirt. He considered the church, moreover, to be his guest-house, while he thought of the solitude of his cell as his dwelling-place. By their irregular lives, his people never allowed him to place the mild yoke of the Lord[8] on their undisciplined necks, but intent on earthly rewards, paid no attention to what their bishop had to say, looking to him for favors as from the hands of a prince. For the more this region is impoverished, the greater is its propensity to vice. Indeed, Gubbio (*Egubium*) seems to derive form the word "destitute" (*egendo*), that is, in need of something good. And therefore, by reason of his oath of office, when forced by my insistence, he again took possession of the diocese he had deserted, but continued to live in the hermitage.

(6) Whenever it was available here, he ate bread, like the kind

8. Cf. Matt 11.30.

of bread made in the hermitage. It was not the kind that was provided for the brothers, or that was usually given to children, but a variety that was made of pure barley, or rather of bran, remnants of the bread eaten by children that were thrown to the dogs. And even though he was content to eat this bread each day except on the greater feasts, he carefully weighed the amount of it on his scales.[9] And so, at a time he complained to me that if he allowed himself the total amount he would feel like a glutton indulging his appetite for this bread. This young man chastised his body with such fasting, that whenever he became aware of his need to eat, he paid little heed to his empty stomach. At times, even on Sundays, passing up the stew, he lived only on fruit, bread, and water. He always wore an iron band round his waist, but took care to hide it under the folds of his stomach when he divested himself before the brothers. He never confessed his faults at a chapter in which he would not receive the discipline, and then was most happy when ordered to be scourged, not only by one, but by two of his confreres. He often took on himself a penance of one hundred years, which he fulfilled in twenty days by lashing himself and applying other penitential remedies.[10] When unable to finish two, he never failed daily to recite at least one psalter. Since he did this while in his cell, he normally said the whole psalter while taking the discipline, which he applied with both hands.

(7) Moreover, whenever he traveled, he would rise in the dead of night, no matter what weather, and continued praying the psalms with bare legs and feet until dawn. When in his cell, he observed this habit, night and day, without letting up. Whatever the rigors of the winter, he wore only stockings on his feet, while his brother was content to wear only sandals. Often he would solemnly charge me by the mercy of Christ, never to hesitate in punishing him if he should perhaps sin in any way, but to apply to him every kind of discipline which monks deserved. In this way he laudably observed the Rule as a monk, and in turn preserved his authority as a bishop. On all occasions[11] he en-

9. Cf. *Letter* 50.21, n. 38.
11. Cf. 2 Tim 4.2.

10. On flagellation, see *Letter* 45.

gaged in preaching, and whatever he was able to spare from domestic expenses, he lavished on the poor. Each year he held a synod, never permitting the accustomed taxes or gifts to be demanded from the clerics, not even a payment from those who had fallen, except only as a penance. "God forbid," he would say, "that I should sell a synod. I would rather lift up the fallen than feast on their dead bodies like a vulture." I should rather not write any more, lest it seem that sorrow over Icarus were keeping his father's hands from his painting.[12]

(8) And so, after being graced with virtues of this kind, like a bright lily he withered in the winter of an untimely death, and when scarcely thirty years of age, departed this unhappy life to return to the Author of true light. "In a short time," as Scripture says, "he came to the perfection of a full span of years. His soul was pleasing to the Lord."[13] And rightly was it said that in a short time he came to the perfection of a full span of years, for in the brief time that he lived, he held to the path of justice, and with all that was in him spent each year in the service of the Creator. Surely, what Wisdom had formerly reported of the holy man so applied to Rodulphus in everything as if it were especially said of him. "It is not length of life," she stated," and number of years which bring the honor due to age. If men have understanding, they have grey hairs enough; for an unspotted life, pleasing to God, is the true ripeness of age."[14] And then she continued, "God accepted him and took him while still living among sinful men. He was snatched away before his mind could be perverted by wickedness or his soul deceived by falsehood. Therefore, he removed him early from a wicked world."[15]

(9) But as I look about for someone to bring this letter to you, and he is not available,[16] I suddenly think of something else, which, if put to writing, would more fully serve to edify you. Perhaps it was divine providence that failed to supply a carrier, so that in the meantime, with nothing else to do, I might write about yet another topic. And so, I come to that man of God, Do-

---

12. Cf. Ovid, *Met.* 8.223ff. and Hyginus, *Fabula* 40.
13. Wis 4.13–14.   14. Wis 4.8–9.
15. Wis 4.10–11, 13–14.
16. On sending letters by carriers, cf. Reindel, *Studien* 1.60.

minic,[17] my father and master, who died about a year ago. If his life should be written, I am afraid that it would be thought incredible by some of the brothers. But God forbid that I should lie in what I write. For as I truly do everything in my power to honor the truth, I will not allow any fabrication or falsehood. Nor am I unaware of the Apostle's statement, who in saying, "If Christ did not rise form the dead, then our preaching is null and void, and so is your faith," at once continued, "and we turn out to be lying witnesses for God, because we bore witness against God that he raised Christ to life, whereas, if the dead do not come back to life, he did not raise him."[18] In these words of the Apostle's statement, not to belabor the case, the reader at once understands that whoever pretends that God or God's servant has performed some marvelous deed, will not only not deserve a reward for his fabricated account, but will be found guilty of giving false testimony against him whom he set out to praise.

(10) And so, while Dominic was still a cleric in the world and the heresy of simony was then prevalent—and would to God it were totally extinct—his parents gave the bishop a piece of soft goat skin that he might be ordained a priest.[19] But since, as the Apostle says, "all things work together for the good for those who love God,"[20] this one fault of this holy man later proved to be the source of many good deeds. For, terrified over this event, he despised the world, became a monk, and like a brave soldier, at once took up the difficult practice of the eremitic life. And because he had been improperly ordained, so long as he lived he never dared to celebrate Mass.[21] He remained chaste until his death, and never left the hermitage where he lived for many years under the direction of that blessed man, John of Montefeltro.[22] In this hermitage, called Luceoli located in the region known as Ponterezzoli, there were eighteen cells that served as

17. For a lengthy bibliography of Dominicus Loricatus, see Reindel, *Briefe* 3.207, n.20.

18. 1 Cor 15.14–15.

19. On the problem of simony in this event, see Calamoneri, *San Pier Damiani agiografo* 183f.

20. Rom 8.28.

21. Here we have evidence that like Dominic, other hermits were priests.

22. Cf. Mittarelli-Costadoni, *Annales Camaldulenses* 1.417f.

residences for the brothers, where he lived under the regimen that they would never drink wine, and never prepare their food with fat. They ate only one warm dish on Sundays and Thursdays, and five days a week fasted on bread and water, engaged only in prayer or manual labor. They did not farm, and owned no lands or other property, except one pack animal.[23] Along with this little ass or horse there was one attendant who faithfully went out either to buy or to mill grain, and only he supplied the hermits with all necessities. This was John, who afterwards became abbot of this hermitage, and governed the community as an upright administrator. The whole week long they observed strict silence, which they broke on Sunday after Vespers and when their meal was finished, when they could then converse with one another until Compline. In their cells, moreover, they always went barefoot, with no covering for their legs. Dominic told me that when he was living with a certain religious named Anso, whom I also met, they used to apply the discipline to one another while reciting all the canonical hours. This same Anso once complained that he had nine daily rations of bread in his stomach at the same time. For they mortified themselves with such fasting, that the dry bread caused constipation, and could be passed only with difficulty.

(11) In that hermitage there was also another brother who often attempted to wander away from his cell. John, the prior, as was only proper, at first severely corrected him, and then commanded that he be thrashed in his presence. But when, at the master's order, he began to put on his clothes, he made some insolent remark. The master again told him to divest himself, and again had him beaten. But as he began to dress himself, he still did not hesitate to show his contempt for what had happened. And so, for a third, a fourth, and if I remember correctly, even a sixth time he was scourged without mending his ways. As he stripped and again put on his clothes, he was unable to respond with humility. But when he was whipped for the seventh time, and then began to clothe himself, he cried out in a loud voice, "Now the devil has left, now that wicked tenant who lived in my

23. On *sagmarius*, the Latin word used here, cf. DuCange 7.268.

heart has fled, and has left me free of the bonds that held me. Now I will gladly obey my lord and master, and I promise to subject myself to his orders in all things." In this way the brother returned to the observance of humility, and as he continued from then on to remain in his cell, he lived there blamelessly.

(12) Many years later, with the consent of his prior, this holy man saw fit in a spirit of marvelous humility to come to me, a miserable and unworthy servant, to ask if I would accept him and allow him to subject himself to me as a monk does to his abbot. But what he offered me, I did not accept. For, instead of receiving him under my obedience as a client, I was happy to accept him into this school of Christ as a true philosopher and teacher. Indeed, his whole life was a learned lecture as well as a sermon, it was both instruction and discipline. But since I have already included many of this holy man's words and deeds in what I have written in my other works, it does not seem out of place to insert them here in what I have in hand, in the very words I used before. Surely, it is an easier task to construct a roof from dressed lumber, than to double the work by planing the wood and building at the same time. For it was written of the temple of Solomon, "In the building of the house, only blocks of dressed and perfect stone were used; no hammer or axe or any iron tool whatever was heard in the house while it was being built."[24] In my clumsy ways, I too have polished stones, which will surely suffice if I simply fit them into the structure just as I found them.

(13) In the letter I sent to Sir Teuzo,[25] I find that I wrote the following, "But when recalling holy men, why do I go about looking in various odd places, since right here at home I have someone at hand whom I cannot even begin to praise sufficiently? He and I are separated from one another by the church that stands between us, with our cells on either side, and if I were to stay up nights recounting his virtues, days would pass, I think, before I ran short of material to write about. I am speaking of Dominic, my lord and teacher, whose speech, to be sure, is the vernacular, but whose life is truly accomplished and elegant. His life is a better

24. 1 Kgs 6.7.
25. Cf. Damian, *Letter* 44.17.

tool for edification when he preaches in living deeds, than some sterile language that foolishly weighs each word in the neat balance of classical usage. For many years he wore an iron corselet next to his flesh,[26] and engaged in implacable combat with the evil spirits. This eager fighter was always ready for battle, armed not only in spirit, but also bodily went forth against the enemy lines.

(14) "He was so accustomed to this way of life, that hardly a day passed without chanting two psalters, beating his naked body with both hands armed with scourges, and that, even at times when we relaxed from our penance.[27] In the Lenten season, or when he had a penance to perform—often he took to doing a hundred years of penance—he then punished himself daily with blows of the scourge, meditatively reciting at least three psalters. Now a hundred years of penance, as I learned from Dominic himself, is performed in this way. While three thousand blows regularly count as one year of penance here, chanting ten psalms accounts for a thousand blows, as we have often proven. Since we know that the psalter contains one hundred and fifty psalms, five years of penance, if we count correctly, are contained in disciplining oneself throughout one psalter. Now if you multiply five by twenty or twenty by five, you arrive at a hundred. And so, when one has chanted twenty psalters while taking the discipline, one is sure that he has performed a hundred years of penance.

(15) "Yet also in this matter our Dominic surpasses many others, for while some use one hand in administering the discipline, he, like a true son of Benjamin,[28] untiringly fights against the rebellious desires of the flesh with both hands. As he himself admitted to me, as is his custom, he easily completes a hundred years of penance in six days. I also recall that at the beginning of one of the Lents that was approaching, he asked me to allow him to take on a thousand years of penance, and completed nearly all of them before the season of fast was over." And then a little farther on, I continued.[29]

26. On the use of iron bands, a widespread practice in oriental monasticism, see the lengthy discussion in Reindel, *Briefe* 3.210–211, n. 32.

27. On self-flagellation, see Damian, *Letter* 44.

28. Cf. Judg 20.16. 29. Cf. Damian, *Letter* 44.

(16) "Now let me return to Dominic about whom I had begun to speak. Even now when he is bent down by old age and frequently weakened, moreover, by sickness, one must wonder at how fervent and eager he is in not letting down, always remaining tireless in his spiritual exercises. For, as I know from his own words, he often continuously recites two psalters while standing and taking the discipline, never once sitting down nor resting for a moment from flogging himself in an unbelievably fervent mood. When once I asked him whether he was able to perform any genuflections with the weight of his iron garment, he answered me in this rather obscure way, 'When my health allows me to do what I wish, I am sometimes accustomed to perform a hundred genuflections for each fifteen psalms of the whole psalter.' At that time I did not pay much attention to what he had said, but later when thinking it over, I marveled that such a weakened man could perform a thousand prostrations in the course of one psalter.

(17) "One day after Vespers he came into my cell. 'Master,' he said—his humility urged him to address me with this title that I did not deserve—'today I did something I do not remember doing until now: I completed eight psalters in the usual way during the course of a day and a night.' His whole appearance seemed to be so beaten with scourges and so covered with livid welts, as if he had been bruised like barley in a mortar. Chanting the psalms has, indeed, become so easy for him because, as he asserted, he does not recite them verbatim, but vigorously runs through their meaning mentally.

(18) "At one time he lived somewhat removed from my cell. When he came over and I asked him what norms he was now living by, he replied that he was now living sensually, and that always on Thursdays and Sundays he relaxed from his normal rigorous abstinence. When asked whether he ate some dish made with eggs or cheese, he said no. 'What about fish or fruit?' I asked. 'If we have any fish or fruit,' he said, 'I give them to the sick, of whom, sad to say, there is quite a number in our area.' When in determined fashion I backed him into a corner, saying, 'How can you claim that on those days you relax a bit from your penance, when you eat nothing that needs cooking or is to be

found on trees?' he answered, 'I enjoy eating fennel with my bread.' So now I was an expert, knowing how sensually a man could live who considered fennel a delicacy.

(19) "He clearly has a copious gift of tears,[30] but only from time to time. When he is all alone, living in the strictest silence, he breaks into tears just as often as he wishes. But if he takes part in conversation, he complains that he has lost the gift of tears. I would often reproach him over the lack of tears caused by my own dryness, saying, 'Alas, my father, these tears of yours do not bear fruit, since they cannot beget tears in others when they ask. For I would surely wish that since you are a father to me, your tears should also beget my tears.' "

(20) I also remember inserting the following in my rule of the eremitic life.[31] "I will speak of another, but who will know whether my statement should be believed or not? Yet one can make light of it if human audacity reproves a person whom the highest Truth does not charge with lying. There is a brother in our community[32] who often spends a whole day and a night meditatively reciting the psalter nine times, and while so doing, almost continuously beats his naked body with scourges held in both hands. It should be noted that while he is so engaged, he does not sleep day or night, but at times while on his knees, he rests his head on the ground, and thus naked, he snatches a little sleep, and with that he is satisfied. At one time as we were engaged in friendly conversation, he confided to me that he had often recited these nine psalters, but could never come to a tenth."

(21) I further notice that I wrote the following in the letter I sent to the Countess Blanche.[33] "I wish it were now possible for you to observe my lord Dominic, who would more readily teach and direct you by the example of his outstanding life than anything I might achieve by my unskilled words. For almost fifteen years now, this man wore an iron corselet next to his flesh, girded himself with two iron bands, and used two others that restricted his shoulders.

---

30. Again, cf. Damian, *Letter* 44.   31. Damian, *Letter* 50.37.

32. Dominic's name occurs in *Letters* 44, 50, and 66. Here Damian omits his name, but it may be presumed that he is speaking of Dominic.

33. Damian, *Letter* 66.

(22) "Since, however, I have already related many things about him in my other works, I will now recount what he told me scarcely six days ago when he came to see me. On that occasion he said, 'I happen to know that you wrote about me reciting nine psalters[34] in one day while taking the discipline. Indeed, when I heard this, I began to tremble and worry, and as my conscience rebuked me, began to weep. "What a fool I am," I said, "without my knowledge, look what was written about me, and I still don't know whether I can bring this off. So, let me try again and find out for certain whether I can do it." Therefore, on Wednesday I took off my clothes, and with a switch in both hands, stayed up the whole night, and did not stop chanting and whipping myself until on the following day, after finishing twelve psalters in this fashion, I slowly dragged myself through the thirteenth up to the psalm, "Blessed are they."[35]'

(23) "Let me further enlighten you with an example of what often seemed to me a harsh and difficult thing, but which he considered child's play and hardly worth noticing. A certain brother was terrified at beating himself, and considered it a fearful burden to scourge himself and bear up under it. But at length he accepted the advice that the lord Dominic frequently gave him, and kept on disciplining himself while chanting the entire psalter, to which he added fifty more psalms.

(24) "This happened during the night preceding a Sunday, the feast of St. Michael.[36] The next morning this brother went to the old man, and fearing that he might be thought guilty of indiscretion, related exactly what he had done. Dominic replied in these words, 'Brother, don't be ashamed and lose courage over your present weakness. God can surely lift you up from lowly things to those that are higher, and toughen the milkfed days of your childhood until you grow to manly strength.' And he added, 'I also began gradually, and even though weak and frail, I slowly reached the goal toward which God's goodness led me.' And so it happened that he did not accuse the young man of excessive fervor, as the brother had feared, but rekindled his spirit, keep-

---

34. Damian, *Letter* 50.37 and *Letter* 66.25 and n. 115.
35. Ps 31.1.   36. Cf. Damian *Letter* 66, n. 117.

ing him from despair for having done so little. Thus, by the example of this holy old man in taking the discipline, the custom spread in our area, so that not only men, but even noble women eagerly took up this form of purgatory.[37] For the widow of Tethbaldus,[38] a woman of noble birth and great dignity, once told me that by taking the discipline according to a predetermined norm, she had satisfied a hundred years of penance."

(25) Also in the letter to John, the prior of the hermitage that lies near Mount Suavicinum,[39] exhorting him and his subjects to pray with arms extended, I first spoke of one of our brothers named Adam,[40] who was most fervent in the love of Christ, and then cited the example of Dominic in these words, "We have here a certain young brother who admitted to me that while chanting the psalter from beginning to end he held his arms aloft, so that often his hands touched the beamed ceiling of his cell. This he did with the proviso that, after completing each fifty psalms, he would lower his arms for a moment, and then immediately elevate them once more. We have another brother, a stooped old man of advanced years, who, as I secretly told you, is Dominic. Once he found a scrap of writing whereon it said, that 'if one should chant the herein mentioned twelve psalms twenty-four times with hands extended in the form of a cross, one would regularly be able to compensate for one year of penance.' At once he began to carry out what was said there, and in one turn, daily chanted the twelve psalms with his arms extended in the form of a cross twenty-six times, as was said, without pausing at all." I perhaps wrote about this topic in other works of mine, but because they are either not at hand, or do not readily come to mind,[41] I shall not now repeat what was already written, and shall move on to something new.

37. This is perhaps an early use of the term *purgatorium*, a substantive, in the sense of a place of reparation after death. Cf. K. Rahner, "Fegfeuer," LThK 4.51. See also Hildebert of Lavardin, *In dedicatione ecclesiae sermo quartus* (PL 171.741C).

38. Cf. Damian, *Letter* 66.

39. Cf. Damian, *Letter* 53, otherwise unknown except for this fragment.

40. Damian addressed *Letter* 92 to him, explaining the events that would precede the Last Judgement.

41. In fact, however, Damian was able to cite from four letters: 44, 50, 53, and 66.

(26) Indeed, it seemed that divine fire always burned in his breast, never allowing him to rest in his spiritual effort. Once on the holy day of Easter, when the other brothers, as was customary, were taking a siesta,[42] I asked him if he too were going to sleep. He said, "Truly, father, I said to myself, why should I sleep during the day, when nights are still so long. So I stretched out my arms in the form of a cross and started the psalter, and thus standing in prayer, I went right on till the three o'clock bell sounded." Thus he combined the victory of the cross with the glory of the resurrection. Occasionally, as is our habit, when we talked together of daily events, he would say, "I will tell you what happened to me last night. As I finished sleeping and got up, I spread my arms in the form of a cross and started a psalter. When I had finished all the psalms, and the hymns and canticles that follow, and was at the point where I had only to say the psalm on the Catholic faith[43] and the litanies, I happened to think that for the moment I would bypass them and recite a psalter for the dead. And so, without lowering my arms, I began the office of the dead, which customarily is composed of fifty psalms with three lessons interspersed. When this was finished, I returned to what I had previously omitted, and completed the remaining prayers of the first psalter. And as I then thought about going on to a third psalter, the blessed signal for Matins, as I call it, suddenly sounded, urging me to lower my arms and celebrate the office with the brothers. Certainly I did not know then that at this time of the year the nights were so short."

(27) Some years before his death, moreover, he discovered a new kind of torture, changing from green branches to a whip for beating himself, and after once trying it, because it inflicted greater pain he adopted this scourge as his discipline. Whenever he left the hermitage, he carried this instrument on his person, so that wherever he might be, he would not omit his scourging. But once when he was in a place where he could not completely take off his clothes, he did not cease from chastising himself, at least about the legs and thighs, and about the head and shoul-

---

42. On the custom of taking an afternoon nap, cf. *Benedicti regula*, c. 48.
43. Probably, the so-called Athanasian symbol is here meant. Cf. G. Owens, "Athanasian Creed," NCE 1 (1967) 995–996.

ders. To the four iron bands, which from long custom had become rather worthless for him, he added four others, wearing two about his hips and two others on his legs. The corselet, moreover, that he wore like a hairshirt or like a woolen garment, he washed every month or after a longer period, that it would be free of rust and would not cause sores on his dry skin. All of us who live in these cells, take precautions to protect our feet from the cold by wearing a habit that reached to the floor. But this, it seemed to me, was intolerable for him, for besides never wearing shoes or stockings in the hermitage he had a habit that barely reached to the middle of his legs. When he had taken off his clothes in chapter to receive the discipline, something he wished never to forego, his body was so emaciated from fasting and so worn by the weight of the rough corselet, that it seemed to have taken on the dark complection of an Ethiopian. His worn and ghastly garments, I might say, seemed to be in tatters with age. He often had this to say to me, "Chanting the psalms quickly, benefits the chanter if he keeps his mind on the words, and if his mind truly understands what the tongue is saying. Otherwise, if the mind wanders, one will only slowly complete the psalms, as the tongue makes mistakes or at times grows tired." He also said that sleep nourishes sleep, while staying awake begets wakefulness; for the human body, at first fed only a little at a time, is thereby afterwards gradually strengthened.

(28) But here, perhaps, someone might object that he is not interested in what kind of life this holy man led, but would like to hear of the miracles for which he was renowned. To such it will suffice to reply shortly, that we do not read of either Mary or John the Baptist performing miracles, but still their life is contained, not in just some ordinary work, but in the Gospel itself. And yet, only by giving birth to her Son, Mary undoubtedly surpassed the miracles and signs of all the saints. I may also say that the remarkable life of holy men is more rewarding for those who hear of it than a display of miracles. The former, in fact, prompts imitation, while the latter promote only admiration. Miracles teach how holy these men were, but their life shows how men today can be holy. Moreover, you who seek miracles, does it not seem admirable to you, that a man still clothed in fragile flesh

could live, I might say, like an angel, so that among countless thousands of men you can scarcely find one who was like him? And certainly, there are many men today leading mediocre lives, through whom almighty God sees fit to work miracles.

(29) As Jesus is my witness, I do not lie when I tell you that hardly three months ago, while I was staying at the hermitage of Gamugno,[44] two young monks came there, one of whom said he was born in the duchy of Spoleto, while the other was a native of the city of Pola in the region of Venice.[45] The Venetian, named Michael, as he told me in confession, at the very beginning of his religious life bound himself with an iron band, with this purpose in mind and resolutely requesting the goodness of almighty God, that when he found a monastery that would be conducive to his eternal salvation, the band would suddenly be broken. Then on the very day he entered this hermitage as a novice, scarcely three hours after his arrival, as he was struggling syllable by syllable through the Rule of St. Benedict, since he was unlettered, suddenly the spirit of compunction caused him to break into tears, and at that very moment the band was broken. Quickly passing over this miracle, because I recall that I have spoken of it elsewhere,[46] I will simply relate another event that has not yet appeared in writing.

(30) Shortly after this had happened, on my orders he traveled to the city of Ravenna to collect his few belongings and the light luggage that he had left behind as he debarked from the ship. While there he went to the blacksmith who made new shackles of iron, and playing the role of both judge and criminal, he encumbered his limbs with many chains. Two pieces hung from his neck over both shoulders, one reaching to the genitals the other to the thigh; two went around the hips, and two around the arms. And thus weighed down by these multiple impediments, he returned to the hermitage, secretly showed me what he had done, and at length barely obtained permission that I should not alter anything that he wished to do. But when these bonds began to cause him more torment than he could bear,

44. On Gamugno, cf. Reindel, *Briefe* 3.218, n. 55.
45. Cf. Damian, *Letter* 56.14.   46. *Ibid.*

and an offensive odor arose from his irritated flesh, it also came to pass that as he rejected all renown for what he was doing, he was greatly disturbed. For the rumor of this wonder began to spread, first among the brothers, and then on the lips of those who came to visit us. He therefore begged almighty God in his mercy to clearly indicate his will in the matter by some sign of his power.

(31) In the meantime, however, as he persisted in this request, he was twice assured in a dream that his iron bonds would soon be loosened by God. An then on the feast of the blessed apostles, Simon and Jude,[47] which we were currently celebrating, as he attended the night office with the brethren, suddenly the two iron chains he wore over his shoulders, both of which hung down to restrict his stomach and waist, were completely broken, one into two parts, the other into three. The remaining bonds, however, were not severed into parts, but became so loose, so soft and flexible, as if they were made of cloth and not of iron, and even if he had wished to restrict himself with these loosely flowing bands, he could not do so. And thus, this brother who was bound by the ardor of such holy devotion, was miraculously freed by God's loving decision. So, what would be so great if God wished to work some wonder through Dominic, who was such a remarkable man, since he saw fit to perform two miracles through this young man at the very beginning of his novitiate, for it is more praiseworthy to have done great deeds rather than novel ones? Hence, when David said, "Marvelous is God in his saints," he at once added, "He will give his people might and abundant power."[48] He does not speak of signs and portents, but he will give might and abundant power.

(32) At one time, moreover, when a certain Roman named Stephen[49] was presiding as judge of the sacred palace in the county of Osimo, Dominic went before him in a case that was pending, and earnestly petitioned him regarding a certain piece of property of the hermitage that he was holding up by authority of the Apostolic See. But the judge regarded him lightly be-

---

47. On 28 October.   48. Ps 67.36.
49. Neither Stephen nor his office can be identified.

cause he was dressed so shabbily, and turned down his every request. When those who were in attendance said to him, "Do not treat him so harshly, for he is a holy man," he bitterly replied, "He may be holy, as you say, but blessed Peter whose rights I protect in this administration, is certainly holier." And so, Dominic returned to his cell empty-handed and shortly after, the judge went back to Rome. But a young man of lowly station, who remained behind to finish some administrative tasks, devoutly carried out whatever Dominic had asked of the judge. Not long thereafter, the latter returned to his home, where he died from wounds inflicted by assassins' swords, and because he had no children, left his extensive wealth to be inherited by strangers.

(33) Dominic, moreover, was very cautious in his speech, so that the statement of James the apostle aptly applied to him, "One who never says a wrong thing is a perfect man."[50] For whenever he was asked what time it was, he would never reply that it was exactly any given hour, but always qualified his answer by saying it was about nine o'clock or about twelve o'clock. When I asked him why he always spoke in this way, he replied, "By so doing I avoid lying. For whether it is already past the hour, or if perhaps somewhat before, it is still close enough, and approximately correct for the moment at which we were conversing."

(34) At one time he had a cell near the monastery known as Santo Emiliano de Conjunctulo.[51] On the vigil of Christmas[52] he went out, prompted by the solemnity of the feast, since during the entire Advent he had stayed in his cell chastising himself with fasting and work, and humbly prostrated himself at the feet of the abbot of that house, begged for a penance, and with tears confessed his sins in thought and deed. But the latter was a young man, easygoing in manner and unaccustomed to giving spiritual advice, who would usually think it sufficient to impose a penance of one psalm or some other slight thing. But for the sins that Dominic had confessed he prescribed that he should chant thirty psalters. When Dominic came to his senses, struck

---

50. Jas 3.2.
51. On the monastery of Santo Emiliano de Conjunctulo near Sassoferrato, see *It. Pont.* 4.91f.; Cottineau, *Répertoire* 1.859.
52. 24 December.

by this sentence as by an arrow, he concluded that this had happened at the disposition of divine judgment. Therefore, going back to his cell, he did not leave it until with the most constant zeal he had completed the prescribed amount of penance that had been given him.

(35) At times he used to drink wine, though most sparingly, yet long before his death he determined to give it up altogether. And now, passing over other items in his career, we come to his death. He suffered from stomach trouble and besides had to endure frequent headaches. And since one thing is usually occasioned by the other, he decided to purge his stomach by taking a cup of some medicine. And so, on Friday he continued either chanting the psalms or scourging himself with his whip for almost the whole day. But that night, after rising from sleep, he took the medicine, and at once suffered great distress, complaining of the severe pain in his stomach. When the night office was over, and after the hymns for the Lauds, and while Prime was being chanted for him by the brothers who were present, he gave back his holy soul to God. Then they found a second corselet besides the one that he wore, wrapped under his ribs like a shroud. Hence the brothers suspected that this could never have happened unless he had always worn it, and since he was used to wearing it under the other when he was in good health, he did not remove it when he was sick.

(36) Now a certain brother dreamt about me that I would lose my sight. When I spoke of this to Hildebrand, the venerable archdeacon of the Roman Church, while we were in the Lateran palace, he said to me, "This is certainly not, as you fear, a sign that you are soon going to die, but it points to someone who is your friend, as dear to you as your eyesight, one who is brilliant in the performance of good works." How true was this foreboding, but bitterer than gall! For three days after I left Rome, the cruel message reached me, every bit as bad as the notion that I would go blind, that Dominic, my lord and guiding light, had recently died. Then it became clear to me, that while he enjoyed the presence of the Author of light, I would have to remain in this world of darkness. The very night he died, the brothers quickly buried his body in the ground dug up in his cell, lest it be

taken away from them by neighboring monks. But on the very Sunday I arrived at the hermitage, I reverently removed his holy body from its resting place, as was only proper, and buried it in the chapter room. And even though it was already nine days since he died, I found his body whole and incorrupt.

(37) Now let those who are so inclined, delight in pampering their flesh; let them drink to the fill of the deepest pleasure, and nourish the eternal flames that await the slaughtered victim. Let them lift themselves up on the wings of pride, claim how innocent they are, and live as voluptuously as they will, so that their inmost being may later be embittered by the pains of avenging punishment. Like unbroken horses, let them now romp through the fields of their voluptuous desires, that afterwards they may be shackled, hand and foot, by the bonds of endless torture.[53] Our Dominic, however, bore in his body the stigmata of Jesus,[54] and fixed the sign of the cross not only on his forehead, but printed it on every part of his body. Burned out, and as dry as a reed without moisture, he was rewarded like the rushes, watered with an abundant rain of heavenly grace. In his life he was girt with an iron corselet, but in heaven he is clothed with the snow-white vesture of angelic glory. Here he was restrained by the harshness of his cell, but there he is comforted in the pleasant company of the patriarchs. His whole life was for him a Good Friday crucifixion, but now with festive splendor he celebrates the eternal glory of the resurrection. Now he sparkles amid the stones that flash like fire in the heavenly Jerusalem,[55] now he lives in triumph with eternal praise adorned with the badge of his victory, and exults in happy union with the blessed.

(38) Saint Dominic died on the fourteenth of October in the reign of our Lord Jesus Christ, who lives and rules with God the Father and the Holy Spirit for ever and ever. Amen.

---

53. Cf. Matt 22.13.   54. Cf. Gal 6.17.
55. Cf. Ezek 28.14.

LETTER 110

Peter Damian to Mainardus, the bishop of Urbino. Written to an obviously wealthy prelate, a man acquainted with the great men and women of his time, this work stresses the value of almsgiving for those who feel that they cannot indulge in more rigorous forms of penance. Damian demonstrates a fine sense of social consciousness: that the rich are only administrators of their wealth, and that when they give alms, they are dispensing only what belongs to others and not to themselves. Here also the author indulges in a bit of autobiography, and provides a source for several contemporary events.

(Summer 1064)[1]

O SIR MAINARDUS,[2] the venerable and holy bishop of Urbino, the monk Peter the sinner sends greetings in the Lord.

(2) He who in the summertime takes his rest in the shade, and is then not engaged in battle, still does not act incongruously if he discusses the martial arts. We are not wasting our time if while resting we are concerned with our work. By so doing, its fruit is even sweeter and its results will grow more plentiful. If one is living at the royal court, he explores all his manly qualities to find out how he might more readily please the prince, and where he discovers he can do his best, he there strives to perfect himself. One, to be sure, may excel in combat, while another is more adept in giving counsel. As the latter pleads cases in court,

1. Dating follows Lucchesi, *Vita* no. 191.
2. Mainardus was bishop of Urbino (1056–1088). In MSS Ut1, V2, and 8 other MSS, this letter is addressed to Adraldus (Aldradus) of Breme, after serving as a monk in Cluny, prior in Peterlingen, and later abbot of Breme near Vercelli. Still later (1069–1075) he was the bishop of Chartres. The dominant MS for this letter is Monte Cassino C2. In view of the multiple addresses, it is possible that Damian sent the same letter to Mainardus and Adraldus, especially since the latter accompanied Damian on his trip to Cluny, and may have hosted Damian's nephew, Damian, during the early years of his education.

227

he will speak in public with distinction and elegance; the former, on the other hand, while not able to equal the urbanity of his speech, perhaps has the advantage in writing or in the art of fowling, or certainly in hunting.

(3) And now, that we might consider our own situation, Moses said to the community of the Israelites, "Each of you set aside a contribution to the Lord. Let all who wish, bring their gifts to the Lord: gold, silver, copper, violet, purple, and scarlet yarn; fine linen, goat's hair and rams' skins; acacia wood and oil for the lamps."[3] Now, since everyone did not have all these things, each offered what he could, and was more lavish with what he had in abundance, so that while all together might offer what the individuals did not possess, the whole nation was able to build a tabernacle to the Lord. We too, who now erect a tabernacle in the desert of this life, after entering the land flowing with milk and honey, under the sway of the true Solomon in that heavenly Jerusalem[4] should dedicate a temple that will not be constructed of various insensate metals, but of living stones. It will not be adorned with the brilliance of flashing jewels, but will be radiant with the beauty of spiritual virtues. Through God's bounty, we will be able to partake of all good things, but will not possess them to the same degree. For also the holy Fathers who went to heaven before us, even though with God's assistance, they practiced all virtues, are not, however, considered to have been equal in everything. Abraham, certainly, excelled all others in faith[5] and obedience, and the shining chastity of monogamy was the mark of Isaac.[6] "Moses," as Scripture says, "was a man of great humility, the most humble man on earth."[7] Freewheeling authority was the distinction of Elijah,[8] the fervent zeal of the avenger forever marked Phinehas as a priest in the sight of God,[9] virginity allowed John to rest on the bosom of the Lord,[10] while outstanding love for the Lord promoted Peter to the office of chief shepherd.[11]

3. Exod 35.5–8
4. On the notion of the heavenly Jerusalem, cf. Reindel, *Briefe* 3.224, n.4.
5. Cf. Gen 17.   6. Cf. Gen 24.
7. Num 12.3.   8. 1 Kgs 18.
9. Num 25.7–11.   10. John 13.25.
11. John 21.15–17.

(4) And thus, although each saint must be resplendent with all virtues, since none of them alone is truly a virtue if not compounded of other virtues, each must choose one virtue in preference to the others, to which he is especially devoted, and must not, so to speak, depart from its service. Nor can we, to be sure, practice all the virtues equally, but as we pay close attention to one of them, we become adept in that which is less than all the rest; and as we strive without ceasing to practice it, through the participation of one member, as it were, we encompass the whole body of virtues.

(5) And so, which virtue should I persuade you to prefer? Should it be fasting? But you will at once reply, "If I chastise my body with unrestrained fasting, I will soon grow weak from the effort required by my unrelenting work and travel." If I should prescribe meditation on the psalms, you will say that you are impeded from constant prayer, since you are daily compelled to meet friends and converse with them. If I should advise you to go barefoot after the manner of the apostles, or like John to subdue your body by wearing a hairshirt, or to go into exile; if I should order you to endure prison life like the penitents, you will at once plead the current state of your health, or more likely, that you are unable to bear such a heavy burden of bodily inconvenience.

(6) Therefore, since you are still afraid to cause pain to your body, or even more, since you are not yet able to sacrifice yourself to God through bitter penance, reach out to those things that are about you; and since you are not prepared to offer yourself, at least give of the things that belong to you. If I should suggest cutting into your flesh, perhaps it would suffice if only I cut your hair; if someone should come forward to amputate your hand, it would be an act of mercy if he only trimmed your nails. There is as great a difference between a man and his property as there is between an injury to a man's body and to his clothes. Thus, Abraham sacrificed an animal to save the life of his son, he killed a ram to safeguard his heir.[12] So, too, Michal put a household idol in the bed to protect her husband from the swords of

12. Cf. Gen 22.13.

her mad father,[13] and that David might truly stay alive, she used a goat's hair rug to simulate his dead body, "Skin for skin! There is nothing a man will grudge to save himself."[14]

(7) You also, should use your personal property in exchange for yourself, and in the meantime make of it a sacrifice, so that afterwards you may deserve to be accepted as a burnt offering. For God is not accustomed to accept a gift and then despise him who offers it, so that he who gives of his property may securely say with the wife of Manoah, "If the Lord had wanted to kill us, he would not have accepted whole-offerings and libations from our hands."[15] In truth, God accepts an alms for the poor from your hands, and securely holds it as an investment for you in his heavenly treasury. And so the Lord says in the Gospel, "Store up treasure in heaven, where there is no moth and no rust to spoil it, no thieves to break in and steal."[16] Clearly, almighty God burdened some people with poverty, and endowed others with great wealth, that the latter might be in a position to atone for their sins, and the former might be able to support themselves in need. Thus it is written, "His riches are the ransom for a man's life."[17] And to this point Daniel said to Nebuchadnezzar, "Therefore, O king, be advised by me: Redeem your sins by almsgiving and your iniquities by generosity to the poor, and perhaps God will overlook your failings."[18]

(8) Therefore, those who are rich[19] should be regarded as dispensers rather than possessors, and should not consider what they have to be their own, because they have not taken possession of passing goods to live in luxury, or to use their wealth for their own purposes, but they should function as administrators in the role of steward. Hence, those who give alms to the poor, return what belongs to others, and do not disburse what is theirs. And so, in commanding almsgiving, the Lord says, "Be careful not to make a show of your justice before men that you may be

---

13. Cf. 1 Sam 19.13.   14. Job 2.4.
15. Judg 13.23.   16. Matt 6.20.
17. Prov 13.8.   18. Dan 4.24.
19. On the relationship betwen rich and poor, see Annick Goulay, "Richesse, pauvreté, aumône chez Pierre Damien," *Recherches sur les pauvres et la pauvreté* 4 (1965/66) 1–4.

observed by them."[20] Now, he does not say "your mercy," but "your justice." For he practices mercy who gives what belongs to him; he, however, practices justice who returns what belongs to another. And so also when the psalmist first stated, "He gives freely to the poor," he did not continue by saying, "his mercy," but added, "his justice shall live forever."[21]

(9) Therefore, when we support the poor, we are undoubtedly giving another's goods and not what is ours. And still, in the eyes of the loving Judge we are perceived as being merciful, since we faithfully dispense things that are not ours, but what is common property; and since we act justly in returning what belongs to others, we are not deprived of the reward for mercy by him who sees the innermost secrets of the heart. On the other hand, those who now turn their backs on the poor, in the terrible accounting at the Last Judgment will be accused not only of avarice but also of plundering, and will be found guilty not of hoarding their own wealth, but rather of stealing that which belongs to others. To such as these the supreme Judge will say at the Last Judgment, "The curse is upon you; go from my sight to the eternal fire that is ready for the devil and his angels. For when I was hungry you gave me nothing to eat, when I was thirsty you gave me nothing to drink."[22] In other words, he will say that because you refused to provide for your fellow servants from the goods you received for their welfare, may the ravenous pit of hell devour you as you stand condemned of despoiling others of their property because of your passionate cupidity. And since what we receive to be dispensed in this life does not belong to us, and our true wealth consists in the glory of heaven for which we hope, that sentence which the Lord handed down in the Gospel will aptly apply to them, "If you have not proved trustworthy with what belongs to another, who will give you what is your own?"[23] He, to be sure, proved trustworthy in handling the property of others, who could confidently say of himself, "The man threatened with ruin blessed me, and I made the widow's heart sing for joy. I was eyes to the blind and feet to the lame; I was a father to the needy."[24]

20. Matt 6.1.
22. Matt 25.41–42.
24. Job 29.13–16.

21. Ps 111.9.
23. Luke 16.12.

(10) Oh, how faithful he had been with other people's property, and how confident in firm hope over what belonged to him, when on another occasion he solemnly swore, "If I have ever withheld their needs from the poor," he said, "or let the widow's eyes grow dim with tears; if I have eaten my crust alone, and the orphan has not shared with me, the orphan who from boyhood depended on my kindness, and came forth with me from my mother's womb."[25] And then he appropriately added, "If I have let anyone go by who was in need of clothing, or a poor man with nothing to cover him; if his body had no cause to bless me, because he was not kept warm with fleece from my flock."[26] Notice what a long list of merciful deeds this is, where hardly anything is left undone in remedying every type of necessity, or in assisting like a physician in healing the wounds of everyone in need.

(11) Moreover, as we help the poor in their extremity, we at once practice truthfulness and mercy. We indeed show mercy, when we lovingly have compassion on the needy; but we observe the law of truth, that is, justice, when we serve them, not with what is ours, but with what belongs to them. That is why Solomon said in the book of Proverbs, "Let your mercy and truth never fail, but bind them about your neck and inscribe them on the tablets of your heart. Thus will you win favor and success in the sight of God and men."[27] And again it was written, "Mercy and truth bring gain, and from every good deed will flow abundance."[28] And lest sluggish inactivity lower the value of kind deeds, but that quick and ready attention might enhance it, he says elsewhere, "Do not say to your friend, 'Come back again, you shall have it tomorrow,' when you could give it to him today."[29] The greedy man's hand trembles when he gives an alms, and like a sick man who delays drinking from the cup because he dreads the bitter medicine, he who is on the point of giving, puts it off till later. The latter, to be sure, is nauseated by the bitterness of the irritating drink, while the former is afraid he will become poor if he should give an alms; and therefore, though the time for acting is at hand, whether for drinking or for giving,

25. Job 31.16–18.   26. Job 31.19–20.
27. Prov 3.3–4.   28. Prov 14.22–23.
29. Prov 3.28.

both in the meantime put off doing what they dread till some future date. Clearly, a generous and openhanded spirit makes a man rich, but anxiety and greediness beget poverty. And so, it was written, "A rich man's wealth is a strong city, but the fear of the poor is their want."[30] For fear causes an ungenerous man to be in want, even though he might appear to be filthy rich.

(12) Now you, my dear friend, do not despise your brother in his present necessity, if you expect God to help you in the moment of your greatest need. "Blessed are those who show mercy, for they shall receive mercy."[31] Moreover, if you give a man your money on interest, you will receive one percent; but if, according to God's command, you give it to the poor, you will gain a hundred percent, and if that should not be enough, eternal life will be given you besides.[32] Is it not better for you to receive a hundred percent than to be satisfied with one percent? So, do not despise your neighbor, if you do not wish to appear contemptible in the sight of God. Wherefore Solomon says, "He who despises his neighbor does wrong, but he who is generous to the poor will be blessed." And then he added, "He who believes in the Lord loves mercy."[33] Obviously, if he who believes in the Lord loves mercy, one must say that he who is guilty of not showing mercy, does not believe. Another statement in the same book explains why such a man does not believe, when it says, "He who is generous to the poor lends to the Lord; he will repay him in full measure."[34]

(13) Therefore, one does not believe in the Lord if he fears to lend him his goods by being unwilling to give to the needy. For if he truly believed in the Lord, he would not fear lending him his wealth, as he would do to a trustworthy debtor. Who would doubt that with such faith he surely does not pay him honor, since it is written, "Honor the Lord with your wealth."[35] And elsewhere it is said, "He who slanders the poor insults his Maker: he who is generous to the needy honors him."[36] And again, "Practicing mercy and justice is more pleasing to God than sacrifice."[37]

---

30. Prov 10.15.
32. Cf. Matt 19.29.
34. Prov 19.17.
36. Prov 14.31.

31. Matt 5.7.
33. Prov 14.21.
35. Prov 3.9.
37. Prov 21.3.

Now, one who gives alms, practices mercy when he has compassion on the poor in their necessity; he practices justice, however, when he distributes to them, not his own goods but what belongs to them. But in giving of his own in this life to provide for another's poverty, he prepares eternal riches for himself in the life to come. And so it was written, "He who gives to the poor will never want; he who despises a beggar will himself suffer poverty."[38] For a rich man has invested what he gives to the poor, and has entrusted to a fund the money he has loaned, which in life eternal he will recover with multiple interest. And he who now becomes a creditor by showing mercy, in the future reckoning will happily collect what is his. Hence it was written, "Poor man and creditor have this in common: the Lord gives light to both of them."[39] And of the capable wife, in whom we see either the holy Church at large, or each faithful and loving soul, it is said in Proverbs, "She is openhanded to the wretched and generous to the poor," and then the text aptly continues, "She has no fear for her household when it snows, for all of them are wrapped in two cloaks."[40] For whoever is now clothed in the twin garments of charity, like being wrapped in two cloaks, need never be oppressed by the cold when it later snows, and he who is now kept warm by the ardor of charity, can then ignore the ice and snow of retribution. Blessed Job spoke of this snow of the suffering to come, when he said of the lost man, "He will pass from melting snows to excessive heat, and his sin will bring him down to hell where mercy will forget him."[41]

(14) It is, indeed, proper that he who in this life was enflamed with the fires of carnal concupiscence, but benumbed by the lack of fervent mercy became cold and stiff, will then pass from melting snows to excessive heat; for just as in this life he sinned in a two-fold way, he will endure double torture in hell, and will there in turn be shown no mercy, since he was guilty of never practicing mercy in this world. Therefore, my brother, dispatch your wealth beforehand, so that you may live hereafter; let your goods precede you, that you may always have them in the life

---

38. Prov 28.27.   39. Prov 29.13.
40. Prov 31.20–21.   41. Job 24.19–20.

that never ends. Remember what was written, "When a rich man dies, he will take nothing with him; he opens his eyes and all is gone. Disaster overtakes him like a flood, and a storm snatches him away in the night."[42]

(15) And so, may you be pleased with this piece of advice from Solomon, "Send your bread across the seas, and in time you will get a return. Divide your merchandise among seven ventures, eight maybe, since you do not know what disasters may occur on earth."[43] And again, "In the morning sow your seed betimes, and do not stop work till evening."[44] And we read in Genesis, that "Isaac sowed seed in Gerar, and that year he reaped a hundredfold."[45] But how much more fortunately does he sow, who in giving aid to the poor, reaps wheat instead of wild oats, a measure rather than a handful, a heap instead of a kernel. With earthly goods he buys those of heaven, with impermanent things he gains those that are eternal. Scripture has it, "Who can say, 'I have a clear conscience; I am purged from my sin'?"[46] Who can boast that his heart is pure?

(16) But always be generous in giving alms, and through God's goodness you can be sure that you are chaste. And so the Savior says, "Let what you can afford be given in charity, and all is clean for you."[47] For, as fire purges rust from all kinds of metal, so almsgiving is wont to cleanse away the filth of the soul. Hence the wise man says, "As water quenches a blazing fire, and almsgiving withstands sins,"[48] and then he continues, "and God foresees when one performs a good deed, he is mindful of him in the future, and when he falls he will find support."[49] And then he adds, "My son, do not defraud the poor of alms, and do not turn your eyes away from a needy man."[50] And again, "Do not tantalize a starving man or drive him to desperation in his need. Do not bring affliction to a poor man, nor add to his troubles."[51] There are many other sayings that, like a prophet, this man composed about showing compassion for the poor; and before ever the

---

42. Job 27.19–20.
44. Eccl 11.6.
46. Prov 20.9.
48. Sir 3.33.
50. Sir 4.1.

43. Eccl 11.1–2.
45. Gen 26.12.
47. Luke 11.41.
49. Sir 3.34.
51. Sir 4.2–3.

Gospel began to shine, he spoke at length like a bishop of the Church. But I do not wish to cite all of them at this time, lest I tire my readers.

(17) Now since almsgiving is advised throughout all the pages of sacred Scripture, and since mercy exceeds all other virtues and holds first place among compassionate deeds, yet that type of mercy is preeminent which comes to the aid of those who had recently been wealthy, but have now fallen upon hard times. For there are quite a few people who are noble by reason of their honorable birth, but impoverished where property is concerned. Many also belong to the knightly order, but are personally in great need.[52] They are compelled to take part in the assemblies of the notables because of the dignity of their family, equal to them in rank but far removed from them in wealth. Although their personal poverty is to them a great concern, and in their extremity they are almost destitute, they are unable to seek support from begging. They would rather die than beg in public; they are ashamed to be recognized as poor, and dread to admit their need. While others advertise their poverty, and at times even exaggerate their impoverished condition so as to receive a more generous handout from those who feel sorry for them, these men hide or dissimulate their sorry state, so that evidence of their poverty may not cause them to appear despicable in the sight of others.

(18) In consequence, it is easier to understand their adversity than to observe it, to conjecture about it from certain indications, than to be sure of it from clear-cut evidence. The prophet speaks of the great reward that awaits those who assist these men whose poverty is not obvious, when he says, "Blessed is the man who understands the lot of the poor and helpless."[53] We need not further probe the case of the poor who appear in tattered rags, with knapsacks and bags, and whose condition is clearly visible; but we need insight to grasp the state of those poor whose misery we cannot observe from their appearance. Indeed, "blessed is the man who understands the lot of the poor and helpless."[54]

---

52. On the problem of the impoverished nobility, see Violante, *Riflessioni* 1066, n. 10.

53. Ps 40.2.   54. *Ibid.*

And why is he called blessed? Because "the Lord will save him in time of trouble."[55] What a marvelous promise: That he who now provides for the poor in their affliction, will afterwards go free in the divine Judgment; that he will later be spared from calamitous suffering, for now having shown mercy to those suffering from want.

(19) But now let us hear what the psalmist has yet to say, "The Lord protects him and gives him life, making him secure and happy in the land; the Lord never hands him over to his enemy, he provides for him."[56] Oh, what a glorious exchange, that for showing mercy to such poor, he will be rewarded by the constant prayer of all Christendom. For the whole universal Church, spread throughout the world, daily intercedes with God on his behalf as it recites this psalm in its daily devotion. In addition, this prayer will never go unheard by the goodness of God, since it was composed by the Holy Spirit who is himself the remission of sins. Who can imagine that God will not accept a prayer that he himself has written? How is it possible that he will not listen to a prayer that he has taught us to pray? Therefore, blessed is he, and truly blessed, who understands the lot of the poor and helpless. And so, Moses says, or rather, the Lord speaking through Moses, "When one of your fellow-countrymen in any of your settlements in the land which the Lord your God is giving you becomes poor, do not be hardhearted or closefisted with him in his need. Be openhanded toward him and lend him on pledge so much as he needs."[57] And elsewhere he says, "The poor will always be with you in the land of your dwelling, and for that reason I command you to be openhanded with your countrymen, both poor and distressed, in your own land."[58]

(20) Almighty God is indeed aware that by practicing justice alone, human frailty can never arrive at eternal life, but always needs to show mercy. And therefore he praises almsgiving throughout all the pages of sacred Scripture, preaches mercy, constantly teaches us to be compassionate toward the poor, so that as one takes pity on his fellowman, he may as his reward obtain mercy from God; and as he gives support to one who is

55. *Ibid.*
57. Deut 15.7–8.

56. Ps 40.3–4.
58. Deut 15.11.

human like himself, he may deserve to have the Author of human nature himself as his support, and that what he provides for his neighbor he may in turn receive from God. For, as the Creator of men from the beginning of the world predestined all the elect for the kingdom of heaven, and yet commanded them to work untiringly to acquire it, so that what the Creator freely granted, man might reach by his efforts, it is likewise necessary that we who are saved by the mercy of the loving Author of all things should not fail to show human compassion for our brothers. Thus Tobias said to his son, "Give alms of what you possess, and do not turn your face away from any poor man, and God will not turn his face away from you."[59] And then he set the standard of discretion, and doubtless established the authentic norm for every amount of wealth that one might possess. For he said, "Let your almsgiving match your means. If you have much, give of your abundance; if you have little, do not be ashamed to give the little you can afford."[60]

(21) He explains why this should be done, when he adds, "You will be laying up a sound insurance against the day of adversity, for almsgiving saves the giver from all sin and from death, and keeps him from going down into darkness. All who give alms are making an offering acceptable to the Most High God."[61]

(22) But that I may encompass the heart of the matter in a few words one will never be pleasing to God without the purpose of practicing almsgiving or of cherishing it, so that he who does not have the means, should have the will, and while not blessed with an abundance of personal wealth, he does not lose the reward that is earned by liberality of spirit. For, if he has no food in the house, perhaps he has a roof over his head. He may be unable to feed the hungry man, but at least he can be hospitable and allow the weary man to get some rest, always keeping in mind what the Apostle says, "Never cease to love your fellow-Christians. Remember to show hospitality. There are some who, by so doing, have entertained angels without knowing it."[62] Indeed, there are certain people who slam the door in the face of

---

59. Tob 4.7.   60. Tob 4.8.
61. Tob 4.10–12.   62. Heb 13.1–2.

Christ's poor, claiming that they fear being robbed. While through avarice they refuse them hospitality, they pretend that the man is a thief and fear the loss of their property. At times they derisively point out how fat they are and how ruddy their appearance, finding fault with their brawny arms and strong shoulders that make them fit for digging in the fields, and that one offends God by helping such fellows, who by working could even be the support of others. Such men should be terrified by what Moses said to the Israelites in Deuteronomy, "No Ammonite or Moabite, even down to the tenth generation, shall ever become a member of the assembly of the Lord, because they did not meet you with food and water on your way out of Egypt."[63] Now, if these peoples who did not possess the Law were forever excluded from the assembly of God because they failed to act humanely even toward their enemies, what a terrible sentence awaits those who refuse to show mercy to their needy neighbors, who do not practice charity toward their brothers? Like them, to be sure, they were begotten at the sacred font of baptism, with them they came forth from the womb of our mother, the Church, and with them they sit at the table of the Lord's Body and Blood, and to these they deny food which is destined for the privy.

(23) And how in good conscience can we be remiss in giving alms, since we enjoy peace and quiet within the Church, and since we read that the apostles, who were seemingly arrayed in battle against the whole world, were so eager to practice this virtue? For if others might do so, they could not readily be freed from such concerns, as they were so intent on sowing the seed of the new faith, and found themselves engaged in such a bitter fight against the world's unbelief. But no hardship or persecution could restrain them from showing human kindness to their brothers, no urgency to engage in preaching could keep them from giving aid to the poor. And so Paul said to the Galatians, "Those reputed pillars of our society, Peter, James, and John, accepted Barnabas and myself as partners, and shook hands upon it, agreeing that we should bring the Gospel to the Gen-

63. Deut 23.3–4.

tiles while they went to the Jews. All they asked was that we should keep their poor in mind, which was the very thing I made it my business to do."[64] And this, moreover, he said to the Corinthians, "And now about the collection in aid of God's people: you should follow my directions to our congregation in Galatia. Every Sunday each of you is to put aside and keep by him a sum that he sees fit. When I arrive, I will give letters of introduction to persons approved by you, and send them to carry your gift to Jerusalem."[65] Such was the apostles' generosity to the poor, that we read in their Acts, "They broke bread outside the homes, and shared their meals with unaffected joy, praising God in the simplicity of their hearts."[66] It says outside and not within the homes. Their example is not followed by those who when preparing to eat, lock and bolt the doors, secure them with bars, and thus protect themselves from the poor, as they would from besieging enemies whose forces are all around them.

(24) In this connection, Gerard di Faroaldo[67] comes to mind, one of the outstanding men of Ravenna, whom I saw as a boy when he was already old and decrepid, and of whom I often heard people telling this story. At one time when the people were suffering from such want that some of them even died of hunger, even though he had grandchildren who would succeed him, he cut his crops and even sold some of his property to provide food for as many people as possible. Throwing open his doors, he then fed the poor who gathered from all around, and when all was consumed and some were still hungry, and he had nothing more for himself or for them, out of compassion for them he broke into tears. Today his descendants are wealthy, having more than their grandfather had left them.

(25) Waldericus, moreover, who died as an outstanding martyr while fighting against the heretics,[68] as Andrew, the venerable bishop of the diocese of Spoleto told me,[69] at one time visited the home where his mother was living. There he found a poor

---

64. Gal 2.9–10.   65. 1 Cor 16.1–3.
66. Acts 2.46.
67. Cf. Mittarelli-Costadoni, *Annales Camaldulenses* 2.287.
68. Nothing further is known of him.
69. On Andrew of Spoleto, see Schwartz, *Bistümer* 240.

man at the door, who complained that he had gathered a bunch of greens, but was unable to procure salt from the lady of the house that he might flavor his stew. After the holy man had entered his mother's house and found salt in a container, he became very angry. He took the bottle and poured the salt in the street as an affront to his mother, saying that what through greed had been denied to Christ must not be consumed by a Christian. But shortly afterwards, the bottle that had stood there empty, to every one's surprise, was found full of salt.

(26) Also the Margrave Mainfredus,[70] whose principality lies on the frontiers of Liguria, along with his wife was renowned for his great generosity to the poor. I will pass over other events in his life, but the following item is still remembered as something special. On Easter Sunday when his house like a royal palace was brilliantly hung with tapestries and purple drapes, the tables groaned under the abundance of food, and glittering crowds of vassals milled around, he ordered the magnificent banquet to be served, and he himself, aided by his servants, acted as headwaiter, meticulously ministering to the poor who were seated here and there at all the tables. After they had had their fill, he and his servants privately took away the leftovers, since this Easter celebration was held especially for the poor, and from them he and his family ate their meal alone. That man of God, my lord Leo,[71] the venerable hermit who still lives as a recluse in his cell after almost twenty years, gave this outstanding account of the Margrave. While he and several brothers were staying in the hermitage on the latter's lands, his wife set this norm for herself, that whenever the messenger from the hermits asked for something that they needed, she would immediately double the amount, so that when he perhaps requested five shillings, she would give ten, and if he asked for ten, she at once counted out twenty.

(27) Now, since I am getting forgetful, I am not sure whether I wrote about the following on some other occasion. But when something is edifying, it is better to repeat the tale than have it

---

70. Cf. Reindel, *Briefe* 3.238, n. 24.

71. Probably the hermit, Leo of Fonte Avellana, to whom Damian addressed *Letter* 28.

passed over in silence and forgotten. And so, since the Margrave was so generous in giving alms to the needy, and, if I recall correctly, had established six or seven good-sized monasteries in his duchy, with great liberality endowing them with lands and furnishings, did his children who succeeded him live in poverty? Far from it! For we see his nephews, young men of great ability, owning also a large part of the kingdom of Burgundy, whose sister,[72] as we know, is betrothed to our emperor. Therefore, should we fear to repay God for what he has given us, since even in this life it is given back to us or to our heirs, and is increased manyfold in the glory of the heavenly kingdom to come?

(28) This story also, which the Margrave Bernard[73] who died this year, often used to tell, I consider worth knowing about. He would say that there was a man from Germany, where he also originated, who owned a fine piece of property that produced bumper crops of various kinds. But he had twelve sons, and he began to worry about what would happen after his death, should he divide this one estate among so many heirs. Then he said, "To be sure, I who am the sole owner of this estate, have enough and can live in peace. But where there are so many who will come forward to divide it, who can put up with their jealousy and with all the hateful quarrels that will break out among them? There can surely be no harmony where there is such a difference of opinion over the property. The serfs, moreover, who are now content to obey one lord, will suffer grave damage if they have to be responsible to such a host of lords. Therefore, almighty God, whatever land I own, I give to you. I make you the sole heir of my possessions, and recommend my sons to you; do for them what seems best to you." Having said that, he at once tied his gauntlet to an arrow, and bending his bow to its limit, shot it high into the air. But in a few moments the arrow fell to the ground without the gauntlet, evidently proving that God's goodness had accepted the gift that he had given in faith.

(29) When the Margrave had thus been assured and relieved over the grant he had made, he handed over his possessions to

---

72. Bertha, who was engaged to King Henry IV.
73. On Bernard, see Mittarelli-Costadoni, *Annales Camaldulenses* 2.288.

a certain church, and confirmed the transfer with his signature. Some time later his sons became so wealthy and were so magnificently endowed with lands and income, that each of them surpassed the holdings of their father, and wherever they turned, prosperity smiled on them. And thus, he who in heaven accepted from the father's hand the title to his land through the symbol of the gauntlet, generously endowed his sons with a shower of blessings. Therefore, whatever is given to God on earth, is received in heaven where one can look forward to the reward that the gift deserves. And so it was that the angel of the Lord said to Cornelius, "Your prayers have been heard and your acts of charity remembered before God."[74] What a fortunate business, in which man is the lender and almighty God becomes the debtor. With confidence we can require compensation for the just debts that are owed us, if beforehand we have invested our gifts with him.

(30) Now as I recall, the following event took place in the days of Pope Gregory, who had previously been known as Gratian.[75] As I learned from the old man, Bonizo, the abbot of the monastery of St. Severus that lies in the vicinity of Orvieto,[76] the king of the Scots, who at the time was still a youth, succeeded to the royal throne of his father who had just died. But as he carefully considered how perishable everything was that flourished in this world, how fleeting all that was preeminent, how quickly eclipsed all that was brilliant, even though he was already married, he decided to put aside royal trappings out of love for the kingdom of heaven, and to exchange his crown for a cowl and the purple for the monastic habit. What more need I say? He took up the practice of prayer, and went on a pilgrimage to Rome. Having completed his devotions at the tomb of the apostles, unknown to the courtiers who accompanied him, he secretly put on the monastic garb, and thus left the world and stole away from his kingdom. Not long afterwards, struck down by sickness, he came to the end of his days, and until his death never stopped repeating these words that were a record of his

74. Acts 10.31.
75. Pope Gregory VI, deposed by Emperor Henry III in 1046.
76. Cf. Cottineau, *Répertoire* IIA, 2150.

agreement, "Lord, I did what you commanded; now fulfill what you promised." Whenever anyone spoke to him, or whatever else happened, as if claiming payment on a debt, he would always say, "Lord, I did what you commanded, now fulfill what you promised." It was somewhat like the man in the vineyard who demanded his money, knowing that he had carried out the householder's orders, and even though he had been hired at the eleventh hour, he expected to rest after his labor, and when he was finished he insisted on his pay. We should now not hesitate to offer God either ourselves or our property, so that afterwards with full authority we may ask for their return. And when we are at table, we should not, by being niggardly in their service, force the poor to lick their plates like frugal men, while we proceed to consume our heaping portions; nor, as some will do, dole out their food by the spoonful, when pots and platters are hardly enough for us.

(31) Then, as Hugh of Cluny, the reverend abbot in Christ, related to me, there was Bishop Fulcranus[77] from a certain region in Gaul, who when asked by his steward what he wished prepared for him, replied, "As you see fit, serve enough for those who will be at table; but for me alone, instruct the waiters to bring the choicest piece of pork, a good size and nicely marbled, so that no one but me must taste even a scrap of it." And so, sitting down with the poor who were dining with him, he ate the whole serving of pork with them and never offered the smallest piece of meat to anyone among them.

(32) The same holy abbot also told me that a certain man who traveled from place to place on a prayerful pilgrimage, came upon a hermitage where some holy brother was living in his cell. After some discussion, the latter casually asked him if he were acquainted with the monastery of Cluny. After that he said to him, "My brother, I beg you for the love of God, that if perhaps you should visit this venerable house, please warn the abbot and the brothers not to grow slack in the practice of almsgiving, but fervently persevere in performing works of mercy as they are

77. Possibly Fulcranus, bishop of Lodève (d. 1006). On Hugh of Cluny, cf. Damian, *Letter* 100.

accustomed to do. For on the one hand, hell burns with its suffocating flames, and on the other, as I have often heard, are the souls of the damned falling into the abyss with cries of anguish and the grating sounds of weeping. But the prayers and alms of that monastery strongly oppose the evil spirits, and like prey rescue many from their hands." Many years later this pilgrim went to the monastery and told the brothers all that he had been commissioned to say.

(33) I am greatly displeased, moreover, at the practice that one can doubtless observe in some men, that while they take their place at sumptuous tables, the poor who receive food from them, sit on the bare ground among a pack of dogs. The former are served on embroidered tablecloths, while for the latter the food is placed in their laps. The celebrated Duke and Margrave Godfrey[78] told me of something contained in the history of his territory, that the emperor Charles went to war fifteen times against the king of the Saxons, who was still involved in the false religion of the pagans. Fifteen times Charles lost the battle, but in three later encounters he won, and at length emerged victorious and captured the king. One day, as was his custom, as Charles dined in imperial splendor, while the poor whom he fed abjectly sat alone, the king who ate far removed from the imperial table, sent a message up to Charles, saying, "Since your Christ declared that he was to be accepted in the poor, how can you dare urge me to submit to him whom you thus despise, and to whom you fail to show reverence and honor?" At that, the emperor blushed with shame, and marveled that such a statement from the Gospel could come from the mouth of a pagan. For the Lord said, "Whatever you did for the least of my brothers, you did for me."[79] And so, the emperor was pleased to be corrected by such a man, who though he had not yet learned the rudiments of the faith, already proclaimed the results that emerged from faith, namely, the works of mercy.

(34) We should take special note, moreover, that washing the feet of the poor is a most salutary act. For the Lord said to his dis-

---

78. On Godfrey of Lorraine, cf. Reindel, *Briefe* 3.243, n. 36.
79. Matt 25.40.

ciples, "If I, your Lord and master, have washed your feet, you also ought to wash one another's feet."[80] And to reinforce this command with greater authority, and to impress it more firmly on their minds, he added, "I have set you an example, so that you shall do the same."[81] For when we wash the feet of the poor out of devotion for him who gave us this command, the soul as well as the body of him who washes is surely purged from sin. Consequently, Peter said, "Then, Lord, not my feet only; wash my hands and head as well."[82] Why did Peter not suggest other parts of the body with the feet besides hands and head, except that he wanted to include in them the deeds of the body and the thoughts of the mind? For the head stands for the mind, and the hands represent the works of the whole body.

(35) It was Mainardus, the venerable bishop of Silva Candida,[83] who told me that Pope Nicholas of blessed memory, who three years ago departed this life to go to the Lord,[84] never let a day pass the whole year long without washing the feet of twelve poor men. If he was unable to do this during the day, he fulfilled this magnificent work of mercy at night. But since I am better able to understand the privilege of mercy and the dignity of almsgiving than to speak of it, I should like to append this brief peroration:

(36) What a virtue is almsgiving! Like a flood from a gushing fountain, you wash away the filth of sin, and extinguish the flames of consuming vices! O blessed alms, you who free the children of darkness from the pit of hell, and bring them as adopted sons to the everlasting light of the kingdom of heaven! From the hands of the poor you fly to heaven and there prepare a home for those who love you. If you are wine, you do not grow sour; if you are bread, you do not become moldy; if meat or fish, you do not spoil; if clothing, moreover, you do not grow old. You always remain fresh and new, and as soon as the donor dies, you at once repay him manyfold. You make illustrious men of those who wallow in the filth of crime, you turn the damned into saints, and

---

80. John 13.14. 81. John 13.15.
82. John 13.9.
83. On Mainardus, cf. Reindel, *Briefe* 3.244, n. 41.
84. Nicholas II, d. July 1061.

convert pagans into Christians. This, indeed, is proven by Cornelius, whose acts of charity went up to heaven to speak before God.[85]

(37) O precious almsgiving that grants an unfading inheritance and the honors of the heavenly court to those who love you. O marvelous power of mercy that wipes away the rust of all sins, tames the incentives of raging vice, and enlightens the darksome souls of men with the splendor of heavenly grace. It makes God man's debtor, so that now he need not seek the kingdom of heaven as something that is not his but may boldly invade it as something that is his property. O happy virtue of mercy, you are indeed born of compassion, but you beget true blessedness for those who possess you. You are a more prudent dealer than any tradesman, obtaining heavenly goods in exchange for those of the earth, eternal ones for those that pass away. Blessed is your marketplace, in which hospitality is offered, and one receives a dwelling place; where for a little bread, one is rewarded with a kingdom, and in exchange for a few coins, one wins the courts of heaven.

(38) Venerable brother, among all the other virtues with which, I have no doubt, your holy prudence is endowed, give special attention to almsgiving. Be tireless in works of kindness, always abound in mercy, so that while here you come to the aid of Christ's poor brothers, you may afterwards receive mercy from Christ.

85. Cf. Acts 10.4.

LETTER 111

Peter Damian to Hugh, the archbishop of Besançon. He came to prize the friendship of this man, with whom he became acquainted on his visit to Cluny in 1063. He here praises Hugh for his quasi-eremitical life and for constructing several cloisters near his cathedral, one of which served as a "seminary" for young clerics. Yet one practice in Besançon and elsewhere in France met with his disapproval: that both clerics and monks sat during the recitation of the divine office and even during Mass. He advised Hugh to reform these abuses, producing cogent scriptural arguments to buttress his position.

(1064)[1]

O SIR HUGH, the most reverend archbishop,[2] the monk Peter the sinner offers his service.

(2) You should know, venerable father, that when I was with you, enjoying your hospitality, I so impressed everything on my mind as if it were a mental picture that nothing would ever be forgotten. I clearly recall the cloister behind the apse of the church where you live alone, where you can engage in such private and secluded prayer and reading that you would seem to have no need for eremitic solitude. I did not, moreover, overlook the other cloister erected to the right of the church, where the splendid group of your clerics shines like a choir of angels.[3] For there, as in a school of the heavenly Athens, they are instructed in the word of sacred Scripture;[4] there they are diligently occupied in the study of the true philosophy, and daily engage in a life of regular discipline.

1. Dating follows Lucchesi, *Vita* no. 180
2. On Hugh of Beasonçon, see B. de Vregille, "Les origines chrétiennes et le haut Moyen Age," *Histoire de Besançon. Des origines à la fin du XVIᵉ siècle*, ed. C. Fohlen (1964) 143–321, esp. 239–272.
3. On the two cloisters of the cathedral of St. John, cf. Reindel, *Briefe* 3.247, n.3.
4. See Lubac, *Exégèse* 283 and Manacorda, *Storia della scuola* 2.122f.

(3) Nor should this be forgotten that besides these buildings you are presently constructing two other canonries simultaneously, one to be associated with the church of St. Mary Magdalene, and the other, if I am correct, with the church of St. Lawrence. And since yours is not a wealthy diocese, one can only wonder how it can sustain the building of such elaborate and magnificent structures, and can daily find sufficient means for such great expenditures.

(4) This too, I must confess, was especially pleasing to me, that on my visit you showed me your tomb, carefully prepared to receive your remains if you were to die that very day, where, like a reward for grave-robbers, five solidi were tied up in handkerchiefs and placed in each of the four corners, so that at the funeral the men in charge of your burial might receive their pay for this work of mercy. In all of this, indeed, you seem to be following the example of the patriarch Abraham. When he was preparing to bury his wife, Sarah,[5] and the Hittites had offered a choice plot free of charge, he turned down their gift and bought a double cave from Ephron, son of Zohar. Also, in using the number four you seem to be imitating his example. For as he bought the cave for four hundred shekels of silver,[6] with four times five solidi you seem to be buying your burial place.

(5) Here we should note how detestable is the avarice of clerics, who in their burials hope to take advantage of the Church, a thing which even the pagans, who do not know God, find abhorrent. The latter turn down the money when it is offered, but the former impudently demand it even when it is denied. In despising Abraham's offer of payment the Hittites said, "Bury your dead in the best grave we have; there is not one of us who will hinder you."[7] But unlike the pagans these clerics say, "Pay us the money and you will have your burial place."[8] You however, venerable father, seem to me to be following the advice of the wise man in deciding to provide for your burial while you are still alive and well. For when this deceitful life allures us, and the mind perhaps prides itself on being promoted to some flattering

5. Cf. Gen 23.1–10.   6. Cf. Gen 23.15–16.
7. Gen 23.6.   8. Cf. Gen 23.13.

high dignity, as soon as one sets eye on the home that awaits him, he will understand that he is really nothing but dust and ashes. And so it is that Solomon says, "Why must a man seek what is greater than himself, since he cannot know what is good for him in this life, this brief span of pilgrimage, this time through which he passes like a shadow?"[9] Nor will seductive pleasures benefit the flesh by immersing it in a flood of debauchery, while the mind is forced to think of crawling worms and of the matter that will flow from this flesh. Hence Solomon says again, "Better to visit the house of mournings than the house of feasting."[10] Here he will be reminded of the end of all men, and while alive will think of what is to come.

(6) But those whose heart is planted in the arid love of this world, if the world smiles on them, if sweet and tranquil happiness caresses them, they will undoubtedly dread the thought of death as they would gall or wormwood. And so the wise man says, "Death, how bitter is the thought of you to a man living at ease among his possessions, free from anxiety, prosperous in all things, and still vigorous enough to enjoy a good meal."[11] But if misfortune and irksome calamity beset him, if he is constantly ill or is in want of the necessities of life, death for him becomes sweet and he begs that it hurry and overtake him. Thus the same wise man says, "Death, how welcome is your sentence to a destitute man whose strength is failing, worn down by age."[12] Then, indeed, man need never fear his approaching end or choose from the vicissitudes of this life, but must only consider whether death or a longer life will serve his or his brother's salvation. Which is exactly what is said by him who remarks, "I am torn two ways: what I should like is to depart and be with Christ; that is better by far. But for your sake there is greater need for me to stay on in the body."[13] This is why blessed Peter said to his audience, "Yet I think it right to keep refreshing your memory so long as I still lodge in this body. I know that very soon I must leave it."[14] Clearly, the good shepherd showed by his words that he wished to live and die, not for himself, but for his disciples.

9. Eccl 7.1; cf. Sabatier 2.363.   10. Eccl 7.3.
11. Sir 41.1–2.   12. Sir 41.3–4.
13. Phil 1.23–24.   14. 2 Pet 1.13–14.

For at once he continued, "But I will see to it that after I am gone you will have means of remembering these things at all times."[15] Therefore, I am pleased by your tomb that you keep in sight as a memorial, so that as you look upon it, the vitality of this evily flourishing life will shrivel before your eyes, and your mind will begin to think earnestly of the future things that it represents. After a man has been placed in his grave, he will there doubtless find that nothing more can be changed. And so Solomon gives us this warning, "Remember the end that awaits you, and you will never sin."[16]

(7) Yet there was one indication of weakness and lack of fervor that I saw in your church, which I then corrected so far as time allowed, and which now I should not overlook writing about. There some of your clerics were seated while chanting the canonical hours, or even when they offered the dread sacrament of the Mass. Such sloth I also discovered among certain monks in other areas of Gaul, an evil custom that should be amended and completely abolished from the choir of the church militant for those who are in good health. Of this one reads in Canticles, "What will you see in the Shulammite maiden but dancers of the castles?"[17] And again, "Your neck is like David's tower, which was built with its battlements; a thousand bucklers hang upon it, and all are warriors' shields."[18]

(8) Indeed, since on all sides implacable warfare with the evil spirits threatens us, it becomes more fierce as we chant the psalms; and when we pray, we fight in battle array against the assaults of a vicious foe, so that the enemy must either feebly yield to us the victors, or exult over us who have fallen in the cause of the Lord. When these enemies see our bodies growing faint as we sit there exhausted, they are at once sure of gaining the victory because our spirit has collapsed. Of such Isaiah says, "I will give it to your tormentors and oppressors, those who said to you, 'Lie down and we will walk over you.' "[19] And then, after speaking of the bending of the spirit, he at once refers to the reclining of the body, "And you made your backs like the ground beneath

15. 2 Pet 1.15.   16. Sir 7.40.
17. Cant 7.1.   18. Cant 4.4.
19. Isa 51.23.

them, like a roadway for passersby."[20] Now both substances, that is, the soul and the body, are so united in us, that usually when one of them acts wisely, the other derives benefit; and when one grows slack and negligent, the other also becomes lazy and is ready to doze off. Indeed, when Joshua saw the angel brandishing a naked sword, he said, "What do you have to say to your servant, my lord?"[21] And the latter gave him no further command and told him there was only this, "Take off your sandals." And why? "For the place where you are standing is holy."[22]

(9) And so, since unshod feet were proper to that place because it was holy, why does the church, which also is a holy place, not deserve that clerics at least show it reverence by standing? The Lord also said to Moses, "Come no nearer; take off your sandals; the place where you are standing is holy ground."[23] What is the purpose of our reading in the sacred Scriptures that God demanded this of the ancient Fathers, except that we believe that we should show reverence for holy places? Is the place where the Body of Christ is offered through the mystery of his life-giving passion less holy than that where God spoke through his angel? One can also read in Deuteronomy that the Lord said to Moses, "Stand here beside me, and I will set forth to you all the commandments, the ceremonies, and the laws."[24] He did not say, sit or recline, but stand beside me, so that in standing he might learn what he should later teach while being seated.

(10) Now, therefore, as we are prepared for battle, God wishes us who are in his service to stand, that later we may deserve to be seated in the peace of the heavenly city. Moreover, if one is so wealthy that so long as he is in office he continually bestows gifts on individuals, he would also continue doing so if his fingers were afflicted with arthritis. And so, while standing he would accept a favor for his body that will die, but by sitting he disdains honors for his soul that will live forever. If we reverently stand while serving a king or any other earthly prince, how dare we sit while joyfully singing our praise in the dread presence of the majesty of God? For Daniel says, "Thousands upon thousands

20. Isa 51.23.
22. Josh 5.16.
24. Deut 5.31.

21. Josh 5.15.
23. Exod 3.5.

served him, and myriads stood in his presence."[25] Note that while countless angels serve God, and others are said to stand in his presence, not one of them is here referred to as seated.

(11) Therefore, as angelic powers stand trembling in his presence, how can earthly and corruptible men dare not to stand? And since we rightly believe that angels are always present at these ecclesiastical functions, because Scripture says, "In the sight of the angels I will sing praise to you,"[26] and not only carefully observe our attention or our slothfulness, but regularly report it all to the heavenly Judge, how quickly will they accuse us when they see us irreverently sitting there in his presence while they stand in awe before him? Indeed, when the priest Zechariah offered incense, he saw an angel, not seated, but standing near the altar. "There appeared to him," the evangelist said, "an angel of the Lord standing on the right of the altar of incense."[27] And blessed John says in the Apocalypse, "I saw a vast throng, which no one could count, from every nation, of all tribes, peoples, and languages, standing in front of the throne."[28] They were standing there, not sitting. And after that he said, "And all the angels stood round the throne and the elders."[29] And when Isaiah opened his remarks by saying, "I saw the Lord seated on a throne, high and exalted, and the skirt of his robe filled the temple,"[30] he promptly added, "About him stood attendant seraphim."[31] Notice that where seraphim did not dare to sit in his presence, should man be seated, a creature made of clay and like a filthy rag, lurid and unclean? Where the powers of heaven do not claim seats, will man there enjoy his rest as he would ordinarily do at home, knowing that he is dust and ashes? When the king comes in to the wedding banquet and perhaps finds a man not only without his wedding clothes,[32] but against all the rules for such a feast, brazenly seated at the table, what do you think he will do but bind him hand and foot and turn him out into the dark? And indeed Scripture says of the priest Eli who was seated, "He fell backwards from his seat by the gate, broke his neck and so he

---

25. Dan 7.10.   26. Ps 137.1.
27. Luke 1.11.   28. Rev 7.9.
29. Rev 7.11.   30. Isa 6.1.
31. Isa 6.2.   32. Cf. Matt 22.11–13.

died."[33] Belshazzar, the king of Babylon, was seated when the hand appeared, writing on the plaster of the palace wall, announcing that that very night he and his kingdom would be destroyed by the Medes and Persians.[34]

(12) Zebah and Zalmunna, kings of Midian, with their army, were resting securely when Gideon attacked them, drew his sword and killed them.[35] The Amalekites also were resting on the ground when David suddenly fell upon them, cutting them down from dusk until evening of the next day without a break.[36] On the other hand, Elijah said, "Long live the Lord of Hosts, in whose presence I stand."[37] "I am standing," he said, not sitting there yawning and falling asleep. And so the Lord spoke to him, "Go and stand on the mountain before the Lord."[38] He did not say sit, but stand before the Lord. Were David and the seven choirs accompanying him seated before the Ark of the Lord, or was it not, as Scripture reports, that "the king danced without restraint to the sound of the harp before the Lord"?[39] And so they brought up the Ark with shouting and blowing of trumpets. Also take note of what the Lord said to Moses, "Bring forward the tribe of Levi, and have them stand before Aaron the priest and minister to him. They shall be in attendance on him and on the whole community before the Tent of the Presence, undertaking the service of the Tabernacle."[40] He did not say that they should sit and yawn and doze off, but have them stand to minister, attend, and serve. While Moses was on the mountain for forty days and forty nights, he never sat for a moment, taking no food or drink, but stood there fasting before the Lord. And you, who daily partake of food, do you find it so difficult to stand in the presence of your Creator for a short period? This is what we read in Exodus, "So Moses stood there with the Lord forty days and forty nights, neither eating bread nor drinking water, and wrote down the words of the covenant, the Ten Commandments, on the tablets."[41] Today when some of the brothers are engaged in

33. 1 Sam 4.18.
35. Cf. Judg 8.21.
37. 1 Kgs 17.1.
39. 2 Sam 6.14.
41. Exod 34.28.

34. Cf. Dan 5.25–28.
36. 1 Sam 30.17.
38. 1 Kgs 19.11.
40. Num 3.6–7.

the divine office, they are not satisfied with just the effort of standing, but are eager to wear themselves out by other bodily practices in addition.

(13) To say nothing of the others, there is a certain brother named Gezo, who lives close to my cell, a man about sixty years old, who prays the whole psalter on bended knees in such a manner, that he recites one verse as he prostrates himself on the ground, and a second as he promptly rises. And thus, through the whole course of the psalter there is always one prostration for each two verses. There is also another in our community, a still older man who is rightly called Dominic. He confided to me that he often performs a thousand prostrations[42] a day while continuously wearing an iron corselet next to his flesh. But whoever wishes to hear more about such practices, should read through the works I have written.[43]

(14) But now it suffices to have called your holiness' attention to this matter, that after first correcting this ill practice in your own church, you should reach out to subsidiary churches in applying the hoe of salutary reprimand. It should be strictly forbidden, not only to clerics, but also to lay persons of both sexes, that except where it is the custom, during the readings at Matins, and elsewhere, when the divine hymns are recited, anyone should be seated unless compelled by bodily infirmity. I have seen some men, not only priests but also laymen, who during the divine office in the church are so disposed, that they would never support themselves with a cane nor any other means at hand. The more effort it requires for them to stand in the presence of the divine majesty that observes them, the sweeter is the pleasure and inner peace that they enjoy, and the more difficult it is for them to bear the heaviness of their limbs, the more plentiful is the merit that brings them closer to God.

(15) As we read in the history of Eutropius,[44] moreover, after the consul Varro had fought at Cannae against Hannibal, and lost the battle, so long as he lived he never again took food while

---

42. On prostrations (*metanea*), cf. Damian, *Letter* 50; also Blum, *St. Peter Damian* 157, n. 79.

43. See esp. *Letter* 109 to Dominicus Loricatus.

44. Paulus Diaconus in Eutropius XI (MGH Auct. ant. 2.54.11).

reclining at table. But if pagans will do such a thing to make themselves famous, how should Christians act that they might be seated in heavenly glory? For if we were endowed with becoming fervor for God, we would not be satisfied to sit during the divine office, but would unceasingly chant with hands extended. The psalmist thus exhorts us when he says, "At night lift up your hands in the sanctuary and bless the Lord."[45] And the Apostle writes to Timothy, "It is my desire that men should pray everywhere, lifting up their hands with a pure intention, excluding angry and quarrelsome thoughts."[46] Indeed, Ambrose, the celebrated doctor of the Church, stated that he saw the blessed martyrs, Gervase and Protase, "praying together with hands extended."[47] From these words we can gather that the bishop himself prayed in the same way, even though, to avoid publicity, he did not expressly say so. It is very likely that when praying together with someone they would not differ from him in the manner of praying; for if Ambrose prayed in some other way, this type of praying was presented to him that in the future he might adapt himself to it. When blessed Paul told him about these martyrs, "whose bodies," he said, "you will find there," he specifically added, "in the place where you are standing and praying."[48] And so, the celebrated bishop stood when he prayed, and like some people did not sit and idly talk. Moreover, the same Apostle says, "There are ministrant spirits, sent out to serve, for the sake of those who are to inherit salvation."[49] Where can we expect the blessed angels to appear more frequently than in the church, where they know that the people of God are gathered, for whose benefit they were sent? And since we quickly rise when some powerful person appears, how dare we not dread to sit in the presence of angelic powers?

(16) And now, my dear friend, since you are preeminent and highly esteemed among the bishops of the West, you should

---

45. Ps 133.2. On reciting the psalms with hands extended (*palmatae*), cf. Damian, *Letters* 50 and 56.
46. 1 Tim 2.8.
47. *Legenda SS. Gervasii et Protasii*, written in the 5th century and falsely ascribed to Ambrose (AA SS June IV, 683C, 18).
48. AA SS June IV, 683D, 18.   49. Heb 1.14.

everywhere and so far as possible destroy this disgraceful practice of sitting during the liturgy, and use every effort to fulfill the
other duties that pertain to your episcopal stewardship. "Proclaim the message, press it home on all occasions,"[50] and as the
same Apostle advises, "Be on your guard at all times; face hardship, work to spread the Gospel, and do all the duties of your
calling,"[51] that when you must stand before the chief shepherd,
you may vouch for the abundant fruit, worthy of him, that accrues to the service you have rendered.

50. 2 Tim 4.2.
51. 2 Tim 4.5.

LETTER 112

Peter Damian to Cunibert, bishop of Turin. This letter, found in 34 MSS, is perhaps one of his more famous utterances on the recurrent problem of clerical celibacy. After a visit with Cunibert in Turin on his return from his mission to France in 1063–1064, Damian wrote to the bishop, reproving him for allowing his clerics to live as married men. His position against clerical marriage is drawn from both Old and New Testament sources, from Gregory the Great and other popes, and from ancient and current councils. This letter is a veritable armory of arguments in favor of clerical celibacy. It should be read in conjunction with *Letter* 114 to the marquise, Adelaide of Turin, the mother of Bertha, the wife of King Henry IV of Germany.

(1064)[1]

O SIR CUNIBERT,[2] the most reverend bishop, the monk Peter the sinner sends his humble service.

(2) It is the norm of true love and friendship that brothers should foster such mutual affection that if anything reproachful be found in either of them, one will not hide it from the other. Such urgency proves to be both useful and upright, for as it brings everything into the open, it repairs that which needs correction and safeguards what is conducive to their wellbeing by a pure and sincere exchange of love. And so it happens, that as the delinquent's fault is called to his attention, he who corrects amasses a greater amount of grace. Among the various virtues, venerable father, with which your holiness is adorned, I must say that one thing greatly displeases me, which, on the occasion of my visit[3] to you, caused me to be very angry with you,

1. Dating follows Lucchesi, *Vita* 54, no. 180, correcting the date in his *Clavis* 81, where he notes that this letter was written in 1063.
2. On Cunibert, bishop of Turin (1046–1081), see Schwartz, *Bistümer* 131f.
3. While he was visiting Cluny at the request of Abbot Hugh, in the latter's dispute with the bishop of Mâcon. Cunibert's name, however, does not occur in the *De Gallica profectione* of John of Lodi, which describes this trip to Cluny.

and which now compels me to bring it up again in this letter. For you have been permissive toward the clerics of your diocese, whatever orders they might have received, allowing them to live with their wives as if they were married men. God forbid that in your great prudence you should be unaware that such a practice is obscene and opposed to ecclesiastical purity, contrary to the commands of the canons, and certainly offensive to all the norms promulgated by the holy Fathers. This is especially true, since these very clerics of yours are otherwise decent people and properly educated in the study of the arts. Indeed, when they met me, they appeared to shine like a choir of angels and like a distinguished senate of the Church.

(3) But after I learned of the hidden discharge flowing from this disease, light was suddenly converted into darkness, and my joy was turned into sorrow, and I at once recalled this saying of the Gospel, "Alas for you, lawyers and Pharisees! You are like tombs covered with whitewash; they look well from the outside, but inside they are full of dead men's bones and all kinds of filth."[4] How is it, father, that you watch out only for yourself, and that in regard to those for whom you must first give an account you are indolently asleep? Certainly, in other individuals productive chastity is not required; but in a bishop chastity is rightly considered unprofitable if it remains so sterile that it does not give birth to chastity in others. This is especially true, since almighty God himself says through Isaiah, "Should I cause others to give birth and myself not deliver, says the Lord?"[5] Here we should note that in saying "I cause other males," and not other women "to give birth," he is speaking rather of men and of the pastors of churches from whom he awaits offspring. With the same prophet the evil shepherd can lament, "I no longer feel the anguish of labor or bear children: I have no young sons to rear, no daughters to bring up."[6] Also, listen carefully to what we read in Leviticus, "If an animal's testicles have been crushed, or bruised, torn or cut, you shall not present it to the Lord."[7]

(4) Wherefore, if God is so opposed to sterility in dumb ani-

4. Matt 23.27.   5. Isa 66.9.
6. Isa 23.4.   7. Lev 22.24.

mals which were offered to him by the hands of priests, how much more will he disdain it in priests who offer the sacrifice of the Mass? For, as from the former carnal offspring is expected, so priests should beget in others a progeny that is holy. Therefore, your chastity will then find approval in the sight of God, if it also extends productively to your clerics. Moreover, as almighty God formerly chose Levites from all the tribes that they might lead the people of Israel in the ceremonies prescribed by the Law, so in the New Testament he selected clerics as members of his family, to whom he entrusted the authority of his Church. For he said to Moses, "Bring the Levites before the Tent of the Presence and call the whole community of the Israelites together. When the Levites are assembled before the Lord, let the Israelites lay their hands on their heads. Aaron shall present the Levites before the Lord as a special gift from the Israelites, and they shall be dedicated to the service of the Lord."[8] Here we should note that when he said, "Let the Israelites lay their hands on their heads, and Aaron shall present the Levites before the Lord as a special gift from the Israelites," it is evident that the Levitical order is a gift offered to God by the people, granted to him as a sacrifice by the hand of the priest.

(5) Therefore, what more need be said, but that they who had already been offered as a sacrifice to God, should be free from the servile works of this world, and should be dedicated only to tasks that pertain to divine service? Why should they be set apart from the people and become a special gift to God, unless they were to observe a life-style different from that of the people, and constantly be engaged in carrying out the ceremonies prescribed in the Law of the Lord? And so, elsewhere he says, "I take the Levites out of all the Israelites as a substitute for the eldest male child of every woman; the Levites shall be mine."[9] But since the Old Law was transmitted through a servant, while the grace of the Gospel was granted by the Lord, obligations were incumbent upon the Levites of the synagogue altogether different from those now required of the clerics in the Church. In keeping with

8. Num 8.9–11.
9. Num 3.12.

the times, the former were allowed to marry, but the latter are bound to hold themselves aloof from all associations involving physical love. For while formerly only the tribe of Levi had been selected for the sacerdotal office, propagation of children was necessary to safeguard the continuation of the priestly ministry, as the Lord said in Leviticus, "A priest shall marry a woman who is still a virgin. He shall not marry a widow, a divorced woman, a woman who has lost her virginity, or a prostitute, but only a virgin from his own people; he shall not dishonor his descendants among his father's kin, for I am the Lord who hallows him."[10]

(6) But now since a priest is selected from the Christian people at large, and since in the promotion of clerics no distinction of race is sought, but only the prerequisite of holiness, the right to marry is rescinded along with the precept contained in the Old Law, as the Apostle said to the Hebrews, "The earlier rules are canceled as impotent and useless, since the Law brought nothing to perfection."[11] And then he added, "But now the ministry that has fallen to Christ is as far superior to theirs as is the covenant he mediates. Had the first covenant been faultless, there would have been no need to look for a second in its place."[12]

(7) This was written because of those who say that if it had been a sin for priests to marry, the Lord would not have ordered it in the Old Law. But those who speak in this way, are undoubtedly either ignorant of the commands of canon law, or falsely pretend to be ignorant. But clearly, we[13] who belong to the household of the Apostolic See, have been publicly announcing throughout all the dioceses, that no one is allowed to hear the Mass of a priest, or the Gospel read by a deacon, or finally, an epistle read by a subdeacon when he is aware that these associate intimately with women.[14] And that I seem not to be handling this question incorrectly, I might cite several statements of the

10. Lev 21.13–15.   11. Heb 7.18–19.
12. Heb 8.6–7.
13. Nicholas II, *Synod. gen.* c. 3; Jaffé 4405 (MGH Const. 1.547); *Concil. Rom.* prius 1059; Jaffé post 4398; *Concil. Rom. 1063* (Jaffé ante 4500); not contained in Leo IX, *Constit. de castitate clericorum*; cf. Ryan, *Sources* no. 182; see also Reindel, *Briefe* 3.262, n. 6.
14. Cf. Reindel, *Briefe* 3.263, n. 7.

Fathers if the limitations of a letter did not stand in the way. But since what I say will otherwise not be believed, I shall at least quote a few of their utterances, that from those I now recall one might gather, if one investigated, how powerful the evidence is that is found in the sources.

(8) First of all, therefore, let us hear what the apostle James wrote to blessed Clement about this matter. "Such ministers of the altar," he said, "whether priests or deacons, should be selected for service of the Lord, who have left their wife before ordination. But if after ordination the minister should go to bed with his wife, he shall not enter the sanctuary, carry the blessed Sacrament, approach the altar, receive the bread and wine for the Mass from those who offer it. Nor shall he come forward to receive communion of the Body of the Lord, pour water for washing the hands of the priest, close the outer doors of the church, perform minor duties, nor bring the cruet for the sacred chalice."[15]

(9) Next, Aurelius, the bishop of Carthage, among other things, had this to say, "It was resolved that venerable bishops and priests of God, and also deacons or those who administer the sacraments of God, be continent at all times, that they might simply obtain what they ask for from God; so that what the apostles taught, and antiquity has preserved, we too may closely guard.[16] Also Faustinus, the bishop of the church of Pontia, elsewhere cited as Potenza, of the province of Picenum, legate of the Roman Church, said, "Be it resolved that a bishop, priest, or deacon, or those who handle the sacraments, safeguarding chastity should abstain from living with their wives."[17] All the bishops have said, "Be it resolved that at all times chastity be safeguarded by all those who serve at the altar."[18]

(10) Also at the Council of Carthage it was again said, "More-

---

15. *Epistola II Clementis* c. 46 (Hinschius, 48): MS class A2; cf. Ryan, *Sources* 95f., no. 183. Cf. Reindel, *Briefe* 3.263, n. 8, where he claims that Damian's ascription of this letter to James is incorrect.

16. Ryan, *Sources* 96f., no. 184. *Coll. Dion., Conc. Carth.* (419), c. 3 (PL 67.186f.); cf. Reindel, *Briefe* 3.264, n. 9.

17. *Coll. Dion., Conc. Carth.*, c. 4 (PL 67.187); Ps.-Isid., *Conc. Carth.* II.2; Hinschius, 295.

18. Cf. Ryan, *Sources* no. 185.

over, when reference was made to certain clerics who were only lectors, living incontinently with their wives, it was resolved that bishops, priests, and deacons in accord with the statutes pertaining to them should also abstain from intercourse with their wives. Unless they did this, they should be removed from ecclesiastical office."[19] In the canons of the apostles it is stated, "Concerning priests and deacons it is the practice of divine law that those who were incontinent while holding these offices, should be deprived of every ecclesiastical dignity, nor may they be admitted to such ministry which should be carried out only by those who live chastely."[20]

(11) Again, to quote the same Aurelius, bishop of Carthage, cited above, "We have also heard, dear brothers," he said, "that certain clerics, although only lectors, were living incontinently with their wives. It was resolved according to the decrees of various councils, that subdeacons who handle the sacred mysteries, that deacons, priests, and bishops according to statutes proper to them, should also abstain from living with their wives, so that it would seem that they do not have them. Unless they did so, they should be removed from ecclesiastical office. I do not involve other clerics in this rule unless they are of mature age. By the whole council it was said, 'We confirm the things your holiness has rightly decreed, things that are holy and pleasing to God.' "[21] But that I do not become boring, it will suffice to cite only what was decreed concerning subdeacons, so that after carefully noting the rules that refer to them, no one can be in doubt about the higher orders.

(12) Among other things, this is found also in the decree of Pope Leo, "Now since living in marriage and begetting children is a matter of choice for those who do not have clerical orders, yet to demonstrate the purity of perfect continence, not even subdeacons are allowed to marry, so that those who have wives should live as though they did not have them and those who are

---

19. *Coll. Dionys.*, *Conc. Carth.*, c. 70 (PL 67.205).

20. Burchard, *Decretum II*, 117 from *Regino* I.90 (Jaffé, 293); CIC I 290; cf. Ryan, *Sources* 98, no. 187.

21. Ryan, *Sources* no. 188; *Coll. Dionys.*, *Conc. Carth.*, c. 25 (PL 67.191); repeated from *Conc. Carth.* of 401.

without wives should remain single. And if it be proper that such
a regulation be safeguarded in this order, which is the fourth
from the top, how much more should it be observed in the first,
second, or third, so that no one be judged fit for the honors of
the diaconate, the priesthood, or for the episcopal dignity if he
is detected not yet refraining from the pleasures of marriage."[22]

(13) Pope Sylvester had this to say in his decree, "While not
permitting a subdeacon to enter the married state, we command
that he dare not do so by recourse to subterfuge."[23] In the Council of Nicea it is said, "We ordain that non-married men who are
promoted to the clerical state may take wives if they so wish, but
lectors and chanters only."[24] But blessed Gregory commanded
Peter, the subdeacon, in these words, "Three years ago, subdeacons in all the dioceses of Sicily were forbidden, according to the
custom of the Roman Church, ever to live with their wives. This
seemed to me to be difficult and out of place that he who was
not used to such continence, and had not previously promised
to observe chastity, should be forced to separate from his wife,
and because of this, which God forbid, would fall yet more
deeply. Hence it seems proper to me that from this day forward
all bishops should be told that they may not presume to ordain
any subdeacon unless he has promised to live chastely, so that
they may not forcibly be provoked to seek past things which by
vow they had promised to avoid, and carefully guard against future circumstances. But those who after the same prohibition
enunciated three years ago, have lived chastely with their wives,
should be praised and rewarded, and exhorted to persist in their
good performance. But we shall not allow those to advance to sacred orders, who, after the above prohibition, are unwilling to
live chastely with their wives. Wherefore, no one shall be permitted to enter the service of the altar unless his chastity has been
demonstrated before he is admitted to the ministry."[25]

22. Burchard, *Decretum II,* 148, *Epist. Leonis,* c. 4; *Coll. Dion., Decretum Leonis,*
c. 34 (PL 67.293); Leon. *Epist.* 14, c. 4 (PL 54.672f.).

23. *Constit. Sylvestri,* c. 8 (Mansi 2.625); cf. Ryan, *Sources* no. 190.

24. *Coll. Dion., Can. Apost.,* c. 27 (PL 67.144); Ryan, *Sources* no. 191.

25. John the Deacon, *Vita Greg.* 2.58 (PL 75.122C); *Reg. Greg I,* 1.42 (MGH
Epist. I.67).

(14) But why proceed any further in heaping up canons, when even they who in their pride oppose them cannot be ignorant of them? At one time when fat bulls of the church of Lodi surrounded me in armed conspiracy, and with fierce noise a herd of calves beset me,[26] as if spewing bile into my mouth, they said, "We have the authority of the council of Tribur on our side," if I have cited the name correctly, "which grants those promoted to ecclesiastical orders the right to marry." To whom I replied, "This council of yours, whatever you wish to call it, is not acceptable to me if it does not agree with the decision of the Roman pontiffs." For they hunt out certain spurious bits of canons, and to these they grant the force of law that they might deprive the canons of their authentic value. But Solomon says, "None of these bastard offshoots will strike deep root";[27] for the inventions of men are far removed from the pronouncements of the Holy Spirit, and those who have no fear of opposing the sacred canons are without doubt offensive to the same Spirit, who made them known. Hence John says in the Apocalypse, "Should anyone add to them, God will add to him the plagues described in this book; should anyone take away from the words in this book of prophecy, God will take away from him his share in the tree of life and the holy city, and of those things described in this book."[28]

(15) But lest anyone accuse me of interpreting the words of sacred Scripture according to my whim, stating that these ideas in no way pertain to the sacred canons, he should listen to what Pope Anaclete, the fifth in line after blessed Peter, says of those who violate the canons, "Those who willfully resist the canons are judged severely by the holy Fathers, and are condemned by the Holy Spirit by whose inspiration and gift they were written. For it is not improper to say that they blaspheme against the Holy Spirit, who freely and not through force, as was previously said, wantonly act contrary to these sacred canons, or who dare to speak against them, or of their own accord agree with those who wish to oppose them. For such a presumption is clearly in

26. Cf. Ps 21.13.   27. Wis 4.3.
28. Rev 22.18–19.

accord with those who blaspheme the Holy Spirit, since as was already said, it opposes him by whose command and favor these same holy canons were published."[29]

(16) Therefore, since all the holy Fathers, who with the aid of the Holy Spirit fashioned the canons, without dissent unanimously concur that clerical chastity must be observed, what will await those who blaspheme against the Holy Spirit by satisfying their own carnal desires? Because of a flux of momentary passion, they earn the reward of burning in eternal fire that cannot be quenched. Now they wallow in the filth of impurity, but later, given over to the avenging flames, they will be rolled about in a flood of pitch and sulphur. Now, in the heat of passion, they are themselves a very hell, but then, buried in the depths of eternal night, they must forever suffer the torments of a savage inferno. In themselves they now feed the fires of lust, but then with their inmost beings they will nourish the flames of a fire that is never extinguished. Oh, unhappy and pitiful men! By observing the law of their putrid flesh which awaits devouring worms, they despise the laws of him who came down from heaven and reigns over the angels. And so, in the words of the prophet, the Lord says to the reprobate, "You have preferred your body to me,"[30] as if to say, "You placed your bodily pleasure before the law, and despised the commands of my precepts." Surely, the law of the human body is contrary to the law of God. Hence the Apostle says, "I perceive that there is in my bodily members a different law, fighting against the law that my reason approves and making me a prisoner to the law of sin that is in my members."[31]

(17) They, therefore, prefer their body to God, who by despising the rule of divine law, obey the pleasures of their own desires; and in unleashing the reins of lust, transgress the norms of restraint imposed upon them. They ignore the fact that for every fleeting enjoyment of intercourse they prepare a thousand years in hell, and those who now ignite the flame of lust, will then be

---

29. JK †241: *Rescriptum beati papae Damasi Aurelio archiepiscopo*, Ps.-Isid., Hinschius, 21. But see Fuhrmann, *Fälschungen* 956f., no. 362.

30. Ezek 23.35.

31. Rom 7.23; cf. Sabatier 3.619 for sources behind Damian's non-vulgate citation.

consumed in avenging fire. But for those who wallow in the filth of wanton pleasure, how can they dare in their pernicious security to participate in the sacrament of the saving Eucharist, since through Moses the Lord said to his priests, "Any man of your descent who while unclean approaches the holy gifts which the Israelites hallow to the Lord shall be cut off from the presence of the Lord."[32] And then the text continues, "No man descended from Aaron who suffers from a malignant skin disease, or has a discharge, shall eat of the holy gifts until he is cleansed."[33] But if he who because of some bodily illness was afflicted with uncleanness of any kind was not permitted to eat of the food offerings, how can he who is willingly contaminated by sexual pleasure offer the sacraments to God? And so we read in Leviticus, "No descendant of Aaron the priest who has any defect in his body shall approach the food offerings to the Lord, nor the bread offered to his God."[34] And then it continues, "He shall not enter through the veil nor approach the altar, because he has a defect in his body. Thus he shall not profane my sanctuary."[35]

(18) The careful reader should note how appropriately the apostolic statement of James, that was cited above, agrees with the divine law.[36] Therefore, if formerly he who had a bodily defect did not dare to enter the sanctuary, how dare anyone who has defiled himself with women serve at the sacred altar, since certainly the tabernacle was only a shadow and served only as a figure? "But the Church," as the Apostle says to Timothy, "is the pillar and bulwark of the truth."[37] And as he said to the Hebrews, "The Law contains but a shadow, and no true image of the good things to come."[38] When the Levites or the priests served in the tabernacle or the temple of the Old Law, they never had relations with their wives. For, as we read in the book of Paralipomenon,[39] David organized twenty-four divisions of priests and the same number of Levites, who would take their turn in the service of the temple, and at their appointed time attend to the rites and ceremonies. Until they had finished the time of

32. Lev 22.3.
34. Lev 21.21.
36. Cf. *supra*, n. 15.
38. Heb 10.1.

33. Lev 22.4.
35. Lev 21.23.
37. 1 Tim 3.15.
39. Cf. 1 Chr 23.

their service, these men remained totally continent and did not fulfill their marriage obligation. This is precisely what the evangelist Luke states, when after saying that Zechariah was of the division of Abiojah, and that in his turn he functioned as a priest before the Lord, he immediately adds, "When his period of duty was completed Zechariah returned home," and then continues, "After these days his wife Elizabeth conceived."[40]

(19) And so, it is clear that the priests of that period completely abstained from granting the marriage right until their time of service was completed. And what is more, they continuously lived in the Temple while performing the duties that fell to them by lot. Hence Moses said to Aaron, "Until the ceremonies of the sacrifice are completed, you shall stay in the Tabernacle night and day, keeping vigil to the Lord, so that you do not die."[41] Now then, since Scripture commands that we should always pray, the ministers of the altar do not have delegates assigned as they offer continual service without any interruption of their ministry. Moreover, the Apostle says, "The husband must give to the wife what is due to her, and the wife to the husband. Do not deny yourselves to one another, except when you agree upon the temporary abstinence in order to devote yourselves to prayer."[42]

(20) Therefore, since intercourse in marriage is preempted by prayer for laymen, how can it be reasonably permitted to clerics serving the sacred altar? How can they ever find time to live as married men, when they are never free from the duty of ecclesiastical service? For the Apostle says to the Corinthians, "The unmarried man cares for the Lord's business; his aim is to please the Lord. But the married man cares for worldly things; his aim is to please his wife."[43] And so he who is dedicated to divine service must always be intent on God's business and should not be distracted by carnal affection. But how can he be solicitous and always attentive to his Maker, when his heart is closely bound to his wife? "Do you not know," he says, "that your bodies are limbs and organs of Christ?"[44] And omitting many things which the

---

40. Luke 1.23–24.
42. 1 Cor 7.3, 7.5.
44. 1 Cor 6.15.

41. Lev 8.34–35.
43. 1 Cor 7.32–33.

same Apostle says on this theme, lest I cause you to be bored, let me at least cite the following, "Do you not know that your body is a temple of the indwelling Holy Spirit?"[45] Elsewhere he says of this temple, "Anyone who destroys God's temple will himself be destroyed by God."[46]

(21) If, therefore, not only the soul but our very body, which is seen and touched externally, is without doubt the temple of the Holy Spirit, how can we say that he who is forbidden to have carnal intercourse, does not destroy the temple of God when in his wanton lust he makes himself a prostitute, rejects the Holy Spirit whose seal he bears, and in his stead welcomes the spirit of impurity? And since the same Apostle says to us, "Do not grieve the Holy Spirit within you, by whose seal you are marked,"[47] does not the Holy Spirit grieve over the loss of him who bans him from his own rightful dwelling and admits his enemy, the very author of lust? Why do we not call to mind the event when Nadab and Abihu, sons of Aaron, put illicit fire on the altar of God, and were at once destroyed by fire that was sent from heaven? "Now Nadab and Abihu, sons of Aaron," it was said, "took their censers, put fire in them, threw incense on the fire and presented from before the Lord illicit fire which he had not commanded. Fire came out before the Lord and destroyed them; and so they died in the presence of the Lord."[48] What else is the illicit fire which priests present to the Lord, except that they approach the most sacred altar while they are inflamed by the heat of passion.

(22) And since Scripture says, "Do not stifle the Spirit,"[49] those who offer illicit fire by approaching the altar of the Lord aflame with lust, so far as they are concerned stifle the Holy Spirit who should be burning within them. But suddenly the fire of God's fury bursts upon them and fiercely destroys them, as Scripture attests when it says, "And a fierce fire will consume God's enemies."[50] And surely it is right that those who are defiled and approach the sacred altar, should be struck down by the sword of divine retribution, as the Lord says to Moses, "You shall warn the

45. 1 Cor 6.19.   46. 1 Cor 3.17.
47. Eph 4.30.   48. Lev 10.1–2.
49. 1 Thess 5.19.   50. Heb 10.27.

Israelites against uncleanness, so as not to defile my Tabernacle where I dwell among them, and so die in their uncleaness."[51] How shameful it is that the sons of Levi should have held the synagogue in greater esteem than the ministers of Christ now show to the Church. The former, indeed, chastised themselves by strict fasting, observing this command upon entering the Tabernacle; while the latter do not even agree to observe the law of chastity. For the Lord spoke thus to Aaron, "You and your sons with you shall not drink wine or strong drink when you are to enter the Tent of the Presence, lest you die. This is the rule binding on your descendants for all time, to make a distinction between sacred and profane, between clean and unclean."[52]

(23) But now the ministers of the Church, who have Christ as their master, him who was crucified, do not shudder at living to enjoy their bodily pleasures, neighing after that to which the desires of the flesh entice them, as the Lord says through Jeremiah, "I gave them all they needed, yet they preferred adultery, and haunted the brothels; each neighs after another man's wife, like a well-fed and lusty stallion."[53] And again, "For prophet and priest alike are defiled; I have come upon the evil they are doing even in my own house. This is the very word of the Lord."[54] But because they are now fed by glutting themselves on the enjoyment of their lust, let them take note of what awaits them for having drunk of the sweetness of these delights, "I will give them wormwood to eat," he said, "and a bitter poison to drink, for a godless spirit has spread over all the land from the prophets to Jerusalem."[55] Indeed, those who now live with abandon, who suck out the last drop of carnal pleasure and feast, as it were, on the honey of wanton lust, must later pay the price and become drunk on bitter poison and wormwood; and those who presently drain the cup of their desires will later be surfeited with bitter gall.

(24) How impudently presumptuous, moreover, is their boldness, that while unable to escape from this foul contagion, they are still unwilling to abandon the practice of their ministry in

51. Lev 15.31.
53. Jer 5.7–8.
55. Jer 23.15.

52. Lev 10.9–10.
54. Jer 23.11.

which they so unworthily persist, since the Lord says to them through Isaiah, "Whenever you come into my presence—who asked you for this? No more shall you trample my courts. The offer of your gifts is useless, the reek of sacrifice is abhorrent to me."[56] Rebuking them also through Jeremiah, he says, "What good is it to me if frankincense is brought from Sheba and fragrant spices from distant lands? I will not accept your whole-offerings, your sacrifices do not please me."[57] And through Malachi he said, "You priests who despise my name, you ask, 'How have we despised your name?' Because you have offered defiled food on my altar."[58] And a bit further on, "I will cut off your arm, fling offal in your faces, the offal of your solemn feasts."[59] And again he says through Isaiah, "When you lift up your hands, I will hide my eyes from you. Though you offer countless prayers, I will not listen."[60]

(25) And so, why do you insolently offer that which, as he declares, is rejected by God? Hence, further on [in Isaiah] he says, "It is your iniquities that raise a barrier between you and your God, and because of your sins he has hidden his face so that he does not hear you."[61]

(26) How much better it would be for these men to withdraw from exercising their orders than provoke God to use the sword of his anger against them; how much more discreet to depart and not serve at Christ's altars than to pollute them by their presence? It is, indeed, an edifying belief, that he who now admits his sins, and after giving them up, humbly refrains from serving in the ministry, will on the day of judgment reacquire the same order which he freely forsook. This seems to be indicated in the book of Ezra, where the priestly genealogy is described.[62] In this work, sacred history relates that certain priests sought a record of their family tree, and because they could not find it, were disqualified for the priesthood. Obviously, they are true descendants of priests and live like priests; they are, indeed, faithful to their priestly lineage and offer their life as a sacrifice to God, and

---

56. Isa 1.12−13.   57. Jer 6.20.
58. Mal 1.6−7.   59. Mal 2.3.
60. Isa 1.15.   61. Isa 59.2.
62. Cf. 2 Ezra 7.

by living according to God's law witness to their sacerdotal descent. And as they imitate the example of holy priests of whom they read, in their sacred preaching they certify that they are the descendants of priests. But those who live for bodily pleasure, and by following in the footsteps of evil men, belong as it were to the lineage of the world, are deservedly expelled from the priestly ranks to which by their wicked lives they do not belong.

(27) We should note that in the same source it then says, "The governor [Nehemiah][63] told them that they should not eat of the sacred offerings until a high priest of God arose, a man learned and perfect."[64] Now in this prohibition what else can be meant by this mysterious allegory, but that one who is unworthy of the priesthood should refrain from receiving the sacraments and from functioning as a priest until Christ, the true priest learned and perfect, comes in judgment? And the psalmist says, "The earth was afraid and kept silence when God rose in judgment,"[65] so that he whose threatening terror causes the sinner in this life willingly to forego his dignity, will at the Last Judgment freely reinstate him and lift him to the heights of the rank that he abandoned, and will say, "Come up higher, my friend. And then all your fellow guests will see the respect in which you are held."[66]

(28) But there are some, which should not be overlooked, who, in the words of the Apostle, despair and abandon themselves to vice;[67] for having lost all hope of living celibately, they refrain from functioning as priest, and thus feel confident that they can sin with impunity, as if the servant were to say to his master, "What you command I am unable to carry out; I will flee to the camp of your enemies and will enroll in their service and fight against you." As if his flight would please his master, and taking up arms against him would not anger him! To these I firmly reply without the slightest ambiguity, that they are deceiving themselves by the vain and hollow expectation that, in not fulfilling their office, they are freed from the duties of their of-

---

63. Probably the meaning of *athersatha*, referring to Nehemiah. Cf. also 2 Ezra 7.65.

64. 1 Ezra 2.63.

65. Ps 75.9–10; cf. Sabatier 2.153.

66. Luke 14.10.

67. Cf. Eph 4.19.

fice. For even though one's order or office is no longer effectively exercised, the sacrament of orders nevertheless persists in him who is ordained. And just as a man who no longer lives with his wife is certainly not freed from the marriage bond, so also a cleric who does not function as a priest, is not divested of the sacrament of orders.

(29) Such men should beware lest that fearsome sentence pronounced by the Apostle be passed on them, "For when men have once been enlightened, when they have had a taste of the heavenly gift and a share in the Holy Spirit, when they have experienced the goodness of God's word and the spiritual energies of the age to come, and after all this have fallen away, it is impossible to bring them again for repentance; for with their own hands they are crucifying again the Son of God and making a mockery of him."[68] Indeed, they seem to be acting as if one of the Israelites, wishing to practice fornication in the service of idols, should say, "Since I am unable to observe the stern and inflexible Law of God, I will go over to the religion of the pagans," as if one who deserts the Law is not bound by the Law. And thus, even though he is not deserving of reward for fulfilling the Law, he thinks himself free from punishment for having despised the Law.

(30) But let us hear what the severe God has to say to such as these in Deuteronomy, "When one hears the terms of this oath, he may inwardly flatter himself and think, 'All will be well with me even if I follow the promptings of my stubborn heart,' and let the drunkard kill the thirsty man and the Lord will not forgive him. For then his anger and resentment will overwhelm this man, and the denunciations prescribed in this book will fall heavily on him, and the Lord will blot out his name from under heaven. The Lord will single him out from all the tribes of Israel for disaster to fall upon him, according to the curses required by the covenant and prescribed in this book of the Law."[69] So, let a cleric who is forbidden intimate association with women, with sacrilegious loathing repudiate the sacred altar, and free as a lusty stallion, seek to indulge his appetite. But when he is free

68. Heb 6.4–6.
69. Deut 29.19–21.

from God and abandons him like one cut off from him, he is unable to escape the snares of his curse and of his own damnation. For the psalmist says, "Cursed are those who turn from your commandments."[70] And in the words of Ezekiel the Lord says, "Let not your thinking be like those who say, 'Let us become like the nations and tribes of the land and worship wood and stone.' As I live, says the Lord God, I will reign over you with a strong hand, with arm outstretched and wrath outpoured. I will bring you out from the peoples and gather you from the lands over which you have been scattered, and I will subject you to my rule."[71]

(31) What I now relate, was said to have taken place in our own day. A priest was living in the region of Gaul,[72] near the lands administered by a venerable abbot named Benedict. The richer this priest became in worldly goods, the more he suffered from a lack of religious spirit and the practice of a virtuous life. When his mistress died, the widowed priest decided to marry again. To make a long story short, he took on a new playmate like one who consults the register of a brothel, invited his friends and neighbors for the wedding, and provided an affluent banquet for his guests. When the abbot, a sick man who expected soon to die, heard of this, he sent two monks to the priest, and under threat of the severest censure forbade him to commit such a shameful crime. But the latter, already carried away by the wicked deed he had planned, would not comply, but with criminal abandon went forward with the marriage preparations. While all the guests were preoccupied with lewd and noisy jokes, the priest, like an ox being led to the slaughter, left the banquet and entered his bedroom that provided, not for his pleasure but for his damnation. O how awesome is God in his dealings with men,[73] for the priest was punished by sudden death! At the very moment when he poured out his semen, he also breathed out his soul. Thus will one be rewarded who decides to abandon the sanctuary of the Lord to enter a filthy brothel and the wallowing-

---

70. Ps 118.21.   71. Ezek 20.32–37.

72. Cf. E. Amann and A. Dumas, *L'Eglise au pouvoir des laiques* (888–1057) (Histoire de l'Eglise 7, 1948) 478; Barstow, *Priests* 36.

73. Cf. Ps 65.3.

place for swine. Perhaps this man thought that he could sin with impunity because he did not often go up to the sacred altar. And yet, he experienced exactly what the Apostle had said, "It is a terrible thing to fall into the hands of the living God."[74]

(32) At another time, Pope Stephen who was afire with the zeal of Phinehas,[75] ordered all the Roman clerics who lived incontinently in defiance of the edict of Pope Leo,[76] to leave the ranks of the clergy and the sanctuary and to do penance, even though they had separated from their wives. Still, while there were some who disobeyed this holy man, and for a time left the sanctuary with no expectation of ever again receiving permission to celebrate Mass, there was a priest living near the canonry of St. Cecilia across the Tiber,[77] who refused to dismiss his mistress and considered this statute to be completely worthless and frivolous. Now one afternoon this man who was in excellent health, strong and robust, lay down on his bed to get some rest. But all of a sudden he suffered a stroke, punished by an avenging God, and the next morning was found dead. At once the holy community of this canonry sent two clerics to me to discuss what should be done about the dead man. If I remember correctly, I advised that they should bury him near the church because he was a priest, but that no hymns or psalms be used in the service so that fear might be engendered in those who live impure lives, and that the glory of chastity might be enhanced. Clearly, it seemed to be the proper procedure that, according to the prophet, the dead man should be buried like an ass, since during his life he refused to be bound by human law. Thus Jeremiah spoke of Jehoiakim, son of Jonah, king of Judah, "He shall be buried like a dead ass, dragged along and flung beyond the gates of Jerusalem."[78]

(33) For one who bears the military mark,[79] no matter where

---

74. Heb 10.31; cf. Sabatier 3.924.   75. Cf. Num 25.7–8.

76. Conc. Rom. 1057; JL post 4375; Hefele-Leclercq 4.2.1126; *Interd. papae Leonis=Constit. de cast. clericorum* (Conc. Rom. 1050, April); cf. Ryan, *Sources* 196, no. 182.

77. On S. Cecilia in Trastevere, cf. *Monasticon Italiae* 1.48, no. 53.

78. Jer 22.19.

79. Cf. RE 2.4.2358, where it is stated that recruits to the Roman army were tattooed under the arm or in the hand during the Late Empire.

he goes, he will always carry the symbol of the service to which he belonged by oath, and whenever one sees the burnt-in stigma of his disgrace, he will recognize a soldier who is a deserter and is guilty of flight. So also a cleric, one who is marked with the seal of the Holy Spirit he received on the day of his ordination, can be recognized when he frequents a filthy brothel. Nor can he ever erase this mark, even though he there received the brand of which John spoke in the Apocalypse, "He will cause everyone, great and small, to be branded with the mark of the beast on his right hand or forehead."[80] But what has the mark of the beast to do with the seal, of which he says, "For those who were on Mount Zion with the Lamb, had his name and the name of his Father written on their foreheads."[81] "Can light consort with darkness? Can Christ agree with Belial? Can there be a compact between the temple of God and the idols of the heathen?"[82]

(34) And now, let me speak to you, you charmers of clerics, tasty tidbits of the devil, expulsion from paradise, venom of the mind, sword that kills souls, poison in the drink, toxin in the food, source of sinning, and occasion of damnation. I am talking to you, you female branch of the ancient enemy, hoopoes, screech owls, nighthawks, she-wolves, leeches, "calling out without ceasing, 'Give, give.' "[83] So come and listen to me, you strumpets, prostitutes waiting to be kissed, you wallow for fat pigs, den of unclean spirits, nymphs, sirens, witches, forest goddesses of the night, and if there are yet other monstrous titles of ill-omen that one can find, they should well be ascribed to you. For you are the victims of demons, destined for destruction and eternal death. On you the devil feasts as on delicious fare, he grows fat on your overflowing lust. As Scripture says, "he lives hidden in the reeds and in the marsh."[84] You are vessels of the wrath and fury of the Lord, stored up for the day of vengeance. You are vile tigresses whose cruel jaws can be sated only on human blood. You are harpies flying about the sacrifice of the Lord to snatch those who are offered to God and cruelly devour them. I might well call you lionesses, who like your wild counterparts, toss your

80. Rev 13.16.   81. Rev 14.1.
82. 2 Cor 6.14–16; cf. Sabatier 3.1017; 3.742.
83. Prov 30.15.   84. Job 40.16

manes and snatch unsuspecting men in your wild embrace and bring them to damnation. You are Sirens and Charybdes[85] who by singing their deceptive song, prepare inevitable shipwreck in the devouring sea. You furious vipers, by the ardor of your impatient lust you dismember your lovers by cutting them off from Christ who is the head of the clergy.

(35) As once the Midianite women in their fine attire enticed the Israelites to have intercourse with them,[86] so by the lure of your charms and your pretty faces you tear unfaithful men from the service of the holy altar in which they are engaged, that you might smother them in the deceitful and tenacious grasp of your love. And as these women of Midian persuaded their victims to worship their idols, so you too compel those who are marked with the sign of the cross to adore the image of the beast. Unless you and your like come to your senses, you will not escape the sentence of the Apocalypse, "Whoever worships the beast and its image and receives its mark on his forehead or hand, shall drink the wine of God's wrath, poured undiluted into the cup of his vengeance. He shall be tormented in sulphurous flames before the holy angels and before the Lamb. The smoke of their torment will rise forever and ever, and they will have no respite day or night."[87]

(36) Moreover, as Adam from among all the fruit in paradise sought only that which God had forbidden, so from the total mass of humanity you chose only those who were prohibited from having any familiar association with women. Through you the forces of Damascus attack the tower of David, when the ancient enemy eagerly uses you to assault the heights of ecclesiastical chastity.[88] I may surely call you vipers and cerastes,[89] which so suck the blood of miserable and unheeding men, that you might fill them with your lethal poison. And so, you belong to those of whom Moses spoke to the commanders of Israel, "Why have you spared the women? Remember, it was they who, at the suggestion of Balaam, set about seducing the Israelites into disloyalty to

85. On this interpretation, see Reindel, *Briefe* 3.278, n. 45.
86. Cf. Num 25.6–18.   87. Rev 14.9–11.
88. Cf. Cant 4.4, 7.4.
89. Cf. Isidore, *Etymologies* 12.4.13; 12.4.18.

the Lord by sinning at Peor."[90] How dare you not be horrified at touching the hands of priests that were anointed with holy oil and chrism, and are also accustomed to leading through the Gospels and apostolic writings? Scripture says of the wicked enemy that he enjoys rich fare.[91] With your assistance, therefore, the devil devours his rich fare, when at your enticement and to your delight he grinds the sanctified members of the Church with his molars, and with your assistance converts them into his very being.

(37) In plenary synod it was Pope Leo of blessed memory, who decreed that whenever these damnable women, living with priests as their mistresses, were found living within the walls of the city of Rome, they were to be condemned from then on to be slaves of the Lateran palace.[92] I have also decided to publicize this salutary law, so replete with justice and equity, throughout all dioceses, so that after first hearing the decree of the Apostolic See, every bishop may acquire as slaves of his diocese all the women in his territory that he finds living in sacrilegious union with priests. It is clearly a matter of justice, that those who have stolen the ministry of the servants of God at the holy altar, should at least reimburse the bishop with their service after forfeiting their civil rights.

(38) But why should I go on speaking to you? You should rather attend to what almighty God says to you through Jeremiah, "Listen, you women," he says, "to the words of the Lord, that your ears may catch what he says. Teach your daughters lament, let them teach one another this dirge: Death has climbed in through your windows, it has entered your homes, it sweeps off the children in the open air and drives the young men from the streets. The corpses of men shall fall like dung in the fields, like swaths behind the reaper, but no one shall gather them."[93] And again, let each one hear what the Lord specifically says to her by the same prophet, "Because you have forsaken me and trusted in false gods, I myself have stripped off your skirts and laid bare

90. Num 31.15–16. 91. Cf. Hab 1.16.
92. Conc. Rom., April 1049; Hefele-Leclercq 4.2.1007; Jaffé ante 4158 (cf. Damian, *Letter* 40; Ryan, *Sources* nos. 88–89); Reindel, *Briefe* 3.280, n. 49.
93. Jer 9.20–22.

your shame, your adulteries, your lustful neighing, your wanton lewdness. On the hills and in the open country I have seen your foul deeds."[94] She should, therefore, fear and tremble lest that curse fall upon her, with which God, the Avenger of evil, threatened impure women in the words of Moses, "These are the curses that will come upon you: May God curse you and make an example of you before all his people by bringing upon you miscarriage and untimely birth. The waters of malediction shall enter your body, bringing upon you miscarriage and untimely birth."[95] She should further reflect on this, that the pleasure of the flesh she now enjoys shall beget the bitterness of which John speaks in the Apocalypse, "For those who were plunged into the lake of fire, gnawed their tongues in agony, and cursed the God of heaven and earth for their sores and pains."[96] But while trying to avoid being longwinded in my writing, from my great outburst of wrath I am, as it were, hardly producing a trace of warming south wind for the cattle.

(39) And now listen to me, you who lead blind clerics by the hand, if you want to regain the kingdom of heaven which is closed to you, withdraw at once from this detestable union, make amends, and submit to the rigors of proper penance. May a holy dissension arise among you that produces and ignites in you the flames of salutary hatred, destroying the affection that is detested by God. Do not turn vessels that are dedicated to God into vessels of reproach. Do not, like Belshazzar,[97] use these vessels for your own pleasure, lest the anger of God be aroused against you in all its fury, and the naked sword of this wrath pierce both of you. I once knew a priest who strictly forbade his dying mistress to do penance for which she urgently pleaded, solemnly promising to perform the penance in her place. She readily believed him since he was a priest and a learned man, and thus she was plunged into hell weighed down by a leaden ballast, as the prophet Zechariah related.[98] Therefore, repel these crafty liars as if they were poisonous serpents, and be quick to free yourselves, as you would from the cruel jaws of a lion.

---

94. Jer 13.25–27.
96. Rev 16.10–11.
98. Zech 5.8.

95. Num 5.21–22.
97. Cf. Dan 5.3.

(40) Nor should you be frightened because, perhaps, he pledged himself to you with a ring of infidelity—I will not call it faith—because the clerk drew up papers and documents of espousal, as if they gave you the right to marry, and because both of you took an oath that presumably allowed you to live together. All that for others was a confirmation of marriage, for you must be considered empty and worthless.[99] For since Scripture says, "A wife is given to her husband by God,"[100] and the Lord observes in the Gospel, "Any tree that is not of my heavenly Father's planting will be rooted up,"[101] that which is opposed to the will of almighty God rests on no firm foundation. Indeed, you abound in the evil that the prophet Isaiah denounces, when he says, "Because the daughters of Zion hold themselves high and walk with necks outstretched and wanton glances, moving with mincing gait and jingling feet, the Lord will give the daughters of Zion bald heads, the Lord will strip the hair from their foreheads. On that day the Lord will take away all finery: anklets, discs, crescents, pendants, bangles, coronets, head charms, signets, nose-rings, fine dresses, mantles, cloaks, flounced skirts, scarves of gauze, kerchiefs of linen, turbans, and flowing veils. So instead of perfume you shall have the stench of decay, and a rope in place of a girdle, baldness instead of hair elegantly coiled, and a loin-cloth of sacking instead of a mantle. Your handsome men shall fall by the sword, and your warriors in battle."[102]

(41) And thus, lest you fall by the sword of God's fury along with the men you consider to be so handsome, bow your heads, forego wanton glances and applause, and be humbly subject to him who is the avenger of all sins. Moreover, if you wish to return to God with unfailing confidence, he is ready to grant you full forgiveness, since through the prophet he says to every soul given to debauchery, "If a woman leaves her husband and then becomes another's wife, will he go back to her again? Is not the woman defiled, believed to be forbidden? You have played the harlot with many lovers, but return to me, says the Lord."[103]

---

99. On marriage and divorce in the central MA, see Reindel, *Briefe* 3.283, n. 52.

100. Prov 19.14.   101. Matt 15.13.
102. Isa 3.16–25.   103. Jer 3.1.

(42) What a fortunate exchange! When you break away from this union with unchaste clerics, the angels will applaud as you enter the bedchamber of the heavenly Spouse. "For there is joy among the angels over one sinner who repents."[104] And in the words of the prophet, "If you will return to me, I will return to you says the Lord."[105]

(43) But to get back to him to whom I was writing, since it was the Apostle who said that "the same punishment awaits not only those who engage in such practices, but also those who consent to them,"[106] you must be extremely careful, venerable father, lest while being personally a model of shining purity, you nevertheless permit impurity, like that bloody Jezebel, to gain the upper hand among your clergy. Of her it was said by the angel of the Church at Thyatira, "I have this against you: you tolerate that Jezebel, the woman who claims to be a prophetess, teaches and lures my servants into fornication."[107] And the statement is certainly genuine that says, "He is guilty of the deed that he fails to correct when able to do so."[108] Of what avail was it to Eli that he himself did not submit to impurity, but with paternal indulgence corrected his sons who practiced fornication, and not with the severity becoming a priest?[109] Therefore, father, you should read the letter I sent to Pope Nicholas of blessed memory on the incontinency of the bishops,[110] and be sure that whatever you find written there, was also meant for you. Is it not true, I ask, that if you discover a monk living with a woman, you retch and become sick to your stomach, disturb heaven and earth with your outcry, and call for him, moreover, to be destroyed in the flames of hell? And yet we know for a fact that canon law does not assess a different amount of penance for a monk and a deacon.[111]

(44) Since, therefore, the measure of sin is the same in both,

---

104. Luke 15.10.   105. Mal 3.7.
106. Rom 1.32.   107. Rev 2.20.
108. John the Deacon, *Vita Gregorii* 3.2 (PL 75.128C).
109. Cf. 1 Sam 2.24–25.
110. Cf. Damian, *Letter* 61. On the idea of an "open letter," cf. K. Reindel, "Petrus Damini und seine Korrespondenten," *Studi Gregoriani* 10 (1975) 203–219, esp. 212ff.
111. Cf. Burch. 17.39 from the *Poenitentiale Egberti* 5.5.

why do we distinguish between sinners, so that while lightly tolerating the one, or even in friendly fashion pat one another on the back, we judge that the other is worthy of suspension? Do we play favorites, and contrary to the law have unequal weights in our bag? "You shall not," Moses says, "have unequal weights in your bag, one heavy, the other light. You shall not have unequal measures in your house, one large, the other small."[112] And do we not act contrary to the Gospel by straining out a gnat and gulping down a camel?[113] Certainly, to the extent that a priest is greater than a monk in ecclesiastical dignity, so is his sin the worse. For while monks have nothing to do with people, priests have the responsibility of bearing the guilt of sins that people commit. As Moses says to Aaron, "Why did you not eat the sin-offering in the sacred place? It is most sacred. It was given to you to take away the guilt of the community by making expiation for them before the Lord."[114] Indeed, how can priests now expiate for the sins of others, when they are always intent on swelling wombs and squalling babies?

(45) But because some of them, while implicated in evil deeds, also defend their actions by slyly asserting that their position is based on established truth, they should not be unaware that they are now caught in the snares of damnable heresy.[115] For when they fall into sin they forfeit their chastity, but when they attempt to defend what they are doing, they are justly considered to be heretics. Therefore, married clerics are called Nicolaitans, and they are given this name because a certain Nicholas proclaimed this heresy as dogmatic truth.[116] I may further note that, if they are successful in their claim, this distinctly new word will take on added meaning, since those who up till now were called Nicolaitans will then be known as Cadalaitans. For they hope that if Cadalus, who burns with hell-like eagerness to achieve his goal, should preside over the universal Church in the role of Antichrist, he will loosen the bonds of lust according to their plans. In reference to him, his supporters also taunt me, charging in-

112. Deut 25.13.   113. Cf. Matt 23.24.
114. Lev 10.17.
115. On Nicolaitism as heresy, see Damian, *Letters* 61 and 65.
116. Cf. Ryan, *Sources* 64 no. 107.

sultingly that he did not die as I had predicted in a verse that I had written. Among other things, I said:

> Nor do I bluff when I warn: In the spring,
> time for you will have ended.[117]

(46) But to prove that I was not lying, let them hear what happened as a marvelous stroke of divine providence. Now Cadalus, contrary to God's resistance and disapproval, was elected antipope on the feast of the blessed apostles, Simon and Jude,[118] and just as that year was ending, on the vigil of the feast of the same apostles, he was condemned and deposed by all the German and Italian bishops and metropolitans who were then present with the king.[119] Therefore, according to the prophet Ezekiel,[120] God allowed him to use cow-dung instead of human dung as he replaced the death of his body by the shattering of his honor. For he surely died so far as his dignity was concerned when he lost his preeminence by the decision of the honorable council. Now, indeed, I will not say that he died a second death,[121] but rather that he died a thousand times, ridiculed, hooted, cursed and excommunicated by the whole world.

(47) So, let my detractors take note, and while they observe the progress of divine providence, let them not accuse me of lying. But you, man of God, with fervent zeal take up the sword of Phinehas, that you might transfix the Israelite who is having intercourse with Cozbi, the Midianite.[123] Also, like Samuel, bravely arm yourself with the spirit of vengeance, and to Saul's consternation, hew the portly Agag in pieces.[124] Elijah, too, hands you the naked sword of the Lord, so that not one of the priests and prophets of Baal brought to the valley of Kishon might escape.[125] Moses, also, because of his affection for a certain Hebrew, struck

---

117. Cf. Damian, *Letter* 88.
118. Cadalus was elected on 28 October 1061; cf. Damian, *Letter* 89.
119. 27 October 1062 in Augsburg. But see also Reindel, *Briefe* 3.287, n. 70.
120. Cf. Ezek 4.15.
121. Biathanatus has the meaning of dying a violent death or dying by suicide. But here it seems to mean a second death, with reference to Rev 2.11 and Rev 21.8.
122. At Rome, April 1063 and at Mantua, May/June 1064.
123. Cf. Num 25.8.   124. 1 Sam 15.32–33.
125. Cf. 1 Kgs 18.40.

down the Egyptian and hid his body in the sand, and for this act
he was afterwards found worthy of the leadership of Israel.[126] But
that we might especially remember the victory that underscores
the mystery of chastity, we should note that David took as his wife
Michal, the daughter of King Saul, immediately after that eager
warrior had slain two hundred Philistines and cut off their foreskins.[127] For since Saul had requested only a hundred, but accepted the two hundred his son-in-law had brought, he too
brings twice the number of foreskins to the king of Israel, who
offers to God not only bodily integrity, but also purity of heart.
Because Adonijah, son of Haggith, requested an unlawful marriage, using Bathsheba to intercede for him, at Solomon's decree
he paid with his life for his incestuous request.[128]

(48) Remember, therefore, what the same Solomon says to
you, "My son, if you pledge yourself for your friend and stand
surety for a stranger, if you are caught by your promise, trapped
by some promise you have made, do what I now tell you and save
yourself, my son: when you fall into another man's power, bestir
yourself, go and pester the man, give yourself no rest, allow yourself no sleep."[129] You were caught by your promise to your friend
when you committed yourself to preside over the people of God.
Nor should you forget what was said by Jeremiah, "A curse on
him who withholds his sword from bloodshed."[130] To be sure, a
man withdraws his sword from shedding blood if he fails to
avenge the sinner's faults. But, perhaps, if you are afraid to stand
up for the cause of chastity and take up the arms of chastity
against the roaring battalions of lust, hear what the voice of God
promises you in the words of Ezekiel. "Man," he said, "I will make
you as brazen as they are and as stubborn as they are. I will make
your brow like adamant, harder than flint. Never fear them,
never be terrified by them."[131] And through Solomon he says to
you, "Do not be afraid when the powers of wickedness suddenly
attack you with terror. The Lord will be at your side, and he will
keep your feet clear of the trap."[132] And again, "God's every

---

126. Exod 2.12.
128. Cf. 1 Kgs 2.13–25.
130. Jer 48.10.
132. Prov 3.25–26.

127. Cf. 1 Sam 18.27.
129. Prov 6.1–4.
131. Ezek 3.8–9.

promise is a fiery shield to all who set their hope on him."[133] But if, perhaps, you are facing the impossible, and, as it were, saying to my face that you doubt that you will ever be able to overcome, listen to what wisdom itself says to you in the words of the same Solomon, "When you see a man being dragged to be killed, go to his rescue, and save those being hurried away to their death. If you say, 'I am not strong enough,' God, who fixes a standard for the heart, will take note. God who watches you—be sure he will know; he will requite every man for what he does."[134]

(49) And so, venerable father, bravely arm yourself for this conflict between chastity and lust. Unsheathe the sword of the Spirit and fatally wound this violent impurity, raging in your diocese, that as a valiant soldier you may snatch the spoils from the bloody hands of this invader, and be worthy of bearing the banners of victory to the Author of chastity himself.

133. Prov 30.5.
134. Prov 24.11–12.

LETTER 113

Peter Damian to Hugh, the abbot of Cluny, and to his community. An excellent piece of rhetoric, based on sacred Scripture, this letter plays on the etymology of the name, Cluniac, deriving it from *clunis* (haunch) and *acus* (goad). In the letter's conclusion, he again reminds the monks of his self-sacrifice in coming over the Alps on their behalf, and of their written promise, made in chapter, to remember him annually in their prayers on the anniversary of his death. If they should forget, he asks that the Lord at the Last Judgment hold them accountable for their broken promise.

(1064)[1]

O SIR HUGH, the archangel of monks,[2] and to his holy community, the monk Peter the sinner, their most humble servant.

(2) After once the hunter has snared his prey and shackled its feet, he allows the animal a certain amount of freedom to move about, without fear of losing it. He, too, who enjoys fowling, after binding the bird's feet with a cord, can safely permit it to fly, seemingly at will. The bird, indeed, tries to get away, flaps its wings as if it were rowing, but in attempting to escape, is held back by the cord that restricts it.

(3) You, too, have safely sent me back to my own monastery, but hold me firmly bound by the glue of your love. Of course, I was physically able to depart, but in spirit I never left your hands. The gluten of your admirable way of life has so bound me, the adhesive of your angelic behavior so held me and caught me fast in the snares of your genuine love, that it would have been easier to forget myself than to tear myself away from remembering you. I have, indeed, beheld a paradise watered by the streams of the

---

1. Dating follows Lucchesi, *Vita* 53, no. 10.

2. On Hugh, see Damian, *Letter* 100, n. 5 and H. E. J. Cowdrey, "Two Studies in Cluniac History 1049–1126," *Studi Gregoriani* 11 (1978) 5–298, esp. 17–175. Damian usually honored only Desiderius of Monte Cassino with this title.

four Gospels,[3] abounding, moreover, with a like number of streams of spiritual virtues. I have seen a garden of delights that contained varied graces of roses and lilies, filled with the sweet smelling fragrance of perfumes and spices, of which almighty God might truly say, "Ah, the smell of my son is like the smell of the open country blessed by the Lord."[4] And what else shall I call the monastery of Cluny but the open country of the Lord, where like a vast field of heavenly grain there dwells in mutual love a similar band of monks. This field is daily furrowed by the hoe of holy preaching, and in it are strewn the seeds of God's word. Here the harvest of spiritual crops is gathered, later to be brought to the heavenly granary.

(4) And so, blessed Cluny, when I think of you, I am sure that the name you bear was not imposed without divine significance. This word derives from haunch (*clunis*) and goad (*acus*), indicating the practice employed with oxen used for plowing. For the ox is pricked in the haunch with a goad that it might pull the plow and break up the earth. In this way we work the field of the human heart, from which the crops are gathered that are stored in heavenly barns. It was such a goad, used on oxen, that was referred to when Scripture said of the still egotistical Saul, "It is hard for you, this kicking against the goad."[5] Obviously, he was still like a haughty untamed bull tossing its proud horns in the field of the Lord, which is the Church. But he was divinely subjected to the yoke of faith, that he might pull the plow on the Lord's land. Hence, later he says of those who spread the Gospels as if he were speaking of plowmen, "The plowman should plow in hope and the thresher thresh in the hope of getting some of the produce."[6] And the Lord was speaking of this plow, when he said, "No one who sets his hand to the plow and then keeps looking back is fit for the kingdom of God."[7] The people of Israel pulled the plow of the Law through the wilderness, when Pharaoh first pricked them with the goad of harsh servitude, and when later Moses urged them on by tugging at the lines, as it were, of heavenly command. The former forced them to build cities of

3. Cf. Gen 2.10.   4. Gen 27.27.
5. Acts 9.5, 26.14.   6. 1 Cor 9.10.
7. Luke 9.62.

clay and brick as he stood behind them, urging them on; the latter went ahead, encouraging them, by promising a land flowing with milk and honey.

(5) But we, who like the Lord's oxen plow in the field of the Church, are thus jabbed in the rear by the goad, when we are terrified by the final ordeal of the Last Judgment. This goad of terror is applied to our rear, so that our neck, chafed by the yoke of the Law of God, may not tire from its labor. Therefore, it is quite apt that I should call Cluny a field, in which the oxen of the Lord plow untiringly as the goad of God's terror stimulates them. And as man's spirit is made to dread the terror of the Last Judgment, it is like the point of the goad piercing his posterior. It pierces the rear, that we might direct our effort toward that which lies ahead, since our past life terrifies our heart, causing it to live in dread of the ordeal at the last accounting. Paul was pierced by this goad that he might strive for what was yet to come, when he said, "I do not reckon myself to have gotten hold of it yet. All I can say is this: forgetting what is behind me, I reach out to win the prize which is God's calling to the life above; I strive to get hold of it."[8] For he was given a sharp, physical pain,[9] that he would not succumb while making this effort, but might plow untiringly in the Lord's field.

(6) This outstanding and admirable ox had two horns on its head, because in carrying out his duties as a preacher, he brandished both Testaments. When he said to the Galatians, "Abraham had one son by his slave and the other by his legal wife,"[10] he at once added, "The two women stand for the two covenants."[11] Like an ox, he was harnessed while plowing, and he often spoke of these strictures. Did he not continue to plow even while he was in prison, when in chains he wrote to Philemon, "I appeal to you about my child, Onesimus, whose father I have become in this prison"?[12] And like an illustrious ox he was led to the slaughter, when he said, "Already I am sacrificed, and the hour of my departure is upon me."[13]

---

8. Phil 3.12–14; but see Sabatier 3.823.
9. Cf. 2 Cor 12.7.   10. Gal 4.22.
11. Gal 4.24.   12. Philem 1.10.
13. 2 Tim 4.6.

(7) Deservedly, therefore, this venerable monastery bears its name, for here the plow is drawn by spiritual oxen, and a vast harvest of heavenly grain is gathered, right down to the last kernel, which is Christ Jesus. For Christ says of himself, "Unless a grain of wheat falls into the ground and dies, it does not bear a rich harvest."[14]

(8) Cluny, moreover, is a spiritual field where heaven and earth are engaged, and it is like a fight arena, where our weak flesh contends with the cosmic powers of wickedness, as in a spiritual wrestling match. "For our fight is not against flesh and blood, but against the authorities and potentates of this dark world, against the spiritual forces of evil in the heavens."[15] There Joshua, not the son of Nun,[16] but the heavenly leader of the army and the instructor of men who are fighting spiritually, taught his soldiers to trample on the proud necks of the five kings.[17] They, indeed, who exert strict discipline over their five bodily senses, will know how to triumph over these kings. There, the walls of Jericho collapsed at the blast of trumpets, and its inhabitants fell before the swords of the Israelites.[18] There Joshua swore a terrible oath, "May the Lord's curse light on the man who comes forward to rebuild the city of Jericho; the laying of its foundations shall cost him his eldest son, the setting up of its gates shall cost him his youngest."[19]

(9) He, indeed, rebuilds Jericho at the cost of his eldest son, if his primary affection is for this world that has fallen before the blast of the apostles' trumpet. And he sets up its gates at the cost of his youngest son, if by despising the world he counts it as naught and esteems it less than all else deserving of his love. Quite clearly, he who is used to this world, does not love it. And fostering the love of the kingdom of heaven like his firstborn and heir, he looks down upon the world as he would on a baby besoiling itself and squalling in its cradle. "Set your mind," says

14. John 12.24–25; cf. Reindel, *Briefe* 3.291, n. 9.
15. Eph 6.12.
16. The Latin MS reading is *Benun*; perhaps it should be read *Ben Nun*, son of Nun.
17. Cf. Josh 10.5.   18. Josh 6.20.
19. Josh 6.26. See Bultot, *Pierre Damien* 129f. and 132, n. 332.

the Lord, "on God's kingdom before everything else, and all the rest will come to you as well."[20]

(10) If the kingdom of God is to be the firstborn in our affection, the world must be thought of as the youngest, and placed in the last place. There, too, one cuts off the thumbs and great toes of Adonibezek,[21] when the evil spirit is deprived of his power to move about and operate among holy men. While this man endured the pain of his mutilation, he bragged that he had done the same thing to others, "I once had seventy kings whose thumbs and great toes were cut off picking up scraps of food from under my table. What I have done the Lord has done to me."[22] Now, these seventy kings are seventy nations, each speaking a different language, which the ancient enemy, down to the coming of the Savior, had utterly deprived of the power to live upright lives and to perform good deeds. But Paul, that physician of souls, applied remedies for both these wounds, when he said, "Come, then, stiffen your drooping arms and shaking knees, and keep your steps from wavering. Then the disabled limb will not be put out of joint, but will regain its former powers."[23]

(11) Now Adonibezek may be interpreted to mean "the Lord of lightning," or "the Lord content with vanity."[24] As soon as lightning flashes, it suddenly lets up. In this we can see the Jewish people who flashed like lightning when they said, "All that the Lord has commanded us we will listen to and obey."[25] But once this light had ceased, they prostrated before the demons of darkness. And in saying that the Lord was content with vanity, the reference was to the gentiles, who were satisfied with idols they could see, and did not bother returning to the mercy of the Creator. And while they were ignorant of the true worship, they kept on performing ceremonies to idols. Of them the Apostle says, "They did not honor God, or render him thanks, but all their thinking has ended in futility."[26] And so, Adonibezek, that is, the

---

20. Matt 6.33.   21. Cf. Judg 1.6.
22. Judg 1.7.
23. Heb 12.12–13; cf. Reindel, *Briefe* 3.293, n. 12.
24. Cf. Jerome, *Nom. hebr.* 31.8 (CC 72.98), where the reading is "despising vanity."
25. Deut 5.27.   26. Rom 1.21.

reprobate spirit of evil, was the Lord of the majority of these two peoples, because the former flashed like lightning and then faded away, while the latter, satisfied with the vain veneration of demons, did not seek for help from their Creator.

(12) But now to get back to my theme, at Cluny the brave Ehud drove his dagger into the belly of Eglon, the symbol of lust;[27] there a tent-peg pierced the brain of the proud Sisera.[28] There they stoned Achan, son of Carmi, as the figure of greed, and the worst of all vices, like the rebellious vanguard of the enemy, did not escape the swords of the brave Israelites.[29] In your monastery, living as it were in the stronghold of Zion,[30] David pierced his adversaries fighting against him from all sides, ran them through with the two-edged sword that went out from his mouth,[31] and cut off the heads of all who resisted him. In this Gilgal,[32] which means "a revelation,"[33] the reproach of the Egyptians was rolled away from the new Israelites as a second circumcision was observed, performed with knives made of flint.[34] Here you celebrate the paschal solemnity, and with Jesus as your leader, pass from the veil of Moses to the vision of revelation.[35]

(13) You are also aware, my dear friends, of the great effort I made to promote your welfare; how at my advanced age I crossed innumerable mountainous crags in the forbidding Alps.[36] And to put it briefly, I underwent the bitter pains of death that you might live in sweet content. I took my life in my own hands, and with the help of him whom you serve, freed you from the hands of your persecutors. Wherefore, when you were all in chapter, you ordained by common consent and decided to enter it as a written record in your archives, that on the anniversary of my death, you and your successors would always perform some special act, namely, that all the trumpets would sound a festive note, and the brothers would celebrate the solemn obsequies

27. Cf. Judg 3.21.   28. Cf. Judg 4.20–22.
29. Cf. Josh 7.25.   30. Cf. 1 Chr 11.5.
31. Cf. Rev 19.15.   32. Cf. Josh 5.9.
33. Cf. Jerome, *Nom. hebr.* 35.24 (CC 72.104).
34. Cf. Josh 5.2.   35. Exod 34.33.
36. Cf. Damian, *Letter* 100.

with prayers and Masses for their brother. Lest it be forgotten, the record of your agreement can be found inscribed on the margin of your obituary.[37]

(14) Therefore, in tears, and prostrate in spirit at your feet, I beg you in your sweet charity that you promptly fulfill what you have promised your servant,[38] as soon as you know for sure that I have been called from this life. And as he promised me, moreover, Hugh, my lord and your venerable father abbot, will give notice of his agreement throughout his monasteries by word of mouth, and order that it be posted in writing in their obituaries, so that each of his true monks will faithfully observe it and not violate the letter of this solemn covenant. I beg you, moreover, in the name of Jesus who gave witness under Pontius Pilate,[39] by his terrifying ordeal in which he will judge the living and the dead, by the angels and archangels, and beseech you by Peter and Paul and all the apostles and martyrs, calling on the name of the blessed and consubstantial Trinity,[40] that both you and those who will come after you remember me in your holy prayers, and that you truly carry out under threat of damnation what you have promised me in writing. And that you fulfill your promise, I hold you to this sacred oath. But if you fail to do so, and as it is in my power by the authority of the Apostolic See, still I will not hurl this terrible sentence at such an angelic band of warriors. But at least, let him who disregards granting me my petition be held guilty of lying, I say, and be under obligation to the truth at the Last Judgment for having broken his word. It is on the tip of my tongue to add: May his name be stricken from the book.[41] But since I have regard for your reverence, I will not presume to utter the words my mind suggests. However, if you carry out my wishes, and as agreed and prescribed, always extend me the help of your holy prayers on the anniversary of my death, may almighty God always watch over this monastery, defend you from

---

37. Cf. Reindel, *Briefe* 3.294, n.17.
38. On Hugh's promise, see Damian, *Letter* 103.
39. Cf. 1 Tim 6.13.
40. See H. Denzinger und A. Schönmetzer, *Enchiridion symbolorum definitionum et declarationum de rebus fidei et morum* ([36]1976) 52, no. 125.
41. Cf. Rev 3.5.

the devices of invisible enemies, and protect your property from
external threat.

(15) May the all-powerful Spirit dwell in your hearts and inflame them with the constant fervor of his love. May he at this
time erect his temple within you, and afterwards bring you
within the walls of the heavenly Jerusalem. Amen.

LETTER 114

Peter Damian to the duchess Adelaide of Turin, heiress to lands in north-
ern Italy and in Burgundy. After explaining his reasons for writing to a
woman about the sexual aberrations of the clergy, he exhorts Adelaide to
use her good offices to second the efforts of Cunibert, the bishop of
Turin, in this regard. Clerical concubines are to be suppressed, and incontinent clerics should be equated with heretics. He praised her generosity, especially to the monastery of Fruttuaria. He calmed her worries
about a second marriage by concluding that twice-married people are not
excluded from the kingdom of God. In conclusion, he sent greetings to
Adraldus, the abbot of the monastery of Breme.

(1064)[1]

O HER EXCELLENCE, the duchess Adelaide,[2] the monk
Peter the sinner sends his constant prayers.
(2) Whatever I wrote to the venerable bishop of Turin[3]
about the harm done to chastity, which this same queen of virtues
suffers at the hands of clerics, I had previously determined to
write to you, except that I feared the calumny of these same in-
sulting clerics. Indeed, they would have complained and said,
"See, how shamefully and inhumanely he acts while preparing to
destroy us, he who is unwilling to discuss this matter cautiously
and discreetly with bishops or with other men of the Church, but
brazenly publicizes to women what should have been handled in
the sacristy." Therefore, fearing this eventuality, I altered the
name of the addressee, and what I had planned to write to you,
I sent to him instead. He, however, is the bishop of only one diocese; but in your lands, which lie in two expansive kingdoms,
Italy and Burgundy,[4] there are many bishops holding office. And

1. Dating follows Lucchesi, *Vita* 54, no. 180.
2. On Adelaide, see F. Cognasso, "Adelaide," *Dizionario biografico degli italiani*
1 (1960) 249ff.; Reindel, *Briefe* 3.296, n. 1.
3. Cf. Damian, *Letter* 112.
4. On the overlordship of the house of Savoy in Italy and Burgundy, see the
literature in Reindel, *supra*, n.2.

so it did not seem improper that I should write especially to you on the incontinency of clerics, since I felt that you possessed adequate means to correct the situation. This is particularly so, for which I praise God, since as a woman you are as strong as a man, and more richly endowed with good will than with earthly power. Therefore, because in the words of the pagan poet, "My champion has need of a man to fight for him,"[5] I beg you and encourage you to join with the lord bishop, so that through your mutual efforts of defense you may take on the fight against the forces of impurity that are attacking Christ.

(3) But while urging you both to join forces against the devil, I recall the battle that the prophetess Deborah, wife of Lappidoth, together with Barak, son of Abinoam, fought against Sisera, the commander of the army. Of her we read, that "she presided as judge over the people, and the Israelites went up to her for justice."[6] Following her example, you too govern your land without a man's help, and those who wish to settle their disputes, flock to you for your legal decision. But notice also, that like her you too sit beneath the palm tree between Ramah and Bethel. Now "Ramah" may be understood to mean "the heights," while "Bethel" has the meaning "house of God."[7] Therefore, you too should dwell beneath the palm tree, and always meditate on the victory of Christ's cross above you. Take your seat also between Ramah and Bethel, that you may not be engaged with the land, that is, with earthly things, but that with the apostles you may live in the upper room, and with the holy widow, Anna, you may always spend your time in the temple. The evangelist says of her, "She never left the temple, but worshipped day and night, fasting and praying."[8] And since "Deborah" means "bee,"[9] you too should produce honey, and always have the sweet praise of God on your lips. "How sweet are your words in my mouth, sweeter on my tongue than honey and the honeycomb."[10]

5. Terence, *Eunuchus* 4.6.770. In this citation Damian substitutes *tutor* for *patronus*.
6. Judg 4.5.
7. Cf. Jerome, *Nom. hebr.* 30.1; 3.18 (CC 72.97, 62).
8. Luke 2.37.
9. Cf. Jerome, *Nom. hebr.* 5.9 (CC 72.64).
10. Ps 118.103; cf. Sabatier 2.242.

(4) Certainly, as I pass over many other things, it seemed to me that honey was flowing from the honeycomb when this truly humble remark came from your lips, "Why should one wonder, father, that almighty God saw fit to grant me, his unworthy servant, some small degree of power over men, since at times he endows even a despicable herb with wonderful qualities?" And so, you acted like the bee as you let the sweetness of the honeycomb proceed from your mouth, as it is written, "Honey comes forth from the lips of the prudent, her tongue has the sweetness of honey, her lips drop sweetness like the honeycomb."[11]

(5) But "Sisera" has the meaning "the shutting out of joy,"[12] a term that aptly applies to the enemy of the human race, who drove out the first man from the joy of paradise that had been his. But since this was not the time for dwelling on an explanation of the mysteries of allegory, Deborah said to Barak, "These are the commands of the Lord, the God of Israel, 'Go and draw an army of ten thousand men from Naphtali and Zebulun and bring them with you to Mount Tabor, and I will draw Sisera, Jabin's commander, to the Torrent of Kishon with his chariots and all his rabble, and there I will deliver them into your hands.' Barak answered her, 'If you go with me, I will go; but if you will not go, neither will I.' 'Certainly I will go with you,' she said, 'but this venture will bring you no glory, because the Lord will let Sisera fall into the hands of a woman.' "[13] For the present, I will quickly pass over these plain words of history, lest in spending too much time in explaining the symbolism, I might bore my readers. Suffice it to say, that "Barak" may be said to mean "a flash."[14] A flash, indeed, gives light, but it does not endure; just as it occurs, it is past. And just so, there are some heads of dioceses who in a way begin to flash when they appear to burn with an avenging zeal for correcting the evil ways of their subjects. But suddenly they grow dark, because their light quickly fails when hindered by some adversity, or when they are overcome by inac-

11. Cf. Cant 4.11.
12. Cf. Jerome, *Nom. hebr.* 33.18 (CC 72.101).
13. Judg 4.6–9.
14. Cf. Jerome, *Nom. hebr.* 77.27 (CC 72.156).

tivity and sloth. And so, Barak, the figure of the weak and slothful pastor, said to Deborah, "If you go with me, I will go; but if
you will not go, neither will I."[15]

(6) Therefore, like this man and woman, namely, Barak and
Deborah, who by assisting one another, entered the battle
against Sisera and destroyed him and his forces armed with nine
hundred chariots equipped with scythes, so should you and the
bishop of Turin take up arms against Sisera, the leader of impurity, and slay him with the sword of chastity for having oppressed
the Israelites, that is, the clerics of the Church. Thus the bishop,
in fact, all the bishops who live in the lands that you administer,
should enforce episcopal discipline on the clerics, and you should
apply the vigor of your worldly power to the women. There were
only three kinds of women whom God knew; more than these
did not come to his attention. In Mary, he knew virgins, in Anna,
widows and in Susanna, wives.

(7) But the women who live with these clerics, legally unable
to contract marriage, cannot properly be called wives but rather
concubines or prostitutes. And since they are not deserving of
recognition by God, they are rightfully deemed to be excluded
from the temple of God. For if Aaron's sister, Miriam, was at once
afflicted with leprosy, and for seven days was removed from the
camp because she spoke belittlingly of Moses,[16] by what right
could these women be allowed to enter the church and come in
with their sordid lust, who appropriate the vessels of the Lord to
their own use, and to speak more frankly, force the ministers of
the altar to serve their own impurity?

(8) Therefore, act at once, be the heroine of the Lord, and
like Deborah together with Barak, that is allied with the bishops,
hound Sisera to his death. And as Heber's wife, Jael, placed the
tent-peg on the skull of Sisera, struck it with a hammer, and
pierced both temples,[17] you too must pierce the head of the devil
with the sign of the cross, and destroy the source of all impurity,
who prevents clerics from participating in the joys of heaven.
Such a victory greatly pleases God, who at times uses women to

15. Judg 4.8. 16. Cf. Num 12.10–15.
17. Cf. Judg 4.21.

achieve a more glorious triumph. As Holophernes sprawled on his bed, bedecked with purple and gold, Judith, the very model of a widow's continence, armed with determination more powerful than any weapon, daringly used the sword to cut off his head as he lay there in a drunken stupor.[18] To be worthy of receiving this strength from God, she had previously censured the diffident and fearful priest, Ozias, who had given God a time-limit of five days, and upbraided him sharply as he deserved, saying to him, "This is not the way to speak if one is to win God's mercy; it is rather adapted to arouse his anger and make him furious. Who are you to test the mercy of the Lord and impose conditions on him to suit yourself?"[19] Esther, who bravely risked her life to save her people, caused Haman to be hanged because he thirsted for the blood of the Jews.[20] The wise woman who lived in Abel, threw the severed head of Sheba, son of Bichri, to Joab, who was in command of the army, and thus saved the city from the impending danger of siege.[21] Another woman in Thebez threw a fragment of a millstone from the battlement of the tower, and crushed the head and brain of the brave Abimelech who was attacking the castle.[22] Abigail, the wife of Nabal, removed from his house the deadly destruction, while she offered a gift to the raging David, so that he disregarded the stupidity of her husband.[23]

(9) You can also turn away the sword of God's anger from your own house and from the ones you have under your authority in these areas, if you strive to overcome impurity that is supported even in the highest circles of the Church by bishops who do not pay attention to it. This namely seems to take place now among the Christians what we read was done in the cornfields of the Philistines. For thus do the old Scriptures tell, "Samson caught three hundred foxes. He joined them tail to tail and bound torches right between their tales; he kindled the torches and set the foxes loose so that they would run all about here and there. These immediately ran through the cornfields of the Philistines. Thus set on fire, the ones carrying grain and the

---

18. Cf. Judith 12–13.
20. Cf. Esth 7.9–10.
22. Cf. Judg 9.53; 2 Sam 11.21.
19. Judith 8.12–13.
21. Cf. 2 Sam 20.16–22.
23. Cf. 1 Sam 25.14–35.

standing grain were totally burnt, so that the flames also consumed the vineyards and the olive orchards."[24]

(10) Clearly this story refers mainly to the heretics, who are identified by the number three hundred, because they confess faith in the holy Trinity with many words, but while under the cover of the orthodox faith they change color at the outer facade of their preaching, they hide the fire of their vile teaching in the back, by which the fruits of all their good deeds are burnt up. Even though, as I say, these foxes may designate the heretics, they can also quite conveniently be applied to unchaste clerics and their mistresses, who walk as if on bound feet, while they pretend to live under the appearance of an honorable life. But they are joined together by lighted torches tied to their tails, because they are bound by the fire of impure love behind them, that they attempt by all means to keep secret. And so, these jackals,[25] joined by the fire that burns between them, and united by the torches of lust, consume in their flames all the crops of the Philistines, because they destroy the spiritual fruits of the Church, and so far as they are concerned, devour the good works of the faithful in the fire of divine wrath. Allegorically the psalmist says of this fire, "He abandoned their cattle to the hailstorm, and their possession to fire."[26] For as good priests offer to God the gifts and prayers of all the faithful, so those who are unworthy to serve at the holy altar, as often happens, dreadfully hinder them. The prophet Ezekiel also states that bad priests are like jackals, "Your prophets, Israel, have been like jackals among ruins."[27] But for now let this suffice in reference to clerics.

(11) I should like to suggest to you, moreover, regarding the dioceses that are in your territory, not to diminish their holdings as some wealthy people of ill repute have done. Indeed, when you were present, and I was speaking with many bishops and heads of monasteries, there was not one of them who complained of having suffered any inconvenience from you or your

24. Judg 15.4–5.
25. Cf. Lothar Kolmer, "Ad capiendas vulpes. Die Ketzerbekämpfung in Südfrankreich in der ersten Hälfte des 13. Jh. und die Ausbildung des Inquisitionsverfahrens," *Pariser Historische Studien* 19 (1982) 9ff.
26. Ps 77.48.
27. Ezek 13.4.

manorial officers. There was only the bishop of Aosta who protested, not that he had incurred any loss on your account but rather that his diocese had not benefited form your generosity. In our day, a wealthy person is indeed fortunate if his subjects, living in close by villages, can accuse him of only such a crime. Certainly, in the monastery of Fruttuaria,[28] where I was a guest for almost ten days, I could see good evidence of your humane and agreeable treatment of the churches. There the brothers served God so securely under the cover of your protection, as if they were featherless chicks kept warm under their mother's wings. And how aptly this monastery bears the name Fruttuaria, which, I think, was not given it by human ingenuity, but rather by divine providence.

(12) Now since "Ephraim" may be said to mean "fertility,"[29] this house is indeed Mount Ephraim where the true Israelites live. As they worked the fields of their mind by diligently reading passages of sacred Scripture, as if these were so many hoes, they produced bumper crops of spiritual grain which were stored in heavenly barns by the angels. This place, I say, is truly Mount Ephraim, where one finds a powerful army whose brave fighters are arrayed for battle. There uncompromising war is eagerly waged against the devil, the forces of Israel on one side and the Chaldaean army on the other, engaging in hand to hand combat. There the fat King Agag was cut to pieces by the weapon of temperance,[30] and Eglon, king of Moab, was killed when the sword of chastity pierced his belly.[31] This "Eglon" may be said to mean "the calf of sorrow,"[32] to indicate a victim of hell. There Zebah and Zalmunna, kings of the Midianites, were slain by the sword of the true Gideon;[33] there the head of the proud Goliath was cut off,[34] the disobedience of Saul was condemned.[35] With Ahithophel, deceit with all its sacrilegious double-dealing, is hanged,[36] and in the case of Achan, son of Carmi, a great pile of

---

28. On Fruttuaria, cf. Reindel, *Briefe* 3.301, n. 16; Lucchesi, *Vita* 50, no. 177.
29. Jerome, *Nom. hebr.* 66.15 (CC 72.142).
30. Cf. 1 Sam 15.33.   31. Cf. Judg 3.21–22.
32. Cf. Jerome, *Nom. hebr.* 27.1 (CC 72.93).
33. Cf. Judg 8.21.   34. Cf. 1 Sam 17.51.
35. Cf. 1 Sam 15.11ff.   36. Cf. 2 Sam 17.23.

stones was raised over avarice.[37] There Jesus, not Joshua, son of
Nun, truly conquered the kings of the Amorites, and had his
troops put their feet on the necks of these kings.[38] There Beza-
lel made the ark for the God of Israel from acacia wood that
would never decay, constructed the tabernacle, put up a can-
delabrum of gold with seven lamps and fashioned also the mystic ornaments for the priests, glittering with gold and precious
stones.[39] There Solomon erected the Temple of the Lord, built
of rare stones, and enforced such quiet on the stonecutters and
masons that no sound of hammer or ax or any iron tool could
be heard.[40] There Zerubbabel, son of Shealtiel, and Jeshua, son
of Jozadak, and a force of strongly armed men, while rebuild-
ing the walls of Jerusalem, constantly had to fight against their
enemies who wished to impede the work. They were always on
their guard, prepared for all eventualities, with one hand busy
on the wall while the other held a ready sword; and as the building progressed, they had to beat back the violent attacks of their
enemies.[41]

(13) And what more shall I say, except that this place is the
workshop in which the drachma, belonging to the woman in the
Gospel,[42] is daily minted by the hammer of regular discipline,
and reshaped in the image of its Creator, in which in the beginning it had been coined.[43] Here, in truth, is the craftsman who
built the fabric of the world, of whom, as the evangelist Mark reports, it was said, "Where does he get all this from, and what wisdom is this that has been given him? How does he work such
miracles? Is not this the son of the artisan and Mary, the brother
of James and Joseph and Jude and Simon?"[44] He, I repeat, is the
son of the artisan, and is himself an artisan, with his own hands
working the bellows, that is, his followers, completely freed from
the weight of temporal things and drained of every drop of
earthly love. The voice of God says of this craftsman in the words
of Isaiah, "It was I who created the smith to fan the coals in the

37. Cf. Josh 7.25–26.   38. Cf. Josh 10.24.
39. Cf. Exod 25 and 36; Num 8; Deut 10.
40. Cf. 1 Kgs 5–6.   41. Cf. 1 Ezra 3.8ff.; 2 Ezra 4.16f.
42. Cf. Luke 15.8.   43. Cf. Gen 1.27.
44. Mark 6.2–3.

furnace, and to forge weapons each for its purpose."[45] And so also Jeremiah said, "All these princes are rebels, mischief-makers, copper and iron; they are all corrupt. The bellows are silent, the lead is consumed in the fire. In vain does the refiner smelt the ore; its impurities are not separated out. Call them spurious silver, for the Lord has spurned them."[46]

(14) And thus, through them the Holy Spirit breathes forth his fire, that by their words and example cold hearts may glow in the love of the Creator. There, too, Jesus[47] often comes to his disciples, even though the doors are closed; and not only does he salute them with greetings of peace, but he also breathes on them and infuses the mystery of the Holy Spirit. In that upper room he daily celebrates the paschal feast with his disciples, and as he imparts to them the strength of his mystic words, he enkindles in them the ardor of his love. It is worth noting how this swarm of bees of the Lord always flies about the hive, busy with various duties, earnestly striving to carry out what was enjoined to them. Truly, they bear all types of burdens, making honey and turning it into nectar, filling the honeycombs with wondrous sweetness and delight that will be served to the most high king. There in the presence of David, the king of Israel, the priests, Levites, and temple-servitors[48] played harps, trumpets, lyres, citharae, and all types of musical instruments, taking their turns in singing mystic songs, saying, "It is good to praise the Lord, for his mercy endures forever."[49] I beg almighty God, O Fruttuaria, that he release me from these bodily chains, rather than allow me to hear that you have abandoned the religious life that I have observed here.

(15) For the rest, venerable sister, strive always to progress from good things to those still better, and since you are forbidden by the Apostle to place your trust in the uncertainty of riches,[50] so too never lose confidence in the generosity of God's goodness. And since I am aware that you are unsure about your

---

45. Isa 54.16.   46. Jer 6.28–30.
47. Cf. Luke 28.36; John 19.26.
48. For the Latin word, *Nathinnei* (temple-servitors), cf. 1 Chr 9.2; 1 Chr 15.16; Schneider, LThK 7.798.
49. Ps 105.1.   50. 1 Tim 6.9.

second marriage,[51] let me say that when the Lord was tested by the Sadducees concerning a woman who had been married to seven brothers, and when asked whose legal wife she would be at the resurrection, he replied, "At the resurrection men and women do not marry; they will be like God's angels in heaven."[52] Now, if a woman with several husbands could never enter the kingdom of God, Truth itself would never have answered, "They will be like angels in heaven," but would have said instead, "They will be like evil spirits in hell." And so, from this remark of the Savior we can be sure that if only one leads a devout life, multiple marriage does not exclude one from the kingdom of heaven. For Jesus is such a bridegroom, that whomsoever he embraces with his love, is restored to lily-white chastity. And I say this, not to encourage multiple marriage in the future, but to assure those already so married, of the remedy of hope or penance.

(16) Be prudent in dispensing justice to those who have sinned, so that you do not impetuously rush to punish them, nor shirk your duty by excusing them. By so doing, you will not act the zealot by dealing with them excessively, nor will too much mercy inhibit you from vigorously applying discipline. Certainly, as soon as one is guilty of injustice, his reason is affected, and then he can scarcely render a proper judgment. For just as quiet waters allow the viewer to see his own reflection, but if they are disturbed, they cause the image to blur; so the human mind does not see the fine line in rendering judgment, if it is at that moment overwrought. Therefore, one must postpone the sentence till later, that with the scales of justice truly in balance, the quiet mind may suspend judgment, a thing which a mind in turbulence can never achieve.

(17) In all of this it will be most instructive to observe how quietly King David acted, and how prudent and serious he was when passing judgment. When Joab and Shimei gravely offended him, so long as he lived, and while anger and revenge might still express themselves, he quietly bore it. But when he was at the point of death and was no longer influenced by his

---

51. On a layman's permission to enter a second marriage, cf. Kötting, *Beurteilung* 5off.

52. Matt 22.30; cf. Luke 20.34–36.

former urge to revenge, he ordered his son to punish them after he was dead, when he was free of human events and could no longer take pleasure in the penalty meted out to those who had done him wrong. "You know," he said, "how Joab, son of Zeruiah, treated me and what he did to two commanders-in-chief in Israel, Abner, son of Ner, and Amasa, son of Jether. He killed them both, breaking the peace by bloody acts of war."[53] And shortly thereafter he said, "Do as your wisdom prompts you, and do not let his grey hairs go down to the grave in peace."[54] And of Shimei he said, "Do not forget Shimei, son of Gera, the Benjaminite from Bahurim, who cursed me bitterly the day I went to the camp."[55] And after several further remarks, he added, "Bring down his grey hairs in blood to the grave."[56] Here we should observe how praiseworthy and admirable was the prudence of this man. When still able to erupt in anger, he did not wish to take his revenge; but when all occasion for rage was past, he exacted punishment so as not to cheat the demands of justice. For when an avenger has nothing personal at stake then is the right moment to pass sentence. Thus David did not burn with vengeance, for he no longer felt outraged by the offense; and hatred did not rouse him excessively, nor did unrestrained generosity cause him to neglect his duty. And so, this prudent avenger did not overlook the injury he had suffered, and did not punish it in savage fashion.

(18) You too, venerable sister and lady, must imitate the example of this holy king. Never abandon the practice of generosity and justice, so that, following the apostolic precept, mercy may triumph over judgment.[57] And thus, let your every legal decision promote the glory of almighty God, that when you have finished your stewardship, he who now holds your soul in his hands may lead you from this earthly realm to the kingdom of heavenly glory. I further recommend to your ever-growing care the monastery of Fruttuaria, truly the bridal bed of Jesus, to which, I say, you should always tender your solicitous service, that

53. 1 Kgs 2.5. 54. 1 Kgs 2.6.
55. 1 Kgs 2.8. 56. 1 Kgs 2.9.
57. Cf. Jas 2.13.

through you, your heavenly Spouse may lie therein and take his rest.

(19) May almighty God bless you and your children[58] of royal descent, and cause them to grow, not only in age, but also in holiness. Through your good offices I send my greetings to Sir Adraldus,[59] the abbot of the monastery of Breme, a truly religious and prudent man. If he should wish me also to write to him, let him so prescribe by writing to me.

58. She had children only by her last husband, Peter, who became duke in 1060; Bertha, the wife of Henry IV, Amadeus, Adelaide, and Otto.

59. On Adraldus, cf. Damian, *Letters* 102, n. 36 and 110, n. 2.

LETTER 115

Peter Damian to Bishop V< > and to the canons of his church. He notes that his diocese does not properly celebrate the octave of the feast of St. John the Baptist, and takes this occasion to remind his correspondents of the great dignity of this feast and its eight-day extension. He equates this observance with the eight great feasts of the Old Testament, which he interprets allegorically. This letter is defective in its conclusion, and perhaps was never finished, or at least was under revision in the two surviving manuscripts of the eleventh century.

(After 1064)[1]

O THE HOLY and venerable Bishop V< >[2] and to the religious canons of his church, the monk Peter the sinner offers his service.

(2) The celebration of divine worship is doubtless worthy of commendation when it is carried out in laudable fashion. Otherwise, what good is served if one properly begins a task, but does not rightly finish it? And so, my dear friends, I am aware that you, indeed, solemnly celebrate the feast of blessed John the Baptist as it should be done,[3] but do not show proper reverence during its octave when you are satisfied in reading three short lessons. For, if we pay special attention to the tenor of the Gospel, there is no saint's day of the Church deserving of greater reverence throughout its octave. Indeed, the angel said to Zechariah, "Your heart will thrill with joy and many will be glad that he was born."[4] We can be sure that this rejoicing was not complete on the day of his birth, but continued on through the eight days that followed.[5] On the eighth day when he was cir-

---

1. Dating follows Lucchesi, *Vita* 2.151.
2. It was impossible to identify Bishop V.
3. On the liturgical cycle of feasts of John the Baptist, see H. Leclercq, "Jean-Baptiste (Saint), " DACL 7.2 (1927) 2167–2184, esp. 2171–2174.
4. Luke 1.14.
5. Cf. Luke 1.59–64.

cumcised, an event announced to Zechariah by an angel to the delight of their many friends, and divinely foretold to Elizabeth, the child received its name, and the lips and tongue of the father, who had for months been dumb, were freed. He who before could not speak even a few simple words, now uttered mystic secrets with the voice of a prophet. And so, on the eight day after his birth, as we know, there was great rejoicing, just as the angel had promised.

(3) Therefore, the birthday of blessed John is not only celebrated in its own right, but its octave is also highly esteemed. Hence, right reason demands that, like the birthday, also its octave should be held in honor, by which the birth is made famous, and from which we understand how distinguished and special an event it is. Indeed, from its octave his venerable birthday receives the distinction of surpassing the birthdays of all other saints. And so, it deserves no lesser honor than that shown to the feast itself. No wonder, then, that every principal and outstanding feast of the Church is prolonged throughout eight days,[6] since we read that in the Old Law the Lord established eight especially solemn days to be celebrated each year.[7] These festivities, then, are commonly observed both by us and by the Jews, but at different times. For them, they were held as rites of the flesh; but for us, through spiritual insight they represent a mystery.

(4) Now the first of these feasts is the continual sacrifice we are commanded to offer as a celebration,[8] that is, by reciting the morning and evening hours on successive days. He, indeed, offers the Lord continual solemn sacrifice who diligently perseveres in meditating on God's word. And since in the morning our light is the Law and the prophets, in the evening, in relation to the passage of time, this light is the Gospel, as the Apostle says, "Upon us the fulfillment of the ages has come."[9] And in the words of the Lord himself, "Let my raised hands be like the evening sacrifice."[10] He always offers a morning and evening sacrifice to the Lord, who cuts himself away from secular affairs and

---

6. See Laqua, *Traditionen* 149, n. 28, who notes that *festivity* includes also the days of the octave.

7. Cf. Reindel, *Briefe* 3.308, n. 4. 8. Cf. Num 28.3–4.

9. 1 Cor 10.11. 10. Ps 140.2.

constantly engages in meditation on the writings of the New and Old Testament; or, we regularly offer a morning and evening sacrifice to God when we give proper thanks to him for our salvation, and living in fear of his terrible judgment, even now stand trembling before the judge presiding in his court.

(5) Next in rank after this perpetual sacrifice we place the Sabbath,[11] that is, the day on which we refrain from all manual labor. For a Christian to observe a spiritual Sabbath, he must rest from his desire for temporal things acquired by labor, occupy himself only with prayer and spiritual reading, throw off from the neck of his mind the burden of secular affairs, engage wholeheartedly in meditating on heavenly things, despise the pleasures of the flesh, and with spiritual delight rejoice in the sole hope of attaining heaven. Of all this the Apostle says, "Therefore, a Sabbath rest still awaits the people of God."[12]

(6) He, moreover, truly celebrates a Sabbath to God, who so frees himself from tasks that pertain to the world, that he does not grow lazy regarding those that are of the spirit. For Truth itself says, "Or have you not read that on the Sabbath the priests in the temple break the Sabbath and it is not held against them?"[13] Therefore, he who refrains from secular work and engages in divine service, observes the Sabbath of the Christian rite. He who guards against committing sin does not perform servile work. "In truth, everyone who commits sin is a slave of sin."[14] Such a person does not light a fire in his house, because in the home of his soul he has extinguished all the embers of vice and the sparks of anger and dissension, guarding against that fire of which it is written, "Go, walk into your own fire and among the firebrands you have set ablaze."[15] Such a one, finally, does not carry a burden on the road, because through penance he has lightened his heart by removing all the rubbish of sin that weighs him down. Of these the prophet says, "For my iniquities have poured over my head; they are a load heavier than I can bear."[16] And shortly

---

11. Cf. Lev 23.1–8. On the Sabbath, cf. Kraus, *Gottesdienst* 98ff.

12. Heb 4.9.   13. Matt 12.5.

14. John 8.34.   15. Isa 50.11.

16. Ps 37.5; cf. Sabatier 2.76, with references to Ambrose, *Explanatio psalmorum*, Paulinus of Nola, *Epistula* 12.10, and Cassiodorus, *Expositio psalmorum*.

after he adds, "I am bowed down and utterly prostrate."[17] He, moreover, does not stray far from the house in which he lives, because he makes Christ his foundation on whom he firmly established his peaceful home. He is the house of which it was written, "Your servants' children shall live there."[18] And he is the foundation of which it is said, "There can be no other foundation beyond that which is already laid; I mean Jesus Christ himself."[19]

(7) The third festival is the first day of the month, that is, the feast of the New Moon.[20] Now the moon is said to be new when it comes near the sun, and from it again receives its splendor after its light has dimmed. The sun of justice is Christ,[21] but primarily, the moon is the holy, universal Church, secondarily, every faithful soul, illumined by the rays of him who is the effulgence of God's splendor and the stamp of God's very being.[22] Therefore, when any holy soul is truly joined in love with its Redeemer, when at length it is united with him as in a bridal chamber by the bond of intimate delight, then without doubt one celebrates the feast of the New Moon, as he shows himself to the view of his brethren, transformed by heavenly light, as the Apostle says, "He who links himself with the Lord is one with him, spiritually."[23] For if in all this only the external ritual of feasts is observed, it would seem that nothing useful would emerge for us, but the outcome would rather be judged superstitious and frivolous. This is why the Apostle says, "Allow no one to take you to task about what you eat or drink, or over the observance of a festival, New Moon, or Sabbath. These are no more than a shadow of what is to come."[24] And so, what at that time was a shadow of things to come for the Jews, is now a display of things present for the Christian; and what was given to them in the guise of external ceremonies, becomes for us a means of spiritual understanding. We truly observe the New Moon at its rise when we put aside our former self and replace it with a holy life that is completely new.

---

17. Ps 37.9; cf. Sabatier 2.77.   18. Ps 101.29; cf. Sabatier 2.199.
19. 1 Cor 3.11.
20. On the feast of the New Moon, cf. Kraus, *Gottesdienst* 96f.
21. Cf. Mal 4.2. See also Reindel, *Briefe* 3.309, n. 13.
22. Cf. Heb 1.3.   23. 1 Cor 6.17.
24. Col 2.16–17.

(8) In the fourth place, they observed the Passover, on which occasion we recall the Lamb who takes away the sins of the world, and who was sacrificed for the salvation of all the world.[25] For "our Passover is Christ himself who was offered in sacrifice."[26] This is a continuation of the feast known as the Unleavened Bread, on which it was prescribed that all leaven be removed from every home. We truly celebrate this feast, which is observed together with the Passover, if we rid the tabernacle of our heart of the leaven of corruption and wickedness and keep the unleavened bread of sincerity and truth.[27] We must, therefore, be on our guard lest our minds contain any shadow of deceit, any corrupting leaven, or that it become a repository of lies, but rather let integral purity and solid virtue flourish in the home that is our heart.

(9) After this followed the celebration known as the feast of the Harvest, when the first fruits of the new harvest were offered. When it came time for the ripening of the grain, they held a festival in honor of God, the Author of all good things, who had given them the new crops. We also observe the solemnity of the Harvest, if first we furrow the field of our heart with the plow of discipline, spread the seed of the virtues, that afterwards we may gather the harvest of good works. And so it was said by the prophet, "Break up your fallow ground and do not sow among thorns."[28] And Solomon says of the good farmer, "The man who tills his land heaps up a multitude of fruits, and he who practices justice will be exalted."[29] The same author also says of the worker who is negligent, "I passed by the field of an idle man, and by the vineyard of a man with no sense. I looked, and it was all overgrown with thistles and covered with weeds, and the stones of its walls had been torn down."[30] And again, "First," he said, "put all in order out of doors and make everything ready on the land; then establish your house and home."[31] But in keeping with the statement of the Apostle,[32] everyone who day by day renews the inner man, everyone who furrows his heart with the hoe of di-

25. Cf. John 1.29.
26. 1 Cor 5.7.
27. Cf. 1 Cor 5.8.
28. Jer 4.3.
29. Sir 20.30.
30. Prov 24.30–31.
31. Prov 24.27.
32. Cf. 2 Cor 4.16.

vine terror, will not sow among thorns, but on land well prepared, that he might reap a hundredfold.[33] And so, the Apostle
says, "For if he sows in the field of the Spirit, the Spirit will bring
him a harvest of eternal life."[34] Now the harvest that is gathered
in the field of the Spirit, even in this life, is carefully enumerated
by the same author, when elsewhere he says, "But the harvest of
the Spirit is love, joy, peace, patience, forbearance, goodness,
kindness, meekness, faith, modesty, self-control, and chastity."[35]
Therefore, anyone who gathers such a harvest into the barn of
his soul, undoubtedly celebrates the feast of the Harvest to his
own profit.

(10) Then follows the feast of the seventh month, which is
known as the feast of Acclamation or of the Trumpets.[36] For just
as in enumerating the days of the week every seventh day is
called the Sabbath, so with the months, the seventh is known as
the Sabbath of months, or also the Sabbath of Sabbaths. But
what do we mean by this sound of the trumpets, at which we are
required to observe the annual feastdays, if not the teaching of
the Gospel and of the apostles, which like thunder from heaven
and a fearful trumpet calls us to the muster of the spiritual army,
and incites us to implacable combat in defense of the stronghold
of the eternal emperor against the spirits of wickedness? Who is
it, therefore, who properly celebrates the feasts of Trumpets or
of Acclamation, except he who strives to store the writings of the
Old and New Testament in the archives of his mind and put to
memory forever their heavenly precepts?[37] To those, then, who
celebrate these feasts, the prophet rightly says, "Blow the horn
for the new month on this day of your special feast."[38]

(11) After this they also observed another feast which was celebrated on the tenth day of the seventh month,[39] on which the
Jews were required to mortify their spirit. We also rightly observe
this solemnity when we chastise our flesh by fasting, when we
curb ourselves by the practice of strict discipline, when we cru-

---

33. Cf. Matt 13.8.   34. Gal 6.8.
35. Gal 5.22.   36. Cf. Lev 23–24.
37. A reference, perhaps, to Damian's own practices of memorizing the
Scriptures.
38. Ps 80.4.   39. Cf. Lev 23.27.

cify the wanton urgings of carnal desires, when for God's sake we
waste our body by work and hardship, when we immolate the
inner man by the lament of compunction and tears. As we celebrate this feast in such fashion, he it is who again expiates for us,
he whom God designed to be the means of expiating sin by his
blood, effective through faith.[40]

(12) The eighth and last solemnity is called scenopegia, that
is, the feast of Tabernacles, the celebration of which begins on
the fifteenth day of the same seventh month. For God rejoices in
you when he sees you as a pilgrim and stranger, living not in the
homes of your own land, but in tents and in exile. "For here we
have no permanent home, but we are seekers after the city which
is to come."[41] In fact, when we are seen living in this world because of our bodily form, we actually dwell in heaven by directing our mind to that purpose; when like travelers and aliens we
pass over all present things by looking down on them, and with
eagerness hasten our anxious steps toward the homeland that is
above; then we are spiritually celebrating the feast of Tabernacles, which long ago was physically observed among the Jews with
appropriate rites and ceremonies. This feast, moreover, begins
on the fifteenth day of the seventh month, and since it was observed for eight days, it undoubtedly came to an end on the
tenth day before the kalends of October (22 September). For it
is said in the book of Numbers, "On the fifteenth day of the seventh month which shall be holy and venerable among you, you
shall not do your daily work, but shall keep a pilgrim-feast to the
Lord for seven days."[42] And somewhat further on it continues,
"The eighth day which is observed in a solemn way, you shall not
do your daily work on it."[43]

(13) Now, it is said that blessed John the Baptist was conceived on this holy and memorable day, in view of which I was
moved to write this letter, and thus I may close on the note on
which my letter began. From here rises the difficult question,
how blessed John could be conceived during the feast that had
not yet passed but was still in progress, since the evangelist Luke

40. Cf. Rom 3.25.   41. Heb 13.14.
42. Num 29.12.   43. Num 29.35.

says, "And it happened that when his period of duty was completed he returned home," speaking, no doubt, of Zechariah. "After these days his wife Elizabeth conceived."[44] How could his period of duty be complete when this feast was not yet over? Certainly this feast, called the feast of Tabernacles, began on the fifteenth of the said month, and it was celebrated for eight days, so that the twenty-fourth of September on which blessed John was conceived, was considered to be more solemn than the other days of that feast, in fact, as was said at this time, the most important. And if, perhaps, it is said that the tradition of the Church has erred, in that he was not conceived on that day, but later, when the entire solemnity was over, this . . . .[45]

(14) Another point, moreover, is worth noting, that if we carefully look at both reckonings, the number of days the Lord remained in the womb of the Virgin, and the time blessed John spent in his mother who was advanced in years, we find that the Lord's period was two days longer. There were two hundred and seventy-six days from the Lord's conception until his birth, while for John the period was only two hundred and seventy-four days. For, since the Lord was conceived on the twenty-fifth of March and was born on the twenty-fifth of December, while John was begotten on the twenty-fourth of September and came forth from his mother's womb on the twenty-fourth of June, the number of days for the Savior exceeds those of John by two days. This occurred because of the month of February which has only twenty-eight days, while all other months have thirty or thirty-one days.

(15) Therefore, because blessed John was hidden in his mother's womb during this month, which was already past when the Lord was conceived, and yet had not yet appeared in the course of the year before he was born, blessed John's period of gestation was found to lack the two days which were wanting in this month. And so, this short month is the reason why the natal period of the Savior exceeds that of John. With this sort of reck-

44. Luke 1.23–24.
45. See Damian, *Letter* 116, where at the conclusion of the letter he corrected his dating of John's conception.

oning, it becomes credible that blessed John the Baptist was conceived before the feast of Tabernacles was complete. But that the Lord remained longer in his mother's womb, while John emerged more quickly, did not happen by chance, but occurred by reason of the persons involved. For the latter, acting as a hosteler, left the house in good time, that he might prepare the way for the emperor who was soon to follow him, announce his coming to kingdoms, provinces, and cities, direct the crowds of people that they would gather to meet his great majesty, and make ready, as soon as possible, all that was necessary for his reception. But our Emperor tarried a bit as he resided in the bed chamber of his virginal˙palace, and while sending ahead his hosteler and steward, decided to come forth somewhat later. But . . . .[46]

46. The MSS break off at this point.

LETTER 116

Peter Damian to the abbots, Gebizo and Tebaldus, and to his fellow hermit, John of Lodi. This letter, which postdates *Letter* 115, is a correction of the latter, in which on his own admission, Damian erred in relating the conception of John the Baptist to the feast of Tabernacles in the Old Testament. In addition, this letter offers evidence of Damian's solicitude for the correction and editing of his dictated works, commissioning his three correspondents to act as censors and editors of his writings.

(After 1064)[1]

O THE HOLY ABBOTS, Gebizo[2] and Tebaldus,[3] and also to John of Lodi,[4] my praiseworthy brother in Christ, the monk Peter the sinner offers his service.

(2) Your holy charity should be made aware, my dear friends, that yesterday as I was taking my noonday nap, it seemed to me that I was in a boat, with a part of the book that I had dictated in my hand, afraid of losing these pages no less than my own life in the midst of a furious storm. As I was terrified and horror stricken by the fear of death, and with every fiber of my body responding to the dread of shipwreck in the treacherous sea, suddenly a monstrous wave broke over me and finally swamped the boat, with me still holding the book in my hand. At that I awoke and began to think over this dream, carefully considering what mystery was here involved and what this vision might portend.

(3) But today as I earnestly reflected on this same event, I remembered the letter in which I spoke of the eight feasts of the Old Testament and of the conception of blessed John the Bap-

---

1. Dating follows Lucchesi, *Vita* 2.153.
2. The abbot Gebizo cannot be clearly identified. On various possibilities, see Reindel, *Briefe* 3.314–315, n. 1.
3. Tebaldus also cannot be identified.
4. On John of Lodi, his biographer, and later prior of Fonte Avellana, see G. Lucchesi, *Il discepolo* 7–66.

tist, and then like a flood coming in from the sea, the waves suddenly engulfed me in the depths of sorrow. At that, I realized that I had erred and had spoken like a fool, clearly aware that I had departed from the rule of right reason. For I had said that blessed John had been conceived on the last day of the feast of Tabernacles,[5] which is the most solemn day of all. But if one carefully thinks this over, one finds that it is at variance with the truth. Now the day blessed John was conceived, which occurred on the twenty-fourth of September, is actually three days after the octave of the feast of Tabernacles, and thus, undoubtedly, was outside that feast. And so, since the feast of Tabernacles ended on the twenty-second of September, and the conception of blessed John took place on the twenty-fourth of the same month, it becomes obvious that blessed John was conceived of the union of this elderly pair at a time when the feast of Tabernacles was over. So you see that the fault I committed by my careless writing, I have now corrected with the help of God who in his mercy called me to do penance.

(4) Therefore now, my dear friends, I enjoin you in your holy prudence as a task under obedience, and more than that, like a servant and disciple I humbly beg you to restore this letter to the accuracy acquired through my correction, and after carefully reading through the other works that I dictated, you should quickly cut out or cast in more exact wording whatever you find that makes no sense.[6] I need not fear that at your correcting hand my writing will lose the grace of its original quality, but rather that your effort will provide that, while my style does not thereby suffer in elegance, the rule of sound reasoning will be kept inviolate. Since, therefore, "all facts may be duly established on the evidence of two or three witnesses,"[7] I appoint you three who, I am sure, are endowed with the Spirit of prudence,[8] to undertake this intellectual task in my place; so that if

5. Regarding this error, see Damian, *Letter* 115, at nn. 43–44.
6. For the history of the transmission of Damian's works, see Reindel, *Studien* 1.63–67; Blum, *The Letters of Peter Damian* 1.14ff.
7. Deut 19.15; Matt 18.16; 2 Cor 13.1.
8. Cf. Gal 6.1.

you should still find in these works anything that departs from the norms of truth, it should be restored and corrected by you, and that through the care with which you inspect it, this book will possess greater value when fully edited, and gain authority for its reader.

LETTER 117

Peter Damian to Ariprandus, his secretary and one of his hermits. The latter had often confided to Damian his regret at not having pursued the liberal arts before entering the hermitage. With exquisite rhetoric, Damian consoled him by stating that secular studies are of diabolic origin, ill become a Christian, provide obstacles to the spiritual life, and lead to pride in one's empty achievements. As a learned man, Damian obviously had to squirm a bit while advising his confrere to be a specialist in asceticism. But tragic humor smoothed over the issue in the story he told of the learned Walter, the assistant to his own teacher, Ivo. After long years of study in many of the cities of Europe, and just as he was beginning his teaching career, Walter was struck down by jealous rivals. As he breathed his last, and without a thought for the welfare of his soul, this final lament escaped his lips, "My God, what a loss!"

(After 1064)[1]

TO ARIPRANDUS,[2] the son of holy expectation, the monk Peter the sinner sends the affection of his fatherly love.

(2) A servant would be most ungrateful if, after receiving spears and swords from the liberality of his lord, and having quickly put on his weapons, he at once rose up in arms against him. A vassal knight would be guilty of treason, if after being endowed with gifts from the emperor, he should assert that a crown rather than the state of vassalage or subjection was more properly his due. You, my son, admit that you are often assailed and suffer from depressing thoughts because, while having a docile mind and a facility for study, you sought first the approach to the light of truth before learning the blind wisdom of the philosophers; and that you fled to the desert, following the footsteps of the fishermen, before you could become dedi-

---

1. Dating follows Lucchesi, *Vita* 2.153f.
2. On Ariprandus, see Damian, *Letter* 54 (Blum, *Letters* 2.344, n. 2) and *Letter* 55 (Blum, *Letters* 2.355, n. 3).

cated, I will not say, to the pursuit but to the folly of the liberal arts.[3]

(3) Divine clemency brought this complaint of yours upon itself for having endowed you with the favor of unusual talent. So it is no wonder that the ancient adversary should assail you at the very beginning of your service, in the same kind of combat in which he overcame the first parents of the human race, just as the world began. For these are the first words of the serpent spoken to the woman, and with these hissing sounds the dragon filled her heart with poison, "God knows," he said, "that on whatever day you eat of it"—without doubt, of the fruit,—"your eyes will be opened and you will be like gods, knowing good and evil."[4] Take note, brother, do you wish to learn grammar? Learn how to decline God in the plural! Now this cunning teacher, while newly laying the foundation for the art of disobedience, announced to the world an unheard of rule of declention suited to the worship of many gods. Moreover, he who had toiled to recruit legions of all the vices, placed the lust for knowledge to lead them like the general of an army, and thus at its heels led all the battalions of iniquity into an unhappy world. Is it any wonder, then, that the ancient enemy should still hurl the same javelin at a son of Eve that once he threw at Eve herself? With his experience behind him, he cannot despair of success while mounting against the sons the same attack in which he recalls that formerly he came away victorious against our parents.

(4) But while our Redeemer is surely the shepherd,[5] not of dogs or wolves or of wild snarling beasts, but of the sheep, and not only of the sheep, but of the very lambs, is it not permitted, I ask, for the shepherd to raise his disapproving staff over his flock, and at his pleasure to lead it to slaughter or to pasture? For the Lord ordained that in the ceremonies of the Law at times oxen, or calves, or bulls, or yearling lambs be sacrificed.

---

3. As generally covering the theme of this letter, see Endres, *Petrus Damiani* 12ff.; Blum, *St. Peter Damian* 129ff.; J. Gonsette, *Pierre Damien et la culture profane* (Essais philosophiques 7, 1956) 13, 28ff., 39; Cantin, *Pierre Damien* 292.

4. Gen 3.5.   5. Cf. John 10.

(5) Since,[6] therefore, every owner may do with his flock whatever he chooses, for what reason would your Creator not be permitted to serve you as a most tender lamb at his own table, and at the same time keep the rest of the flock in the pastures of the secular world, that by a kind of special intimacy he might incorporate you into his very self, while in the meantime at the direction of his loving providence, he waits for others to be converted at their appointed time? Indeed, little Samuel was placed, I might say, on the table of the Lord like a tender lamb, along with three measures of flour and an amphora of wine, when he was consecrated by his parents to Eli, the priest, and to the temple of God, which was in Shiloh.[7] John the Baptist was selected from the flock of a sacerdotal lineage, not only as a lamb, but as one destined to proclaim "the Lamb who takes away the sins of the world,"[8] and hastened into the desert that the Lord might delight in being nourished with him as at a banquet set with the choicest food.

(6) For men are not chosen for battle in the army of the spirit only because of their own decision, but he, who inspires them to be converted to him, arranges in their regard each moment of their life and time, so that some he invites to his service who have already reached a ripe old age, and others are enjoying the full vigor of surging youth. Some he takes in the very flower of tender adolescence, others, however, while they are still nursing infants, taking them, as it were, like unfledged chicks from the nest. Ahijah, you know, was blind because of his old age, but with a clear prophetic eye he beheld the approaching wife of Jeroboam while she was still some distance away, and said to her, "Come in, wife of Jeroboam. Why do you pretend to be another? For I am charged with heavy tidings for you."[9] Ezekiel was in the vigor of his thirtieth year, living near the river Kebar, when he was appointed to the office of dispensing prophetic gifts.[10] David was elected when he was still a lad in the first flush of youth, tending the ewes that belonged to his father, and was promoted

---

6. On the various age levels among those who enter the monastery, see Cantin, *Pierre Damien* 483, n. 4.

7. Cf. 1 Sam 1.24.   8. John 1.29.

9. 1 Kgs 14.6.   10. Cf. Ezek 1.1–3.

to plucking the harp of spiritual allegory and to accepting the dignity of the royal scepter.[11] To Jeremiah it was said, "Before I formed you in the womb I knew you, before your were born I dedicated you, a prophet to the nations I appointed you."[12] And why should I mention others? For he who inspired Eleazar, already in the winter of his years, with the fervor of triumphal martyrdom,[13] also confirmed the young sons of blessed Felicitas in the constancy of an unconquered faith.[14]

(7) But perhaps you may say, "I will convert many if I should be endowed with the grace of preaching, and should possess a great facility with words." And I reply that Eleazar also could have rallied many from idolatry if he had lived, and both the Maccabees and countless martyrs of Christ would have been able to fortify many for the supreme test of faith if they had resolved to defer the torments of persecution they had endured. But since one gives greater inducement for bearing the suffering of execution by martyrdom rather than by preaching, while disregarding encouraging words they bequeathed to their followers an example that they might imitate. You too will find it easier to influence those who see you following in the footsteps of Christ, than to persuade those who hear you by any amount of words you speak.

(7) Nor does almighty God have any need for our grammar to attract men to himself, since at the outset of man's redemption, when indeed it seemed more necessary for disseminating the seeds of the new faith, he did not commission philosophers and orators, but instead sent simple and unlettered fishermen. For this reason one reads that Samson seized the jawbone of an ass that was lying there, and with it killed a thousand Philistines.[15] What is meant by slaying a thousand men with a worthless jawbone of an ass, but to divert a perfect number of unbelievers from their state of depravity by means of the words of humble and simple men, and by the use of holy preaching to bring them to submit to the lowliness of Christ. But now, since "Samson"

---

11. Cf. 1 Sam 16.11ff.; 2 Sam 7.8; 1 Chr 17.7; Ps 77.70.
12. Jer 1.5.   13. Cf. 2 Macc 6.18ff.
14. For Felicitas and her seven sons, see AA SS Jul. 3.5–26.
15. Cf. Judg 15.15.

means the "sun,"[16] after the Sun himself shone upon the world, after he had shed on the earth the rays of his miracles and wonders, he quickly bent the necks of all those who resisted him and cast them to the ground, abandoning the rigidity of their proud lives.

(9) You too, my son, if you wish to obtain the office of preacher, should imitate the example either of the ass, of which we have spoken, or also of the sheep. The latter while it is alive, bleats unpleasantly, and after it is dead sings sweetly in musical instruments. In the same way, those who live according to the flesh, can blather unprofitably with the sheep, but are unable actively to fulfill the office of preacher. For the prophet says, "Praise the Lord in timbrel and dance."[17] To be sure, a skin does not give sound unless moisture is removed and it is left to dry. Therefore, if you wish your timbrel or string to sound clearly in the hearts of your listeners, all moisture of carnal living must disappear from you, and your soul must become dry by removing every current of poignant pleasure. On the other hand, a benumbing cold usually hoarsens the voice in the throat. So, if you wish to proclaim the word of God in a clear tone, see to it that the flame of divine love in you does not burn low and that the cold of the prince who resides in the north does not surprise you.[18] Such a chill was already experienced by him, who in a somewhat hoarse voice, replied to the Lord as he walked in the garden in the cool of the afternoon, "I heard your voice and I was afraid because I was naked, and I hid myself."[19] Moreover, to the fact that the noonday heat had passed, and that the breeze is brought on by the cold, we should add that he had also with the loss of innocence, become naked.

(10) What do all these things mean but that, with the stifling of love, the cold constricted his inner being, and therefore his voice sounded harsh to the ears of the Lord? Of old, the priest Eli had become numb with this constraining cold, and he said to his sons, "It is no good report that I hear, my sons, that you cause the people of the Lord to sin."[20] Indeed, since the cold of the loss

---

16. Jerome, *Nom. hebr.* (CC 72.101).   17. Ps 150.4.
18. Cf. Isa 14.13.   19. Gen 3.10.
20. 1 Sam 2.24.

of God's love had closed the throat of this preacher, his voice, in consequence, became so rough that it did not resound effectually in the heart of his sons. If, therefore, you wish to have the rolling voice of the preacher, or one that is efficacious in prayer make sure that the love of God inflames you at every moment, lest the shocking cold strike you dumb. Indeed, no one will listen to a prayer or a sermon that emanates from an icy spirit, for like a raspy voice it is not heard. From such cold Abraham completely shielded himself, of whom Scripture tells us that "the Lord appeared to him in the valley of Mamre as he sat at the door of his tent in the heat of the day."[21] Also the heavenly Spouse, as it is said in Canticles, pastures his flock and makes it lie down at noon.[22]

(11) Now, when your talented mind prompts you to complain, do you realize that you are fighting against God with the very weapons that he gave you? And since it is no small crime to be ungrateful to God, you should anxiously be on your guard not to rebel against him in the very things in which you should show him your gratitude; and while intemperately pursuing knowledge that breeds conceit, you foolishly cause damage to love that builds up.[23] How, then, do you know that almighty God, the treasurer of merits, has not endowed you with the discrimination and agility of a talent more subtle than usual, for the purpose of now somehow giving you a sign of future reward and of compensating with the keenness of an active mind for knowledge that brings death which, for his love, you have despised? For since learning began from understanding, and not understanding from learning, for him who possesses a sound understanding, learning is not necessary. As we know, in grammar school where boys are given the rudiments of articulate speech, some are called "abecedarians," others "syllabarians," still others "nominarians," while others also are known as "calculatorians," and when we hear these names we immediately recognize in them the progress that the boys have made.[24]

21. Gen 18.1.   22. Cf. Cant 1.6.
23. Cf. 1 Cor 8.1.
24. On education in the monastery cf. Manacorda, *Storia della scuola* 1.137; Cantin, *Culture* 253.

(12) For him, however, whose mind is opened by the gift of the Holy Spirit, there is little need of this graded learning because he easily grasps everything by the natural vigor of his nimble talents. Thus it is said of the three young men that "God gave them knowledge and proficiency in all literature and science, and to Daniel the understanding of all visions and dreams,"[25] so that the learned men of Babylon had not acquired the level of their knowledge, nor had the astrologers, the soothsayers, or the diviners equaled them in revealing heavenly mysteries.

(13) But let us omit further reference to the ancients and turn again to the moderns. St. Benedict was sent to study, but was soon recalled to the learned folly of Christ, and by having exchanged school for a pious life on the farm, he occasioned the story written about him and the country-girl's winnow, that the learned men of this world could not tell of themselves in the councils of geometrical or astronomical science.[26] Martin also was uneducated, but this simple and unlettered man called back from hell the lost souls of three dead men.[27] Anthony was not skilled in the art of rhetoric, but he was so famous throughout the world that we read of him, I might say, in a script written in uncial letters.[28] Hilarion renounced Plato and Pythagoras, and content with only the Gospel, confined himself in a burial grotto that was his cell.[29] Yet see what power he wielded over the demons, even though he had not been endowed with the wisdom of the philosophers. But if you had pursued such studies when you were in the world, as you now earnestly request to do, perhaps today the Lord would not have you as a share of his inheritance. For there is a wisdom, of which it is written, "For men, who from the start have learned what was your pleasure, O Lord, were saved by wisdom."[30] And there is a wisdom of which it is said,

25. Dan 1.17.

26. See Gregory I, *Dialogi* 2.1, 2 (SC 260.128ff.).

27. See Sulpicius Severus, *Vita sancti Martini* c. 7, 25 and c. 8, ed. J. Fontaine, *Sources Chrétiennes* 133 (1967) 268–270.

28. Cf. *Vitas patrum I: Vita beati Antonii abbatis* c. 61 (PL 73.168B). On the use of uncial letters, see Jerome, *Prologus in libro Job*, ed. R. Weber, *Biblia sacra iuxta vulgatam versionem* 1 (1975) 732.

29. On Hilarion, see AA SS Oct. 9.16–58.

30. Wis 9.19.

"This is not the wisdom that comes from above; it is earth-bound, sensual, demonic."[31] And oh, to how many this earth-bound, sensual wisdom has not granted a happy life, so that they first come to the point of death before enjoying the benefits they desired.

(14) Let me tell you about Walter,[32] who was an assistant to my master Ivo.[33] For almost thirty years he sought an education throughout western Europe, moving from one kingdom to another, and traveling to the cities, burghs, and regions not only of Germany and France, but even to those of the Saracens in Spain. But after he had scoured the world for its learning, so to speak, he gave up his wandering, settled down, and quietly began to teach boys. But the relatives or partisans of one of his rivals, another teacher, killed him from ambush while he was taking a walk. Horribly cut up by the swords, he did not ask for a priest, as it was told me, I believe, and was not concerned about having made his confession or having repented, but to his last breath kept calling out only these words, "Oh, what a loss! What a loss!" And if anything was said about whether he needed to go to confession, or about any other concern, now in his delirium he merely repeated this cry, "Oh, what a loss!" Like a spider, he had indeed woven the fibers of the fabric, so that to him they seemed inextricable, but as soon as the storm of death burst upon them, in a flash all was reduced to nothing. "Surely our years," as the Prophet asserts, "will be considered as the work of a spider."[34]

(15) I will not stop to enumerate the many advantages that Hugh,[35] a cleric of the church of Parma, possessed, because I would annoy you with too many digressions. But he was so ambitious in his study of the arts, that he acquired an astrolabe[36] of

---

31. Jas 3.15.

32. On Walter, cf. Reindel, *Briefe* 3.322f. n.20, where he notes the *Rhythmus Gaulterus* of Adelman of Lieges (d. 1061), ed. A. Clerval, *Les écoles de Chartres au moyen âge* (1895, reprint 1965).

33. Neukirch, *Das Leben des Petrus Damiani* 15, n. 5 thought it possible that Ivo was later the bishop of Piacenza (1040–1045). On Ivo, see the literature cited in Reindel, *Briefe* 3.323, n. 21.

34. Ps 89.9.

35. On Hugh, see Schwartz, *Bistümer* 186, noting that he was chancellor from 1023–1027 and from 1027–1040 is referred to as bishop.

36. On the astrolabe, see Reindel, *Briefe* 3.323, n. 23.

the finest silver. And since he aspired to the episcopal dignity, he took the position of chaplain to the emperor Conrad. On his return from the court, loaded with the king's promises and with never a doubt in his mind that he would win the high office, he was attacked by brigands. In fact, a certain German priest, accompanied by a layman, tried to seize his horses while they were grazing. But just as he rushed in to save them, the priest killed him by running him through with a lance. Then, indeed, he clearly understood that what he had learned was of no value, for together he lost both the sweetness of life that had smiled upon him, and the high dignity to which he aspired.

(16) Moreover, it frequently happens that some men who are wise in sensual things enjoy a long life and are never able to find what they are looking for. Confident in the vanity of their wisdom, and at the same time, hoping for easy success in all their efforts, they decide that they can do without the help of religion; and while bragging about their senseless knowledge, are not afraid to live like fools. Therefore, their conduct is deplored by those who observe them, their life is despised, their morals are ridiculed, their good name is besmirched and their testimony is impugned. Consequently, those who have decided to live according to the desires of the flesh, once the verdict has gone against them, often find themselves impoverished, while on the other hand, people who live simple and tranquil lives have more than they need. Hence the Lord says through the words of Isaiah, "Since when I called, you did not answer, when I spoke, you did not listen, but you did what was evil in my sight, and preferred that which displeases me: therefore behold, my servants shall eat, but you shall be hungry; my servants shall drink, but you shall be thirsty; my servants shall rejoice, but you shall be put to shame; my servants shall sing for gladness of heart, but you shall cry out for pain, and shall wail for anguish of spirit."[37]

(17) Today, in fact, there is a confrere living in Rome, born of the highest nobility of France, whose name I shall not reveal for fear of defaming him. To me it seems that no advantage is denied him, for such is the splendor of his many outward graces,

---

37. Isa 65.12–14.

that he is as noble as an emperor, and to the manner handsome to behold. He has the eloquence of Cicero and writes verses like Vergil; a mighty trumpet in the Church, he is keen and penetrating in propounding the law of God. When arguing with scholars,[38] he spouts learned passages like a book; when speaking in the vernacular, he does not offend against the rules of Roman elegance. But what can I say of him relative to the monastic life, or of his authority in regard to regular discipline? His knowledge of these matters, certainly, is of such high quality that he is completely competent to teach them. But his life, I am sad to say, leaves so much to be desired that no one prefers him to another, no one is eager to introduce himself to him, and, to be brief, to this wise fool the door to his living in the monastery is closed while at the same time access there is not denied to peasants, or to the uneducated, or to the undisciplined. So it was reasonable for the wise man to say, "Better is a man of little wisdom and of less understanding, but who fears God, than he who has great understanding and violates the law of the Most High."[39]

(18) This is surely borne out by the example of my holy lord Leo,[40] the recluse. I have just shown you a foolish sophisticate; let me also introduce you to a profound but unlettered man. Our Leo, in fact, who besides the psalms, had little or nothing of an education, was so superior to any grammarians and philosophers of the world in his understanding of Scripture and in the insights of his spiritual guidance, that whoever of us approached him seeking counsel in any matter of the soul and received a word of advice from him, was as assured of him as if he had received a response from a prophetic spirit. But because he is well known to you and has frequently been mentioned in my writings, it suffices here to include just one of the remarks that he recently dropped, quite offhandedly, but which I was not able to take so casually. Once, having especially asked him, among other topics on the spiritual life, whether he was able to sleep if he wished, after attending the divine office at night, he replied that he really did not know. And when I often returned to the same

---

38. Cf. Manacorda, *Storia della scuola* 2.166; Cantin, *Pierre Damien* 270.
39. Sir 19.21.
40. On Leo of Prezza, cf. Damian, *Letter* 44.

question and inquired whether he did not get some sleep about day break, he assured me that he was absolutely in the dark about this in that it had never happened to him. He added, moreover, that he usually said to himself, "I might be overcome by mental weariness, my eyes may grow weary, I may never stop yawning and snorting, and my head may bob and droop; but since none of these can overwhelm me, they are not going to make me give in to sleep at this time." I once wrote a couplet on this subject that, I think, is not out of place in this context:

> The rule is not observed by him who, Matins done, again turns in;
> Nor, surely, does he fill the gap, who girds for choir with a nap.

(19) But what a fool I am! Between me and my lord Leo, there is as much disparity as between the valiant David and some crazy actor. The one performs great deeds of strength, but the other is content to declaim in song only the hero's conquests. Leo, indeed, is able to sacrifice himself to God by his struggle with sleep, while I write indifferent verses like a schoolboy. Tell me, what kind of a man is this, drained of his strength and wasted away from living the monastic life for almost seventy years, and yet does not know whether he dare go to sleep at the first crack of dawn? He, indeed, is learned and must be called a wise man, for while turning his back on the world, he mocks the very prince of this world with his own philosophy.

(20) Therefore, my dear son, do not search for the kind of wisdom that can put you in a class with reprobates and pagans. For who, indeed, ever lights a lamp to see the sun? Who uses a torch to observe the stars that shine overhead? In the same way, whoever seeks God or his saints with an unaffected purpose, does not require an alien light to discern the true light. Actually, the only true wisdom reveals itself to those who seek it, and the brilliance of that never fading light shows itself without the aid of a spurious light. And so it is written, "Ever resplendent and unfading is Wisdom, and she is readily perceived by those who love her, and found by those who seek her. She hastens to make herself known in anticipation of men's desire."[41] You should,

41. Wis 6.13–14.

therefore, search for this wisdom and embrace it with all the ardor of your being, that with its help you may not only be wise, but may also live, and with it rejoice forever.

(21) And so, make of God, who is true Wisdom, the goal of all your seeking and understanding. Constantly let your restless meditation rest in him, to whom these words of the Book of Wisdom were also addressed, "For to know you is complete justice, and to know your justice and your might is the root of immortality."[42] Therefore, direct your total concentration on him; from this font of Wisdom quench your thirsty spirit, so that when this life-giving draft has invigorated your very being, you may always be strengthened with a flood of heavenly grace and may transfuse into others the waters that gush from this fountain. And I beg that through your good offices the omnipotent God may one day grant to your brethren what he promised to his poor in the words of Isaiah, "The poor and the needy seek water, and there is none, and their tongue is parched with thirst. I, the Lord, will answer them. I, the God of Israel, will not forsake them."[43] And then he continues, "I will open rivers on the bare heights, and fountains in the midst of the plains; I will turn the desert into a pool of water, and the dry land into springs of water."[44]

(22) Since, therefore, dear son, you have sacrificed yourself to God as a most tender lamb, and on that account a swarming flight of devils assaults you, either to snatch the offering from your hands, or to corrupt it by a filthy suggestion of evil thoughts, like Abraham drive off these birds swooping to the attack, that you may succeed in keeping your holocaust pure and intact.[45] Without doubt, the poisoned arrow of this thought of yours is taken from the quiver of those of your contemporaries who have remained in the world and whose study of letters you envy, and in this you consider them discreet and foresighted, and yourself deceived and foolish, so that if you yourself had so acted, you would then have offered a more acceptable sacrifice of your life to God. But in truth, you offered to God all that you

---

42. Wis 15.3.   43. Isa 41.17.
44. Isa 41.18.   45. Cf. Gen 15.11.

had despised for love of him, in your haste to achieve a richer and more permanent life; for it is better to offer everything once and for all, than to give it piecemeal. For certainly, just as it is better to give a sheep than the product of a sheep, so it is more laudable to offer God one's entire genius at once, than the fruit of that genius.

(23) The emperor Julian and the martyr Donatus studied at the same time; the former continued in school, but the latter followed in the footsteps of truth. The former was so prominently successful in his learning that he wrote eight books against the Galileans, as he called the Christians or the apostles, and against the Gospel.[46] Donatus, however, was such a fool, that he reached the heights of heaven, crowned with the aureola of triumphal martyrdom.[47] John, the evangelist, had learned almost nothing in the world, but after turning his back on the subtleties of the orators and dialecticians, he left all as a boy to pursue the simple foolishness of Jesus;[48] yet, when at the beginning of his book he announced the awful mystery of supernal light, the blind astuteness of the philosophers groped helplessly in the dark profundities of their own studies.

(24) The blessed Pope Gregory, moreover, mentions the study of grammar in his letters only to say that it is not fit for Christians.[49] Jerome was dragged before a dreadful tribunal and was there severely beaten for no other crime but that of being called a Ciceronian. He vowed that if he ever read the books of the pagans again he should undergo the same punishment, just as if he had denied Christ through the sacrilegious heresy of apostasy. When they charged him, "You are a Ciceronian and not a Christian," he replied, "If I ever again read the pagan books, I have denied you."[50] How respectable, indeed, and how profitable is the wisdom that is given as a premium for denying Christ; that is considered to be the same as heresy, so that choosing to have it is equivalent to denying God.

---

46. On Julian and his three volumes against the Christians, see Reindel, *Briefe* 3.327, n. 32.

47. Cf. Reindel, *Briefe* 3. 327, n. 33.

48. Cf. Acts 4.13; R. E. Brown, "John, Apostle, St." NCE 7 (1967) 1005f.

49. Cf. Ryan, *Sources* 122, no. 265; Cantin, *Culture* 251.

50. Jerome, *Epistula* 22, c. 30 (CSEL 54.189ff.); Reindel, *Briefe* 3.328, n. 37.

(25) If, therefore, one who had acquired this learning of the world is to be restrained from using it, how much more is one forbidden access who has not yet tried his hand at it? If it should have limited use by those who are trained in the classics, how much more carefully should it be withheld from those who would like to learn? Brother, take your seat at the table of God and be satisfied with a banquet of the heavenly words of sacred Scripture. Throw away the darnel that induces madness in the minds of those who eat of it; have some of the good grain that strengthens hungry souls with a sensible diet. Your spiritual taste should not reject the nourishment of the food of life, but should completely throw off the foibles of falsehood and the rebirth of vanity.

(26) May almighty God, dear son, instruct you in the knowledge of his law, and illumine your heart with the light of true wisdom. May he accept from your own hands the sacrifice of yourself as a living victim, and form you to grow in the spiritual life. May he allow you to stay in him and may he delight to repose in your heart, so that, as he had promised, like a branch on the vine you may never stop growing in good works.[51] Amen.

51. Cf. John 15.4.

LETTER 118

This letter of Peter Damian lacks a salutation, but it is clear from the context that it was written to his "beloved brothers," perhaps meant only for the hermits of Fonte Avellana. He deplores the recent custom in some quarters of not fasting on the vigils of eight outstanding feasts: the Assumption, Christmas, Epiphany, Holy Saturday, the Major Litany at the time of the feast of St. Mark; feasts of the apostles, St. Philip and St. James, St. James the brother of St. John, and St. Bartholomew. He exhorts his hermits to disregard this modern innovation, and to practice the ancient discipline of the Church by fasting on these vigils.

(Before 1065)[1]

T IS NATURAL that human infirmity should suffer from the malady that readily causes it to abandon the rigors of self-control, but finds it difficult to rise to the life and practice of virtue. And so it happens, that when we strive to attempt something severe for God, we find that we must tread the path of exertion all alone, with hardly anyone to keep us company. But if we should let up ever so little to indulge in pleasure, we suddenly discover many of our fellows willing to imitate us.

(2) This, therefore, dear brothers is my complaint: that most of the venerable fasts occurring throughout the year, which up to now we have observed, in keeping with the ancient tradition of our predecessors, we now sadly see being neglected and exchanged for hardy meals, introduced by certain people like new heresies.[2] Consequently, I do not think it useless to enumerate them, so far as the limitations of a letter will allow, and also to propose arguments why none of them should be omitted.

(3) So now, let me begin. Why do we no longer observe with fasting the vigil of the Assumption of the blessed Mary, ever vir-

---

1. Dating follows Lucchesi, *Vita* 2.155.
2. For a general coverage of monastic fasting, cf. Zimmermann, *Ordensleben* 38–45, 50ff., and 77ff. On Damian's earlier writing on fasting, see *Letters* 18 and 50.

gin,[3] a custom that was transmitted to us, and which we doubt-lessly know was practiced in ancient times down to our own day? Is it because the Mother of God did not die as a martyr? But if that is the reason why we should not fast, then there is no basis for fasting on the day before the birth of Christ's blessed precur-sor, since we are not celebrating this boy-prophet's death by the sword, but rather his coming forth from the womb. But if we carefully view the significance of the matter, both feasts are wor-thy of being anticipated by fast days, because the blessed Virgin by her death experienced the burden of the flesh, and blessed John by the circumstances of his birth came squalling and weep-ing from his mother's womb.

(4) Rightly, therefore, do we suffer through fasts with them on the day preceding their feast, that when their solemnity dawns we may rejoice together with them; and as we mutually experi-ence sorrow, we may also feast with them at a banquet in a holi-day spirit. But perhaps someone will say that because the blessed Virgin gave birth to the Author of life without pain, she did not experience the agony of dying.[4] But by what authority can one conclude that she did not suffer at the death of her body, when a sword pierced her heart even when she was still in the flesh?[5] This is especially so, since even the Mediator between God and men said when he was dying, "My heart is ready to break with grief."[6] Of him Peter also said, "But God raised him from the dead, setting him free from the pangs of hell."[7] Yet whether at her death she did not suffer pain, which, indeed, God could have effected, or whether she experienced it, which perhaps he allowed, whence, I ask, comes this proclaimer of feasting, this enemy of salutary abstinence except from the ranks of those of whom the Apostle complains when he says, "For as I have often told you, and now tell you with tears in my eyes, there are many whose way of life makes them enemies of the cross of Christ. They are heading for destruction, appetite is their god, and they

---

3. 14 August.

4. On the death of Mary, see M. Schmaus, "Aufnahme Marias in den Himmel (4)," LThK 1.1070–1071, where the likelihood of Mary's death is stated. See also Peter Damian, *Sermo* 64 c. 5, 380.

5. Cf. Luke 2.35.   6. Matt 26.38.

7. Acts 2.24.

glory in their shame. Their minds are set on earthly things."[8] When Moses and Aaron had paid their dues to death, all of the Israelites mourned for each of them for thirty days.[9] Also when Jacob died, all Egypt extended their sad obsequies for seventy days.[10] And do you try to escape even one day of mourning at the death of the Mother of God, and thus deserve to rejoice on her feast?

(5) Furthermore, at the nativity of the Savior something no less ugly and indecent takes place, when on the vigil some not only eat as usual, but indulge in wine and variously prepared dishes.[11] Surely, since that bread came down from heaven[12] that it might become the ordinary food also of men, while until then it had been the special repast only of angels, it would be too absurd if through the refreshment coming down from heaven the divine nourishment would not immediately give way to earthly nourishment. Thereafter, swallowing wine thick with sediment would dull the mind's sense of smell, if now the odor of heavenly grace gave forth its honeyed sweetness.

(6) Now when someone especially wishes to meet a friend who has traveled a long distance, he will not sit down and have his meal but will gladly wait for him before he eats. And although this singular birth of the Savior was completely free of pain, labor pangs are still the ordinary experience of childbearing, as Truth asserts when he says, "The woman in labor is in pain because her time has come; but when the child is born she forgets the anguish in her joy that a man has been born into the world."[13] And so, just as the whole blessed Church rightly experiences the death of the dying Christ, rises with him at his resurrection, ascends with him at his ascension into heaven, so, as it were, it joins with his blessed mother in giving birth, and together with her is in labor as it grieves on the vigil. The Church so reacts, that when this saving childbirth is over, it may celebrate

---

8. Phil 3.18–19. 9. Cf. Num 20.30; Deut 34.8
10. Cf. Gen 50.3.
11. Cf. V. Vailati, "La devozione all' umanità di Cristo nelle opere di San Pier Damiani," *Divus Thomas. Commentarium de philosophia et theologia* 46 (1943) 78–93.
12. Cf. John 6.50. 13. John 16.21.

with her this blessed nativity. Thus, at the grandeur of such a feast it is not only the soul that erupts in spiritual dance, but even the body that was distressed, can join in the feast as it experiences relief. To this point the prophet says, "My soul thirsts for you and my body is wasted with longing for you."[14]

(7) Now there are some brothers in the army of the spirit, something we must not overlook, who on these aforesaid vigils are more indulgent in eating, under the pretext that they may be in better physical condition to chant the melodies of the liturgical office. But if we hope that divine rather than human ears will enjoy the much more refined sweetness of our voices, the timbrel of our body will produce a higher tone when dry, than when dampened with wine or besmeared with oil. And it is better that because of the effort of fasting our singing be restrained and soberly discreet, than by the elaborateness of our song to demonstrate to laymen our profligate departure from spiritual norms.

(8) Obviously, since we are aware of the extensive fast of forty days prescribed by the fathers that serves as a preparation for the nativity of the Lord, one can only marvel that this outstanding feast itself should be deprived only of the distinction of its vigil. Moreover, how is it that we are not ashamed to drink water, as said before, in anticipation of the birth of the servant, namely, blessed John the Baptist, but on the vigil of the Lord's birth intemperately reek of wine? This is especially so, since the first-mentioned feast is on one of the warmest days of the summer, and one of the longest, while the latter is on a day that is short and damp. And certainly, if we are to observe vigil, we should be more willing to keep watch abstemiously than to burden ourselves by indulging in wine that puts one to sleep.

(9) It is also proper that we fast[15] on the vigil of Epiphany, because of the greatness of this feast on which so many mysteries come together, even though those who cannot otherwise be persuaded, are not forbidden to have wine along with other liquids. Here, I think, the defender of an easier life will grow angry, here the promoter of steaming dishes will furrow his brow, shouting

14. Ps 62.2; cf. Sabatier 2.123 for variants from the Vulgate.
15. The observance of the fast for the vigil of Ephiphany appears to have been first celebrated in Milan in the Gallican liturgy. Cf. Hall-Crehan, *Fasten* 53.

that I am introducing novel and strange fast days, which I am unable to support by any evidence from the Fathers. But that I may not waste more time with him, and get on with the subject, tell me, why did blessed Gregory in his sacramentary assign a special Mass to this day, and entitle it the vigil of Epiphany?[16] Why, therefore, does he call that day a vigil, on which he does not curb the freedom to eat by prescribing fasting? And since Masses for the vigil by ecclesiastical custom are always celebrated at three o'clock in the afternoon, so that they seem to belong to the feast of the following day, why is this one called a Mass of the vigil and is celebrated at nine o'clock,[17] that is, before the midday meal, and is never considered as belonging to the following day? So, let our gluttons search through every day of the year, and since they will never find days that are called vigils, on which Masses are celebrated without fasting, there can be no doubt that fasting must be observed along with the celebration of the Mass at the vigil of Epiphany.

(10) Also in the case of Holy Saturday that precedes the glory of the Lord's resurrection, there is an obvious reason why one must strictly fast. For if we, his members, are truly to suffer with the Author of life who was dead and buried, if in union with the disciples we are to lament together with the apostles, it would be a shame for us to belch after a full meal, while he for whom we mourn still lies in his grave. Indeed, according to the Scriptures,[18] the apostles were filled with grief so long as the Lord was dead, but after three days rejoiced at seeing him again at his resurrection.

(11) But to have some respite from this tedious controversy, I will send this counsel for the stomach to the definitive evidence of blessed Sylvester.[19] Surely, if we give credence to his words, all this disagreement of ours will be put to rest. Now this is what Sylvester says, "If every Sunday is observed and celebrated be-

16. Gregory I, *Liber sacramentorum: In vigilia Theophaniae* (PL 78.38B).

17. On the times at which Mass is celebrated, Jungmann, *Missarum sollemnia* 1.320–329.

18. Cf. Mark 16.10; John 20.20.

19. *Vita s. Silvestri* (Mombritius, *Sanctuarium II*, 1910) 510; Levison, *Misc. Ehrle* 2.168; Ryan, *Sources* no. 207.

cause of the Lord's resurrection, it is proper that on each Saturday there should be fasting because of his burial, so that while we weep with the apostles over the death of the Lord, we may deserve to rejoice with them at his resurrection." And again he says, "If we believe that every Sunday is adorned with the glory of the resurrection, every Saturday that precedes it should be observed in fasting over his burial, so that one may deserve to rejoice over the resurrection after he has mourned at the Lord's death." Certainly, I can see no reason to add anything further to these words that are so plain and, because of the dullards, so often repeated, except to say, that if this holy man thought that all the Saturdays of the whole year should be devoted to fasting because of this one Saturday when the Lord was in his grave, how can it be used as a norm and model of abstinence for all the rest, when that one Saturday, which is primary and special, is spent in feasting?

(12) Therefore, one must firmly assert that as Good Friday surpasses all Fridays of the year because of its strict observance; as the day of the resurrection exceeds all other Sundays by the solemnity of its celebration; so also the Saturday that comes between them, must be observed with abstinence, more than all other Saturdays. For as Good Friday is the day of the cross and of sorrow, so too this Saturday is recognized as the day of Christ's burial and of sadness. But if, because of the effort of those who travel far to be at the ceremony of baptism, or because of the weakness of various people in poor health it is customary in some quarters to relax somewhat the restrictions of fasting, this should be overlooked by religious, and not made the rule. This is so, lest the latter, by now spending their time in eating while all the apostles are still mourning, show that they do not, which God forbid, belong to their company.

(13) Nor do I object to the singing of the "Glory to God in the highest" during the celebration of Mass on this day. This is done for the benefit of those who are about to be baptized, that as the glorious day of the resurrection is dawning, one may say that they are baptized in the death of the Lord.[20] Thus, the Mass which is not allowed during the day, must be celebrated at night,

20. Cf. Rom 6.3.

so that the saving mystery of general baptism may be held, as it were, between these events, the death of Christ on the one hand, and his resurrection on the other. For in the sacrament of baptism we die and rise again in imitation of Christ. We die as we are immersed in the water; we rise when we are lifted out again. Hence the Apostle says, "When we were baptized into union with Christ Jesus we were baptized into his death. By baptism we were buried with him, and lay dead, in order that, as Christ arose from the dead in the splendor of the Father so also we might set our feet upon the new path of life."[21] Clearly, for this purpose we are immersed in this salutary bath, that we might be dead to all sin. For this we were lifted from the water, that in rising we must now and for all time live for Christ, the Sun of justice. As the same Apostle says, "Jesus Christ died for our misdeeds, and rose to justify us."[22]

(14) Consequently, the same Mass seems to belong at once to the lenten and to the paschal season, since after the Alleluia is sung, we say the Tract, which is proper to Lent. But if Easter is wholly in force after the Mass and so continues, as our opponent stubbornly insists, we need no longer contend the point, with this stipulation, that laymen may immediately eat meat. Nor is there any reason why the liberty to partake of the Easter meal be put off till later, since Easter, as said above, is now fully in force. But since this is clearly contrary to the discipline of the Church, our opponent must admit that the day of the Lord's burial is not Easter, but rather the vigil of Easter, and because of that fact, is subject to fasting, at least by reason of the rule of vigils.

(15) Shortly after I had written these lines, the following happened to me by chance, or rather, by divine providence, and I must tell you about it. A certain older brother,[23] who for almost thirty years now had lived in his hermit's cell, came to me, and in private told me about a vision he had had. "Master," he said, "I often experienced animosity and anger toward you because you constantly insisted that we fast on Saturdays. In the meantime, I longed to travel to Jerusalem. As this desire grew daily stronger,

21. Rom 6.3–4.   22. Rom 4.25.
     23. It is noteworthy that this "older brother" here addressed Damian as "master."

while I was asleep one Sunday night, a certain cleric, brilliantly
clad, appeared to me in a vision, and said, 'Brother John,' for
that was his name, 'do you wish to go to Jerusalem?' When I replied that this was what I wanted, in my dream he promptly took
me there, where we visited many graves of the saints, and especially pointed out whose graves they were. As he led the way, I
came at length to the sepulcher of the Lord. And there, near the
sepulcher, stood a handsome cleric whose appearance was most
peaceful, properly wearing a white stole about his neck. And he
said to me, 'The day before yesterday, as you were fasting, you
truly venerated the life-giving cross, and yesterday you also paid
your respects to the Lord's tomb. And now, without the slightest
doubt, you should recognize that you certainly celebrate and
venerate the cross on Friday and the tomb of Christ on Saturday
if you fast on those days while you chant and pray.' After being
thus instructed by what he said, I lost the ill-feelings that I had toward you, father, and from then on, when I had the strength, I
fasted on Saturday with no less devotion than on Friday." This
holy brother told me these things while totally unaware that I
was writing about them, and still does not know about it.

(16) What is more, on the day of the Greater Litany[24] some
act disgracefully and clearly violate the decrees of the canons,
because they do not then observe the fast on the feast of St. Mark
also celebrated on that day. But since my remarks cause those
who support full bellies to jest and scoff, to avoid all subterfuge,
let me simply cite the canonical text. For the Council of Mainz
says, "We have agreed that the Major Litany shall be observed by
all Christians on the same day, on 25 April, as we found it prescribed in the Roman Church, and as our holy Fathers have decreed: we should fast by not riding, by avoiding costly clothes,
and rather be sprinkled with ashes and wearing sackcloth, unless
impeded by illness."[25]

(17) But if this text is still not sufficient for some people, it
should be enough to cite the Apostolic See, enough to cite all

24. 25 April. On the "Greater Litany," see Stephen J. P. van Dijk, *Sources of the
Modern Roman Liturgy* (Studia et documenta Franciscana 2 vols., 1963) 1.78f.
and 2.368.

25. Cf. Ryan, *Sources* no. 208, citing Burchard, *Decretum* 13.6 ex con. Mo-
guntinense (813) c. 33 (MGH Conc. 2.1, 1906) 269.

Rome, which confirms this fast, not only by publishing its decretal, but year after year observes it in actual practice.[26] We should here note that the holy Fathers prescribed that fasting be observed between the two feasts, namely, St. Mark's day and Pentecost, which period is often concluded with that day, but in such a way that they still solemnly carry out the ecclesiastical office.

(18) Again, this too is not to my liking, that many brothers, while refraining from fasting on the vigils of the blessed apostles, Philip and James,[27] bring up the feast of Pentecost as an excuse for their license, saying that no one should be bound to fast at that time, since this season calls rather for feasting with paschal joy. To such I briefly reply in a few words, that if the feasts of the Church and the fasts ordained by Church discipline are so opposed to one another that they cannot be observed together, then neither the Major Litanies of which I spoke above, nor the three Rogation days before the Lord's Ascension, nor the vigil of Pentecost can be ordained as fast days. And if this is not enough, even that fast is eliminated, which was unanimously and properly decreed by the holy Fathers to be observed during the week that follows the coming of the Holy Spirit. And since, as is said, fasting cannot be associated with a solemn feast, and according to the opinion of some people fast days cannot be enforced when a feast day occurs, and that the feast day always prevails, then fasts should be removed from the octave of blessed John the Baptist, from the vigils of the apostles, Peter and Paul, and also from the octave of Lawrence the martyr, and should be eliminated on the vigil of the blessed Virgin Mary. Moreover, on all feast days during the greater Lents, one should eat twice a day.

(19) But if ecclesiastical regulations do not allow this, and the world which has now grown old[28] under the guidance of apostolic tradition in no way acquiesces in these modern teachings, it must be said that feast days, unless they are the principal ones,

---

26. Cf. Ryan, *Sources* no. 209 citing Amalarius *Statutum Gregorii = Liber officialis* IV.24 (Studi e testi 139.481 and also PL 105.1207). Among the books which Damian provided for Fonte Avellana (cf. Damian, *Letter* 20), was also a volume of Amalarius, on which see Pierucci, *Inventari* 163; Reindel, *Briefe* 3.337, n. 20.

27. 11 May.

28. Cf. Damian, *Letter* 88 (Blum, *Letters* 3.319.20).

do not disadvantage fast days, so that each retains its right, the office of the Church is performed in all its solemnity, and bodily penance does not lose its function. Hence it follows, that if anyone rejects fasting on the vigils of two such venerable apostles as James and Philip, he is not persuaded to do so out of love for their feast day, but following the advice of his gluttony and all its rhetoric, is enticed by the sweetness of soft living.

(20) Besides all this, many make light of the vigil of blessed James, the brother of John the Evangelist,[29] and irreverently and with little thought pass it by. They presume to do this, perhaps, because the feast is not celebrated at its proper time. Now as we learn from the testimony of Luke in the Acts of the Apostles, it was about Easter time that James was killed by Herod. For, after first saying that "Herod killed James the brother of John with the sword,"[30] he immediately added, "This happened during the festival of the Unleavened Bread."[31] And about the same time blessed Peter was released from his chains,[32] and somewhat earlier James was beheaded by Herod's sword.

(21) And since neither feast could be properly and freely celebrated within the octave of Easter, at the discretion of the ancient Fathers it had to be transferred to another time. But if this solemn day were to be deprived of the dignity of its vigil on this account, then the feast itself should not be celebrated. But if it was proper to transfer this apostolic feast to another date out of respect for Easter it is surely correct that its vigil should inseparably accompany it.

(22) Indeed, the authority of the canons is the last word, and in general it orders all vigils of the apostles to be celebrated.[33] But if my opponent should still stubbornly insist on his point of view, I will also observe that, if this feast is rightly deprived of its dignity because the time of celebration was changed, then the great feast of Easter should not be observed, since it does not occur at an exact and certain time, but rather follows the rule of

---

29. James the Elder: 25 July.   30. Acts 12.2.
31. Acts 12.3.   32. 1 August.
33. Cf. Ryan, *Sources* no. 210, citing Burchard, *Decretum* 2.77 (PL 140.640AB). He notes that the text derives from Haito, *Capitula ecclesiastica* c. 8 (MGH Capit. 1, 1883) 363f.

the full moon. For it is the belief of the Church that our Redeemer was crucified on the twenty-fifth of March, the same day on which he was earlier conceived in the womb of the Virgin.[34] But if we should wish to follow this temporal line of reasoning, we should celebrate the Lord's resurrection each year on the twenty-seventh of the same month. But this is actually not done, because it was seen fit first to pass through the fourteenth day of the new moon together with the Passover of the Jews (*azymitae*), that we might arrive at the new Passover, just as if we were leaving the shadow of the Law and entering the true light of grace.

(23) Therefore, let these enemies of holy vigils, these destroyers of time-honored fasts go on teaching that the feast of Easter should not be celebrated, saying that since it occurs at various times it should be denied popular observance and the dignity of its accustomed liturgy. And what they evil-mindedly assert of Easter, they must consequently state of the Ascension and of Pentecost. But if they should contend that the beheading of blessed John does not have a vigil because the feast is customarily transferred from the time of the Lord's passion when the holy Baptist was killed, to the month of August, I will reply that this is the case, not because the feast was changed, but since we observe his blessed birthday with a vigil, on his beheading we are satisfied in having only one day of solemnity lest we inconvenience the people.

(24) And lastly, the same reasoning applies to the vigil of St. Bartholomew,[35] which some people are already beginning to omit. Now some time ago on this day, a certain abbot in the company of men who were in good health, from far away came to us here in the hermitage, having already had his breakfast, and expecting to eat his dinner with us. But on the next day, namely, on the feast of the apostle, as he was about to leave, we asked him if he would have breakfast, but he refused and would not listen as we pleaded with him. How he was repaid by the judgment of God! Whether in a convent of nuns where he then stopped, or at the homes of certain laymen whom he visited, throughout the

---

34. On this, see E. Schweizer, "Jesus Christus I," *Theologische Realenzyklopädie* 16 (1987) 671–726, esp. 711.

35. 24 August.

whole day he was unable to get a single drop of wine. And so, by divine providence he was compelled to fast on the feast day whose vigil he had dared to violate, contrary to the law of the Church. And as I might put it, he suffered on the feast what he had failed to do on the vigil.

(25) And now, my dear brothers, in my uncultured style I have addressed these words to your holiness on the eight vigils that should be celebrated at their precise time, and I exhort you as true soldiers of Christ manfully to arm yourselves in correcting the practices that are now so daringly appearing on the scene. Through your effort may the prescriptions of ecclesiastical discipline remain in force, may the regulations of patristic tradition endure, the estate of religious observance retain its dignity, and the vigor of the Church not grow soft. For, I have no doubt that if this letter should fall into the hands of those who detest fasting, it will be shamefully abused. I refer to those who pride themselves on their anointed and well-kept skin, and who, while waging unabating war against sobriety, glow like fat men with ruddy lips. But neither out of love nor hatred for anyone am I allowed to hide what I think when it is correct. And since I am not unaware that the emperor Julian wrote eight volumes against the Gospel of Christ,[36] I experience no shame at having my little dissertation torn to bits by biting words, even from those who are opposed to the discipline of the Gospel. Let them, along with their old foodmongers, say, "Let us eat and drink, for tomorrow we shall die."[37] And we along with the servants of Christ should respond, "Let us fast and observe the sacred vigils, that on the heavenly feast day, when we shall be endlessly victorious, we may dine with joy."

36. Cf. Damian, *Letter* 117, n. 45; K. Gross, LThK 5.1195–1196.
37. Isa 22.13; 1 Cor 15.32.

LETTER 119

Peter Damian to the abbot Desiderius and the monastery of Monte Cassino. This letter on the omnipotence of God is perhaps the prime example of Damian's philosophical writing. It is a mixture of philosophical and theological argument. The text that appears in the volume of *Medieval Philosophy* noted below is a bowdlerized version of the original, omitting most of the theological arguments based on Scripture and rearranging the philosophical sections to fit the purpose of the editors. Flowing from the question whether God is able to cause created things to become uncreated, Damian discusses problems about the omnipotence of God, whose solution, in his opinion, cannot be found by using human logic.

(Beginning of 1065)[1]

On Divine Omnipotence

TO THE LORD DESIDERIUS, the most reverend abbot of the monastery of Monte Cassino,[2] and to all his holy community, the monk Peter the sinner sends the kiss of peace in the Holy Spirit.

(2) For him who alone was rescued from the swells of a high-flowing sea it would be an act of inhumanity if, while seeing his

---

1. Dating follows Lucchesi, *Vita* no. 193. The translator herewith calls attention to a previous, partial translation of this letter done by him and published as follows: In *MEDIEVAL PHILOSOPHY*: From St. Augustine to Nicholas of Cusa, edited by John F. Wippel and Allan B. Wolter, O.F.M, pp. 140–152. Copyright c1969 by the Free Press, a Division of MacMillan, Inc. Reproduced by permission of the publisher.

2. On Desiderius, see Damian, *Letter* 82 (Blum *Letters* 3.233 n. 2). In general on this letter, see Endres, *Petrus Damiani* 16–30; Gonsette, *Pierre Damien* 61–99: Andreoletti, *Libertà*; R. P. McArthur and M. P. Slattery, "Peter Damian and Undoing the Past," *Philosophical Studies* 25 (1974) 137–141; A. Brinton, "Omnipotence, Timelessness, and the Restoration of Virgins," *Dialogos* 45 (1985) 149–156; Resnick, *Peter Damian*; Brezzi-Nardi, *S. Pier Damiani*, who comment especially on (Pseudo-) Dionysios Areopagita, *De divinis nominibus* as a general reference for this letter, and Cantin, *Pierre Damien*, who refers to Augustine as the source for Damian's thought.

boat[3] still foundering amid threatening and towering waves and in danger of rocks and cliffs, he did not deplore the condition of his companions who were fighting for their lives. And so, after putting down the episcopal burden,[4] I rejoice as one who safely reached the shore; but with brotherly solicitude I am concerned[5] that you are still shaken by winds and storms and are tossed about amid the ocean's yawning depths. He errs, father, he errs, indeed, who assures himself that he can live as a monk and at the same time devote himself to the Curia. What a poor bargain, to abandon the monastic cloister to serve in the world's militia. A fish is caught intact from the water not to live for itself, but to become the food of others. We are called and attracted, but only to live for others and to die to ourselves. The hunter loves the deer, but only to provide him food; he pursues goats and chases young rabbits, but only for his own benefit and for their destruction. Men indeed love us, but not for ourselves; they love themselves and seek to make of us one of their luxuries. Hence, while cultivating such friends in the world, what else do we achieve but the repudiation of the monk who lies hidden within us? Presently, the life of striving for perfection is subverted, austerity is weakened, the severity of discipline and silence is dissipated, and our lips are loosed to pour forth whatever caprice might suggest. This is the background for what now comes to mind.

(3) As you might remember, one day as we both sat talking at table, the topic turned to this passage of St. Jerome, "I speak boldly," he said, "while God can do all things, he cannot cause a virgin to be restored after she has fallen. He may, indeed, free her from guilt, but he cannot award her the crown of virginity which she lost."[6] Although I was fearful and hardly dared to dispute the statement of such a man, I told you exactly what I thought, speaking to you as to a father who agreed with my ideas. "I confess," I said, "that this opinion has never satisfied me; and I consider not by whom a thing is said, but what is said. It

---

3. Cf. Damian, *Letter* 48 n. 6, where he first uses the word *sagena* to mean *boat* and not *net*.

4. On Damian's lengthy effort in this regard, see his *Letter* 57.

5. Cf. Cantin, *Pierre Damien* 385 n. 3.

6. Jerome, *Epistula* 22.5 (CSEL 54) 150.

seems altogether unbecoming that impotence be so lightly ascribed to him who can do all things, unless it be affirmed on the
secret evidence of a higher intelligence."

(4) On the other hand, you replied that it is certain and quite
worthy of belief that God cannot cause a virgin to be restored
after rape. Then, after we had gone far field with long and wordy
arguments, you at length reduced your thinking to this brief
statement, "God is unable to do this for no other reason than
that he does not wish it."

(5) To this I replied, "If God can do none of the things that he
does not wish to do, he does nothing but that which he wishes;
therefore, he can do none of the things at all, which he does not
do. Consequently, if I may speak freely, God does not cause it to
rain today because he is unable to do so; therefore, he does not
heal the bedridden, because he is unable; for the same reason,
he does not destroy the unjust, nor free the faithful from their
oppression. These, and many other deeds God does not perform
because he is unwilling, and because he does not so wish, he is
unable. It follows, therefore, that whatever God does not do, he
is totally unable to do. This seems clearly to be so absurd and so
ridiculous, that such an assertion not only fails to agree with divine omnipotence, but is incompatible even with the weakness
of man, since there are many things that we do not do, and yet
are able to do."

(6) However, if in the Scriptures we should find such statements to have mystical and allegorical significance, we should
accept them cautiously and with reverence, rather than interpret
them boldly and freely in a literal sense. Such is the case when
the angel spoke to Lot who was hurrying to Zoar, "Make haste,"
he said, "escape there; for I can do nothing until you arrive
there;"[7] and again, "I regret that I made man;"[8] and the further
saying that God, looking into the future, was grieved to the
heart, and many similar examples. If, therefore, statements of
this kind are found included in sacred Writ, they must not be
quickly and indiscriminately publicized with a daring and self-

7. Gen 19.22.
8. Gen 6.7.

conceited air,[9] but treated with restraint in temperate and modest language; for if the assertion should reach the common folk that God were in any sense impotent—which would be an impious thing to say—unlettered people would be immediately confused and the Christian faith would be disturbed to the grave detriment of souls.

(7) In the same sense that one asserts that God cannot do a thing one may also say that he is ignorant of something: namely, since he cannot do anything that is evil, he does not know how to do evil. Thus he has neither the power nor the knowledge to lie, or to commit perjury or any injustice, even though he says in the words of the prophet, "I am the Lord, I form light and create darkness, I make peace and create evil."[10] However, concerning his statement in the Gospel, "But about that day and hour no one knows, not even the angels in heaven, not even the Son; only the Father,"[11] this undoubtedly is to be understood in the sense that, while in himself he is ignorant of nothing, he was uninformed of this fact only in relation to the disciples. Since Jesus, the Word of the Father, is the author of all time, through whom certainly all things came to be,[12] by what logic can he who knows the whole of time be ignorant of the day of Judgment, which is a part of time? Yet, of the same Savior the Apostle writes, "In him lie hidden all treasures of wisdom and knowledge."[13] And why are they hidden except that they have not been clearly made known to all? In fact, when he was again asked by the disciples after the resurrection about the day of Judgment, he replied, "It is not for you to know about dates or times, which the Father has set within his own control;"[14] as if to say: It is not to your benefit to know this, so that anxiety over this doubt might continually stimulate you to greater effort in works of piety and repress all vain glory that might possibly surprise you. Therefore, for himself he knew what for the apostles he did not know: a thing that he certainly demonstrated when stating that this was known to

---

9. Cantin, *Pierre Damien* 390 n. 1 refers to a similar type of argument in Othloh of Saint Emeram, *Dialogus de tribus quaestionibus* (PL 146.60A).

10. Isa 45.7.   11. Mark 13.32; Matt 24.36.
12. Cf. John 1.3.   13. Col 2.3
14. Acts 1.7.

the Father, with whom he is one substance, saying, "I and the Father are one."[15]

(8) In this way he asserted, in the accepted use of the word, that he somehow did not know what the Father knew, just as once he indicated that he somehow did not have what the Father had. Accordingly, also the Apostle stated, "When he delivers up the kingdom to God the Father,"[16] as if to say that the Father did not possess the kingdom while the Son had held it, and that when the Son delivered it up to the Father, he no longer held it. Since, according to sound interpretation, by delivering up the kingdom to God the Father he meant merely to say that he conducted the believers to contemplate the form of God the Father; the kingdom was then surely delivered by the Son to God the Father when, through the action of the Mediator between God and men, the host of the faithful was conducted to the contemplation of eternal divinity, that is, that it was no longer necessary to provide examples of divinity by the work of angels, or principalities, or authorities, or powers. In their person one can easily understand what is said to the spouse in the Canticle of Canticles, "We will make you ornaments of gold, studded with silver, until the king is on his couch,"[17] that is, until Christ is in his secret place, when "our life lies hidden with Christ in God." For "when Christ, who is your life, is manifested," he added, "then you too will be manifested with him in glory."[18] But before that occurs, "we see now only puzzling reflections in a mirror," that is, in images; "but then we shall see face to face."[19] Such contemplation is promised to us as the objective of all our deeds and as the eternal perfection of all enjoyment. "For we are his children and what we shall be has not yet been disclosed; but we know that when it is disclosed we shall be like him, because we shall see him as he is."[20] This, in fact, he said to his servant Moses, "I am who I am;" and "Say therefore to the people of Israel, 'He who is, has sent me to you;'"[21] this we shall contemplate when we see him in eternity. For this reason he said, "This is eternal life: to

---

15. John 10.30.
17. Cant 1.10–11; cf. Sabatier 2.376.
18. Col 3.3–4.
20. 1 John 3.2.
16. 1 Cor 15.24.
19. 1 Cor 13.12.
21. Exod 3.14.

know you who alone are truly God, and Jesus Christ whom you have sent."[22] This will occur when the Lord will come and will bring to light what darkness hides, when the darkness of this mortal and corruptible life shall pass away. Then our morning will arrive, of which he spoke in the Psalm, "In the morning I prepare a sacrifice for you, and watch."[23] This contemplation is understood in the saying, "When he delivers up the kingdom to God the Father,"[24] that is, when he has conducted to the contemplation of God the Father the just, in whom, while they now live by faith, reigns "the Mediator between God and men, Christ Jesus, himself man."[25]

(9) In short, many such assertions are found in the passages of Scripture, and if we are content to accept them only at their surface meaning, they cannot project light for us, but will rather generate darkness. Hence, the statement that God is unable to do or to know something evil, does not refer to ignorance or impossibility, but to the uprightness of the eternal will. Precisely because he does not wish evil, it is correct to say that he can neither know nor do something evil. In all other respect he undoubtedly can do whatever he wishes, according to the evidence of Scripture, "But though you have might at your disposal, you judge with clemency, and with much lenience you govern us; for power, whenever you will, attends you."[26]

(10) The will of God is truly the cause of the existence of all things, whether visible or invisible, in that all created things, before appearing in their visible forms, were already truly and essentially alive in the will of their Creator.[27] "All that came to be," says John, "was alive with his life."[28] And he testifies in the Apocalypse to the same statement by the twenty-four elders, "You are worthy, O Lord our God, to receive glory and honor and power, because you created all things; by your will they have their being and were created."[29] In the first place it is said that "they have

---

22. John 17.3.   23. Ps 5.5.
24. 1 Cor 15.24.   25. Cf. 1 Tim 2.5.
26. Wis 12.18.

27. Cantin, *Pierre Damien* 398 n. 1, here cites Augustine, *Enarrationes in Psalmos* 134.10.1945; Augustine, *De Genesi contra Manichaeos* 1.2 (PL 34.175); Augustine, *De trinitate* 3.4.135f.

28. John 1.3–4.   29. Rev 4.11.

their being," and then that "they were created," because the things that were externally expressed by their making, already existed internally in the providence and in the design of the Creator.

(11) Moreover, as the will of God is the cause by which the things that were not yet made, originally came into being, so it is no less the efficient cause whereby those things that have been lost might return to the integrity of their state. "Do I have any pleasure in the death of the wicked, says the Lord, and not rather that he should turn from his way and live?"[30]

(12) But to resume the discussion we were having at the beginning: what should hinder God from being able to restore a virgin after she had been violated? Is it for the reason that he is unable because he is unwilling, and that he does not wish it because it is evil, as was said before, that God neither wishes nor is able to lie, to swear falsely, or to commit an injustice? But it is unreasonable to state that it is evil for a girl who was violated to again become a virgin; on the contrary, as it is evil to violate a virgin, so doubtless it would be something good for a violated girl to be restored to virginity if this were favorable to the order of divine providence.

(13) To pose an example, it was an evil that man, after the fall, should suffer the penalty of death even though this occurred by the just judgment of God; for God did not make death, since he is rather the death of death,[31] as he says through the prophet Hosea, "O death, I will be your death."[32] Nevertheless, at least after the mystery of our redemption, it would certainly have been something good for man to have become immortal, if divine forbearance had annulled the sentence he had once pronounced. The omnipotent God cannot, in fact, be said to be unwilling or unable to do this for the reason that it is evil for a mere man to become immortal, but because, in his just judgment and for the greater assurance of our salvation, which was known to him, he wished death to remain merely as a penalty owed by man already redeemed.

---

30. Ezek 18.23.   31. Cf. Wis 1.13.
32. Hos 13.14.

(14) In the same way, it is an evil for a virgin after rape to remain violated; on the other hand, it would be something good for God to restore in her the seal of virginity. But even though God never does this, either to terrify a young girl so that she will fear to lose what afterward she cannot recover; or for reasons of the equity of justice, in that she should be unable to restore by tears of penance what she had discarded as worthless in satisfying carnal pleasure; or, at least, while she was aware that the marks of her fall were still upon her, that she might more earnestly persevere in applying the bitter remedies for her misfortune: if therefore, for these or for other reasons of high providence a violated virgin does not revert to her former integrity, it is totally improper to say that the omnipotent God is unable to do this, but rather that he does not wish to do so; that freedom might be affirmed to his most just will, and that, unthinkably, impotence might not be ascribed to omnipotent majesty. Indeed, God cannot do something evil for the very reason that he cannot even wish it; but this should never be attributed to impossibility, but rather to the natural goodness of his exceptional forbearance.

(15) On the other hand, he can both wish and do that which is good, although there are some good things which he rarely or never does, following, as it were, the judgment of his caution or of his wisdom. Otherwise it could be said that before the coming of the Savior, God was not able to bring forth a son from the womb of the Virgin, something, indeed, which he had never done, and which was never to be done but once. And yet, even though he had never done it, he was able both to wish it and to do it simply because it was good. And so, how is it impossible for God to restore a virgin after violation, since without doubt he is omnipotent and that action is something good?

(16) That a virgin may be restored after her fall, is to be understood in two ways: either in relation to the fullness of merits, or in relation to bodily integrity. Let us see, then, whether God is not able to do both.

(17) In reference to merit, the Apostle calls the community of the faithful a virgin when speaking to the Corinthians, "For I betrothed you to one spouse, thinking to present you as a chaste

virgin to Christ."[33] Certainly, there were not only virgins in this people of God, but also many women who had married or who had lived in continence after they had abandoned virginity. And the Lord said in the words of the prophet, "If a man divorces his wife, and she turns away and takes another man, will he ever return to her? Would not that woman be thought contaminated and impure? You have played the harlot with many lovers; nevertheless, return to me, says the Lord."[34] This return to the Lord, in so far as it concerns the quality of merits, is exactly that by which a woman becomes pure after she has lost her virtue, or by which a virgin is won back from prostitution. To her the same Spouse repeats his words, "And I will no longer remember any of your sins."[35]

(18) Indeed, for a wife preoccupied with sex the embrace of the husband is the corruption of the flesh; the contract of love becomes a sacrifice of chastity; and most frequently she surrenders herself as a virgin at the marriage bed only to come away from it raped. But on the other hand, if the heavenly Spouse unites himself with her, he will suddenly wash away all stains of dishonor and will revive the flower of most fragrant chastity; he will rescue her virginity from the brothel and will restore her integrity after her defilement.

(19) Consequently, we know that many persons of both sexes, after enjoying the abominable delights of passion, have attained such purity in the spiritual life, that they not only advanced in sanctity beyond some who were chaste and pure, but actually surpassed the considerable merits of many virgins. These, doubtless, are not to be repaid merely on the basis of former merit, for with the remission of their guilt the accumulation of greater reward is actually increased. So it is proved, I think, that in the area of merit God can bring renewal to a virgin after she has fallen.

(20) In relation to the body, moreover, who in his right mind can doubt that he who "lifts up those who are bowed down, who sets the prisoners free,"[36] who finally "cures every illness and every infirmity,"[37] is unable to restore the virginal hymen? Indeed, for

33. 2 Cor 11.2.
35. Jer 31.34.
37. Cf. Matt 4.23.

34. Jer 3.1.
36. Cf. Ps 145.7–8.

him who constructed the human body from a minute drop of semen, and who by the varied design of its members gave to the human form its proper beauty; in short, for him who produced a creature which had not yet existed, is it beyond his power to restore a despoiled woman already existing? In my opinion, and I state and affirm this without fear of abuse or captious arguments to the contrary, the omnipotent God has power to restore virginity to any woman, no matter how many times she has been married, and to renew in her the seal of integrity, just as she was when taken from her mother's womb. I have said these things, however, not to lessen respect for St. Jerome, who spoke with pious purpose, but to refute with invincible reasons of faith those who take occasion from his words to charge God with impotence.

(21) And now I feel obliged to respond to an argument which, on the subject of this controversy, many put forward on the strength of the opinion of your holiness. They say, "If God," as you assert, "is omnipotent in all things, can he act so that things that were made become things that were not made? He can certainly destroy all things so that they no longer exist, but it is impossible to understand how he can cause things that were made to become unmade. One might grant that it is possible that from this moment on and thereafter, Rome does not exist, since it can be destroyed; but there is no way to explain how it is possible that it was not founded in antiquity."

(22) As I prepare to reply to these objections, as God may inspire me, I feel obliged in the first place to call my critic's attention to the words of Solomon, where he says, "With what is too much for you meddle not, and do not search out the things which are beyond you."[38] Then one must say: what God makes is something; what God does not make, is nothing. "And through him all things came to be; no single thing was created without him."[39] Of him certainly it was written elsewhere, "He who made the things that are to be,"[40] and in the same sense also, "He who lives forever created all things together."[41] And the Apostle says, "He who calls into existence the things that do not exist."[42]

38. Sir 3.22–23.
39. John 1.3.
40. Eccl 3.15.
41. Sir 18.1.
42. Rom 4.17.

(23) Clearly, all these citations from Scripture testify that God has made that which was not, and did not destroy that which existed; that he created future things without forgetting things past, although one often reads that God had overthrown something to make provision for something better, for example, the earth by means of the flood, and the Five Cities (Pentapolis) by means of fire.[43] These things, in fact, he so deprived of being and of future being, although he did not at all deprive them also of past being. But if you should closely note the deeds of the evil men who were then destroyed, seeing how in pursuing vain and worthless things they tended not toward being but toward nothing, you might reasonably conclude that they had not existed. For this reason Scripture asserts that they cry out from the fullness of their affliction, "Brief and troublous is our lifetime: neither is there any remedy for man's dying, nor is anyone known to have come back from the nether world, for from nothing were we born, and hereafter we shall be as though we had not been."[44] "We shall be as though we had not been," they say, because even at the time when they seemed to be, they belonged rather to nonbeing than to real being. " I am who I am," he said, and, "Say this to the people of Israel, 'He who is, has sent me to you.' "[45] But he who withdraws from him who truly is, must cease to be, because he tends toward nothing. Consequently, they again lament and say, "Our body will become quenched ashes and our spirit will be poured abroad like unresisting air; our life will pass away like the traces of a cloud, and will be dispersed like a mist pursued by the sun's rays; our name will be forgotten, and our lifetime is the passing of a shadow through time."[46] Hence, also, the prophet says, "All the nations are as nothing before him, and they are accounted by him as nothing and emptiness."[47] And Solomon says, "Before you the whole universe is as a grain from a balance, or as a drop of morning dew."[48] Countless similar statements are to be found in the Scriptures, in which wicked men are compared to the smallest or the most trifling things, or are said to be nothing, even at the time they seem to be powerful. To

43. Cf. Gen 6–8 and 19.   44. Wis 2.1–2.
45. Exod 3.14.   46. Wis 2.3–5.
47. Isa 40.17.   48. Wis 11.23.

this point David said, "I have seen a wicked man, overbearing and towering like a cedar of Lebanon, and I passed by and, behold, he was no more."[49] For just when they are elated over their wealth and arrogantly promote themselves to positions over others, when finally they oppress their subjects through tyrannical violence, then, I say, they are more surely nothing, the farther they depart from him who is the true and highest being.

(24) But what is the purpose of these vain men, of these sacrilegious innovators in doctrine, who, while devising their ensnaring questions for others, were not aware that they themselves had first been trapped in them; and of those who, while placing obstacles of frivolous investigation in the path of simple wayfarers, themselves stumble over the "stumbling-stone"?[50] "Can God," they ask, "bring it about that once something happened, it did not happen?" as if this impossibility should appear to be restricted only to past events and were not to be found similarly in things present and to come. For truly, whatever exists at the moment, so long as it exists, must undoubtedly exist.[51] For it is not true that so long as something exists, it is possible for it not to exist. In like manner, for something that will happen, it is impossible for it not to happen, even though there may be some things whose happening or not happening is a matter of indifference, as, for example, my riding or not riding today, seeing or not seeing a friend, our having rain or clear weather. These and similar cases secular scholars are wont to call "indifferent alternatives" (*utrumlibet*), because generally they are just as likely to happen as not to happen; but these are called "indifferent alternatives" more properly in relation to the variable nature of things than to the logical consequence of speech. Thus, according to the natural order of inconstant phenomena, it can happen that today it may rain, and it can also happen that it may not rain; but by the logic of words, if it is going to rain, it is absolutely necessary that it rain, and consequently, altogether impossible not to rain. Likewise, what is said of past events may be applied with equal cogency to present and to future things; in this sense,

49. Ps 36.35–36.   50. Cf. Rom 9.32.
51. Cf. Boethius, *In librum Aristotelis de interpretatione commentarii* 1.9, ed. C. Meiser (1877) 103 ff.

that, just as everything that happened, necessarily had to happen, so also everything that exists must exist so long as it exists, and everything that will happen, must happen in the future. And so, in relation to the logical order of speech, for whatever was, it is impossible not to have been; for whatever is, it is impossible not to be; and for whatever will be, it is impossible that it will not be.

(25) Notice, therefore, how the blind foolhardiness of these pseudo-intellectuals who investigate non-problems, by boldly attributing to God those things that refer to the art of rhetoric, cause him to become completely impotent and deprived of strength, not only regarding things past, but also relating to things present and to come. These men, indeed, because they have not yet learned the elements of style, lose their grasp of the fundamentals of simple faith as a result of the obscurity produced by their dull tricks; and, still ignorant of those things boys study in school, they heap the abuse of their contentious spirit on the mysteries of God. Moreover, because they have acquired so little skill in the rudiments of learning or of the liberal arts, they obscure the study of pure ecclesiastical doctrine by the cloud of their curiosity.

(26) Clearly, conclusions drawn from the arguments of dialecticians and rhetoricians should not be thoughtlessly addressed to the mysteries of divine power; dialecticians and rhetoricians should refrain from persistently applying to the sacred laws the rules devised for their progress in using the tools of the syllogism or fine style or oratory, and from setting their inevitable conclusions against the power of God. However, if the techniques of the humanities be used in the study of revelation, they must not arrogantly usurp the rights of the mistress, but should humbly assume a certain ancillary role, as a maidservant to her lady, so as not to be led astray in assuming the lead, nor to lose the enlightenment of deepest virtue, nor to abandon the right road to truth by attending only to the superficial meaning of words.[52]

52. Brezzi-Nardi, *S. Pier Damiani* 80 n. 1 call attention to Gerard of Csanád, *Deliberatio supra hymnum trium puerorum* 2.128–130, ed. G. Silagi, CC Continuatio mediaevalis 49 (1978) 15, and to Manegold, *Contra Wolfelmum* c. 5, 52ff.

(27) Surely, it is obvious to all that, if one should trust these arguments based on the meaning of words, the power of God would appear impotent on many occasions. For, in keeping with this abusive and frivolous inquisition, God would be unable to act so that things that had already happened, should not have happened; nor, contrariwise, that things which did not happen should have happened; nor that those things which now exist, so long as they exist, should not exist; nor that things that will happen, should not exist in the future; nor, on the contrary, that things which will not happen, should happen in the future.

(28) The ancient authorities in the liberal arts, not only pagans but also members of the Christian faith, have studied this question at length, but none of them dared to promote the mad opinion that would attribute the quality of impotence to God, and especially, if he were a Christian, to doubt his omnipotence. But they disputed the real problem of dialectical necessity or impossibility in such a way as to keep it solely within the framework of this art, without ever mentioning God in the course of their arguments. But those who today take up this ancient problem, while striving to comprehend higher things beyond their capacity, instead blunt the keenness of their minds because they have not feared to offend the very Author of light.

(29) Therefore, this question, in that it is proven that it pertains neither to the investigation of the power of divine majesty, but rather to the skills of the art of dialectic, nor to the perfection or to the nature of things, but rather to the method and order of speech and to the relationship of words, has no place amidst the mysteries of the Church, which are loosely discussed by young lay students in the schools.[53] This question, in fact, does not relate to the norms of faith nor to the probity of conduct, but to the fluency of speech and to the elegance of language.[54] Therefore, we are satisfied that in this brief summary we have defended the faith which we hold, while granting to the wise of this world the things that are theirs. Let those who wish,

53. Cf. Cantin, *Pierre Damien* 418 n. 1.
54. Cassiodorus, *Institutiones* 2.4, ed. R. A. B. Mynors, *Cassiodori Senatoris Institutiones* (1963) 91.

retain the letter that brings death, so long as, by the mercy of God, the life-giving Spirit does not depart from us.[55]

(30) It is evident, therefore, that the omnipotent God encloses all ages within the treasure of his eternal wisdom in such a manner, that nothing can be added to him and that, through the alteration of time, nothing can pass away from him. And so, while enduring at the ineffable summit of his majesty, he contemplates in one simple insight all things marshaled in his presence for review, so that for him it can never happen that past events will completely disappear or that future things will come to pass. While it is his prerogative for eternity to be forever and to be the same, and while he encompasses everything that changes, he contains within himself the march of all time; and just as he holds within himself all times without their changing, so too within himself he encloses all places despite their spatial difference. To this point he clearly says, "I fill both heaven and earth";[56] and similarly his wisdom says, "The vault of heaven I compassed alone."[57] And of this wisdom Salomon says that "she, who is one, can do all things, and renews everything while herself perduring."[58] And elsewhere he says, "If heaven and the heavens of heavens cannot contain you, how much less this house, which I have built for you?"[59] Of his spirit also it is written, "The spirit of the Lord fills the world and is all-embracing";[60] of whom it is said again that "he is the artificer of all," "all-powerful and all-seeing."[61] And the Lord spoke through the prophet, "Heaven is my throne and the earth is my footstool;"[62] and again it is written of him, "He measures the heavens with a span and encompasses the whole earth in the hollow of his hand."[63] However, he remains immanent and transcendent in relation to the throne on which he presides, for, by measuring the heavens with a span and gathering the earth in the hollow of his hand he demonstrates that on every side he is external to all the things that he has created. Whatever, in fact, is enclosed inside remains external to the container; hence, rel-

---

55. Cf. 2 Cor 3.6.   56. Jer 23.24.
57. Sir 24.8.   58. Wis 7.27.
59. 2 Chr 6.18.   60. Wis 1.7.
61. Wis 7.21, 7.23.   62. Isa 66.1.
63. Isa 40.12.

ative to the throne on which he sits, he is considered to be within and above; by the hollow of the hand in which he is enclosed, however, it is indicated that he is external and beneath. And since he remains within all, external to all, above all, and beyond all things, he is superior through his power, inferior by reason of his support, external relative to his greatness, and internal because of his subtle penetration. Consequently, where is there anything that exists without him who, while occupying no place by corporal extension, is nowhere absent because of his unlimited substance? Of him the Apostle says that "all things are held together in him,"[64] and again, "for from him and through him and in him are all things."[65] He is, in fact, one might say, a nonlocal place, one who embraces all places within himself without need to move from place to place; and since he at once fills all things, he does not with parts of himself occupy parts of space, but is totally everywhere. He is not more widely diffused in more expansive places, not more compressed in those that are narrower; he is not higher at greater altitudes, nor lower in the depths; he is not greater in vast things nor smaller in the slightest things, but he is one and the same, simple and equal everywhere,[66] in need of no creature, but on him every creature depends.

(31) In fact, even before he had created the angels, before time or before anything temporal had existed he possessed the full and perfect riches of immortality and glory.[67] Nevertheless, no sense of solitude or need persuaded him to create that which was not, but only the urging of his loving goodness;[68] nor could the creation of the world add anything to his blessedness, since he is so complete and perfect of himself and in himself that nothing accrues to him from an existing creature, and nothing escapes from him if it perishes; for "all streams run to the sea, yet the sea is not filled"[69] with them.

(32) It is clear that the power to do all things is coeternal to

---

64. Col 1.17.   65. Rom 11.36.

66. Cantin, *Pierre Damien* 422 n. 1 cites here Augustine, *De civitate Dei* 11.10.330f.

67. Cf. Boethius, *Philosophiae consolatio* 5.6.101: "Aeternitas igitur est interminabilis vitae tota simul et perfecta possessio."

68. Cf. Augustine, *Enarrationes in Psalmos* 134.10.1945.

69. Sir 1.7.

him in the same way that he knows all and always remains the same. At the critical summit of all nature where he regulates the right of all things, he so embraces all times past, present, and future within the mysteries of his providence that nothing new at all befalls him, and nothing escapes his attention as it passes on its momentary way. He does not view dissimilar things in various ways so that, while attending to past events, he is unaware of the present and the future; nor, on the other hand, does he take his attention from the past while considering things present and to come; but with merely one simple glance of his ever present majesty he comprehends all things in an instant.[70] This, moreover, he achieves, not in some confused and unaccountable manner, but he discriminates all things and distinguishes each from the other according to its essential property.[71]

(33) Certainly, he who attends the theater does not view everything at once, because as he directs his attention to the action before him he does not see behind him; but if one is not sitting in the theater but is stationed high above it, he takes in the complete interior sweep of the theater at a single glance. Thus, since almighty God rises incomparable above everything that happens, he sees all things as simultaneously present to his gaze.

(34) And so, that not only the quick-witted, but even a duller mind might easily understand what I am saying, I maintain that for us a greater chain of events transpires during the briefest moment that it takes to pronounce the word "heaven," than is needed for God to view in a single instant the infinite period of all the ages. For when one pronounces the first syllable of this little word the second is yet to come, and when the second is sounded, the first has already passed by. But God, on the other hand, in a single and ineffable twinkling of an eye sees everything at once and on sight distinguishes one thing from another: by encompassing he penetrates all things, and by penetrating he encompasses all things.

---

70. Cantin, *Pierre Damien* 424 n. 1, citing Augustine, *De civitate Dei* 11.21.339f.
71. Brezzi-Nardi, *S. Pier Damiani* 90 n. 1 cite (Pseudo) Dionysios Areopagita, *De divinis nominibus* c. 7 (PL 122.1154CD).

(35) To this point the apostle Peter says, "Do not ignore this one fact, my friends, that with the Lord one day is like a thousand years and a thousand years like one day."[72] And since the number one thousand is a perfect number,[73] he substituted a thousand years for the length and duration of all ages. Hence also the psalmist says, "A thousand years in your sight are as yesterday when it is past."[74] He does not say, "like today," but "like yesterday, which is past," for whatever we expect to happen in the future is already completely known by God as if it were past. He is, indeed, as he says of himself, "the Alpha and the Omega, the beginning and the end,"[75] and he proclaims through the prophet, "Before me no god was formed, and after me there shall be none."[76] Indeed, since while presiding ineffably at the very summit of things, he embraces within the ambit of his vast and eternal council not only the total spectrum of time but also all places and creatures, and always discerns each of these beings in an instantaneous act of contemplation and simple insight, not without justice is it claimed that he alone is powerful, he alone is eternal, and he alone is immortal. Hence the Apostle says, "To the King of all worlds, immortal, invisible, the only God, be honor and glory."[77] And the same Apostle says, "He is the blessed and only Sovereign, the King of kings and Lord of lords, who alone possesses immortality, dwelling in unapproachable light. No man has ever seen or ever can see him."[78]

(36) For also the energy of the angels, even though it is powerful, is not, however, self-engendered but derives from him; although it is immortal and possesses its blessed life utterly without end, because it changes in regard to places and times, it cannot be considered coeternal with its Creator, who by nature and by essence is power, immortality, and eternity itself. Hence, also, Moses said, "The Lord has reigned forever and beyond."[79] On the other hand, the blessedness of the angel, if judged according to its nature seems, with some justification, to be eternal

---

72. 2 Pet 3.8.   73. Cf. Meyer, *Zahlenallegorese* 190f.
74. Ps 89.4.   75. Rev 1.8, 21.6.
76. Isa 43.10.   77. 1 Tim 1.17.
78. 1 Tim 6.15–16; cf. Sabatier 3.879.
79. Exod 15.18.

in that it is in no wise subject to ending; and it is rightly said to live forever because its blessed life never ends. But God reigns not only forever, but forever and beyond, he includes within the depths of his foresight all the records of the ages, grasping it in a most penetrating insight, not only as past or as future, but as truly present and subject to his view; he governs all with absolute sovereignty, to whose laws all things submit; he regulates all creatures at the pleasure of his will; for all he directs and moderates the course of living, he arranges the form and species of all beings, and at will distributes to all the capacity that is adequate for action; from him and through him exists everything that exists, and without him, whatever exists would undoubtedly be nothing.[80]

(37) And so, almighty God possesses neither a yesterday nor a tomorrow but an everlasting today, from whom nothing is subtracted and to whom nothing is added, from whom nothing is at variance, and with whom nothing is in conflict. This today is an immutable, unfailing, and inaccessible eternity, to which nothing can be added and from which nothing can be removed; in that today all things remain firm and endure immovably that with us fleetingly pass us by or that vary with changing times. In his today, moreover, the moment at which the world began is still unspent, and in that moment the day is already present on which the world will be tried by the justice of the eternal Judge. Nor does any defect of changeableness appear in that light, which without increase illumines all that he has chosen, and without dimming recedes from what he has rejected, because, while it remains immutable by its very nature, he directs all things that change, and has produced in himself all transitory things in such a way that whatever he has created is unable to pass away at all. Time, that for us moves along outside in relation to external things, for him is something internal and does not pass; hence it happens that in his eternity a fixed permanence pervades all things that outwardly, with the passage of the ages, flows on incessantly in instability. With God, consequently, his eternity is but a single day, which the psalmist observes as never

80. Brezzi-Nardi, *S. Pier Damiani* 94 n. 3.

ending and never beginning, when he says, "One day in your courts is better than a thousand (elsewhere)."[81]

(38) How is it possible, therefore, that he, who without any change determines and establishes in his majestic presence all things made or to be made, should be ineffective concerning all past and future events? Why, indeed, since he is immovably present in the time that preceded the things that were made, and the period in which he decided that all things should successively follow?

(39) It is for this reason, obviously, that among the statements of Scripture that are spoken in a prophetic mood, one often finds past deeds described as future events, and others that would occur long afterwards as having already happened. So it is that the Lord, who had yet to undergo his passion, should say in the words of the prophet, "I gave my back to those who beat me, my cheeks to those who plucked my beard; my face I did not shield from buffets and spitting."[82] Before the Resurrection he says, "I have arisen and I am still with you;"[83] and speaking of the future Ascension and of the future grant of the gifts of the Holy Spirit, he says, "He ascended into the heights with captives in his train; he gave gifts to men;"[84] because all times stand at once in the sight of his wisdom, whence they have emanated, and future and past events stand always before him as actually present, fixed and unmovable. And so he could just as readily say, "They gave me gall for food,"[85] as to say: they will give me; and he also says, "They have pierced my hands and my feet,"[86] as saying: they will pierce.

(40) So now let us hear from those others who raise useless questions, or rather who strive to advance false doctrines, and who ask, "Does God have the power to act in such a way that events that have happened, should not have happened?"[87] To these on first sight I reply, that this is not a question of divine goodness producing something from nothing, but rather of reducing something to nothing, since, of course, it is written,

---

81. Ps 83.11.   82. Isa 50.6.
83. Ps 138.18.   84. Eph 4.8; cf. Ps 67.19.
85. Ps 68.22.   86. Ps 21.17.
87. Endres, *Petrus Damiani* 17; Brezzi-Nardi, *S. Pier Damiani* 98 n. 6.

"Through him all things came to be, and no single thing was created without him."[88] I wish to prove that God makes something from nothing, while you endeavor to show that he makes nothing from something.

(41) But now, if you please, disgorge everything at once, spit out with one hawking effort all the phlegm of a noxious sluggishness, so that one swallow of medicine may suffice to cure your compounded disease, and that we are not compelled to prepare a mixture of drugs for your cure. So tell me, please: in relation to the past, does God have the power to cause something not to have happened that has happened; or in respect to the present, to cause something now existing, so long as it exists, not to exist, or what will certainly take place, that it will not take place, or, on the other hand, is all the contrary true, which would seem to me deserving of abomination rather than being put to writing?

(42) Tell me, you who play the role of accuser in this cunning matter: do you also believe that whatever God does is good and is therefore something, and that anything that he has not made, is nothing? Listen to what Scripture says, "God saw everything that he had made and it was very good."[89] And again, "Without him nothing was made."[90] But since you cannot deny this, you say, "I agree." You, therefore, while demanding that one and the same thing has been and has not been, that it be and not be, that it shall be and shall not be, you are surely trying to make things that have happened indistinguishable from those that will happen, and to demonstrate that they are tottering between being and nonbeing. This, certainly, the nature of things will not tolerate;[91] for nothing can simultaneously exist and not exist, and anything that does not exist in accord with the nature of things, without doubt is nothing. You, therefore, acting the role of unyielding extortioner, demand that God make that which is contrary to his nature, that is, nothing; but take note that the evangelist stands opposed to you, saying that "without him nothing was made."[92]

---

88. John 1.3.
89. Gen 1.31.
90. John 1.3.
91. Cf. Andreoletti, *Libertà* 319 n. 68.
92. John 1.3.

God has not as yet learned to make nothing. Now you instruct him and command him to make nothing for you.

(43) Once again, please, what have you to say to this: Do you believe what the prophet says and with which all the evidence of Scripture agrees, "All that the Lord wills he does in heaven and on earth, in the sea and in all the deeps"?[93] But it is clear that this too cannot be denied by you. Since, therefore, God has power over all things, why are you inclined to doubt that God should be unable to act so that a thing may simultaneously be and not be, provided it were good that this should happen?[94] However, if it serves no purpose to have things suspended in confusion between being and nonbeing, and God has made all things not to be useless but to be good;[95] if moreover it is evil and in that case, nothing, this God does not do at all, because "without him nothing was made."[96]

(44) To this one may add, that the will of the most high and omnipotent Maker is such an efficacious cause of the existence or nonexistence of things, that whatever he wills to exist cannot but exist and whatever he does not will to exist, is not capable of existence. The power of God has, in fact, established that what he has ordered to have happened, is impossible not to have happened; and what he has ordained to be, so long as it exists, is unable not to exist; and what he has appointed to happen in the future, can no longer not happen in the future.[97] Is it not the case, therefore, that from this the power of God appears to be the greater and more wonderful in that it is judged by wise fools to be weak and impotent? If, then, whatever is comes from him, he has given to things such an energy for existing, that after once they have existed, it is impossible for them not to have existed.

(45) All manner of evils, in that they are iniquities and crimes, even when they seem to exist, do not exist because they are not from God and are therefore nothing simply because

---

93. Ps 134.6.
94. Cf. Brezzi-Nardi, *S. Pier Damiani* 102 n. 2; Andreoletti, *Libertà* 315 n. 59.
95. Cantin, *Pier Damien* 434 n. 1.
96. John 1.3.
97. Cf. Brezzi-Nardi, *S. Pier Damiani* 102 n. 4.

God, "without whom nothing was made,"[98] has in no sense made them. On which account if anything good is done by men, it cannot lose its being or its past being because it is the work of God, even though it is achieved by men. Hence the prophet says, "For it is you who have accomplished in us all we have done."[99] Good deeds, in fact, belong equally to God and to us because he operates in us and gives efficacy to our labors. And Solomon states, "For both we and our works are in his hand, as well as all wisdom and the knowledge and discipline of craft."[100] "In him, moreover," as the Apostle says, "we live and move and have our being."[101]

(46) But if an evil was done, even then it was nothing at the moment that it seemed to be. Consequently, Scripture attests that the very authors of evil and of depravity suffer in hell, "All of them passed like a shadow and like a fleeting rumor; like a ship traversing the heaving water, of which, when it has passed, no trace can be found, no paths of its keel in the waters;"[102] for a path cut into the waves is soon swept away. And Scripture continues, "or like a bird flying through the air; no evidence of its course is to be found;" and a third figure is added, not unlike the others, "or as, when an arrow has been shot at a mark, the parted air straight way flows together again so that none discerns the way it went through."[103] Clearly, every trace of the passage of a ship, or a bird, or an arrow disappears the moment it occurs, in such a way all things adverse, as soon as they begin, readily fail. And so holy Writ continues, "Even so we, once born, abruptly ceased to be."[104] What is more, at the very moment they seem to be, they are no longer, because they are far from him who truly is. On the contrary, of the just man it is said, "Having become perfect in a short while, he reached the fullness of a long career, for his works were pleasing to the Lord."[105] And Scripture says of them, "You hurled them down while they were rising."[106] It does not say, "after they had risen," but "while they were rising," be-

98. John 1.3.
99. Isa 26.12.
100. Wis 7.16.
101. Acts 17.28.
102. Wis 5.9–10.
103. Wis 5.11–12.
104. Wis 5.13.
105. Wis 4.13–14.
106. Ps 72.18.

cause they become worthless in the very act of becoming proud, they fall to their ruin just as they reach the heights. One must not assert, therefore, that they become nothing after they arrive at their peak, but unquestionably they are nothing at the moment they appear to be something; nothing, in relation to the evidence of the truth, something, under the shadow of darkness.

(47) Perhaps he still feasts in great magnificence,[107] is bolstered by a host of clients, is surrounded by troops of fighting men, whom the prophet saw as an overbearing and towering man;[108] but just as he turned to view the most exalted, he recognized that he, whom perhaps he took for one of the great, was nothing. So it is written, "Yes, the hope of the wicked is like thistledown borne on the wind, and like fine, tempest-driven foam; like smoke scattered by the wind, and like a passing memory of the nomad camping for a single day."[109] Certainly, he who compiled so many examples of fleeting things, recognized that every glory of the reprobate is not so much something trifling as it is nothing. Therefore, evil things even when they seem to be, do not exist because they are not made by the good Creator and are far from him who is the true and highest being.[110]

(48) Good things, however, that is, those that the good Maker has produced, as you, whoever you are, investigate, cannot simultaneously be and not be, because this concurrent alternation has no place in the nature of things, which the rational Creator brought into being. Since namely it is an evil thing to be confused between being and nonbeing, and it is rather nothing, therefore this confusing alternation is not made by the good Creator, who has made all good things. This confusing mutuality, on the other hand, can be seen in one way or another in evil things, which indeed seem to be and are not, and hence, in a certain sense, exist and do not exist: they exist indeed, in external form, but not according to the truth; although, moreover, we cannot with precision grant such reciprocal diction to these evil things, that, because they seem to be, but are not, they should be and not be at the same time; and therefore, it would be more

---

107. Cf. Luke 16.19.
109. Wis 5.15.

108. Cf. 1 Macc 1.4.
110. Cantin, *Pierre Damien* 440 n. 1.

true to say that they are always nonexistent, than that they possess existence and nonexistence.[111]

(49) It is clear, therefore, that this concurrent alternation of which we have been speaking, namely, whether it can be accepted that something simultaneously has been and has not been, is and is not, will be and will not be, can in no way be made compatible with the nature of existing things; and that we are here concerned only with the conflict in terminology proper to the rules of rhetoric and logic. Therefore, we must believe with unquestioned faith that God has power over all things, whether he acts or does not act.[112] For whatever is evil should rather be called nothing than something, and so it does not prejudice our saying that to God all things are possible, even though he cannot produce evil, since evil should preferably be excluded from all things and not counted among them.

(50) So it is that divine power often destroys the armored syllogisms of the dialecticians and their subtleties and confounds the arguments of all the philosophers that are judged by them to be so necessary and inevitable. Listen to this syllogism: If wood burns it is surely consumed; but it is burning, therefore it is consumed. But notice that Moses saw the burning bush that was not consumed.[113] And to this other: if wood is cut from the tree it does not bear fruit; but it was cut off, therefore it does not bear fruit. Yet notice that the rod of Aaron is found in the meeting tent, having borne almonds contrary to the order of nature.[114]

(51) Moreover, what is the significance of so many miracles and mighty deeds that threatened the Pharaoh in Egypt;[115] of the passage of the troops of the faithful through the parted seas while the Egyptians were perishing;[116] of the gushing of a most generous flow of water from an arid rock;[117] of the demolition of the walls of Jericho not by clash of arms but by the blast of trumpets?[118] Finally, what is the meaning of the event that startled all the world when at Josue's command the sun in the heaven stood

---

111. Cf. (Pseudo) Dionysios Areopagita, *De divinis nominibus* c. 4 (PL 122.1137ff); Brezzi-Nardi, *S. Pier Damiani* 108 n. 2; Cantin, *Pierre Damien* 142 n. 1.
112. Brezzi-Nardi, *S. Pier Damiani* 110 n. 2.
113. Cf. Exod 3.2.   114. Cf. Num 17.23.
115. Exod 14.   116. Exod 17.
117. Cf. Josh 6.   118. Cf. Josh 10.12–13.

still for a day,[119] and at Hezekia's order went back ten steps to the east;[120] of the extinguishing of the roaring flames surrounding the three young men;[121] or of restraining the cruel jaws and rabid mouths of the lions around Daniel?[122] Why did all these events occur, I say, except to confound the frivolous notions of the wise of this world and to reveal to mortal men the glory of divine power over the established order of nature?

(52) Now, let us hear from the dialecticians or rather from the heretics, as they should be called, let them look into these events; let them come forward, I say, these weighers of words, these verbalizers of noisy questions, "proposing," "assuming," and, as they think "inevitably concluding,"[123] and let them argue, "If she gave birth, she had intercourse with a man; but she gave birth, therefore she had intercourse."[124] Did this not seem to be an argument impregnably strong before the mystery of man's Redemption? But the sacred event took place and the argument was resolved.

(53) And, indeed, God could both cause a virgin to become pregnant before she would lose her virginity and restore virginity after it was lost. Each, of course, was good, but even though he had as yet done neither one nor the other, there is no doubt that he has the power to do both. To be sure, it is more wondrous and more imminently excellent that a virgin remain inviolate after giving birth than that one after losing her integrity should recover her virginal purity after its loss, because it is more difficult for one to enter after the doors were shut than to be enclosed by doors that had just been opened. If, therefore, by being born from a virgin, our Redeemer had performed a deed that was something greater and far more outstanding, should he not be able to restore integrity to a woman who had lost it, a thing that was less significant? The God-man had power to come forth from a virginal womb without violating virginity; should he not be able to repair the loss of defiled virginity? How, therefore, is a

---

119. *Ibid.*
120. 2 Kgs 20.8–11; Isa 38.8.
121. Cf. Dan 3.46–50.
122. Cf. Dan 6.17–25.
123. Cf. Cantin, *Pierre Damien* 444 n. 1, with reference to Boethius, *De syllogismo hypothetico libri duo* 1 (PL 64.844A).
124. Brezzi-Nardi, *S. Pier Damiani* 112 n. 5 cite the long history of this syllogism, on which see Reindel, *Briefe* 3.366, n. 74.

murderer restored so that after a fitting penance he should no longer be a murderer? How can a thief, or a perjurer, or a robber, how indeed can those who are guilty of all crimes, after they have truly reformed themselves, be no longer what they were? So it is written, "Transform the wicked and they will be no more."[125]

(54) But you say, "Now I admit that a violated woman after she has done penance is no longer what she was, even if she is accused of fornication; nevertheless she does not recover the glory of virginity." But on the contrary I reply that he who could come from his mother's womb without impairing her virginity, can also, if he wishes, restore the seal of virginity for any woman who has been violated.

(55) There are still those who promote opposition in this useless argument. So let us investigate the origin from which it springs so that this stream, worthy of being swallowed by the earth, may dry up at its source, lest by its headlong rush it overwhelm the abundant fruits of sincere faith. To confirm their position that God cannot restore a virgin's integrity after her fall, opponents add this apparent inference, "Does God perhaps have the power to cause what has happened, not to have happened?" so that, once it is apparent that a virgin had lost her integrity, it was now impossible for her to be again restored.

(56) In respect to nature this is certainly true, as is also the statement: it is impossible for one and the same thing to have happened and not to have happened; for, indeed, they are mutually contrary in the sense that, given the one, the other cannot exist. For assuredly what was, cannot in truth be considered not to have been, and antithetically, what was not, cannot rightly be said to have been: for things that are contrary cannot coincide in the same subject.[126]

(57) This impossibility, moreover, is properly maintained in reference to the needs of nature. But God forbid that it be applied to divine majesty; for he who brought nature into being, at will easily abrogates the necessity of nature. For the need that governs created things, by law is subject to the creator; but he

---

125. Prov 12.7.
126. Macrobius, *Commentariorum in somnium Scipionis libri duo* 2.14.25, ed. L. Scarpa (1981) 334.

who created nature has power to change the natural order at his pleasure; and while ordaining that all created things should be subject to the dominion of nature, reserved to the dominion of his power the obedience of a compliant nature.

(58) To anyone giving it some thought, it is quite apparent that from the very moment the world was born, the Creator of things changed the laws of nature in any way he pleased, and even, I might say, made nature itself to a certain extent against nature: for is it not against nature that the world was made from nothing, even though it is stated by philosophers that nothing is made from nothing;[127] that at his mere command animals were created, not from animals, but from lifeless elements; that a sleeping man should lose a rib and not feel pain;[128] that a woman should be produced from a man alone without a woman's intervention, and that from a single rib should emerge all parts of the human body; that they should see themselves nude and should not only not be ashamed, but should not even have had intercourse, and many other such things too numerous to mention?

(59) What should one wonder, therefore, if he who prescribed for nature its law and order should exercise his right of decision over nature herself, without natural necessity rebelling against him, but instead serving in the role of handmaid submissive to his laws. Indeed, the very nature of things has its own nature, namely, the will of God,[129] in the sense that, just as any created things observe her laws, so also she, upon command and forgetting her own rights, reverently obeys the divine will.

(60) What do we make of a thing that we see even today, that the salamander remains alive in a fire, and not only is not harmed by burning, but seems rather to be stimulated by the warmth?[130] Certain worms, moreover, are born and live in boiling water.[131] How is it that straw is so cold that it preserves for the longest time snow that is covered by it, and so warm that it matures unripened fruit?[132] How does it happen that fire, which is

---

127. For this Aristotelian thought, see Brezzi-Nardi, *S. Pier Damiani* 120 n. 2.
128. Cf. Gen 1–2.
129. Cf. Brezzi-Nardi, *S. Pier Damiani* 120 n. 4.
130. Cf. Isidore, *Etymologies* 12.4.36.
131. Cf. Pliny, *Naturalis historia* 2.106.
132. Cf. Isidore, *Etymologies* 17.3.19.

transparent, blackens everything that it burns, and while it glows in all its beauty it discolors all that it licks and engulfs?[133] Moreover, stones that are fired at candescent heat themselves become white; and although the fire becomes rosier and the stones grow white in the flames, whiteness nevertheless corresponds to the light, and blackness to the dark. And while a wood fire blazes and fire stones glow, [fire] produces contrary effects in substances that are not contrary: for although stone is different from wood, still they are not contraries, as white and black, one of which occurs when stones are fired and the other in charred wood; in fact, as it grows in intensity it brightens the former, and while it is completely extinguished darkens the latter.[134] Why, moreover, is coal so weak that it is broken by the slightest blow and crumbles at the lightest pressure, and, on the other hand, possesses such durability that it is neither destroyed by humidity, nor worn away by age, to the degree that they who mark boundaries will bury a layer of coal to convince suitors in law when it is shown in evidence, if after a long span of years they should contend that the set stone does not mark the boundary? Who could have caused coal that was extracted from a humid pit, where trees would rot, to endure indefinitely without disintegrating, unless it were done by fire that destroys all things?[135]

(61) Lime moreover, holds fire so secretly confined and dormant within itself that no one touching it is aware; but when it is slaked, it is then ignited and is felt. Consequently, for lime to expel the force of its latent fire, one must douse it with water, and while before it was cold, it now begins to boil by the same agent that causes all other boiling things to cool. But if in place of water, one should use oil, which is obviously an incentive to fire, not the least bit of heat is generated when it is used.[136]

(62) Why should one marvel, therefore, if the omnipotent God is revealed as magnificent in grand things while in the smallest and the least of all things he works so wondrously? What is more worthless than the skin of a snake? Yet, if it is boiled in oil

---

133. Augustine, *De civitate Dei* 21.4.762.
134. Isidore, *Etymologies* 19.6.3.   135. Isidore, *Etymologies* 19.6.7.
136. Isidore, *Etymologies* 19.10.19.

it is wondrously helpful in soothing earache.[137] What is lower than a bug? If a leech snatches it in its mouth, it is immediately vomited once its odor is detected, and by its application it relieves urinary troubles.[138] What shall I say of the diamond, which neither fire nor iron nor any other force can break, but which is cut only by the blood of a goat.[139] What causes the magnet to have that wonderful attraction for iron? However, if a diamond is placed near it, not only does it not attract the iron, but even if it has already attracted the iron, at the diamond's approach, it releases it, just as if one stone feared the other and lost its own powers in the presence of the greater force.[140] It is known, of course, that asbestos, the stone of Arcadia, is so called because, once it is ignited it cannot be extinguished.[141] Again, why is the stone, pyrite, which is found in Persia, named for fire, if not because it burns the hand that holds it if it is grasped too tightly?[142] Also, in Persia there is a kind of stone called selenite whose inner glow increases with the waxing of the moon and afterwards decreases with its waning.[143]

(63) Moreover, what is it that makes the salt of Agrigento in Sicily to flow when it is brought close to fire, and when it is poured into water, to crackle as if it were in fire?[144] Why is it that in the region of the Garamantes a certain fountain flows so cold during the day that one cannot drink from it, and so hot at night that it cannot be touched?[145] Who is responsible for that other extraordinary fountain in Epirus, which, although it is cold to the touch, extinguishes a burning torch as in other fountains, but unlike others, can ignite one that has been extinguished?[146] Who produced the fig tree in Egypt of such quality that its wood, when tossed into the river, does not at once float as wood will do,

---

137. Cf. Pliny, *Naturalis historia* 28.48.174.
138. Cf. *Ibid.* 29.17.62 and 32.42.124.
139. Cf. Isidore, *Etymologies* 12.1.14 and 16.13.2.
140. Cf. Augustine, *De civitate Dei* 21.4.763.
141. Cf. Isidore, *Etymologies* 16.4.4.
142. Cf. Isidore, *Etymologies* 16.4.5.
143. Cf. Isidore, *Etymologies* 16.4.6.
144. Cf. Isidore, *Etymologies* 14.6.34 and 16.2.4.
145. Cf. Isidore, *Etymologies* 14.5.13.
146. Cf. Pliny, *Naturalis historia* 2.106.228.

but sinks to the bottom, and what is stranger still, after being submerged for a time on the ground again comes up to the surface of the water, when it should stay down because it is waterlogged? Why is it that in the regions of Sodom there are fruits that seem to be ripe, but when one tries to bite into them or peel them and the skin is broken, they vanish into smoke or into ashes?[147] How does it happen that in the area of Cappadocia horses are sired by the wind and that their foals do not live more than three years?[148] How does one explain that Ceylon, an island of India, is so endowed that all the branches of its trees never lose their foliage?[149] Moreover, why are the western areas of this land so favored that birds are born from the branches of trees and that a living and feathered harvest that looks like fruit bursts forth?[150] For, as they relate who swear they saw it, gradually something is seen hanging from the branch, then it assumes the appearance and form of a bird, and finally while it begins gradually to grow feathers it separates itself from the tree with a peck of its beak, and thus a new inhabitant of the air learns to fly almost before it had the knack for living. Truly, who is wise enough to enumerate the mighty deeds of divine power that occur contrary to the universal order of nature and which, surely, are not to be explained away by human arguments, but should rather be left to the power of the Creator?

(64) Why should one marvel therefore, that he, who ordained the natural course of all things, should alter the very order of nature to the dominion of his omnipotent will, so that he, who by being born preserved the virginity of his mother, should, if it were his will, restore the integrity of any woman whose virginity had been violated? Certainly, it is quite the same for God first to keep Enoch and Elias living in the flesh[151] and then to bring forth Lazarus and the widow's son alive from the grave.[152]

(65) I do not know if I read it, but it was told by many within the city of Rome and often repeated, that Romulus, who is called

147. Cf. Flavius Josephus, *De bello Judaico* 4.8.4.
148. Cf. Augustine, *De civitate Dei* 21.5.765.
149. Cf. Isidore, *Etymologies* 14.3.5 and 14.6.13.
150. Cf. Pliny, *Naturalis historia* 12.12.24; 12.21.38 and 16.80.221.
151. Cf. Sir 44.16; 2 Kgs 2; Heb 11.5.
152. Cf. Luke 7.11–15; John 11.

the founder of the city, after building a palace whose ruins, although half destroyed, are still to a great degree extant, shouted these words as if he were convinced of the permanence of his work, "It is certain and unalterably established that unless a virgin gives birth, this house will not fall to pieces."[153] And so, if it is indeed true what is told, by the mouth of a pagan a prophecy was uttered as the facts prove. For on the night in which the Savior came forth from the womb of a virgin for our redemption, the palace reportedly collapsed.

(66) To a man who was ignorant of God, both events, namely the virgin birth and the destruction of the house, seemed impossible; yet that God could always do both, but for a long time held them within the secret recesses of his providence, and that he wished to do both, he announced at the proper time by actual deeds.

(67) Indeed, it is an amazing thing that men who are now not only reborn within the family of the Church but also born there, should so shamelessly and presumptuously reproach the omnipotent God with the false charge of impossibility and are not afraid to immediately engross themselves in the whirl of incidental worldly affairs. And now let their frantic tongue be ashamed, and if it does not know how to be eloquent, it should learn instead to be silent; if it is unversed in promoting edification, let it know at least how to be silent without subverting the faith.[154] Otherwise, as a punishment, let his foreskin be cut off with a knife if he does not restrain himself by the discipline of silence. Let those who so desire, air their questions according to the manner and rules of dialectic, so long as by their circumlocutions and the trifling song of their school days they do not outrage the Creator, and let them know that the impossibility of which they speak lies in the very nature of things and in the logical consequence of words resulting from this art, that it does not belong to divine power and that nothing can escape the capacity of divine majesty, as one might say in speaking only in terms of the natural order and the use of words, "If something exists, so long as it exists, it is impossible not to exist, and if it was, it is

---

153. Cf. Brezzi-Nardi, *S. Pier Damiani* 128 n. 2; Reindel, *Briefe* 3.372, n. 100.
154. For similar formulations of this idea, see Damian, *Letters* 38 and 121.

unable not to have been; and if it will be, it is impossible not to be." On the other hand, what thing is there that God is unable to destroy contrary to the order of natural rights and of existing matter? What is it that God cannot create under new circumstances? Let them discuss, therefore, in their own small measure, merely the element of grammar, which they still need to do, and not usurp the field of the higher mysteries of God.[155]

(68) A certain philosopher,[156] while observing at night the course of the constellations and the motion of the stars, suddenly fell into a mud-hole. Shortly after, his maid, Iambi, composed the following verse about his fall, "My master did not know of the ordinary mire that lay beneath his feet, yet he attempted to explore the secrets of the heavens." And so from her name was derived the iambic meter.

(69) This should be a lesson for those who exceed the limits of their capacity and who rush proudly out attempting to do something beyond them, lest, while being unaware of what they are saying against God, they also learn from the punishment to which they were justly sentenced that they had spoken like heedless fools.

(70) From the account of a certain deacon I learned the story of this prudent and respected man in the world, of whom I now speak. In the region of Bologna, he told me, two men who were related by friendship and, if I remember correctly, the one was godfather to the other, sat down to a fine meal. A cock was served them and one of the men took his knife, carved the bird into pieces, as was customary, sprinkled it with ground pepper, and poured over it the gravy. When this was finished, the other at once said, "Godfather, you have so hacked up this rooster that St. Peter himself could not reconstruct it, even if he wanted to." To which the other replied, "Yes, indeed, not only St. Peter, but if Christ himself should order it, this bird would never rise again." At that the cock suddenly came alive, jumped

---

155. Cf. Brezzi-Nardi, *S. Pier Damiani* 132. n.1.

156. This account is found in Plato, *Theaitetos* 174 a (c.24) and in Diogenes Laertius, *De vitis, dogmatibus et apophthegmatibus clarorum philosophorum libri decem* 1.1.34. Damian also recalls this event in *Letter* 121. See also Reindel, *Briefe* 3.373, n. 103.

up completely covered with feathers, beat its wings and crowed, shook its feathers and splattered all the gravy over those who were at table. At once, a fitting and avenging punishment follows a rash and blasphemous sacrilege, for in being splattered with pepper they were struck with leprosy. It was not only they who carried this calamity to their death, but they bequeathed it to their descendants for all generations as some sort of inheritance. And so it came about that they were reduced to slavery in the service of the church of Bologna, which bears the name of St. Peter the apostle. And so for their posterity, they are to this very day marked with leprosy, as my reporter asserts, and are forced by law to bring to the church wooden basins from the work of their hands. Afflicted in this way with paying a double penalty, both of leprosy and servitude, they are taught not to speak lightly of the power of God. And the cock that once accused Peter of his denial on earth now proved that Peter reigned in heaven with him whom he had denied.[157] And perhaps it was not without divine judgment that they are condemned to pay this fine, so that, as wheat is separate from the chaff by shaking it in the winnowing basin, they may learn, taught by discretion, which words to reject as chaff, and which as worthy of eating they should speak.

(71) Indeed, all wicked men, in doing whatever appeals to them, and in thoughtlessly and wantonly spouting anything that tickles their tongue, if at some time they are not impeded by chastisement, go about saying either that God does not exist, or that he has no concern for human affairs. For, "the fool says in this heart, 'There is no God.' "[158] And again, "How does God know? and, Is there any knowledge in the Most High?"[159] And hence, in the very instant of their evil deed or at the moment immediately after committing sin, many suddenly incur the divine fury, so that they may no longer mock the patience of God, and that others might constrain themselves from similar deeds by the example of their punishment.

(72) On another occasion, when I was living in the city of

---

157. Cf. Matt 26.74; Mark 14.72; Luke 22.60; John 18.27.
158. Ps 13.1.   159. Ps 72.11.

Parma and there toiling with my classical studies,[160] I happened
to learn of an event that does not appear unprofitable for those
who will come after us and that might be included in my present
article. To the west of the city, outside the walls, a basilica is located bearing the double title of the blessed martyrs Gervase and
Protase.[161] One night, on the eve of the feast of these martyrs, a
certain fellow rose earlier than usual and drove his oxen to a pasture some distance away. One of his neighbors, overwhelmed by
sexual desire, watched for a chance to violate his wife. And so,
that same night this crafty prowler came to his house, and finding his opportunity not very long after the other had left to feed
his animals, pretended with devilish cunning that he had a fever,
and went to bed for the other's wife as if he were her husband.
And when he shook as though chilled through and through, and
with chattering teeth frequently uttered shivering cries, the poor
woman taking pity on her sick husband, began to embrace him
in her arms, to cover him with a blanket, and to warm him as
best she could. But as he had planned this injury in his mind, so
now he brought it about in action: in consequence, he violated
another's bed and won death for himself, and now quickly departed. But shortly after he had gone the husband returned and
went back to bed. At once his wife began to complain and argue
with him, saying, "You will surely be in great shape to go to the
church of the holy martyrs today, which is almost here, and assist
at the divine mysteries with other Christians." And when the husband asked with astonishment what she was talking about and had
learned in every detail just how this thing had happened, both realized that they had been made a laughing stock and deceived by
the foulest joke, and were overcome by a feeling of intolerable distress. In the meantime, while the people were gathering at the
church from far and wide to attend devoutly at Matins, they too arrived, having recovered somewhat, and putting aside all sense of
shame, lodged their complaint before all present, and especially
the wife, tearing at her hair, and with a flood of tears pouring

---

160. On Damian's study in Parma, cf. *Letters* 70 and 117. See also, Lucchesi,
Vita no. 53; Silvio Celaschi, "La chiesa di Parma nel tempo di S. Pier Damiani,"
Ravennatensia 5 (1976) 35–40.
    161. Cf. Reindel, *Briefe* 3.376, n. 105.

down her unhappy cheeks, she cried to heaven her wailing lament. "O Lord," she said, "you know the hearts of men, you are the witness of my conscience that on this holy night I avoided even the conjugal embrace of my own husband, and especially was completely unaware that I was sleeping with another man. Therefore, O Lord, I beg you, do not regard my sins, but may it please you to avenge in your presence the injury that was done your saints. Now, therefore, show your power in the sight of your people, and to the glory of your most holy name reveal the man who has dishonored me. He must be publicly exposed and let him not win immunity from this barbarous crime by flight from his deception." After the woman in the bitterness of her soul had poured out these and many similar expressions in a shout that could be heard by all, and the people, moved with pity for her, had implored the divine mercy with unanimous petitions and prayers, the author of the crime was suddenly seized by a dia- bolical spirit in the place where he lay hiding, and became a mad and raging beast. Suddenly he sprang into the church where the people were more startled than ever, causing all to marvel at him cutting and tearing himself to pieces. With growls and roaring he cruelly mutilated himself with his own hands, now leaping into the air as if trying to fly, now throwing himself to the ground with a mightily force, now smashing his head against the wall, now groveling on the pavement like a madman, doing himself frightful internal injuries all over. In this way his evil spirit con- tinued to batter him until he wrested his unhappy soul from his body before the very eyes of the people who were present. When the congregation saw what had happened, they gave great glory to God, the source of justice, who did not suffer the sinner to go unpunished and brought comfort to the innocent woman. When this story was related to me, it was said that one could still see the stones which he had struck, red with his blood and gore.

(73) Indeed, he had perhaps thought that the Lord was either unaware of what he had secretly done, or that he was totally un- able to punish those who had committed crimes, saying to him- self, "The Lord will not see; the God of Jacob will not perceive."[162]

162. Ps 93.7.

But whoever in his arrogance sins, either by trampling under-
foot the commandments of God, or by goading him with slander, is guilty of no small crime; and in the case of the few whom
divine justice has unexpectedly struck, either for their evil deeds
or for their insolent speech, he shows what those others, who
seem to be exempt, deserve at any hour. Stop, I beg, let him stop
whoever sets his mouthings in place of heaven, so that his pronouncements may roam the earth.[163] For so indeed it is, that he
so offends God by his calumnies that he may also forcefully
demonstrate to one of God's servants his own impotence.

(74) Consequently, when the question is asked in these
words: How can God bring it about that something that had happened, will not have happened,[164] a brother endowed with a
sound faith should reply that whatever has happened, was not
something but was nothing, if it was evil. Hence, it must be considered not to have existed because it did not possess the
grounds for existence, which the Maker of things had not provided so that it might exist. However, if what happened was
good, it was surely made by God, "For he spoke, and it was made;
he commanded, and they were created."[165] "For through him all
things came to be, and no single thing was made without him."[166]
And so, it is much the same thing to ask: How can God bring it
about that what once happened, did not happen? or to ask: Can
God act in such a way, that what he once made, he did not make?
as to assert that what God has made, God did not make.[167] And,
indeed, whoever affirms this proposition should be thought contemptible and he is not worthy of a reply, but should rather be
sentenced to branding.

(75) Nevertheless, for purposes of confuting wicked and
sharp-tongued men, one should call to mind what was said
above. At this point, however, I avoid mentioning this, even
briefly, so that verboseness of style may not annoy my reader; for
I did not set out to compose a book, but a letter. Among other

---

163. Cf. Ps 72.9.
164. Cf. Cantin, *Pierre Damien* 131 n. 1 and 139 n. 1, with reference to Anselm of Canterbury, *Cur Deus homo* 2.17, ed. F. S. Schmitt (1970) 134ff.
165. Ps 32.9; Ps 148.5.   166. John 1.3.
167. Cf. Brezzi-Nardi, *S. Pier Damiani* 144 n. 1.

things that I noted, however, this one point that I talked about should not be forgotten: that as the *ability* to do all things is co-eternal to God, the Creator of all things, so also is his power to know all things; and that he contains, determines, and forever confirms within the compass of his wisdom all times past, present, and future in such a way, that nothing new at all can happen to him, nor can anything pass away from him through forgetfulness.[168]

(76) What sort of power is this by which God can do all things? What is the nature of the wisdom by which he knows all things? Let us inquire of the Apostle. "Christ," he says, "is the power of God and the wisdom of God."[169] In him, surely, there is true eternity and true immortality; in him there exists that eternal today that never ends; in him an everlasting and modern present is so firmly and perpetually fixed that it is capable of neither passing away, nor of changing at some time into the past.

(77) If, therefore, I must refute the insolence of these impudent opponents, for whom the above solution to the proposed question is still not satisfactory, I can say without appearing foolhardy, that God, in that immutable and ever uniform eternity of his, is able to bring it about that what had happened relative to our passing time, did not happen. For example, we may say: God *can* so cause it to happen that Rome, which was founded in antiquity, had not been founded. In saying *can*, that is, in the present tense, we use the word properly insofar as it relates to the unalterable eternity of almighty God; but in relation to us, in whom there is continuous movement and perpetual change, we should more correctly say *could have*, as we normally do, and as we may also understand the following: God can so act that Rome *would not have been* founded, that is, in respect to himself, with whom "there is no variation, no play of passing shadows."[170] For us, however, this is equivalent to saying: God *could have*. But in respect to his eternity, whatever God could do, he also can do, because his present never turns into the past, his today does not change into

168. Cf. (Pseudo) Dionysios Areopagita, *De divinis nominibus* c. 10 (PL 122.1163B–C).

169. 1 Cor 1.24.   170. Jas 1.17.

tomorrow or into some other alteration of time; and hence, just as he is always what he is, so also whatever is present to him, is always present. Therefore, as we may rightly say that God *could* cause Rome, before it was established, to be nonestablished, so no less rightly may we also say: God *can* cause Rome, after it was founded, to have been nonfounded; he *could have* relative to us, he *can* relative to himself. Indeed, the very potency that God possessed before Rome existed, remains forever immutable and intransigent in the eternity of God, so that we can say about anything, that God *could have* caused it, and we may equally say, that God *is able to* cause it, since his potency which is coeternal to him, remains forever fixed and immutable. Only in relation to ourselves can we say that God *has been able*; relative to himself, however, there is no *has been able*, but always a motionless, constant, and unchangeable potency: for whatever God *could* do, he doubtless also *is able to* do.

(78) In truth, as there is within him no being and having been, but everlasting being, so consequently there is no having been able and being able, but always a perpetual potency that can never change. For, just as he did not say, "I am who was and am," but rather, "I am who am," and, "He who is, has sent me to you";[171] so it undoubtedly follows that he does not say, "I am who could and can," but, "Who unalterably and eternally can." In fact, the potency that was in God before all ages is the same today; and the same potency that he possesses today was his before all ages and it eternally endures still firm and immutable through all the ages yet to come.[172] Since, therefore, God could have caused things not to exist before anything was made, so even now he has that power that the things which were made should not have existed; for the same potency that he then possessed has been neither changed nor removed, but just as he always is what he is, so also God's potency cannot be changed. Truly, it is he who speaks through the prophet, "I am God and do not change";[173] and in the Gospel, "Before Abraham was born, I

---

171. Exod 3.14.

172. Brezzi-Nardi, *S. Pier Damiani* 148 n. 2 refers to (Pseudo) Dionysios Areopagita, *De divinis nominibus* c. 9 (PL 122.1160C–1161A).

173. Mal 3.6; cf. Sabatier 2.1010.

am."[174] For, in the manner of our human condition, he does not change from future being to present being, or from present being to past being; but he is always the same and is always what he is.

(79) Therefore, since God is always one and the same, so in him the power to do all things is always present, is unfailing, and cannot pass away. Moreover, as in all truth and without any fear of contradiction whatsoever I say that God is now and forever what he was before all time, so in all truth I say that what he was able to do before all time, God is able to do now and forever. If, therefore, in every instance God is always able to do whatever he could do from the beginning, if he was able before the creation of things to cause whatever now exists not to have existed in any way, he has the power, consequently, that the things that were made would not have been made at all. Indeed, his potency is fixed and eternal, so that whatever he could have done at any moment, he always has the power to do, nor does the diversity of times suggest the presence of the slightest change in eternity; but as he is the same as he was in the beginning, so also he has the ability to do everything that he could have done before time began.

(80) We must, therefore, allow the following conclusion to the problem here set forth: if the potency to do all things is co-eternal to God, then it follows that God could have caused things that have happened, not to have happened.[175] But all potency is eternal to God, therefore, it follows that God can cause things that have happened, not to have happened. And hence we must firmly and surely assert that God, just as he is in fact said to be omnipotent, can in truth, without any possible exception, do all things, either in respect to events that have happened or in respect to events that have not happened. And so I may end by placing the following testimony from Esther as an unbreakable seal at the conclusion of this work, "Lord, almighty King, all things are in your power, and there is none who can resist your will. You have made heaven and earth and all things that are

174. John 8.58.
175. Cf. Brezzi-Nardi, *S. Pier Damiani* 150 n. 3.

under the cope of heaven. You are Lord of all, and there is none that can resist your majesty."[176]

(81) Without doubt, this charge, although it is idly brought against God, presents other hidden facts and still retains obscure bypaths and recesses, which I have refrained from exploring with greater subtlety, simply to avoid writing a lengthy volume, in that I proposed to offer an abridgment in the form of a letter. This is especially so since I have judged that nothing more remains to be done about the subject of this dispute but by adducing the truth to reject the false accusation brought against me of having claimed too much for the power of God.

(82) But in dictating these lines I am unable to refrain from telling you the extent of my affection for you without revealing something of its warmth. Addressing myself, therefore, to all of you together, I wish you to know, venerable brothers, that from the moment I departed from your glorious monastery, I have constantly kept you in mind and have had you in my warmest affection; and, as I must admit, that in returning from the sacred temple of Monte Cassino I experienced the same reaction as that of the woman who had returned from the tabernacle of Shiloh, namely, that my countenance "was no longer sad."[177] I live in your midst as if you were present and am always at your service. On the other hand, if it is said that I am not in your company because I do not look at you physically with my eyes, then neither are the eyes in the head because they cannot view the head, and furthermore the eyes are even nonexistent to oneself, because no one sees himself nor do two persons see one another in the same glance.

(83) Blessed, indeed, are they who live in your community, blessed are they who die in your midst while engaged in your holy work! One can truly believe with pious faith that the staircase, which was once seen rising from the heights of Monte Cassino into heaven, was all draped in raiment and gleaming with lamps.[178] While at that time it welcomed our leader [St. Benedict] it now conveys the array of his followers to the kingdom of

---

176. Esth 13.9–11.   177. 1 Sam 1.18.
178. Cf. Gregory I, *Dialogi* 2.37, vol. 2, 244.

heaven; nor do those now dead, who while living in this exile followed in his steps, wander away from its glorious course. Such is the ardent fervor that burns unquenchably in my heart, and such are the words that constantly come to my lips.

(84) But among other flowers of virtue that I discovered in that fertile field which the Lord has blessed,[179] I confess that this pleased me not a little that I did not find there schools for boys[180] which often weaken and dissipate the rigor of the religious life; but all of you are either elders, in whose company, indeed, that noble churchman will sit at the gates,[181] or enjoying the vigor of manhood and as sons of the prophets are fit to seek Elijah in the desert;[182] or you are still in the flower of youth, who in the words of the apostle John, have overcome the evil one.[183]

(85) Something that just now comes to mind I will tell you, to console my friend Peter,[184] the bishop, who was at one time a citizen of Capua, but is at present enrolled in the army of the eternal King.

(86) A small boy of five, the son of the nobleman Herbaldus,[185] who lived for a while with me in the hermitage, became a monk in my monastery. Once, in the dead of night while the brethren were sleeping, the youngster either left the house or was carried off, I am not sure. But it happened that the miller who was asleep in his mill woke up for a moment, and when he was about to cover himself with the blanket that lay close by to ward off the cold, in reaching out his arm, he discovered the boy sleeping beside him. Suddenly wide awake and thoroughly disturbed, he quickly arose, lit the lamp, and carefully checking around the entire house, found that all the entrances were closed and barred. When it was morning, the brethren were greatly surprised and wondered how the boy, whom without doubt they had seen the previous evening resting in his bed, had been able to enter the mill with the doors closed.

(87) Indeed, one can read about the apostles, that when they were about to be led away from the public prison, "an angel of

---

179. Cf. Gen 27.27.
181. Cf. Prov 31.23.
183. Cf. 1 John 2.13.
185. See Peter Damian, *Letters* 67 and 158.

180. Cf. Reindel, *Briefe* 3.382, n. 117.
182. Cf. 2 Kgs 2.
184. Cf. Reindel, *Briefe* 3.382, n. 119.

the Lord came during the night and opening the gates of the prison and freeing them, said, 'Go, take your place in the temple and speak to the people, and tell them about this new life and all it means.' "[186] Again, one also reads of Peter, that while the angel preceded him from the prison "to the iron gate, it opened for them of its own accord";[187] and also of Paul, that "suddenly there was such a violent earthquake that the foundations of the prison were shaken; all the doors burst open and all the prisoners found their fetters unfastened."[188] If, however, the angels themselves did not release the blessed apostles from their prisons without first opening the doors, it is very strange how the boy, either by the arts of men, or by the deceptions of unclean spirits could enter a house that was completely locked, without opening the doors. For the boy himself, when carefully interrogated, stated that some men in taking him with them, brought him to a great dinner, where one could find all kinds of delicious foods, and there made him eat. He told also how they had brought him to the castle that stands high above the monastery, and placed him even above the bell that hangs high up near the basilica.

(88) I was led in these circumstances to narrate this account that everyone of us monks, while realizing that boys are subject to the wiles of the malicious adversary, even though they still are unable to commit sin, he may also bear with patience whatever suffering may be his lot. For, with what patience should sinners bear the afflictions of the evil spirit, when even innocent persons must at times suffer from his deceits? I therefore exhort the brother whom I have mentioned to rejoice in the midst of his distress and to trust confidently that his soul, wounded by the blows of temptation, will return to health; for what he endures is not a token of future damnation, as the devil himself tries to misrepresent by terrifying him, but is rather a proof of eternal salvation.

(89) May the Holy Spirit, who is everlasting light and the remission of sins, illumine and absolve all of you, and may he instruct you to remember me constantly in your holy prayers.

---

186. Acts 5.19–20.   187. Cf. Acts 12.10.
188. Acts 16.26.

LETTER 120

Peter Damian to the young King Henry IV. Writing on the occasion of Henry's reaching his majority and of his investiture at Worms, Damian exhorts him to use his sword against the disturber of the Church's peace, Cadalus, the bishop of Parma, the antipope Honorius II. In this letter he clearly explains his position on the relationship of Church and State. The two are in alliance to bring peace and well-being to all men. The king should not heed the advice of those royal counselors, who are using the papal schism for temporary profit. If he hopes to acquire the imperial title, Henry should oppose those who would rend the seamless garment of the Church and avert, in consequence, a future rising of his own subjects who might divide his kingdom. As the emperor Nerva brought peace to the Church, as Constantine confirmed it, and Theodosius exalted it, will it be to the young king's glory should it be said of him, "And Henry divided it"? "But if you should compromise," he wrote, "and refuse to abolish this scandal . . . I hold my breath, and leave the consequence to the imagination of my readers."

(1065–1066)[1]

O THE LORD HENRY, most excellent king,[2] the monk Peter the sinner offers his service.

(2) All subjects fear the king; the king must fear the Creator. But since Scripture says that where much has been given a man, much will be expected of him,[3] it also behooves a king to be more inclined to dread the account he must give in many things, to him from whom the secrets of the heart are not withheld. Therefore, since in an ordeal a king may try a man, and God may try a king, is it proper that dust should fear dust, and that the same dust in a king should despise the divine majesty?

(3) In your day, O king, such a dangerous situation has arisen,

1. Dating follows Lucchesi, *Vita* no. 195. On variant dating, cf. Reindel, *Briefe* 3.384, s.v. Datierung.
2. Cf. Schubert, *Petrus Damiani* 98; see Reindel, *Briefe* 3.385, n. 1.
3. Cf. Luke 12.48.

that it exceeds almost every evil that the world has ever seen. The Apostolic See is torn asunder by the prince of heretics of the church of Parma,[4] the Christian religion is in disarray, the work of the apostles is overturned, and the splendor of the universal Church is eclipsed by the lusting darkness of one schismatical man. And what do you say to these events, you who function as the defender of the Church, succeeding to the royal prerogatives of your father and grandfather?[5] Or perhaps, will you plead that you are still not endowed with the strength of mature years? But note that Joash, king of Judah, while still a youth, contended with the priests on quickly restoring the structure of the temple,[6] forbade them also to retain the money given by the people, and decided that the total amount be spent to pay the workers on the job. When David had scarcely reached the age of adolescence,[7] he fought against Goliath, not with a sword, but with small stones in the manner of a boy, and like a brave man he cut off his head with one stroke of his sword.[8] While Josiah was still a youth, he threw out of the temple of the Lord all the vessels made for Baal, along with the priests, and with an all-engulfing fire burned them in the valley of Kidron.[9] These men did honor to the temple in which the blood of dumb animals was shed; and do you refuse to help the Church in which the body of Christ is offered for the salvation of the world?

(4) And now I should like to cite from pagan history. The famous Hannibal, later to become the commander of the Carthaginians, when still only nine years old, swore by the altar of his father, Hamilcar, that at his first opportunity he would do severe battle against the Romans.[10] Noncombatant boys can hardly wait to go to war for the honor of an earthly city, and are you not aroused to prepare for action in defense of the liberty of the universal Church?

(5) An ugly rumor among the people has it, that certain coun-

---

4. On Cadalus, see Damian, *Letters* 88 and 89, addressed to Cadalus, the bishop of Parma.

5. He here refers to the emperors, Henry III and Conrad II.

6. 2 Kgs 12.4–11.

7. A boy reached adolescence at 15 years of age.

8. Cf. 1 Sam 17.49–51.

9. Cf. 2 Kgs 23.4.   10. Livy, *Ab urbe condita* 21.1.

selors of yours,[11] specifically, some of the administrators at your court, are overjoyed at the persecution of the Church of Rome. While supporting and gently flattering both sides, they first assert with fawning adulation that they are loyal to the venerable pope, and then assure the firstborn of Satan the pleasure of spurious success. That this should be true of some of the holy men habitually in your service, is shocking to believe. Certainly, whoever attempts to divide the holy Church should fear, as the Gospel has it, lest he too be divided, "Then the master will arrive on a day at which that servant does not expect it, at a time he does not know, and he will cut him in pieces, and give him his place among the unbelievers."[12] Moreover, of Peleg, the son of Eber, it was written, that "in his time the earth was divided."[13] You too must beware lest it be said that in your time the Church was divided. Annals were written and history was composed, in which it states that Nerva, the most gentle of emperors, brought peace to the Church, that Constantine confirmed it, and Theodosius exalted it.[14] And when the history of your time is written, will it redound to your glory if it is said, "And Henry divided it"? God forbid that posterity should read such an account of you.

(6) Therefore, do not be a Peleg, dividing what was assembled, but be a disciple of Christ who puts together what was divided. Surely, those who succumb to the diabolical impulse to divide the Apostolic See would call to mind Dathan, Abiram, and Korah,[15] and from their fall let them consider that their fate awaits also those who have pursued similar objectives. The for-

---

11. Laqua, *Traditionen* 313 places Adalbert of Bremen among the counselors to whom Damian refers.

12. Luke 12.46.   13. Gen 10.25.

14. Nerva (96–98) ended the persecution of Domitian by releasing all those on trial for atheism (Christianity) and for following the Jewish way of life (cf. Dio Cassius, *Historia Romana* 68.1; Eusebius, *Ecclesiastical History* 3.20). Under Nerva the decrees of Domitian were annulled by the Senate (Paulus Orosius, *Historiae* 7.11). All exiles were recalled, among them the apostle John, and freed in the general amnesty. On this, see J. Speigl, *Der römische Staat und die Christen* (Amsterdam 1970) 26, 35f., 44; K. Baus, *Handbuch der Kirchengeschichte* 1.157. Baus follows Dio Cassius. It is difficult to believe that Damian knew the work of Dio Cassius, even though in another letter he appears to cite Dio Cassius in Latin translation. This comparison of the three emperors seems to be Damian's own doing.

15. Cf. Num 16.1–3.

mer, to be sure, fostered schism in the synagogue, while the latter plot division in the Church. And as the earth swallowed up the former alive, so the latter, as the reward of their schismatic misdeeds, with full knowledge will be buried in hell.

(7) On the other hand, there should be no boasting by those who, while not openly promoting schism in the Roman Church, by their approval or negligence do not resist the destroyers. Since not only he who said, "I will scale the heavens, I will set my throne high above the stars of heaven,"[16] but all his supporters as well were suddenly cast out of heaven, so too, not only Korah but his accomplices also, namely two hundred and fifty men, were consumed by the fire coming down from heaven. Hence, one must be careful lest the wickedness of subjects redound to the king, who, although not committing wrong, has not forbidden their deeds with all the power at his command. For a Gregorian judgment has it, "He is guilty of the deed, if he failed to correct it when he could."[17]

(8) Be careful, I repeat, O king, lest while allowing the *sacerdotium* to be divided, your empire too, which God forbid, should be divided. For as sacred history reports, when Saul caught the edge of Samuel's cloak, and it tore, Samuel promptly said to him, "Thus has the Lord torn the kingdom of Israel from your hand today and given it to another, a better man than you."[18] Moreover, just as this cloak was the garment of Samuel, so too, indeed, is holy Church the garment of the Redeemer. To him the prophet says, "You are clothed in praise and splendor."[19] For the Lord is clothed with praise when he gathers sinners to himself who have been healed by repentance; with splendor, when he gently makes the sinless his associates, beautiful with the luster of justice. And so, Saul rent the cloak of Samuel and lost his kingdom; the garment of Christ is torn, and will the empire remain for those who permitted the rending, even though they did not rend it? The pagan soldier feared to tear the seamless tunic of Jesus,[20] and

---

16. Isa 14.13.

17. Ryan, *Sources* n. 202, 105 cites John the Deacon, *Sancti Gregorii Magni vita* 3.2 (PL 75.128C). Damian quotes the same passage also in *Letters* 61 and 112.

18. 1 Sam 15.28.   19. Ps 103.1.

20. Cf. John 19.23.

should Christians not be afraid to partition the Church by schismatical error? For since holy Church is called the tunic of Christ, the rending of this garment threatens division for the power of the king. This is perhaps the reason why in our day we see cities and towns and even provinces of this kingdom occupied by foreign nations.

(9) Because Belshazzar gave the vessels of the Lord to be profaned by the lips of pagans, he at once heard these words from the mouth of Daniel, "Your kingdom has been divided and given to the Medes and Persians."[21] Eli was dispossessed of the priestly dignity when, instead of threatening his sons with blows, he treated them lightly. To be sure, he corrected them, but lighthandedly like a father and not with the severity of a high priest.[22] And so, he fell and broke his neck because with untimely mercy he showed kindness to the sinners.[23] The prophet Ahijah tore his cloak into twelve parts, and said to Jeroboam, "Take ten pieces, for this is the word of the Lord, the God of Israel, 'I am going to tear the kingdom from the hand of Solomon and give you ten tribes.' "[24]

(10) Therefore the division of this garment signifies the rending of royal authority. But since the Lord did not fulfill this judgment in Solomon's time, but carried it out in the days of his posterity, we would like to believe that in your case, too, your kingdom will remain intact because you are guiltless. After your reign, however, as a just retribution for the sins of your subjects unless perhaps they correct their ways, the kingdom will be handed over and given to foreigners. As it was said in the words of Daniel, "The Most High is sovereign over the kingdom of men and gives it to whom he will."[25] For a definite span of time Assyrians, Spartans, and other peoples retained their kingdoms and, as their histories attest, they were unable to go beyond the limits fixed by God. The Greeks temporarily ruled this kingdom of Italy, for a time the Gauls, and more often the Latins. I plead with you, O glorious king, disregard the advise of wicked coun-

---

21. Dan 5.28.
22. Cf. 1 Sam 2.22–25.
23. Cf. 1 Sam 4.18.
24. 1 Kgs 11.30–31.
25. Dan 4.29.

selors as you would turn a deaf ear to the poisonous hissing of snakes, and with manly vigor rouse yourself to spiritual enthusiasm. Reach out your hand to your fallen mother, the Roman Church, and like the archangel Raphael exorcise Sarah, the daughter of Raguel, and drive out the devil by which she had been widowed.[26] Octavian Augustus could boastfully claim, "I found the city of Rome made of bricks; I leave it built of marble."[27] May you, too, be able to say with much more pride, "As a boy I indeed found the Roman Church prostrate, but before I was fully an adult, with God's help I restored her to her original glory." As people used to say of him, may they with singular devotion later also say of you, "Would that he had either not been born, or had not died."[28] And to use an example from sacred Scripture, may the same thing be true of you which David recalls the God of Israel saying to him, "May you be like the light of morning at sunrise, sparkling like a morning that is cloudless, and like one making the grass spring from the earth with the rain,"[29] so that you too might rightly be able to sing with David, "My whole salvation and all my desire, nor is there any of it that puts forth no shoots."[30]

(11) And as both dignities, namely, the royal and the sacerdotal, are primarily joined to one another in Christ by the reality of a unique mystery, so are they united in the Christian people by a kind of mutual agreement.[31] Each, in truth, needs the other for what he there finds useful, since the *sacerdotium* is protected by the defensive capability of the empire, and royal power is supported by the holiness of the priestly office.[32] The king wears a sword, that so armed he may confront the enemies of the Church; the priest engages in watchful prayer, that he may appease God for the benefit of the king and his people. The former, using the scales of justice, is required to compose earthly af-

---

26. Cf. Tob 8.1–3.

27. Suetonius, *De vita caesarum* 2.28.3.

28. Cited also in *Letter* 89 (Blum, *Letters* 3.331) with attribution to Paul the Deacon, *Historia Romana* 7.10 (MGH Auct. ant. 2.121.19 and 104.15).

29. 2 Sam 23.4.   30. 2 Sam 23.5.

31. Cf. Gelasius I, *Tractatus* 4.11 (A. Thiel, *Epist. Rom. Pont.* 1.567); Ryan, *Sources* no. 203, 105.

32. Cf. Gelasius I, *Tractatus* 4.11; Ryan, *Sources* no. 204, 106.

fairs; the latter must provide for the thirsty a stream of heavenly eloquence. The former is established that he might compel evildoers and criminals by using the severity of legal sanctions; the latter is ordained to apply the keys of the Church that he has received, in binding some with the zeal of canonical vigor, while loosing others with the tenderness of ecclesiastical devotion.[33] But listen to what Paul has to say of kings, as he lays down the proper course that the royal office is to follow. For after he had said much previously he continues, "He is God's agent working for your good. But if you are doing wrong, have fear; it is not for nothing that he has the power of the sword. For he is God's agent, an avenger punishing the offender in his anger."[34]

(12) And so, if you are God's agent, why do you not defend God's Church? Why put on arms if you are not prepared to fight? Why gird yourself with the sword if you are not ready to resist those who are arrayed for battle?[35] He who in the summer takes his midday nap under a sunshade, can safely discourse of war. This too can truthfully be said, you carry a sword in vain unless you are going to thrust it through the throats of those who resist God. Nor are you an avenger, punishing the offender in his anger, if you do not rise up against the defilers of the Church, and with Simeon and Levi,[36] do not remove the shame of their violated sister from the house of Israel. Let your experienced hand grasp the hilt of your sword, and with David attack the Amalekites in a lightning stroke,[37] and as he subdued the brigands, so you too should pierce the enemies of the Church with the unsheathed sword of justice.

(13) Let that ancient dragon, Cadalus, take note. Let this disturber of the Church, this destroyer of apostolic discipline, this enemy of man's salvation understand. Let him beware, I say, this root of all sin, this herald of the devil, this apostle of Antichrist. And what else shall I call him? He is the arrow drawn from the

33. Cf. Matt 16.19.

34. Rom 13.4. For biblical commentary on this text, see Reindel, *Briefe* 3.389 n. 21.

35. Henry IV was invested with the knightly sword on 29 March 1065 in Worms; cf. *Reg. Imp.* 3.2.3.1 (1984) n. 360. But it is unclear whether Damian here refers to this event.

36. Cf. Gen 34.25.   37. Cf. 1 Sam 30.17.

quiver of Satan, the rod of the Assyrian, the son of Belial, "the son of perdition, who rises in his pride against every god, so called, every object of men's worship,"[38] the whirlpool of lust, the shipwreck of chastity, the disgrace of Christianity, the ignominy of bishops, the progeny of vipers, the stench of the world, the filth of the ages, the shame of the universe. Still more epithets for Cadalus can be added, a list of darksome names: slippery snake, a twisting serpent, the dung of humanity, the latrine of crime, the dregs of vice, the abomination of heaven, the expulsion from paradise, the fodder of hell, the stubble of eternal fire. Let him who dares to provoke the prince of heaven to battle, experience royal majesty when it is aroused, and fear the earthly prince. And since "the fool says in his heart: there is no God,"[39] let him come to learn of the devotion to the Christian faith that resides in the king's heart as he valiantly fights on the side of the army of God.

(14) Let your kingdom now take up arms, that the *sacerdotium* may stand firm with Melchizedek;[40] let the *sacerdotium* pray that the ancestral empire of David might be exalted. In this cause the whole Church prays for you, that by your effort it may enjoy peace, and by its intercession a glorious triumph may accrue to your name. Just so, Moses prayed, and while he prayed, Israel was victorious; but when Moses lowered his hands, Amalek had the advantage.[41] Therefore, the Apostle says, "First of all, I urge that petitions, prayers and thanksgivings be offered for all men; for sovereigns and all in high office."[42] And why is this? Listen to what follows, "That we may lead a tranquil and quiet life in full observance and in chastity."[43] Moreover, just as your father, the distinguished emperor of illustrious memory, brought the church to an exalted position, may you too, as the heir to his empire, succeed to the honor of guarding the Church. Therefore, in watching over the integrity of the Church, his eminent offspring should follow the practice of his father. And may the branch of this tree not produce less quality fruit than that, which through

38. 2 Thess 2.3–4.   39. Ps 13.1.
40. Cf. Gen 14.18–20; Laqua, *Traditionen* 316f.
41. Cf. Exod 17.11; see also Reindel, *Briefe* 3.390 n. 25.
42. 1 Tim 2.1.   43. 1 Tim 2.2.

hereditary virtue and grace, distinguished it at its origin. Just as formerly through his efforts a fallen Church was able to rise again, so henceforth through your's may ecclesiastical discipline that has suffered disorder once more be restored.[44]

(15) Perhaps I have spoken too harshly to the king, especially since Solomon says, "Do not disparage the king in your thoughts or speak ill of a rich man in the recess of your bedroom; for a bird in the sky will carry your voice and a winged messenger will repeat what you say."[45] And indeed a man who is guilty of embezzlement is compelled, in financial difficulty, to hide what he took. One must then honor the king if the king obeys the Creator; otherwise, if the king resists God's commands, he too is rightly despised by his subjects.[46] The king is judged to be his own man and not God's if, at the time of battle, he is not fighting for the cause of the Church. And thus, he may have his own special interests in mind and feel that he is not called upon to save a tottering Church from ruin. And also, since the Lord says through Isaiah, "Come and reprove me,"[47] why should one object to being censured by another, since he is obviously bound by the same law of mortality. And as civil law[48] provides that one who is not punished for killing his parents can never be admitted to the rights of inheritance, should I, who have no desire to be penalized for the murder of my mother, the Roman Church, at least not attempt to arouse the avengers?

(16) Think of me, therefore, my king, as a man who faithfully counsels you, not as one who impudently reproaches you. Or, if it suits your pleasure, judge me insane with grief for my murdered mother, and not as one who insolently takes a stand against your excellency's royal majesty. But would that I were judged guilty of treason before your court, if only you, as the ar-

---

44. See H. P. Laqua, "*Refloreat disciplina*: Ein Erneuerungsmotiv bei Petrus Damiani," *San Pier Damiano nel IX centenario della morte (1072–1972)* 2 (1972) 279–290.

45. Eccl 10.20.

46. For the question of whether or not Damian is here promoting a right of removal from office, see Reindel, *Briefe* 3.391 n. 31.

47. Isa 1.18.

48. For Damian's reference here to the *Codex Iustinianus*, see Reindel, *Briefe* 3.391 n. 32.

biter of justice, were to punish the opponents of the Apostolic See. Let the unsheathed sword savage my throat, so long as the Roman Church, restored by you, rises once again to the dignity that is its due.

(17) But if, like another Constantine in the case of Arius, you quickly destroy Cadalus and strive to restore peace to the Church for which Christ died, may God shortly cause you to progress from kingship to the sublimity of empire, and gain a singular victory over all your enemies. But if you should still compromise, if you should refuse to abolish the scandal endangering the world, even though you can . . . I hold my breath, and leave the consequences to the imagination of my readers.[49] Amen.

49. From these words, as Leclercq, *Pierre Damien* 153 suggests, Damian seems to refer to the publishing of this tract as an open letter to the king's subjects.

INDICES

INDEX OF PROPER NAMES

INDEX OF PROPER NAMES

INDEX OF SACRED SCRIPTURE

Books of the Old Testament

Books of the New Testament